EXAMPLES & EXPLANATIONS

California Community Property

Sixth Edition

EXAMPLES & EXPLANATIONS

California Community Property

Sixth Edition

Charlotte K. Goldberg
Professor of Law Emerita
LMU Loyola Law School

Jan C. Costello
Professor of Law Emerita
LMU Loyola Law School

ASPEN PUBLISHING

To contact Customer Service, e-mail customer.service@aspenpublishing.com, call 1-800-950-5259, or mail correspondence to:

Aspen Publishing
Attn: Order Department
1 Wall Street
Burlington, MA 01803

1 2 3 4 5 6 7 8 9 0

ISBN 978-1-5438-0570-3

Library of Congress Cataloging-in-Publication Data

Names: Goldberg, Charlotte K., 1946- author. | Costello, Jan, author.
Title: California community property / Charlotte K. Goldberg, Professor of Law Emerita, LMU Loyola Law School; Jan C. Costello, Professor of Law Emerita, LMU Loyola Law School.
Description: Sixth Edition. | Burlington : Aspen Publishing, 2025. | Series: Examples & explanations | Includes bibliographical references and index. | Summary: "California community property law is the property system of married couples. To understand that law, we must learn some new property concepts and apply concepts from other disciplines such as contracts, evidence, and constitutional law. There is no question that it is complicated and technical in some areas and decep-tively simple in others. The goal of this book is to explain and illustrate California community property"—Provided by publisher.
Identifiers: LCCN 2025023898 (print) | LCCN 2025023899 (ebook) | ISBN 9781543805703 (paperback) | ISBN 9798889065906 (epub) | ISBN 9798889065890 (ebook)
Subjects: LCSH: Community property—California—Problems, exercises, etc.
Classification: LCC KFC125.C6 G647 2025 (print) | LCC KFC125.C6 (ebook) | DDC 346.79404/2—dc23/eng/20250516
LC record available at https://lccn.loc.gov/2025023898
LC ebook record available at https://lccn.loc.gov/2025023899

ABOUT ASPEN PUBLISHING

Aspen Publishing is a leading provider of legal education content and digital learning solutions in the United States and globally. Our innovative products and platforms—designed based on best practices in learning science—engage students and enhance outcomes. From textbooks and audiobooks authored by renowned experts to digital platforms and products like LEAF, Connected eBooks, Connected Quizzing, PracticePerfect, and JD-Next, we empower the next generation of legal professionals with innovative, trusted, and accessible resources.

The Aspen Casebook Series, affectionately known as the "red and black" casebooks among law faculty and students, includes hundreds of highly regarded textbooks across more than 80 disciplines. These range from foundational courses like Torts and Contracts to emerging electives such as Sustainability and the Law of Policing. Our study aids, including the popular *Examples & Explanations* series, help law students master complex topics with clarity and confidence.

Aspen's expertise extends to undergraduate education with our Paralegal, Criminal Justice, and Business Law series, offering the same hallmark quality to a broader audience. JD-Next, our groundbreaking online law school prep course and admissions test, provides a realistic preview of law school, equips students with essential skills for academic success, and evaluates their readiness for legal studies.

Aspen Publishing Is Proud to Be a UWorld Company

Since 2003, UWorld has been a global leader in developing high-quality learning tools for students preparing for high-stakes exams. With a commitment to excellence, UWorld has helped millions of students in undergraduate, graduate, and professional programs in fields such as medicine, nursing, finance, and law achieve their academic and career goals.

Founded by Chandra S. Pemmasani, M.D., during his medical residency, UWorld began focusing on medical education and has since expanded into various academic fields, including law. In 2020, UWorld launched its Legal vertical, starting with its comprehensive Multistate Bar Exam (MBE®) Question Bank, followed by the acquisition of Themis Bar Review, which integrated resources to provide a complete bar exam preparation experience. In 2024, UWorld expanded its offerings by acquiring Aspen Publishing, enhancing its suite of legal education products.

Today, UWorld offers an unparalleled range of study materials that blend active learning methods with expert content, ensuring students and educators can access the most effective resources. From bar preparation to law school success, UWorld is committed to supporting the next generation of legal professionals. Learn more at uworld.com.

To My Husband
Howard

To My Husband
Dick Rothschild

Summary of Contents

Contents

Preface

Over the years, students have frequently asked for more examples so they could test their understanding of the complexities of California community property law. Although they found the community property concepts interesting, many students also struggled with their application. There are several reasons why California community property law is so challenging and why applying it can be so difficult. First, California law protects competing interests: community property that belongs to both spouses and separate property that belongs to each spouse. Second, the courts and the legislature have wrestled with how best to protect those competing interests. Third, changing perceptions of marriage and women's rights provided another overlay to community property law. Finally, California community property law is often not retroactive, which means that for several topics, it is necessary to learn two sets of law.

To help you master California community property law, this book presents a comprehensive framework for addressing the myriad characterization issues that arise at either divorce or death. That framework is called FIT and stands for "funds, intentions, and titles." It is explained in the Introduction and should be an aid in approaching characterization of property as either community or separate. Also, this book breaks down the topics into manageable chunks. This is necessary because there are technical rules that apply to each distinct topic. For instance, specific rules apply to bank accounts where both separate and community funds are commingled. Also particular formulas determine whether the community has an interest in separate property businesses.

Since the publication of the Fifth Edition, almost a decade ago, there have been significant changes or developments in California community property law. The California Legislature has passed new statutes and amendments, and the California courts have interpreted and applied them. This Sixth Edition identifies and explains such changes, with special focus on premarital agreements, title presumptions, transmutation of the nature of separate or community property, separation of spouses and the end of the economic community, and registered domestic partnerships. We hope that you will find it useful whether taking a California Community Property course or in other contexts such as bar exam preparation, research, and law practice.

Charlotte K. Goldberg
Jan C. Costello
March 2025

Acknowledgments

LMU Loyola Law School has provided significant support and encouragement for the creation of this book. We are pleased that Professor Jan Costello has joined as a co-author for the Sixth Edition. Both authors have taught California community property law for many years. The authors greatly appreciate the support and feedback of others who teach California community property law: Grace Blumberg, Lisa Ikemoto, and Herma Hill Kay. This book could not have come to fruition without the support of many Loyola student research assistants. Also, the feedback of our students has been tremendously helpful.

Finally, our families deserve recognition. Professor Goldberg thanks her husband, Howard, who always encouraged and supported her writing efforts, and to their children, Yehoshua, Ethan, Suri, and Dvora, for always understanding when Mommy had "to work." Professor Costello thanks her husband Dick Rothschild, her daughter Laura Rodriguez, and her granddaughter Lennaiya Rodriguez, the first two for asking tactfully about progress on "the book," and the third for providing irresistible distraction.

EXAMPLES & EXPLANATIONS

California Community Property

Sixth Edition

CHAPTER 1

Introduction

California community property law is the property system of married couples. To understand that law, we must learn some new property concepts and apply concepts from other disciplines such as contracts, evidence, and constitutional law. There is no question that it is complicated and technical in some areas and deceptively simple in others. The goal of this book is to explain and illustrate California community property.

HOW DID WE GET TO WHERE WE ARE TODAY?

To understand the California community property system of today, it is worthwhile to look back and examine the events and concepts that led to the creation of the system. Several historical events led to the amalgam of civil law and common law ideas that gave birth to our peculiar marital property law. For those who desire to skip this section, please feel free to do so; however, examining some of the original concepts may help you understand our present system. Also, some ideas persisted for many years and have influenced the confusing hodgepodge of doctrines you will be learning about in this book.

California was acquired by the United States in 1848 through the Treaty of Guadalupe-Hidalgo, which ended the Mexican-American War. The early settlers of California operated under a community property system that derived from European civil law. As most students remember, the next event that influenced California's growth was the discovery of gold in 1849. Imagine the gold seekers trekking to California with their picks and pans, and, of course, following not far behind were lawyers from the East Coast with their common law backgrounds.

Community Property and Common Law Concepts Converge

Community property concepts were enshrined in the California Constitution. The Constitution defined the *separate* property of the *wife* but left open her rights regarding that property and property held in common with her husband. Distinctions between the rights of husband and wife probably jar the twenty-first-century ear. Who speaks of the wife, or the husband, without being reminded to use the gender-neutral term "spouse"? Yes, we must return to the nineteenth century to understand that mindset toward married couples, husbands and wives. The civil law concept of marital property that was in existence at the time of California statehood only had two categories: "common" property and "separate" property. "Common" property was all property that was not separate property. Separate property was that property owned before marriage or acquired during marriage through gift, devise, or descent.

The idea of separate property appealed to some early lawmakers as a way of protecting the wife who came into the marriage with wealth from the "idle habits, carelessness, or dissipation of the husband." Mr. Norton, *Report of the Debates in the Convention of California on the Formation of the State Constitution in September and October 1849*, found in Blumberg, *Community Property in California* 58 (6th ed. 2012). One legislator, a bachelor, favored protection of a wife's separate property as a way of encouraging "women of fortune to come to California." Mr. Halleck, *Id.* at 56. The most persuasive reason for retaining the civil law concepts in the California Constitution was "to take into consideration the feelings of the native Californians, who have always lived under this law." Mr. Tefft, *Id.* Despite this respect for wives and native Californians, common law concepts soon overwhelmed the constitutional provision regarding the wife's separate property.

Statutes passed by the first California Legislature in 1850 incorporated common law concepts. The Easterners' common law ideas regarding marital property were derived from the doctrine that when husband and wife married, they became "one," and that "one" was the husband. Almost all incidents of ownership of property belonged to the husband—at marriage, a wife's personal property became his, and *he* had sole possession and control of his wife's real property with no duty to account to her even though the title to that property was in her name. At the time of California's statehood, a change was at work in the East with the passage of Married Women's Property Acts. These acts were aimed at removing a married woman's legal dependence on her husband. The most radical of these acts considered a wife the separate and independent owner of all property that would have been hers but for the marriage. She would be considered the owner of all property she owned before marriage, all gifts or inheritances received during marriage, and any property earned by her during marriage.

Common Law Ideas Dominate

However, the legislators and jurists of early California statehood were not radicals. Although they retained the civil law/community property distinctions of separate and "common" property, they enacted into statute their traditional common law way of thinking. The husband was given almost all the power: (1) to manage and control the "common" property as if it were his own separate property; and (2) to manage and control the wife's separate property, with the only exception that he could not convey or encumber it without her consent. In contrast, he could manage and control his separate property however he wished without seeking his wife's consent to any transaction. A wife could not even make a valid will without her husband's consent. Clearly, when husband and wife married in California in the nineteenth century, it was the husband who was in control. Over the years, the husband's total management and control of the couple's property was diminished through various legislative enactments, but it was not until 1975 that equal management and control of community property by husband and wife went into effect.

One concept that persisted for many years was that a wife's interest in community property was a "mere expectancy" that materialized only at divorce or death. The "mere expectancy" phrase was uttered in 1860 by no other than then-Chief Justice of the California Supreme Court, Stephen J. Field. Students may recognize Justice Field, who was the first United States Supreme Court Justice from California. In 1877, he was the author of that memorable case, *Pennoyer v. Neff.* The 1860 case that he authored, *Van Maren v. Johnson*, 15 Cal. 308, discussed the power of creditors to reach community property for the wife's premarital debt. Justice Field obviously thought in common law terms because he noted that the "title" to the community property was in the husband and thus the wife's interest was a "mere expectancy." We can see that a distinctively common law idea—title—resulted in the husband actually being considered the "owner" of the community property and the wife reduced to waiting for her expectancy to materialize. It was not until 1927 that the Legislature declared that the spouses' interests in community property were "present, existing, and equal" thus explicitly overturning the "mere expectancy" doctrine. Yet the "mere expectancy" concept persisted regarding employee pensions until 1976 when it was abandoned in *Marriage of Brown*, 15 Cal. 3d 838, 544 P.2d 561, 126 Cal. Rptr. 633. Pensions are discussed in Chapter 5.

As you progress through this book, try to examine your own thinking—has it been influenced by your "common law" courses of Property and Contracts? Also try to immerse yourself in the community/separate property concepts and how they have developed in California law.

LET'S GET TO THE BASICS

Consequences of Characterization

The most basic premise of California community property law is that there are only two types of marital property: community property and separate property. Before even defining the terms, we examine the consequences of classifying (in California parlance, characterizing) marital property as either community or separate. At divorce, community property is divided equally between the spouses. That 50/50 split is mandatory, and there are almost no deviations from equal division. Separate property belongs to each spouse and is not divided by the court. At death, if a spouse dies without a will (intestate), all the community property goes to the surviving spouse. The separate property also goes to the surviving spouse if there are no other heirs; otherwise, the surviving spouse receives either one-half or one-third of the decedent's separate property. If a spouse dies with a will (testate), that spouse may devise one-half of the community property and all of his or her separate property to anyone he or she may choose. Thus the characterization of marital property as either community or separate property has momentous consequences at divorce and at death. Most litigation over marital property in California and most of this book concern characterization problems.

Let's take some simple scenarios to illustrate those consequences. Husband and Wife marry in California. Although same-sex marriage is now part of California law, this book will often use opposite-sex scenarios to illustrate hypothetical problems. After many years, their marriage falters and they seek a divorce. During their marriage, they have accumulated community property worth $500,000. Husband has separate property worth $100,000. Wife has separate property worth $200,000. The community property will be split 50/50 and Husband will receive $250,000 and Wife will receive $250,000. Neither Husband nor Wife's separate property will be divided by the court. After their divorce, Husband will have assets totaling

$350,000 and Wife will have assets totaling $450,000. So we can see that, at divorce, California community property law mandates equal division of community property, but their separate property is not subject to division and is retained by each spouse.

Again take our couple, Husband and Wife with the same assets. But instead of their marriage ending in divorce, they have a long and happy marriage and Husband dies first. He did not have a will and therefore died intestate. Under the Probate Code, all the community property goes to the surviving spouse, Wife. If Husband has no other heirs, his separate property will also go to Wife. Therefore, she could receive all the family wealth in the event Husband dies intestate. Depending on whether there are other heirs, such as parents or children, Husband's separate property would be divided between Wife and those other heirs. However, Wife would receive at least one-third of Husband's separate property in addition to all of the community property.

Now let's change the scenario. Husband died with a will (testate), in which he specified that all his property goes to Nephew upon his death. Since a spouse may devise one-half of the community property, Nephew will receive $250,000 as specified in Husband's will. The other one-half of the community property is the surviving spouse's share and thus Wife will also be entitled to $250,000. Husband may also devise all of his separate property to anyone that he chooses. Therefore, Nephew will be entitled to Husband's $100,000 separate property as specified in Husband's will. Wife has no rights to Husband's separate property.

These rules seem very clear-cut. However, the results of these simple scenarios could change drastically if there was a controversy over whether the property accumulated during marriage was community or separate property.

Only Two Categories

With only two categories, community and separate property, one might think that all we need to know are the definitions of those categories and it would be easy. Not so. The reason is that the California community property system is overlaid with a long history of not only favoring community property but also of protecting separate property. Therefore, doctrines have developed to try to balance the interests of both the "community" and the "separate property spouse." To begin to understand, we must try to define the categories by reference to the statutory definitions. Community property is defined in Family Code §760 as "all property, real or personal, wherever situated, acquired by a married person during marriage while domiciled in this state." That is an exceedingly broad definition, but Family Code §770 carves out separate property as "all property owned before marriage" and "all property acquired . . . after marriage by gift, bequest, devise, or descent." In addition, the "rents, issues, and profits" of separate property are separate property.

The basic definition of community property is the concept that labor or effort of either spouse during marriage is community property. For instance, let us take an imaginary married couple, Harry and Wilma. It is a marriage where Harry is the breadwinner and Wilma is the homemaker. All of Harry's earnings are community property—that means that they belong to the community, to *both* Harry and Wilma. Wilma's ownership rights are not dependent on any monetary contributions she may make to acquire the property or on any "paid" labor she contributes to the community. The appealing aspect of community property is that it values *each* member of the community, whether they work inside or outside the home. However, it goes against the ingrained idea of payment for labor: "I earned it. It is mine." The community property concept is "I earned it. It is *ours*."

On the other hand, the community property definition does not extend to property owned before marriage, gifts and the like during marriage, and earnings after the economic community ends. If Harry owned stock before their marriage, that stock is his separate property, and any dividends that accrue from that stock are also his separate property. If Wilma receives a gift of stock from her parents during marriage, that stock is her separate property, and any dividends that accrue from that stock are also her separate property Similarly, inheritances received during marriage are also the separate property of the spouse who receives the inheritance. Once the spouses are living separate and apart, the economic community ends. Earnings of the spouses after separation are the separate property of the earning spouse. The time of the acquisition, before marriage or after separation, is a significant determinant of the character of the property of the spouses. The type of acquisition, either through labor or through a gift or inheritance, will also determine whether the property is community or separate property.

DOES IT FIT?

The main challenge in the characterization process is determining whether the property FITs into either category. FIT stands for "funds, intentions, titles." In first-year Property courses, one question is always pounded into students' heads: What does the title say? In community property law, the title in many cases plays a much less significant role. The most striking example is when property acquired during marriage is placed in one spouse's name. For example, Harry and Wilma buy a new car with community property funds and take the title in Wilma's name. There are various reasons for doing this. One reason might be that they want the car to be Wilma's separate property—a gift to her. Another reason might be that it is just convenient because Wilma handles all family financial affairs. Then how do we know how to characterize the car? According to California law, when the title is in one spouse's name, the title does *not* determine the character of the property. Instead, we look to the source of the *funds* that are used to acquire the car. If Wilma can prove that separate property funds were used to buy the car, then the car will be characterized as her separate property. Otherwise, because the car was acquired during their marriage, it will be presumed to be community property unless rebutted by tracing to separate property funds. Presumptions regarding community property will be treated in more detail in Chapter 3. The separate property proponent in our scenario, Wilma, will have the burden of proving that the car was purchased with separate property funds. If she cannot, the car will be characterized as community property. The same analysis applies to all property acquired during marriage that does not have a title. The source of the *funds* controls. The technical name for this process is called tracing. Property acquired during marriage that is untitled or titled in one spouse's name is presumed to be community property unless the funds used to acquire the property can be *traced* to a separate property source.

FIT also refers to *intentions*. In the above examples, we said that couples may have various reasons for putting the title in one spouse's name. Harry and Wilma may have *intended* or agreed that the car was to become Wilma's separate property even if community funds, such as Harry's earnings, were used to buy the car. When do their intentions control? How do the spouses go about changing the character of property from community to separate property of one spouse? As of 1985, the answer is "with great difficulty." To change property from one category to another, which is called *transmutation*, there must be an "express declaration in writing . . . by the spouse whose interest in the property is adversely affected." Family Code §852(a). In our car example, putting the car in Wilma's name would not be sufficient. Although the title is in writing, the "express declaration" requirement is more stringent. The title would have to read "to Wilma, as her separate property," to show clearly that Harry knew that he was giving up any interest he might have in the car, which was purchased with community funds. Transmutation of property is treated in Chapter 2.

Examples

Example 1—Who Gets the Chair?

Alice and Bob, who have lived in California their whole lives, have been married for many years. Alice is a lawyer who practices family law and Bob is a sculptor. Alice earns approximately $100,000 a year; Bob has only sold a few of his sculptures for a very minimal amount. Alice has been able to save $10,000 a year and put the funds into a savings account in her name. Alice and Bob also like to frequent garage sales where they try to find antiques to add to a collection they have started. One weekend they find an old child's rocking chair at a garage sale and buy it for $25.00. Alice buys it with funds that she had withdrawn from her savings account. Unfortunately, Alice and Bob have separated. Alice's friend notices the rocking chair and realizes that it is very valuable since it is the child's rocking chair of a famous president. It is valued at $25,000. In a divorce proceeding, how will the rocking chair be characterized and divided?

Example 2 — Alice Uses Aunt Sarah's Bequest

Assume the same facts as Example 1, except that Alice receives an inheritance of $10,000 from Aunt Sarah. She opens a different savings account in her name and puts the $10,000 from Aunt Sarah in that account. Before the garage sale, she withdraws $1,000 from the account. She uses $25.00 from that cash to buy the rocking chair. In a divorce proceeding, how will the rocking chair be characterized and divided?

Example 3 — Does the Stock Belong to Alice?

Assume that recently Alice and Bob use Alice's savings from her earnings to buy $10,000 worth of stock in XYZ Company. They direct their stockbroker to put the stock in Alice's name. The stockbroker does so. They also agree orally that the stock will be Alice's separate property. Unfortunately, Alice and Bob have separated. Alice wants to claim the stock as her separate property. Will she succeed?

Explanations

Explanation 1 — Who Gets the Chair?

The rocking chair is untitled personal property that was acquired during Alice and Bob's marriage while they were domiciled in California. Therefore, it is presumptively community property. The funds used to purchase the rocking chair are community property because they were earned during marriage. Even though Alice's earnings were in a savings account in her name, that does not transmute the funds into her separate property. When the title is in one spouse's name, that does not indicate a change in the character of the property. That is not enough to transmute the funds into Alice's separate property. Because there is no possibility of tracing the funds to separate property, the conclusion is that the rocking chair is community property. Just as the rents, issues, and profits of separate property are separate property, the rents, issues, and profits of community property are community property. Thus, the rocking chair valued at $25,000 would be split

50/50 in a divorce proceeding. It could be sold and the couple could split the proceeds. If Alice wanted to keep the rocking chair, Bob could receive another item of equal value from the community property or she could buy him out.

Explanation 2 — Alice Uses Aunt Sarah's Bequest

Alice's inheritance received during marriage would fall under the definition of separate property. Again, putting the funds into a bank account in Alice's name does not affect the character of the property in the bank account—it is the source of the funds that determines the character. Again, we start with the acquisition of the rocking chair. It is untitled personal property acquired during Alice and Bob's marriage while they are domiciled in California. It is presumptively community property. However, Alice, who is the "separate property proponent," would try to rebut the community property presumption by tracing to separate property funds. If Alice can show that the funds used to purchase the rocking chair came from the inheritance from Aunt Sarah, she would be able to rebut the community property presumption. The rocking chair would be characterized as Alice's separate property. Separate property is not divisible at divorce, and Alice would keep the rocking chair as her own.

Explanation 3 — Does the Stock Belong to Alice?

Let's get the facts straight and see how it FITs. The *funds* used to buy the stock are community property because they came from earnings during marriage. Even though Alice earned them, they belong to the community. The *title* is in Alice's name, but by now we know that the title in one spouse's name is *not* determinative of the character of the property. The *intentions* of the spouses are that the stock will be Alice's separate property, but their intentions are expressed orally.

We start with the presumption that the stock was acquired while Alice and Bob are married and before they separate; therefore, the stock is presumed to be community property. Alice, the separate property proponent, cannot rebut the presumption by tracing because the funds used to buy the stock are community property. They came from her earnings. The title in her name is also insufficient to show that they intended to transmute the property into Alice's separate property. That is because couples put the title in one spouse's name for various reasons, not always because they intend to transmute the property from community property to the separate property of one spouse.

Their oral agreement will also be insufficient to rebut the community property presumption. As of 1985, transmutations must be in writing and "expressly declare" that the spouse adversely affected, here Bob, consented to give up his interest in the property. Thus, the conclusion is that the stock will be characterized as community property. At divorce, the value of the stock will be split evenly between Alice and Bob. This is an example of the dominance of the *funds* in characterization of property as either community or separate. It also shows the policy of California law to protect the community (both Alice and Bob). In addition, it shows that at present it is very difficult to change the character of property, especially from community to the separate property of one spouse.

CHAPTER 2

The Community Chameleon: How Property Can Be Changed by Agreement

PREMARITAL AGREEMENTS: PURPOSE AND BACKGROUND

Not everyone embraces the sharing concepts of community property that earnings during marriage are community property. Not everyone believes that the rents, issues, and profits of separate property should be considered separate property. For those couples who want to marry but do not accept the tenets of California community property law, they may opt out by entering into a premarital agreement specifying their own property system.

Before the advent of widespread divorce, premarital agreements (also called antenuptial or prenuptial agreements) were used primarily by couples who wanted to arrange their financial affairs in the event of the death of either spouse. Often it was the wealthy spouse, sometimes called the economically superior spouse, who wanted to guard assets earned during the marriage. Sometimes it was the poorer spouse, sometimes called the economically inferior spouse, who wanted to ensure that upon the death of the other spouse that he or she would be provided for. This was particularly true of second marriages where there were children from a prior marriage. Typically, the premarital agreement provided that each spouse's earnings during marriage would be the separate property of the earner spouse, contributing to

That change would have great consequences upon the death of the earner spouse because, at death, all separate property can be devised to whomever the separate property owner desires. That differs from community property, because a spouse has the right to devise only *one-half* of the community property. If a spouse dies without a will, *all* the community property goes to the surviving spouse; depending on whether there are other heirs, either one-third, one-half, or all the separate property will go to the surviving spouse. Thus, premarital agreements that provide that earnings are separate property give maximum control over those earnings to the earner spouse in the event of the death of that spouse.

Before divorce became common, it was considered against public policy to "contemplate" divorce and to include in a premarital agreement provisions that spoke about how to divide property in the event of divorce. It is hard to understand that thinking today, but the idea was that if a premarital agreement "contemplates" divorce, then the spouses are not serious about marriage. Thinking about divorce before you even marry—what kind of commitment does that represent? It was against public policy to contemplate that a marriage would not last until "death do us part." Then came "the Sixties" and what was called "the (Second Wave) Women's Movement." Passed in 1964 the federal Civil Rights Act prohibited discrimination in the workplace on the basis of sex, opening up to women employment positions and professions which had been largely limited to men. It was thought that women who had work experience could bargain as equals and no longer needed economic protection provided by "public policy." It became more common for married women to work outside the home, and to manage their separate assets and their income. In 1970 California adopted no-fault divorce, and in 1975 the wife as well as the husband had the power to manage community property. These changes in law to treat women as equals to men in the workplace and in marriage led to a reassessment of the public policy objections to premarital agreements. Premarital agreements contemplating divorce were thought to be positive. Couples could decide in advance the details of a divorce settlement. Having full disclosure of each person's economic status and assets would reduce the likelihood of fraud or misrepresentation. Having the details worked out would reduce the acrimonious litigation surrounding the increasing volume of divorce proceedings. Premarital agreements would encourage couples to marry because they would know the property division and other details if their marriage ended in divorce.

The case of *Marriage of Dawley*, 17 Cal. 3d 342, 355, 551 P.2d 323, 331, 131 Cal. Rptr. 3, 11 (1976) established that a premarital agreement could be valid even though it was made in the expectation of divorce. The major provision in that agreement concerned mutual separate property clauses as well as spousal support provisions. The husband agreed to support the wife (and her daughter from different father) for a minimum period of 14 months. Although the *Dawley* Court stated that waivers of spousal support are generally not enforceable, they found that the Dawleys' support provision did not violate public policy because it stated a minimum but no maximum amount. Therefore, it was enforceable because it did not waive all spousal support.

Dawley established the following principles that applied to premarital agreements made before 1986:

1. The agreement need not be made in expectation that marriage will terminate only by death.
2. The terms of the agreement must not promote or encourage divorce.
3. The objective terms of the agreement control, not the subjective contemplation of one or both parties.
4. The parties must enter into the agreement freely (voluntarily) without fraud, duress, coercion, or undue influence.
5. The agreement may deal with property rights of spouses, and may limit but not waive spousal support.

PREMARITAL AGREEMENTS IN CALIFORNIA, 1986 TO THE PRESENT

The 1986 Premarital Agreement Act

The growing need for uniform legal guidance in the area of premarital agreements sparked the enactment in 1986 of the California version of the Uniform Premarital Agreement Act. The Uniform Premarital Agreement Act was promulgated initially by the National Conference of Commissioners on Uniform State Laws, to encourage certainty and uniformity in enforcement of premarital agreements. The Uniform Act also promoted freedom of spouses to contract regarding their property. The 1986 California Act followed those directives, delineating expanded parameters of subject matter of premarital agreements as well as enacting rules guaranteeing their enforceability. Family Code §1601 of the Premarital Agreement Act makes it clear that the Act only applies to premarital agreements executed on or after January 1, 1986. Former law continues to apply to agreements made prior to 1986.

General Requirements

Under the 1986 Act, premarital agreements made on or after January 1, 1986 are required to be "in writing and signed by both parties." Family Code §1611. Simply adhering to these two requirements, however, will not automatically render a premarital agreement enforceable. Although consideration is not required for a validly executed premarital agreement, premarital agreements generally must abide by contract law. For example, the Court of Appeal in *Marriage of Shaban*, 88 Cal. 4th 398, 105 Cal. Rptr. 2d 863 (2001), stated that the agreement's terms, in addition to being in writing, must also be stated with sufficient certainty to be an enforceable contract. Parol evidence is not allowed to insert missing terms and conditions absent from the agreement in order to make the agreement enforceable, although such evidence would be allowed to interpret existing terms.

In the *Shaban* case, the parties married in Egypt and obtained a divorce in California after living in the United States for approximately 17 years. The husband claimed that the parties had a written premarital agreement and offered a one-page piece of paper written in Arabic as evidence of such claims. The husband and the wife's father (as a representative) signed the paper, but it only outlined a dowry arrangement between the parties. At trial, the husband unsuccessfully attempted to introduce parol evidence in the form of an expert witness who would testify that, based on the one-page document, it was intended for the marriage to be interpreted by "Islamic law" in lieu of California's community property law. The Court of Appeal affirmed the trial court's rejection of the husband's alleged contract, holding that, because the Statute of Frauds applied to the formation of prenuptial agreements, parol evidence was properly excluded, because it was offered to establish the substance of the agreement. Language in the document indicating a general desire to be governed by the rules of the Islamic religion bore too attenuated a relationship to any actual terms of a prenuptial agreement to satisfy the Statute of Frauds.

The writing requirement of the Premarital Agreement Act is also subject to most Statute of Frauds exceptions. According to *Hall v. Hall*, 222 Cal. App. 3d 578, 271 Cal. Rptr. 773 (1990), the traditional exception to the Statute of Frauds of promissory estoppel applies to premarital agreements. In *Hall*, the wife, Carol, would not accept the proposal of a premarital agreement from the husband, Aubrey, because she feared that she would lose all her money during the marriage and have no place to live for the rest of her life. Aubrey orally promised Carol that if she married him, she could live in his house until she died if she would also give up her job, apply for Social Security at age 62, and give him $10,000. The title of the house in question was in a revocable trust, with Aubrey as trustee and sole beneficiary during his lifetime and his sons from a previous marriage as residuary beneficiaries. After they married, Carol fulfilled her side of the bargain in full and had their attorney draft a trust amendment, giving Carol a life estate in the house. Aubrey, however, died unexpectedly without ever having signed the trust amendment. The trial court held that Carol's partial performance of the couple's oral agreement qualified as an exception to the requirements of the Statute of Frauds. *Id.* at 582-583, 271 Cal. Rptr. at 775. The appellate court affirmed, holding that although the Premarital Agreement Act requires a premarital agreement to be in writing and signed by both parties, the traditional promissory estoppel exception to the Statute of Frauds should be applied to premarital agreements as it does to all other contracts.

The scope of *Hall*, however, is limited to where the party seeking enforcement "performed his/her part of the bargain and in so doing irretrievably changed his position." Thus, partial performance of acts typically common in marriage would not be sufficient to be considered "irretrievably changing position" for purposes of getting around the writing requirement. In *Hall*, however, Carol did irretrievably change her position by quitting her job and applying for early Social Security in reliance on Aubrey's promise to give her a life estate in the house.

One major change produced by the 1986 Act concerned the amendment or revocation of premarital agreements after marriage has taken place. Case law prior to 1986 generally allowed evidence of implied modification or retraction based on oral agreement or conduct. In contrast, with the enactment of the 1986 Act, "after marriage, a premarital agreement may be amended or revoked only by a written agreement signed by the parties." Family Code §1614. Keep in mind that the Act only applies to premarital agreements entered into on or after January 1, 1986, and agreements prior to the Premarital Agreement Act will still be controlled by prior case law.

Subjects of Premarital Agreements 1986 Act

The 1986 Premarital Agreement Act also outlined what can and cannot be proper subjects of a premarital agreement. The applicable section, Family Code §1612, lists the broad subject matter that can be included in such agreements. Among the subjects permissible in premarital agreements are: property (including all rights thereto), choice of law (separate property versus community property principles), and any other matter, including personal rights and obligations, not in violation of public policy or a statute imposing a criminal penalty. The only subject matter that is specifically prohibited from being included in a premarital agreement is child support: "The right of a child to support may not be adversely affected by a premarital agreement." Family Code §1612(b).

The expansive nature of the subject matter provision of the 1986 Premarital Agreement Act led to highly disputed issues in the California courts. Most troublesome of the provisions seemed to be Family Code §1612(a)(7), which was the catchall provision, allowing for personal rights and obligations not against public policy to be a permissible subject matter in premarital agreements. The highly controversial issue of spousal support waivers in premarital agreements was broached in *Pendleton v. Fireman*, 24 Cal. 4th 39, 5 P.3d 839, 99 Cal. Rptr. 2d 278 (2000).

In *Pendleton*, the wife, Candace Pendleton, an aspiring writer and holder of a master's degree, and husband, Barry I. Fireman, a businessman and holder of a doctorate in pharmacology and a law degree, entered into a premarital agreement in 1991, which provided: "[B]oth parties now and forever waive, in the event of a dissolution of the marriage, all rights to any type of spousal support . . . from the other." The agreement acknowledged that both parties had been represented by independent counsel in the negotiation and preparation of the agreement, that counsel had advised them of the meaning and legal consequences of the agreement, and that both parties had read and understood the agreement and its legal consequences. When the couple split in 1995, Candace filed for divorce and subsequently sought spousal support despite the spousal support limitation in the premarital agreement. The trial court, consistent with prior case law, ruled that the waiver of spousal support was against public policy in California and thus unenforceable.

The Court of Appeal reversed the trial court's decision, stating that the Legislature, although omitting a subdivision from the Uniform Premarital Agreement Act that would have expressly permitted the parties of a premarital agreement to contract for the modification or elimination of spousal support, intended to leave the question of whether spousal support waivers violated public policy to the courts. The California Supreme Court ultimately agreed with the Court of Appeal on the premise that "changes in the law governing the spousal relation warrant[ed] reexamination of the assumptions and policy underlying the refusal to enforce waivers of spousal support." *Id.* at 48, 5 P.3d at 845, 99 Cal. Rptr. 2d at 285. Spousal support waivers "executed by intelligent, well-educated persons, each of whom appears to be self-sufficient in property and earning ability, and both of whom have the advice of counsel regarding their rights and obligations as marital partners at the time they execute the waiver" were deemed to not violate public policy and not to be per se unenforceable. *Id.* at 53-54, 5 P.3d at 848-849, 99 Cal. Rptr. 3d at 289. The majority specifically declined to decide whether enforcement of one of these waivers might be unjust under other circumstances, only ruling that such waivers would not violate public policy per se.

Defenses to Enforceability

The enforceability of premarital agreements executed on or after January 1, 1986, is delineated in Family Code §1615. There are two methods to invalidate a premarital agreement by the party against whom enforcement is sought. As outlined in Family Code §1615(a)(1), the first way to invalidate a premarital agreement is to prove that the agreement was not executed "voluntarily." This would require a showing of fraud, coercion, or lack of knowledge. We must then ask what exactly constitutes "involuntary" for purposes of premarital agreements and how does the party go about proving this standard. These issues were discussed and decided in *Marriage of Bonds*, 24 Cal. 4th 1, 5 P.3d 815, 99 Cal. Rptr. 2d 252 (2000).

In the *Bonds* case, Barry and Susann ("Sun") Bonds had entered into a written premarital agreement in February of 1988. Barry was a professional baseball player whose annual salary at the time of the agreement was approximately $106,000. Sun had immigrated to Canada from Sweden in 1985, had worked as a waitress and bartender, and had some training as a cosmetologist, although she was unemployed at the time she entered into the agreement. Barry and Sun executed the premarital agreement in which each party waived any interest in the earnings and acquisitions of the other party during marriage. That same day, the parties flew to Las Vegas and were married the following day.

After Barry petitioned for legal separation in 1994, Sun challenged the validity of the premarital agreement, claiming it was not entered into voluntarily. The California Supreme Court rejected the ruling of the Court of Appeal, which stated that a determination of voluntariness in premarital agreements was subject to strict scrutiny where one of the parties was not represented by independent counsel. The Supreme Court concluded that while retention of independent legal counsel was a relevant factor in determining voluntariness, it is only one of several factors that need to be considered in determining whether a premarital agreement was entered into voluntarily. Factors articulated by the Supreme Court were: (1) proximity of execution of the agreement to the wedding; (2) surprise from the presentation of the agreement; (3) the presence or absence of independent counsel or an opportunity to consult independent counsel; (4) inequality of bargaining power (indicated in some cases by the relative age and sophistication of the parties); (5) disclosure of assets; and (6) the understanding and awareness of the intent of the agreement. *Id.* at 17-18, 5 P.3d at 824-825, 99 Cal. Rptr. at 262. In the instant case, the Supreme Court held that Sun had entered into the agreement voluntarily, as there was sufficient evidence to show that she had reasonable opportunity to retain independent legal counsel (admonitions were given to her up to a week prior to execution of the agreement), she understood and even concurred with the terms of the agreement, and she executed the agreement without being subject to fraud, coercion, or undue influence.

The second method of invalidating a premarital agreement is provided by Family Code §1615(a)(2). The party against whom enforcement is being sought has to prove both that the agreement was unconscionable when it was executed and that before execution of the agreement, the spouse was not provided with fair and reasonable disclosure of the property or financial obligations of the party. Also there must be proof that the party did not voluntarily waive, in writing, his/her right to disclosure of the property or financial obligations, and the party did not have actual or reasonably could not have had adequate knowledge of the property or financial obligations. Under Family Code §1615(b) an issue of unconscionability of a premarital agreement is to be decided by the court as a matter of law.

The most important point regarding §1615(a)(2) is that it states that the unconscionability of the agreement must have been present at the time "it was executed." Thus, we know that even if circumstances in the spouses' lives have changed since the time of execution of a premarital agreement, and this change in circumstance now renders the previously executed agreement unconscionable, the agreement is still valid and enforceable. In addition, fair and reasonable disclosure of property or financial obligations will save even an unconscionable agreement. Because the spouse arguing against enforcement is required to prove both an unconscionable agreement and inadequate disclosure of property/financial obligations, it is implied that if there is adequate disclosure, the premarital agreement will be upheld regardless of the degree of unconscionability at time of execution.

The 2002 Premarital Agreement Act Amendments

The controversial decisions in *Pendleton v. Fireman* and *Marriage of Bonds* were the impetus for amending the 1986 Premarital Agreement Act. The 2002 Premarital Agreement Act amendments revised §§1612 and 1615 of the California Family Code, the two portions of the 1986 Act that were the subjects of litigation in those cases.

One question left open by the Legislature was the retroactivity of the 2002 amendments. The 1986 Act had specifically provided that its requirements were prospective, applying only to premarital agreements executed on or after January 1, 1986. Even though the amendments did not go into effect until January 1, 2002, the Legislature did not specify whether the new requirements applied to premarital agreements that were executed prior to 2002. Before the California Supreme Court decided the case of *Marriage of Fellows*, 39 Cal. 4th 179, 138 P.3d 200, 46 Cal. Rptr. 3d 49 (2006), most practitioners assumed that the new requirements in §§1612 and 1615 would not be retroactive. The *Fellows* case highlighted a little-noticed section of the Family Code, §4, that established the general rule that the Family Code and, more importantly, amendments to the Family Code, are retroactive. That general rule, however, is subject to certain exceptions in §4 and due process.

Despite the *Fellows* case, the Courts of Appeal have not applied the 2002 amendments retroactively. *Marriage of Howell*, 195 Cal. App. 4th 1062, 126 Cal. Rptr. 3d 539 (2011), held that the statute providing that a premarital waiver of spousal support without independent counsel is unenforceable does not apply retroactively to premarital agreements signed before the effective date of the statute, since the statute does not merely clarify prior law, but rather substantially changes it. *See also Marriage of Hill and Dittmer*, 202 Cal. App. 4th 1046, 136 Cal. Rptr. 3d 700 (2011).

Seven-Day Waiting Period: Case Law

In addition, the Court of Appeal clarified the meaning of the "seven-day waiting" period in Family Code §1615(c)(2). *Marriage of Cadwell-Faso and Faso*, 191 Cal. App. 4th 945, 119 Cal. Rptr. 3d 818 (2011). In this case, Faso's attorney presented a premarital agreement to Cadwell-Faso's attorney six months before the wedding and advised Cadwell-Faso to seek independent counsel. Cadwell-Faso asked her attorney to draft a modification. After many modifications the final version of the agreement was delivered to Cadwell-Faso's attorney five days before the wedding, and signed two days before the wedding. During their divorce proceedings, Faso sought to have the premarital agreement set aside because he did not have seven days (only three days) between the time he received the final draft and his signature. Cadwell-Faso argued that the seven- day rule of §1615(c)(2) only applied to parties who did not have attorney representation (self-represented parties). The trial court decided in favor of Faso, finding that the seven-day rule applied without distinction to attorney represented and self-represented parties. However, the Court of Appeal reversed the trial court, finding that §1615 (c)(2) was ambiguous, and that because Faso was represented by an attorney from the beginning, he did not need seven days to consult with his counsel before signing.

In another case interpreting the seven days provision, *Marriage of Clarke and Akel*, 19 Cal. App. 5th 914, 228 Cal. Rptr. 3d 483 (2018), husband Clarke downloaded a premarital agreement from Nolo Press (a self-help website) and emailed it to Akel. Clarke hired an attorney to represent Akel but remained self-represented. After negotiations, Akel's attorney sent the final version to Clarke, who signed it one day after receiving it. At divorce, Akel sought to enforce the premarital agreement, but Clarke argued in opposition that he was not represented and did not have seven days before signing the final version. The trial court ruled against enforcement, because Clarke did not have seven days before signing. The Court of Appeal affirmed, emphasizing that Clarke was self-represented and the changes to the original draft were significant.

2020 Amendment Seven-Day Rule

The California Legislature addressed the disparate treatment of self-represented parties and parties represented by attorneys, by passage of amendment to Family Code §1615 (c)(2). The amendment, effective January 1, 2020, requires that for premarital agreements signed after January 1, 2020, the party against whom enforcement is sought must have seven calendar days between the time that party was first presented with the final version and advised to seek independent counsel—and the time the agreement is signed, regardless of whether the party is represented by an attorney. This requirement does not apply to non-substantive amendments that do not change the terms of the agreement. Self-represented parties and parties represented by attorneys are now treated the same under the seven-day rule, and the seven-day period begins to run again each time a version of the agreement with significant changes is presented for signature.

> (A) For an agreement executed between January 1, 2002, and January 1, 2020, the party against whom enforcement is sought had not less than seven calendar days between the time that party was first presented with the final agreement and advised to seek independent legal counsel and the time the agreement was signed. This requirement does not apply to non-substantive amendments that do not change the terms of the agreement.
>
> (B) For an agreement executed on or after January 1, 2020, the party against whom enforcement is sought had not less than seven calendar days between the time that party was first presented with the final agreement and the time the agreement was signed, regardless of whether the party is represented by legal counsel. This requirement does not apply to non-substantive amendments that do not change the terms of the agreement

Subject Matter of Premarital Agreements

Spousal Support

The 2002 amendment to the 1986 Premarital Agreement Act, regarding subject matter, tackles the topic of spousal support. New §1612(c) makes it clear that spousal support provisions in premarital agreements will not be enforceable unless independent counsel represented the party against whom enforcement is sought at the time the premarital agreement was signed. Even if independent counsel represented that party, spousal support provisions can still be held unenforceable if they are unconscionable at time of enforcement. The new section clearly states that an unconscionable spousal support provision will never be enforced, regardless of representation by independent counsel.

Voluntariness and Legal Representation

The 2002 Act added a new subsection to §1615 of the Family Code, which governs premarital agreement enforceability. Under §1615(a)(1), the party seeking to invalidate the premarital agreement had to prove that he/she did not execute the agreement voluntarily, "voluntariness" being determined by the series of factors set out in the *Bonds* case. However, newly added §1615(c) has expanded the *Bonds* factors by adding precise requirements regarding voluntariness.

Under this newly added subsection, an agreement shall not be deemed voluntarily executed unless legal counsel represented the party against whom enforcement was sought at the time the premarital agreement was signed or, after being advised to seek independent legal counsel, expressly waived representation in a separate writing. Moreover, the party against whom enforcement was sought also must have had not less than seven calendar days between the time that party was first presented with the agreement and advised to seek independent legal counsel and the time the agreement was signed.

The amendment to §1615 also includes additional requirements to enforceability where the party against whom enforcement is sought chooses to expressly waive, in a separate writing, representation by independent counsel. If the party is not represented by legal counsel, that party must be fully informed of the terms and basic effect of the premarital agreement as well as the rights and obligations he/she would be giving up by executing it. A writing that describes the rights and obligations that the unrepresented party would be giving up must be delivered to the party prior to the signing of the agreement, and the party must be proficient in the language of the explanation of rights as well as in the language of the premarital agreement. The unrepresented party must also, on or before the signing of the premarital agreement, execute a document declaring that he or she received the explanation of rights and indicate who provided that information. Finally, the premarital agreement and all other writings, including the explanation of rights, must not have been executed under duress, fraud, or undue influence.

Provisions Concerning Infidelity or Spousal Misconduct

California revoked the prior fault grounds for divorce and established "no fault" divorce in 1970. As a result of the change to "no fault," provisions in premarital agreements imposing penalties for infidelity were unenforceable. In *Diosdado v. Diosdado*, 97 Cal. App. 4th 470, 118 Cal. Rptr. 2d 494 (2002), the Court adopted the reasoning of the trial court that the provisions were not enforceable "as contrary to the public policy underlying California's no-fault divorce laws." *Id.* at 473. The Family Code §2310 states that "fault is not a relevant consideration in the legal process by which marriage is dissolved. Recovery in no-fault proceedings 'is basically limited to half the community property and attorney fee orders—no hefty premiums for emotional angst.' In this case, the agreement purports to award a community property premium because of the behavior of the husband. As such, its objective is illegal under Civil Code Section 1667." A California court will not investigate the misconduct of either spouse in a divorce proceeding.

Retroactivity of Family Code Amendments

The issue of retroactivity of statutes relating to family law and, in particular, to community property statutes, has been controversial since 1897. In *Spreckels v. Spreckels*, 116 Cal. 339, 48 P. 228 (1897), the California Supreme Court refused to apply a community property statute retroactively to property acquired prior to the date of the statute. For many years after the *Spreckels* decision, *non-retroactivity* seemed to be the norm regarding community property statutes. In 1976, the California Supreme Court revisited the retroactivity issue and approved retroactivity of a community property statute in the case of *Marriage of Bouquet*, 16 Cal. 3d 583, 546 P.2d 1371, 128 Cal. Rptr. 427 (1976). It was thought that the issue was then settled in favor of *retroactivity* of community property statutes. However, controversy erupted again when the Legislature tried to make statutes regarding joint titles and reimbursement retroactive. The retroactivity of those statutes was not settled until 1995 in *Marriage of Heikes*, 10 Cal. 4th 1211, 899 P.2d 1349, 44 Cal. Rptr. 2d 155. There the Court allowed only very limited *retroactivity*. See Chapter 4 on joint tenancy deeds and titles.

The issue of retroactivity again came before the Court in the family law case of *Marriage of Fellows*, 39 Cal. 4th 179, 138 P.3d 200, 46 Cal. Rptr. 3d 49 (2006). That case involved a Family Code amendment that eliminated the defense of laches in private actions to enforce a child support order. The Legislature had been silent about application of the amendment to child support orders entered prior to the date of the amendment. The Supreme Court turned to Family Code §4 to provide guidance regarding retroactivity. Family Code §4 is a general section that was enacted when the Legislature pulled together provisions from various other statutes in the California codes to create the Family Code. The main purpose of §4 was to make sure that those various provisions still applied to events prior to the effective date of the Family Code, 1994. More significantly, §4(c) made retroactive not only the Family Code itself but also made retroactive *amendments* and *additions* to the Code. Family Code §4(a)(1)(B). As stated in *Fellows*, "[t]hus, as a general rule, future changes to the Family Code apply retroactively." *Id.* at 186, 138 P.3d at 204, 46 Cal. Rptr. 3d at 54. The Supreme Court also found that due process was not offended by retroactively applying the amendment barring the laches defense to the child support order in that case. *Id.* at 189-190, 138 P.3d at 205-206, 46 Cal. Rptr. 3d at 56.

The *Fellows* holding contradicts the usual rule that legislation is considered prospective unless the Legislature makes it retroactive. The *Fellows* interpretation of §4(c) reverses that usual rule regarding the Family Code and amendments to the Family Code: Legislation is considered retroactive unless the Legislature makes it prospective. This reversal of the usual rule potentially affects the 2002 Premarital Agreement Act amendments. Under the *Fellows* holding, because the Legislature was silent about retroactivity of the 2002 amendments, §4(c) should control and the amendments would seem to be considered retroactive.

In fact, one case involving the 2002 amendments was on appeal at the same time as the *Fellows* case was decided. The California Supreme Court dismissed that case, *Marriage of Rosendale*, 15 Cal. Rptr. 3d 137 (2004). The Court cryptically stated that "In light of Family Code section 4 and section 1612, subdivision (c), review . . . is dismissed." *Marriage of Rosendale*, 115 P.3d 417, 31 Cal. Rptr. 3d 95 (2005). It is instructive to flesh out that cryptic statement by applying the *Fellows* reasoning to the *Rosendale* facts. That case involved a pre-2002 premarital agreement that waived spousal support. Both the husband, Warren, and the wife, Carol, were represented by independent counsel. The agreement was signed shortly before their wedding. Eight years later, Carol was involved in a life-shattering auto accident, which caused her extensive and continuing health problems. In divorce proceedings, she challenged the spousal support waiver, citing the new requirements in §1612(c). Even though represented by independent counsel, she claimed the spousal support waiver was unenforceable because the spousal support provision was "unconscionable at the time of enforcement." §1612(c). Warren claimed that the new §1612(c) was not retroactive and therefore did not apply to their premarital agreement that was executed before 2002. Even if §1612(c) did apply retroactively to their premarital agreement, Warren also could have argued that retroactive application would deprive him of a vested right without due process. Under the *Fellows* holding, both Warren's arguments would probably fail.

First, under the *Fellows* holding, §4(c) controls the retroactivity issue. In the face of legislative silence about retroactivity, §4(c) provides that amendments are retroactive. The 2002 amendments were silent about retroactivity. Under the usual rule, those amendments would be prospective. To the contrary, under the *Fellows* holding, silence means retroactivity. Thus, Warren's first argument would be rejected. Warren's second argument would be that applying §1612(c) retroactively would violate due process. He would argue that he had a right to rely on the law as it was when he signed the premarital agreement and applying §1612(c) would deprive him of a vested right without due process. The *Fellows* Court addressed the main considerations regarding due process, which it found codified in an exception to Family Code §4. Family Code §4(h). Those considerations are: (1) the significance of the state interest served by the law and the importance of applying the law retroactively to effectuate that interest, and (2) the extent of reliance on the former law, the legitimacy of that reliance, the extent of actions taken based on that reliance, and the extent that retroactive application of the new law would disrupt those actions. *Marriage of Fellows*, 39 Cal. 4th at 189, 138 P.3d at 205-206, 46 Cal. Rptr. 3d at 56.

The state interest served by §1612(c) is clear. It is to assure that ex-spouses will receive support if unexpected catastrophic circumstances render them unable to be self-sufficient. The public policy is that an ex-spouse rather than state coffers should support a spouse who does not have reasonable means of support. The importance of applying the law retroactively is also evident—spouses need to be assured that when catastrophic circumstances occur, a premarital agreement will be open to reconsideration at the time of divorce. The "rank injustice" cured by §1612(c) is that of a spouse trying to evade support obligations through a premarital agreement. *Marriage of Fellows*, 19 Cal. 4th at 190, 138 P.3d at 206, 46 Cal. Rptr. 3d at 56.

Reliance on the former law is a more difficult issue. At the time the Rosendales signed their premarital agreement, a premarital agreement was unenforceable if the agreement was unconscionable *when it was executed* not *at the time of enforcement*. Family Code §1615(a)(2). The purpose was to provide certainty that premarital agreements would be enforced and not open to reconsideration at the time of divorce. Warren would argue that he relied on the certainty that the premarital agreement would not be reconsidered at the time of divorce. Carol's argument would be that the state policy of support of incapacitated spouses is so important that Warren would never be justified in relying on a premarital agreement that waived that right. Since the Supreme Court dismissed the appeal in the *Rosendale* case based on §4(c) and §1612(c), it can be inferred that Warren's arguments would be rejected and Carol would succeed in having the spousal support waiver declared unconscionable. See Charlotte K. Goldberg, "If It Ain't Broke, Don't Fix It": Premarital Agreements and Spousal Support Waivers in California, 33 Loy. L.A. Rev. 1245 (2000).

The Court of Appeal in *Marriage of Howell*, 195 Cal. App. 4th 1062, 126 Cal. Rptr. 3d 539 (2011), directly addressed the retroactivity of the other requirement of Family Code §1612(c), that a spousal support waiver is not enforceable absent representation by independent counsel. The *Howell* case presented that exact scenario. Michael, who had previously been divorced, wanted a premarital agreement. Pamela reluctantly agreed and signed a premarital agreement that waived spousal support in the event of divorce. The agreement specified that Pamela was advised to seek counsel and waived that right.

The major issue on appeal was whether the 2002 "independent counsel" requirement for spousal support waivers applied to this premarital agreement that was signed in 1998. If the 2002 requirement applied, the spousal support waiver would not be enforceable. If the 2002 requirement did not apply, the spousal support waiver would be enforceable and Pamela would be precluded from seeking spousal support from Michael. The Court of Appeal considered the following issues: (1) whether the 2002 amendment changed the law rather than merely clarifying the law, and (2) if yes, whether the Legislature intended the 2002 amendment to apply retroactively. The Court concluded that the 2002 amendment did change the law, but the Legislature did not intend to apply it retroactively. Thus, the lack of independent counsel did not automatically invalidate the spousal support waiver.

The Court of Appeal did not ignore the *Fellows* Court's rule of retroactivity of Family Code amendments. Instead the Court distinguished this case from *Fellows*. Because the independent counsel requirement imposed new duties on the parties, "the holding and reasoning in *Fellows* . . . are inapposite to the facts and circumstances presented in the case before us." Thus the Court of Appeal concluded there was no need to decide the due process issue. *Id.* at 1077, 126 Cal. Rptr. 3d at 551.

In conclusion, the *Rosendale* and *Howell* decisions together represent the peculiar situation that one part of the spousal support waiver requirements in §1612(c) is retroactive and that the other is not. Under *Rosendale*, the unconscionability of a spousal support waiver can be considered at divorce no matter when the premarital agreement was executed. Under *Howell*, the requirement of independent counsel applies only to those premarital agreements executed on or after January 1, 2002.

The question of the retroactivity of the 2002 amendments enforcement provisions was raised in *Marriage of Hill and Dittmer*, 202 Cal. App. 4th 1046, 136 Cal. Rptr. 3d 700 (2011). There, the Court of Appeal considered whether the "seven-day" rule applied to a premarital agreement executed in 2001. Based on the reasoning of *Howell*, the Court of Appeal concluded that the "seven-day" rule in §1615(c)(2) was like the independent counsel requirement in §1612(c) in that there was a substantive change in the law. Therefore, the "seven-day" rule did not apply retroactively. This Court of Appeal also followed the *Howell* Court's application of the prior law regarding the "voluntariness" of the premarital agreement.

It is doubtful that most of the new requirements in the 2002 amendments that changed both spousal support waiver and enforcement requirements will be applied retroactively despite the Supreme Court's statements in *Fellows* and *Rosendale*. It is most likely that there will be three sets of law depending on when the premarital agreement was executed: (1) before 1986, (2) from 1986 to 2002, and (3) from 2002 to the present. For instance, in *Marriage of Melissa*, 212 Cal. App. 4th 598, 151 Cal. Rptr. 3d 608 (2012), a spousal support waiver in a 1985 premarital agreement was controlled by pre-1986 law and was thus unenforceable because spousal support waivers were against public policy at that time. Also in *Marriage of Facter*, 212 Cal. App. 4th 967, 152 Cal. Rptr. 3d 79 (2013), the unconscionability of a spousal support waiver in a 1994 premarital agreement was controlled by the requirements in the *Pendleton v. Fireman* case, not the 2002 amendments. In *Marriage of Zucker*, 76 Cal. App. 5th 82, 291 Cal. Rptr. 3d 183, modified 75 Cal. App. 5th 1025 (2022), the trial court upheld the validity of a premarital agreement, made after 1986 but before 2002, that kept as his separate property the husband's earnings and assets acquired with separate property funds. The marriage of 20 years had produced six children. Enforcing the agreement against the wife would leave her with only the little separate property she owned at the time of the marriage. The husband would leave the marriage as a multi-millionaire.

The trial court found that the spousal support provisions that limited the wife to $7,500 per month in spousal support were unconscionable. The trial court awarded the wife $40,000 per month in spousal support. The Court of Appeal upheld the trial court's judgment that the property provisions were valid but the spousal support provision was unconscionable and unenforceable at the time of divorce. "We hold that in considering whether a spousal support agreement executed between 1986 and 2002 is enforceable, the court is not limited to a determination under Family Code section 1615, subdivision (a)(2) whether the agreement was unconscionable when executed. Rather, the court retains the power under Family Code section 1612, subdivision (a)(7) to shape public policy regarding premarital spousal support agreements to the extent not inconsistent with Legislative declarations of such policy, and to declare that a premarital spousal support agreement is unenforceable as against public policy solely because it is unconscionable at the time of enforcement." *Id.* at 107.

Examples

Example 1 — Lonely and Neglected?

Harry is a former construction worker currently not working due to disability. Wilma is the CEO of a Fortune 500 company. Prior to their marriage in 1995, Harry and Wilma orally agreed to waive any and all interest in the other party's earnings and acquisitions during marriage. Due to Wilma's rigorous working schedule, Harry often felt lonely and neglected at home. After several years of marriage, Harry petitioned for divorce. At divorce proceedings, Harry argues that the premarital agreement that he and Wilma entered into should be held unenforceable, because a premarital agreement needs to be in writing in accordance with the Statute of Frauds. How does the court rule on Harry's argument, and will the court ultimately uphold the premarital agreement?

Example 2 — Coast-to-Coast Marriage

Herman and Wendy were college sweethearts who planned to get married post-college. Both Wendy and Herman planned to work in investment banking. Herman, however, stayed in California, while Wendy moved to New York to work on Wall Street. Although Herman and Wendy desired to get married, they could not decide where they would live. Herman wanted to live in California, but Wendy loved New York and insisted on staying there. In 2014, Herman orally promised Wendy that if she would quit her job and move to California, upon divorce or his death he would give her title to a Manhattan Beach apartment, which he inherited from his rich uncle. Wendy agreed, quitting her job and moving to California. The two were wed later that year. Recently, it became clear that distance had created a rift in their relationship and Herman filed for divorce. Wendy, in her response, wants to enforce the orally executed premarital agreement and take title to the Manhattan Beach apartment. How will the court rule? Will the premarital agreement be upheld?

Example 3 — Spousal Support Waiver Valid?

George, a lawyer at a successful law firm, and Brenda, a tenured schoolteacher at a prestigious private school, are in a long-term relationship and contemplate getting married. In 2020, they execute a written premarital agreement, with a term that provides that both parties waive their respective rights to receive spousal support from the other in the event of divorce. George's attorney drafted the agreement. Brenda was advised to seek independent legal counsel but declined. The agreement indicated that she waived her right to independent counsel. Brenda was also informed of her rights and obligations at the time the agreement was executed. They marry soon after signing the agreement. They recently separated and are now getting a divorce. Brenda wants to challenge the spousal support waiver of the premarital agreement, claiming it to be invalid under Family Code §1612 since it violates the public policy of the state. How will the court likely rule?

Example 4 — Will Success Spoil Lucy and Ricky's Marriage?

Lucy and Ricky executed a written premarital agreement in January 1990, prior to their wedding in June of that year. Lucy and Ricky decided a premarital agreement would be prudent to "simplify" matters in the case of divorce. Ricky was represented by his attorney friend, who offered his services pro bono. Lucy is unrepresented despite the numerous admonitions from Ricky's attorney to seek independent legal counsel. Ricky and Lucy tell the attorney friend that they want to simplify their financial affairs with an agreement that "what is mine is mine and what is yours is yours." The agreement drafted and signed ultimately provided that both parties waive all rights to the other spouse's earnings and acquisitions during marriage.

Ricky is a 32-year-old Cuban-born immigrant who is struggling to break into show business. Lucy is a 30-year-old housewife with a high school diploma at the time of their marriage. Ricky and Lucy had little to no assets but a wealth of love for each other. A year ago, however, Ricky found sudden success as a club owner and entertainer. He is now making millions. Caught up in the glitz and glamour of his newly found fame, he petitions for divorce from Lucy and begins to date a supermodel. Lucy is incensed and wants to attack the enforceability of the premarital agreement during dissolution proceedings. What defenses to enforceability might Lucy raise and how successful will each argument be?

Example 5 — Chris, Get Your Own Lawyer!

Jennifer is a highly successful actress and singer worth millions of dollars. She meets Chris, a struggling backup dancer, at one of the auditions for her music video. They instantly fall in love and become engaged to be married. On December 1, 2002, Jennifer's attorney presents Chris with a premarital agreement in which each party's earnings and acquisitions during the marriage will be treated as their own separate property. Chris is not represented by independent legal counsel, despite the multiple admonitions from Jennifer and her attorney that he should seek his own lawyer. Because of Chris's stubborn refusal to seek counsel of his own, Jennifer's attorney calls Chris on his cell phone and fully informs him of the terms and effect of the premarital agreement and the rights and obligations he would be giving up by signing it. Chris says he is fully aware of what he is relinquishing by signing the agreement and accordingly executes the agreement on January 1, 2003. They marry that day. Upon divorce, would this be an enforceable premarital agreement?

Example 6 — Chris Gets His Own Lawyer

Assume the same facts as Example 5, except that Chris takes the advice of Jennifer's attorney and is represented by his own independent legal counsel. On December 6, 2002, they sign the agreement and are married the same day. What result?

Example 7 — What About Spousal Support?

Assume the same facts as Example 5, except that there is an additional provision added to the premarital agreement on wedding day that spousal support will be limited to $50 a month. Will this provision be enforceable? Is it a substantive addition or not? What if Chris had been represented by independent legal counsel?

Explanations

Explanation 1 — Lonely and Neglected?

The court will rule that the premarital agreement between Harry and Wilma is unenforceable. Under the 1986 Premarital Agreement Act (Family Code §1611), premarital agreements must be in writing and signed by both parties. Here, we have an oral agreement. Thus, Harry's argument against enforcement will be successful.

Explanation 2 — Coast-to-Coast Marriage?

The general rule is that premarital agreements must be in writing and signed by both parties (Family Code §1611). However, these agreements are also subject to most of the Statute of Frauds exceptions, as are other contracts. As illustrated in *Hall v. Hall*, 222 Cal. App. 3d 578, 271 Cal. Rptr. 773 (1990), promissory estoppel is one exception to the writing requirement. Under *Hall*, where one party performed his/her part of the bargain and in doing so, irretrievably changed his/her position, even an oral premarital agreement will be upheld.

Here, the court could rule that there was an enforceable premarital agreement based on promissory estoppel principles. By quitting her job and moving to another state, Wendy irretrievably changed her position in reliance on Herman's promise to provide her with the Manhattan Beach apartment upon divorce or death. Herman would argue that the facts of this case differ significantly from *Hall*. There, the couple was older, and the wife was living on Social Security after she quit her job. Here, Wendy is young and has the possibility of resuming her career in investment banking. Also Wendy's moving to reside with her spouse is arguably an act common in marriage and would not be considered "irretrievably changing position." Finally, in *Hall*, providing a home for a widow overcame the strictures of the Statute of Frauds. The equities are weaker in a divorce case where a spouse can "change position" again to retrieve her losses.

Explanation 3—Spousal Support Waiver Valid?

According to the law prior to the 2002 amendments to Family Code §1612(c), spousal support waivers were not per se unenforceable. *Pendleton v. Fireman*, 24 Cal. 4th 39, 5 P.3d 839, 99 Cal. Rptr. 2d 278 (2000). The issue here is whether the 2002 Premarital Agreement Act amendments, especially §1612(c), apply retroactively. According to *Marriage of Fellows*, 39 Cal. 4th 179, 138 P.3d 200, 46 Cal. Rptr. 3d 49 (2006), the Family Code and Family Code amendments are retroactive unless application would violate due process. The amendment to §1612(c) requires independent counsel at the time the premarital agreement is signed. That requirement was not met in George and Brenda's case. In *Marriage of Howell*, 195 Cal. App. 4th 1062, 126 Cal. Rptr. 3d 539 (2011), the Court of Appeal held that the independent counsel requirement of §1612(c) was not retroactive to premarital agreements executed before January 1, 2002. Therefore, the spousal support waiver would likely be enforceable against Brenda.

The 2002 amendment also provides that even if there is independent counsel, a spousal support waiver can be reexamined at the time of enforcement and will be unenforceable if unconscionable at that time. According to *Marriage of Rosendale*, 115 P.3d 417, 31 Cal. Rptr. 3d 95 (2005), the unconscionable-at-time-of-enforcement requirement would apply to premarital agreements prior to January 1, 2002. Therefore, Brenda would be able to challenge the spousal support waiver as unconscionable. Unconscionability is a matter of law that would be decided by the court.

Family Code §1615(b). Here there would probably be a disparity in the earning capacity between George, who is a lawyer at a successful law firm, and Brenda, who is a schoolteacher. However, since they have been married since 2000, they probably have accumulated community property that may be sufficient to provide Brenda reasonable means of support. Unless Brenda has fallen to the level of needing state support, it is likely that a court would enforce the spousal support waiver.

Explanation 4—Will Success Spoil Lucy and Ricky's Marriage?

Lucy and Ricky's agreement involves property rights and does not address the issue of spousal support. Thus, enforceability of the agreement depends on Family Code §1615, not §1612. It is clear that property rights are a proper subject of premarital agreements. §1612(a)(1). Under §1615, Lucy can invalidate the premarital agreement in only one of two ways. She has the burden of proof because she is the "party against whom enforcement is sought." She can first try to argue that she did not execute the agreement voluntarily. Her second option is to argue that (1) the agreement was unconscionable when it was entered into and (2) before execution of the agreement, the spouse was not provided with fair and reasonable disclosure of the property or financial obligations of the party.

Lucy's first argument is that she did not execute the agreement voluntarily. Prior to the 2002 Premarital Agreement Act Amendments, the term "voluntarily" was not defined. Courts would look at the factors outlined in *Marriage of Bonds*, 24 Cal. 4th 1, 5 P.3d 815, 99 Cal. Rptr. 2d 252 (2000). Unfortunately for Lucy, she does not have a strong argument based on those factors. There was no surprise in presentation of the agreement, as both parties jointly decided to get a premarital agreement. There was no inequality of bargaining power, as both parties were approximately the same age, there was no great disparity of sophistication, and neither party was wealthy at the time of execution. Lucy understood the intent of the agreement, and Ricky disclosed all assets he had to Lucy.

One major issue that must be resolved is Lucy's lack of independent legal counsel. The *Bonds* Court considered that to be only one factor among all the other factors that determined whether a premarital agreement was voluntary. Following *Bonds*, a court might find that Lucy executed the agreement voluntarily. Even though the *Fellows* case suggested that changes to the Family Code are presumptively retroactive, the Courts of Appeal in *Marriage of Howell*, 195 Cal. App. 4th 1062, 126 Cal. Rptr. 3d 539 (2011), and *Marriage of Hill and Dittmer*, 202 Cal. App. 4th 1046, 136 Cal. Rptr. 3d 700 (2011), declined to apply the 2002 amendments retroactively. Thus, the *Bonds* requirements would apply to this case and Lucy would probably have no rights to Ricky's earnings.

Lucy could argue that (1) the agreement was unconscionable when it was entered into and (2) before execution of the agreement, the spouse was notprovided with fair and reasonable disclosure of the property or financial obligations of the party. This argument will also fail. With Ricky's new wealth, an agreement to waive rights to the other spouse's earnings during marriage seems very unfair to Lucy, and possibly "unconscionable." Family Code §1615, however, looks at whether the agreement was unconscionable *at the time it was entered into*. At the time of execution, both Ricky and Lucy did not have any substantial assets. It is thus unlikely the agreement was unconscionable. Even if the court believed the agreement to be unconscionable, we see that Lucy would not have been able to fulfill the second prong of the analysis, as Ricky provided her with fair and reasonable disclosure of his assets before execution of the agreement. Could *Zucker* public policy reasoning apply?

Explanation 5 — Chris, Get Your Own Lawyer!

Under the 2002 Premarital Agreement Act amendments, the premarital agreement would be deemed unenforceable by Family Code §1615(c), which states that an agreement is "not executed voluntarily" where the party against whom enforcement is sought was not represented by legal counsel at the time the agreement was signed. In our example, Chris, despite claims of knowledge of the rights he would be giving up, was still unrepresented by legal counsel.

If Chris had expressly waived, in a separate writing, representation by independent counsel after being advised to seek counsel, then we might have had a different result. Not only must the waiver of independent counsel be in writing, but an oral explanation of the terms and effect of the agreement and the rights and obligations given up must also be "memorialized in writing." But Chris did not execute an express written waiver. In addition, he received the required explanation orally and it was not memorialized in writing. The premarital agreement will be unenforceable against Chris.

Explanation 6 — Chris Gets His Own Lawyer

This agreement would likely be enforceable. The "independent legal counsel" requirement prescribed by §1615(c) has been met. The only question that remains is whether the "seven-day" requirement was met. Here Chris was presented with the agreement and advised to seek independent counsel on December 1 and signed the agreement on December 6, less than the seven days mandated by §1615(c). Therefore, if the "seven-day" requirement applies, the agreement would not be enforceable because it would not be considered voluntarily entered into. However, under *Marriage of Cadwell-Faso and Faso*, 191 Cal. App. 4th 945, 119 Cal Rptr. 3d 838 (2011), the "seven-day" requirement applies only to unrepresented parties. Since Chris was represented by legal counsel, there is no waiting period and the agreement would likely be enforceable.

Explanation 7 — What About Spousal Support?

Under the 2002 Premarital Agreement Act amendments (§1612(c)), spousal support provisions are not enforceable unless the party against whom enforcement is sought is represented by independent counsel at the time the premarital agreement was signed. In our original example, Chris is unrepresented. Thus, the agreement is unenforceable.

Even if Chris was represented by independent counsel, however, this spousal support provision is likely to be held unenforceable. Under §1612(c), even if the party is represented by his/her own counsel, an unconscionable spousal support provision will not be enforced. A limit of $50 of spousal support a month is likely to be considered unconscionable, especially in light of Jennifer's wealth and earning capabilities.

TRANSMUTATION: PRIOR TO 1985

A chameleon can change color depending on its environment. The law regarding transmutation in California was like a chameleon prior to 1985. It was surprisingly simple to change property from separate property to community property and vice versa. It could be done by a conversation. It could be done by conduct. It led to much litigation about what the spouses said and thought and did.

The classic example of how easy it was, prior to 1985, to transmute property is the case of *Estate of Raphael*, 91 Cal. App. 2d 931, 206 P.2d 391 (1949). In that case, in a dispute between the son and wife of Raymond Theodore Raphael, the wife, Bertha, claimed that all of Raymond's separate property had been transmuted to community property by their oral agreement. That agreement occurred at tax time. Bertha testified:

> He told me that now that we were married, that we were partners, and marriage is a partnership, and we had to file taxes and he said that everything he had was mine and everything that I had was his; that we were partners, and everything was fifty-fifty.

The Court of Appeal stated, "The object of the oral agreement of transmutation was fully performed when the agreement was made for it immediately transmuted and converted the separate property of each spouse into community property and nothing further remained to be done." *Id.* at 939, 206 P.2d at 394. The sharp law student will say, "OK, here we have a poor widow and the husband was not there to testify, so that could justify the decision in *Raphael*." Also, we favor community property as a matter of policy.

On one point, the sharp law student is correct. It is much more difficult to prove an oral agreement when a spouse is there to testify to the contrary, as in a divorce proceeding. Memories of conversations are often blurry and memories sometimes change when the consequences of the conversations are explained in a lawyer's office. In the case of *Marriage of Jafeman*, 29 Cal. App. 3d 244, 105 Cal. Rptr. 483 (1972), the only evidence supporting an agreement to convert husband Edward's house he owned before marriage to community property was wife Mary's testimony that "they always referred to the residence as 'our home'" and Mary's belief that the home was "our property." The Court looked at whether referring to the home as "our home" was sufficient to transmute the property and answered, "No." It was the intent of the spouse whose interest was affected that controlled, and their conversations were not enough to indicate that Edward agreed to transmute his separate property to community property. The Court added that "Mary's beliefs" were insufficient to show Edward's intent to transmute his separate property to community property. Here we learn that, in terms of property concepts, the question is really not one of "agreement" but of a "gift" by the spouse who would be giving up his or her interest in the property.

What compelled the Legislature to change the law regarding transmutation was the litigation resulting from the ease with which transmutation could be accomplished. The example that struck the legislators most forcefully was *Marriage of Lucas*, 27 Cal. 3d 808, 614 P.2d 285, 166 Cal. Rptr. 853 (1980). In that case, the transmutation was from community property to the separate property of the wife, Brenda. There, Gerald and Brenda purchased a mini-motor home partially with community property and partially with Brenda's separate property funds. Brenda's funds made up 75.4% of the cost of the motor home. The Supreme Court affirmed the trial court's determination that Gerald transmuted his interest in the motor home as it was supported by sufficient evidence: Brenda wished to have title in her name alone, and title and registration were taken in Brenda's name alone. Although the purchase agreement was in Gerald's name alone, Gerald did not object to the title and registration being in Brenda's name. As we know, the evidence that the title was in Brenda's name is not necessarily determinative of the character of the property. Also, the funds used to purchase the motor home show apportionment, part separate/part community, not that Brenda's separate property was the exclusive source. So, in essence, it was Gerald's silence that resulted in transmutation of the entire asset into Brenda's separate property. That failure to object was sufficient to transmute Gerald's interest in the community property to Brenda's separate property. That decision, criticized by noted Professor William Reppy and the Law Revision Commission, spurred the Legislature into action. *See Estate of MacDonald*, 51 Cal. 3d 262, 794 P.2d 911, 272 Cal. Rptr. 153 (1990). In 2015, the California Supreme Court stated that this "portion of the decision is no longer good law." *Marriage of Valli*, 58 Cal. 4th 1396, 1406 fn.2, 324 P.3d 274, 280 fn.2, 171 Cal. Rptr. 3d 454, 462 fn.2 (2014).

TRANSMUTATION: 1985 TO THE PRESENT

As of January 1, 1985, it became much more difficult for the property chameleon to change its color. The statute applies to transmutations on January 1, 1985, or thereafter. The "easy transmutation" doctrine applies to transmutations prior to 1985. Family Code §852(e). Please be clear here—the critical time is the date of the alleged transmutation not the date of the acquisition of the property. Therefore, the Legislature clearly intended the new rules regarding transmutation to apply to all property owned by *spouses no matter when the property was acquired*. The Legislature put all married couples on notice that, as of January 1, 1985, if they wanted to transmute their property, new rules applied.

In addition, the scope of the 1985 statute is broad. Those rules apply to transmutations of community property to separate property of either spouse and to separate property of either spouse to community property or to separate property of the other spouse. Family Code §850(a)-(c). The transmutation may be by written agreement or transfer, with or without consideration. §850.

The major questions are (1) how to accomplish that transmutation, and (2) whether there are any exceptions to the rigorous requirements of the statute. First, the transmutation must be accomplished "in writing by an express declaration." §852(a). Second, it is the spouse "whose interest in the property is adversely affected" who must make, join, consent to, or accept the express declaration in writing. Clearly, the statutory writing requirement reverses the "easy transmutation" doctrine and opts for a very strict requirement to transmute the property. Oral agreements will not work; the conduct of the parties will not change the character of the property. Informality of transmutation has been changed to a very formal procedure. However, the statute also makes clear that it is the intention of the spouse adversely affected by the transmutation that controls. Although a transmutation may be accomplished by a written agreement, what really matters is the written understanding of the spouse whose interest is affected by the transmutation.

How to Transmute: *Estate of MacDonald*

The first California Supreme Court case that defined what type of document will actually accomplish a transmutation was *Estate of MacDonald*, 51 Cal. 3d 262, 794 P.2d 911, 272 Cal. Rptr. 153 (1990). Because the Legislature included the language "express declaration," the Court concluded that not all written documents would be sufficient to transmute the property. The case involved the sad situation of Margery MacDonald, facing terminal cancer and trying with her husband, Robert, to arrange their financial affairs prior to her demise. The property in question was Robert's IRA accounts. Robert designated his trust as the beneficiary of the IRA, and Margery signed a form that stated, "I hereby consent to the above designation [of the trust]." The question in the case was whether that writing was sufficient to transmute Margery's community property interest in the IRA accounts to Robert's separate property. The Court held that it was not.

The Court explained that to meet the "express declaration" requirement, the document must "contain language which expressly states that the characterization of ownership of the property is being changed." No such language was found in the "I consent" form. The Court indicated that "magic words" would suffice: "transmutation," "community property," or "separate property." However, the Court also held that "magic words" are not required but the language must show that the spouse affected knows that he/she is giving up his/her interest in the property. The Court suggested the following language in a *MacDonald*-type situation: "I give to the account holder any interest I have in the funds deposited in this account." California banks promptly adopted that language in IRA agreements.

Even more important, the Court interpreted the language of the statute to preclude the introduction of extrinsic evidence to supplement the words in the written document. The Court recognized that extrinsic evidence in some cases could show an intent to transmute, but that the Legislature intended to eliminate reliance on that type of evidence in enacting the "express declaration" requirement. Thus it is the documentary language that controls, not extrinsic evidence of the spouse's intent. A clear-cut rule that will minimize litigation has replaced the informality of most spouses' treatment of property. Perhaps it is only lawyers who will be able to assist in validly transmuting property. Most spouses will find that their informal understandings will probably not control. Written documents will be the major determinants of the character of marital property. Extreme informality has given way to extreme formality.

Since the California Supreme Court decided *Estate of MacDonald*, the lower courts have adhered to the strict writing requirement enunciated in that case. In *Marriage of Barneson*, 69 Cal. App. 4th 583, 81 Cal. Rptr. 2d 726 (1999), the Court of Appeal discussed whether particular language in a document was sufficient to meet the express declaration in writing requirement. In *Barneson*, at the time when Robert Barneson married Evelyn Kaiser in 1988, he was 65 years old and she was almost 36. The next year, Robert suffered a stroke. The following year, after recovering from the stroke, Robert signed a letter instructing his stockbroker to "transfer" certain stocks into Evelyn's name. The transfer was accomplished according to the procedural requirements of the Securities and Exchange Commission. In 1992, Robert filed for divorce and sought return of the "transferred" stock. After the couple divorced but before the property issues were resolved, Robert died. The trial court found that the transfer of the stock met the requirements of Family Code §852 and constituted a valid transmutation to Evelyn.

The executor of Robert's estate appealed. The Court of Appeal reversed and held that the word "transfer" did not accomplish a transmutation. Although the letter was in writing, the word "transfer" did not specify that Robert's interest in the stock was to be transferred. According to the Court, "a direction by a spouse to transfer stock into his spouse's name does not unambiguously indicate the ownership of the stock is being changed." *Id.* at 591, 81 Cal. Rptr. 2d at 732. The Court of Appeal stressed that the writing itself must show that a spouse "truly intended a transmutation," such as "adding a sentence indicating he was giving his interest in the stocks" or directing that the stock should be transferred to her name "as her sole and separate property." *Id.* at 593-594, 81 Cal. Rptr. 2d at 733.

In *Marriage of Lafkas*, 237 Cal. App. 4th 921, 188 Cal. Rptr. 3d 484 (2015), the Court of Appeal held that the transmutation statute was not satisfied by the language "husband and wife as owners" in the modification of a real estate partnership agreement. This illustrates again how strictly the lower courts have followed the mandate of *MacDonald*.

In *the Marriage of Begian and Sarajian*, 31 Cal. App. 5th 506, 242 Cal. Rptr. 3d 692 (2018), the court considered whether the term "grant" in a "trust transfer deed" met the transmutation requirements of Family Code §852. Husband, wife, and wife's mother were co-owners of real property in Glendale, California. The three of them executed a "Trust Transfer Deed" which provided as follows: for no consideration, the three co-owners "hereby grant" ownership of specific real property [Avonoak] to Ida Sarajian. The deed states that the conveyance was not subject to a documentary transfer tax because "this is a bona fide gift." At divorce, husband claimed that the real property was community property because the Trust Transfer Deed did not alter the fact that the portion of the property in the names of husband and wife was community property. Wife claimed that the deed complied with Family Code §852 and transmuted the community property to separate property. The trial court agreed with wife that the community property had been transmuted to her separate property by the used of the word "grant." However, the Court of Appeal reversed, finding that the term "grant" was ambiguous because the word only established husband's intention to transfer an interest in real property, without specifying what interest was to be transferred.

Extrinsic Evidence

The Supreme Court in *MacDonald* also stated that the Legislature intended to eliminate reliance on extrinsic evidence to prove transmutations. Therefore, reference to the written documents will determine whether a particular asset has been transmuted and evidence of oral agreements will be excluded. This attitude toward extrinsic evidence and oral agreements was reflected in *Marriage of Campbell*, 74 Cal. App. 4th 1058, 88 Cal. Rptr. 2d 584 (1999). In that case, the wife, Jean, had used her separate property to improve the home that her husband, Robert, owned prior to their marriage. Jean claimed that they had an oral agreement to add her name to the title to the property. It was not added before the couple separated. In the divorce proceedings, Jean wanted the court to consider their oral agreement. The trial court refused to consider evidence of the oral agreement that would have transmuted the home from Robert's separate property to community property. The Court of Appeal agreed with the trial court and rejected all of Jean's arguments concerning extrinsic evidence and oral agreements. In other words, the original characterization of property will control unless the transmutation is in writing. The transmutation statute "precludes the admission of extrinsic evidence to prove an oral transmutation of property between spouses." *Id.* at 1065, 88 Cal. Rptr. at 585.

One argument in the *Campbell* case was that extrinsic evidence should be permitted when an exception to the Statute of Frauds is involved. The Court of Appeal in *Campbell* concluded that the Supreme Court in *MacDonald* had precluded the consideration of extrinsic evidence whenever a transmutation was under consideration. *Id.* at 1064, 88 Cal. Rptr. at 584. Instead, only the documents involved should control. In *Marriage of Benson*, 36 Cal. 4th 1096, 116 P.3d 1152, 32 Cal. Rptr. 3d 471 (2005), the California Supreme Court agreed with the *Campbell* Court's narrow reading of the transmutation statute. In *Benson*, the husband, Douglas, argued that the exception to the Statute of Frauds for partial performance should apply. The Supreme Court rejected his argument, stating, "we see no evidence the Legislature intended to incorporate traditional exceptions to the statute of frauds into section 852." *Id.* at 1109, 116 P.3d at 1160, 32 Cal. Rptr. 3d at 480. In that case, the wife, Diane, had a trust that was her separate property. She and her husband, Douglas, also owned a home. Douglas had a pension and a gumball business. The home (at least a 72% interest in the home), the pension, and the gumball business were all community property. During their marriage, Douglas signed a deed that transferred his interest in the home to the wife's trust, thereby transmuting his community property interest in the home to the wife's separate property. Douglas testified that he agreed to sign the deed only because Diane agreed to give up her interest in his pension benefits. That agreement was not in writing.

Let us now examine these facts using the strict transmutation requirements and the rule that requires exclusion of extrinsic evidence to prove an oral agreement. The deed that Douglas signed is the transmutation. That deed was in writing and signed by Douglas, whose interest was adversely affected. That deed meets the express declaration in writing requirement of Family Code §852(a) and means that Douglas's community interest was transmuted into Diane's separate property. The agreement regarding the pension was oral. Since there was no writing that showed Diane gave up her right to Douglas's community property pension, it should have been characterized as community property. Evidence of their oral agreement is extrinsic evidence that must be excluded. The inequity to Douglas was that the application of the rules means that Diane receives the home as her separate property *and* retains her right to one-half of Douglas's retirement assets.

Douglas made a contrary argument that was accepted by the trial court. The court noted the inequity that Douglas gave up a very valuable interest in the house of between $400,000 and $500,000 in return for retirement assets valued at a little over $91,000. That would be the result if the court upheld the oral agreement. If not, Diane would also have a right to one-half of the retirement assets. How then did the trial court avoid the rule that required exclusion of extrinsic evidence to prove an oral agreement? The court reasoned that the writing requirement could be ignored if there was an exception to the Statute of Frauds. Here that exception would be partial performance of the oral agreement—when Douglas transferred his interest in the home to Diane, he partially performed and therefore was justified in relying on her oral promise to waive her interest in his retirement assets. Thus, the trial court concluded that Diane had no community property interest in the retirement benefits.

The Court of Appeal agreed with the trial court's analysis and its reliance on the case of *Hall v. Hall*, 22 Cal. App. 3d 578, 271 Cal. Rptr. 773 (1990). Even though *Hall* involved an oral premarital agreement, the Court of Appeal supported the notion that partial performance provides an exception to all Statute of Frauds requirements and therefore it was proper to consider the extrinsic evidence of the couple's oral transmutation agreement. *Benson*, 7 Cal. Rptr. 3d at 910-911. The Court of Appeal also read the *MacDonald* decision to apply to solely oral transmutations, and this case involves "an express written transmutation with a contemporaneous oral promise to waive wife's interest in a community property retirement fund." *Benson*, 7 Cal. Rptr. 3d at 912.

The Supreme Court rejected the partial performance exception to the strict writing requirement of the transmutation statute. *Marriage of Benson*, 36 Cal. 4th 1096, 116 P.3d 1152, 32 Cal. Rptr. 3d 471 (2005). The Court suggested that the proper course was for Douglas to try to undo the transmutation by claiming that the wife, Diane, breached her fiduciary duty under Family Code §721(b). Family Code §721(b) states that "neither [spouse] shall take any unfair advantage of the other." Here, the only writing was Douglas's signing of the deed transferring his community property interest to Diane's separate property. In a concurring opinion, Justice Moreno pointed out that §721(b) could apply "when . . . one spouse unfairly gains a benefit from the other spouse in exchange for an orally promised transmutation that in fact has no legal effect." *Id.* at 1112, 116 P.3d at 1162, 32 Cal. Rptr. 3d at 483.

That seemed to be the case in *Benson* because Diane gained what could be characterized as an unfair benefit because she received Douglas's community property interest in the home and also retained her right to Douglas's community property pension. That benefit was based on her oral promise to give up her right to the pension; that oral promise had no legal effect because it did not meet the writing requirement of §852. However, the Court's suggestion was of no help to Douglas because his main argument on appeal was based on the partial performance exception to §852's writing requirement and he had settled any claim he had regarding the deed.

Thus, the Supreme Court clarified that the strict writing requirements of §852 are very strict—no extrinsic evidence allowed, no exceptions to the Statute of Frauds allowed. However, *dicta* in *Benson* direct attorneys to challenge transmutations based on breach of fiduciary duty. See Chapter 6 on fiduciary duty.

Marriage of Valli: Rule and Application

The Supreme Court addressed a major issue in *Marriage of Valli*, 58 Cal. 4th 1396, 324 P.3d 174, 171 Cal. Rptr. 3d 454 (2014). Did the transmutation statute apply only to "interspousal transactions," or did it also apply to "acquisitions from a third party"? The acquisition in question was a life insurance policy acquired with community property by the husband, Frankie Valli. He named his wife, Randy, as the "owner" of the policy. At the time of the dissolution of their marriage, the policy had a cash value of $365,000. Frankie argued that the policy was community property because it was purchased with community funds. Randy argued that the policy was her separate property because Frankie arranged to have the policy put in her name, therefore changing the policy to her separate property. The trial court agreed with Frankie; the Court of Appeal agreed with Randy.

At the Supreme Court, Randy argued that the transmutation statute and its strict requirements did not apply to this transaction because Frankie purchased the policy from a third party and thus placing it in her name was not an "interspousal transaction." The Supreme Court rejected Randy's argument. The Court traced the history of the transmutation statute and the cases that led to the perception that there may be a difference if a purchase is made from a third party. According to the Court, the transmutation statute should apply to both interspousal and third-party transactions because "it is difficult to conceive any justification for treating these two . . . scenarios differently." *Id.* at 1402, 324 P.3d at 277, 171 Cal. Rptr. 3d at 459. If they were treated differently, the purpose of the transmutation statute to prevent easy transmutation would be undermined.

Because there was no evidence that the "express declaration" requirement of the transmutation statute was met, Frankie never "gave up his community interest in the policy bought with community funds." *Id.* at 1407, 324 P.3d at 280, 171 Cal. Rptr. 3d at 462. Thus, the Court determined that designating a spouse as "owner" is insufficient to establish a transmutation. The California Supreme Court in *In re Brace*, 9 Cal. 5th 903, 470 P.3d 15, 266 Cal. Rptr. 3d 298 (2020), reaffirmed that the "community property presumption" of Family Code §760, overrides a "separate title" presumption. The Court had to determine whether property acquired by husband and wife using community property funds had been transmuted to separate property by the spouses taking title as Joint Tenants. The husband had filed for Chapter 7 bankruptcy and argued that the bankruptcy creditors could only reach his 50% of the property. The wife had not joined her husband in filing for bankruptcy, and claimed that her share of the property was separate property and not reachable by the bankruptcy trustee. The Court held that "[F]or property acquired with community funds on or after January 1, 1983, titling of a deed in joint tenancy, is not sufficient to transmute community property to separate property under Cal. Fam. Code 852." *Id.* at 947.

Gift Exception

The Legislature did recognize that not all transmutations of marital property should be in writing. The 1985 transmutation statute excludes certain gifts from the express declaration requirement. Family Code §852(c). There were, however, limitations on the gift exclusion. The gift in question is required to be

> A gift between the spouses of clothing, wearing apparel, jewelry, or other tangible articles of a personal nature,
>
> That is used solely or principally by the spouse to whom the gift is made, and
>
> That is not substantial in value taking into consideration the circumstances of the marriage.

All three requirements must be met, or there has to be an express declaration in writing to transmute the gift to the separate property of the donee spouse. For instance, in *Marriage of Steinberger*, 91 Cal. App. 4th 1449, 111 Cal. Rtpr. 2d 521 (2001), the couple purchased an expensive diamond from funds conceded to be community property. For their fifth wedding anniversary, the husband, James, took the diamond and had it mounted in a gold setting. He gave it to his wife, Buff, with a card. Based on the first two criteria, that should have worked a transmutation of the diamond ring into the wife's separate property without an express declaration in writing. The husband gave her the ring, an item of jewelry, and she wore it. However, the trial court found that the ring was "substantial in value considering the circumstances of their marriage." Therefore, the Court of Appeal concluded, "Under the clear statutory provision of section 852, gifts of personal property that are substantial in value taking into account the circumstances of the marriage will not be considered converted to separate property without the writing required by section 852." *Id.* at 1466, 111 Cal. Rptr. 2d at 534. Thus, since the ring was purchased with community funds and there was no express declaration in writing that the husband was giving up his interest in the community property, the ring was community property. Thus, if the wife wanted to keep the ring, she would owe the husband one-half of the value of the ring.

At the end of the list of gifts that are not subject to the "express declaration in writing" requirement is the catchall phrase "tangible articles of a personal nature." The question of whether an expensive Porsche automobile could be a "tangible article of a personal nature" was raised in *Marriage of Neighbors*, 179 Cal. App. 4th 1170, 102 Cal. Rptr. 3d 387 (2009). There the wife, Tatia, purchased a Porsche for $60,000. The husband, Walter, considered the Porsche a gift from her because it was bought shortly before his birthday. The trial court found that the Porsche had been transmuted to Walter's separate property.

Tatia appealed, arguing that the Porsche was not a tangible article and for it to be transmuted to Walter's separate property would have required her to create an express declaration in writing. There was no such writing. The Court of Appeal accepted part of the trial court's analysis: that the general community property presumption applied to the Porsche. The Court stated that unless the Porsche was a tangible article, it would be considered community property. There was also evidence that the Porsche was purchased with Tatia's separate property funds.

Automobiles have a special place in California culture. Californians spend much of their time driving, and many feel that a car is personal enough that it could even be considered part of their persona. The Court, however, held that an automobile is not a tangible article of a personal nature. *Id.* at 1175, 102 Cal. Rptr. 3d at 390. Knowing the place cars hold in California culture, the framers of the gift exception probably considered this particular issue since the California Law Revision Commission used the gift of an automobile as a specific example of what is *not* an article of a personal nature. *Id.* at 1175, 102 Cal. Rptr. 3d at 390 (quoting from the commission report).

The Court of Appeal reversed the determination that the Porsche was Walter's separate property and remanded. The Court supported Tatia's second argument that if the Porsche were to be characterized as community property, she would have a right to reimbursement of her separate property funds. This part of the Court's analysis raises some questions. If, on remand, the trial court applies the general community property presumption and Tatia can trace the purchase to her separate property funds, she would be able to rebut the community property presumption and the Porsche would be *her* separate property. Perhaps she does not really want the Porsche but would prefer to receive the funds she used to buy it, or at least the value of the Porsche if it has depreciated in value. See Chapter 3, Evidentiary Presumptions, and Chapter 4, The Role of Title in Characterization of Property.

"Commingled or Otherwise Combined"

Another exception to the express declaration in writing requirement is more problematic and enigmatic. Family Code §852(d) states that "nothing in this section affects the law governing characterization of property in which separate and community property are commingled or otherwise combined." Only one part is clear and that is "commingling." Commingling is a term of art that refers to separate and community funds being deposited in a bank account or other type of account. The rules regarding commingling are treated in Chapter 5. The statute says that the commingling rules, not §852, will govern characterization of commingled property.

The enigmatic part here is the phrase "otherwise combined." It could mean that when personal property that is untitled or titled in one spouse's name is acquired using both community and separate property funds, characterization is controlled by the source of the funds not by an express declaration in writing. That interpretation seems to undermine the entire purpose of the express declaration in writing requirement. So far that part of the statute has not been successfully invoked to circumvent the statutory requirement of an express declaration in writing.

The argument that "combining funds" overcomes the requirement of an express declaration writing was made in *Estate of Murphy*, 2001 WL 16040734 (not certified for publication). Julie Murphy argued that she had used her separate property to make mortgage payments and pay for remodeling of the home she and her husband had lived in. When Julie's husband died without a will, his sons from a former marriage claimed the home as the husband's separate property. Julie argued that she and her husband had an oral agreement that the property "was now community property." Because "combined" funds were used for the house, the express declaration requirement did not apply and thus their oral agreement controlled the characterization of the home. The Court of Appeal rejected her argument and left her with the possibility of seeking reimbursement for her separate property contributions to the improvement of the property. The case itself was not certified for publication so the status of the arguments made in the case is questionable.

The only other common scenario where funds are "combined" is where spouses use separate property and community property funds to purchase an asset and take the title in joint form. At divorce, when property is held in joint form and there are "combined" funds used to purchase the asset, Family Code §2581 controls characterization of that property. If a spouse argues like Julie Murphy that an oral transmutation controls when there is a joint title and "combined funds," the best counterargument is that the law governing characterization is Family Code §2581 only. It is likely that a court will accept that argument because the Legislature has provided specific requirements for characterization of property held in joint form regardless of the funds "combined" to purchase the property. Characterization of property held in joint form is explained in Chapter 4.

"Statement in a Will"

Finally, Family Code §853 indicates that in some cases "a statement in a will" can effect a transmutation. For instance, let's say Harry puts in his will the following statement: "I bequeath to my beloved wife, Wilma, my coin collection as her separate property." It would hold up as an express declaration in writing as it is clear that Harry wants her to have the coin collection as her separate property and knows that he would be changing the character of the property from either community property or his separate property. Section 853 puts a limitation on the use of that statement. It would not be admissible "as evidence of a transmutation of the property in a proceeding commenced *before* the death of the person who made the will." That means that in a divorce proceeding, the statement in Harry's will could not be used to show that the coin collection was transmuted into Wilma's separate property. It makes sense both emotionally and legally! If Harry and Wilma divorce, Harry would in all likelihood have changed his mind about giving the coin collection to Wilma as her separate property. Also, it makes legal sense because a will does not become effective until the death of the decedent, and therefore, Harry may change his will at any time up to his death. As a matter of practicality, it would be good advice for Harry to change his will as soon as the couple has separated.

A will is not the only document that can be used for estate planning. The other major document used for estate planning is a trust. Married couples often consult a lawyer to draw up documents that provide for favorable estate tax treatment in the event one spouse dies. Generally, community property receives more favorable tax treatment at death than separate property. In two recent cases, the creation of a trust was accompanied by an agreement containing language that was considered to denote a transmutation of one spouse's separate property into community property. *Marriage of Holtemann*, 166 Cal. App. 4th 1166, 83 Cal. Rptr. 3d 385 (2008); *Marriage of Lund*, 174 Cal. App. 4th 40, 94 Cal. Rptr. 3d 84 (2009). In *Holtemann*, the agreement used express language of transmutation: "Husband agrees that the character of the property . . . is hereby transmuted from his separate property to the community property of both parties." *Holtemann*, 166 Cal. App. 4th at 1172, 83 Cal. Rptr. 3d at 390. Similarly, in *Lund*, the language signified a transmutation: "All of the property . . . is hereby converted to the community of Husband and Wife." *Lund*, 174 Cal. App. 4th at 52, 94 Cal. Rptr. 3d at 94.

In both cases, the marriage resulted in divorce rather than death. The husbands argued that estate-planning documents should not control in a divorce proceeding. First, it was argued that the transmutation was limited to estate planning and was therefore ineffective in a dissolution proceeding. Second, it was argued that estate-planning documents are equivalent to a will and therefore, under Family Code §853, were "not admissible as evidence of a transmutation in a proceeding commenced before the death of the person who made the will." The Court of Appeal in *Holtemann* rejected those arguments.

Concerning the first argument, the *Holtemann* Court thought that the husband wished "to have his cake and eat it too." *Holtemann*, 166 Cal. App. 4th at 1174, 83 Cal. Rptr. 3d at 392. In other words, in the event of death, the surviving spouse would obtain the tax advantage of community property, but in the event of a divorce, the spouse with the separate property would be able to retain the advantage that the separate property would not be subject to division. The Court held that transmutations cannot be "conditional or temporary." *Id.* at 1174, 83 Cal. Rptr. 3d at 391. The transmutation was effective from the time it was made, and only another transmutation would change it back to the husband's separate property.

The second argument was rejected because a will differs from an estate-planning document in that a will does not become effective until the death of the testator, whereas an estate-planning document becomes effective upon execution. Also, Family Code §853 provides that only a "will" is inadmissible. Because the Legislature did not include language of "will substitutes," the Court was not willing to extend the clear language of Family Code §853 to cover estate-planning documents. *Id.* at 1175, 83 Cal. Rptr. 3d at 392.

Examples

Example 8 — Thanks for the Treasure!

Alice and Bob were married in 1970 in California. Alice was an antique collector who specialized in collecting snuffboxes. She bought them with her earnings from her job as a bookkeeper. One Sunday in 1979 she found an especially beautiful one at a garage sale. It was silver and quite tarnished. She bought it for $25. After it was cleaned and appraised, it turns out it was worth $10,000. On their tenth anniversary, Alice gave the snuffbox to Bob and said, "I want you to have this snuffbox as yours forever." Bob said, "Thanks! I will treasure it." Unfortunately, Alice and Bob have recently separated and are considering a divorce. She comes to you for advice. She thinks that the snuffbox belongs to her because she bought it. How would you advise her?

Example 9 — Happy Anniversary!

Assume the same facts as in Example 8, except that Alice gave Bob the snuffbox on their twentieth anniversary in 1990. Advise Alice on how a California court would treat the snuffbox.

Example 10 — No More Mozart?

Wolfgang and Constanze were married in 2010 in California. Wolfgang was an accomplished concert pianist and composer and played the piano all the time. In fact, he played so well that he earned millions of dollars from his performances around the world. Constanze did not play the piano but enjoyed listening to Wolfgang play his repertoire of classics. In 2014, using earnings from Wolfgang's performances during their marriage, Constanze purchased an antique grand piano for $25,000. On Wolfgang's birthday, she gave him the piano and told him it was his forever. He graciously thanked her and began playing away. Unfortunately, Wolfgang started becoming more in tune with his new piano than with the marriage. They recently separated and are considering a divorce. Wolfgang comes to you and tells you he thinks the piano belongs to him because Constanze gave it to him as a birthday gift.

Example 11 — Martha's Claim to the Stock?

Martha married Stewart who, prior to marriage, was a wealthy investor owning numerous stocks. All of Stewart's stocks were held in a brokerage account at Merrill Lynch. As Stewart was recovering from a stroke, he wanted Martha to handle all of his investments. In 2014, he wrote a letter to Merrill Lynch that instructed them to "transfer" his stocks into the name of his wife, Martha. Merrill Lynch did so. After Martha and Stewart separated, Martha claimed the stocks as her separate property. How would a court in their dissolution proceeding characterize the stocks?

Example 12 — Life and Love on Hickory Lane

Edward and Mary lived across from each other on Hickory Lane. Mary lived at 122 Hickory Lane, and Edward lived at 123 Hickory Lane. Each owned their own home. When they married, Mary moved into Edward's home, which was larger than Mary's home. Mary kept the house at 122 Hickory Lane and rented it out. They often talked about adding each other's name to the homes so that they would share both homes. They agreed to take steps to accomplish that goal. Edward went first, and they both signed a deed stating that Edward and Mary, as husband and wife, own the property at 123 Hickory Lane as community property. Mary promised that she would do the same but never got around to it. Unfortunately, life on Hickory Lane has lost its luster, and Edward and Mary have separated. Mary is claiming that she has a one-half share in the home at 123 Hickory Lane. Edward is claiming that he has a one-half share in the home at 122 Hickory Lane. How would a court characterize and divide the homes?

Example 13 — Hank Strikes Out

In 2005, Jackie married Hank, who was an avid baseball memorabilia collector. In 2014, Jackie set out to find the perfect anniversary gift for Hank. She purchased a game-used baseball autographed by Babe Ruth on eBay for $1,000. She used funds from an inheritance she received when her grandfather passed away. It turns out that the baseball is worth $25,000. On their anniversary, Jackie gave Hank the autographed baseball and told him it was his forever. Hank graciously said thank you. Jackie also put in her will the following statement: "I bequeath to my beloved husband, Hank, the Babe Ruth autographed baseball as his separate property." Unfortunately, Hank began spending too much time admiring his new baseball instead of his wife, Jackie. Jackie and Hank are considering a divorce. How would a California court characterize the autographed baseball?

Example 14 — Hank Hits a Homer

Assume the same facts as in Example 13, except that Jackie created a trust instead of a will and that the trust was executed in 2015. Additionally, assume that the agreement accompanying the trust contains the statement, "All of the Wife's separate property is hereby converted to the community property of Husband and Wife." Jackie created the trust so that they could receive favorable estate tax treatment. Jackie and Hank are considering a divorce. Advise Jackie on how a California court will treat the Babe Ruth–autographed baseball.

Explanations

Explanation 8 — Thanks for the Treasure!

Although Alice bought the snuffbox with her earnings, which are community property, there is a question of whether she transmuted the snuffbox to Bob's separate property when she gave it to him on their tenth anniversary in 1980. Up until 1985, oral agreements were sufficient to transmute property from community property to the separate property of one spouse. The essence of the transmutation is that the spouse, here Alice, was giving up her interest in the property. When Alice gave Bob the snuffbox "as yours forever," it indicates that she was giving up her interest in the property. It would not even have been necessary for Bob to say anything, but here it is clear that he took the snuffbox.

The 1985 transmutation statute does not apply to this situation because it applies to transmutations in 1985 and thereafter. The "easy transmutation" doctrine applies to transmutations prior to 1985. Depending on the testimony regarding their conversation in 1980, the court will determine whether the snuffbox is community property or Bob's separate property. It will essentially be Alice's word against Bob's word. It may also depend on their conduct regarding the snuffbox between 1980 and the present, although the oral agreement would be sufficient without any other actions necessary.

Explanation 9 — Happy Anniversary!

In this case, the transmutation occurred in 1990 and would be controlled by the 1985 transmutation statute. An "express declaration in writing" is required to transmute property, here from community property to Bob's separate property. Here there is only the conversation when Alice gave the snuffbox to Bob. That would be insufficient to accomplish the transmutation.

The statute also provides the express declaration in writing requirement that does not apply to certain gifts. The first requirement of the gift exception is that the gift is "clothing, wearing apparel, jewelry, or other tangible article of a personal nature." Here a snuffbox is a tangible article and may have been considered an article of a personal nature in the eighteenth or nineteenth century, but not today. Clearly it is an antique. In addition, we do not have facts that would allow us to consider the other requirements of the gift exception. We do not know if Bob used the snuffbox, and that is unlikely since it is an antique. Also we do not have information about the financial circumstances of Alice and Bob's marriage that would allow us to determine if the gift was "substantial" or not. Therefore, under the 1985 transmutation statute, the snuffbox would be considered community property, and its present value would be split between Alice and Bob.

Explanation 10 — No More Mozart?

The piano was purchased during the marriage with Wolfgang's earnings. His earnings are community property; therefore, the piano is initially community property. The question is whether it was transmuted to Wolfgang's separate property when Constanze gave it to him on his birthday. Because she gave it to him in 2014, the 1985 transmutation statute applies. For the transmutation to be valid, Constanze would have had to consent to the transmutation of the piano from community property to Wolfgang's separate property by an express declaration in writing. Her oral statement that it was his forever is insufficient to effect the transmutation to his separate property.

Under Family Code §852(c), there is an exception to the writing requirement for gifts. The exception is limited to clothing, wearing apparel, jewelry, and other tangible items of a personal nature, used solely or principally by the spouse who receives the gift, and the gift is not substantial in value considering the circumstances of the marriage. At first glance, it seems as if the piano falls under the gift exception and was validly transmuted to his separate property, even though there was no express declaration in writing. The piano was used solely by Wolfgang. The piano's value is not substantial, considering Wolfgang earned millions of dollars.

However, the main requirement is that the piano must be like clothing, wearing apparel, jewelry, or in this case, "a tangible item of a personal nature." It is conceivable that Wolfgang felt that the piano was part of his persona. He played the piano all the time and it was a huge part of his life. Therefore, the piano could possibly be considered a tangible article of a personal nature. Yet the Court of Appeal's holding in *Marriage of Neighbors* indicates that the piano would probably not fall into that category. In *Neighbors*, the Court determined that an automobile is not an item of a personal nature that would exempt it from the "express declaration in writing" requirement. If a person's automobile is not considered personal in nature—even in a car-obsessed state like California—a piano would not be either. Therefore, the characterization of the piano as community property would stand. If Wolfgang wanted to keep the piano, he could buy out Constanze's share or substitute another item of property of equal value. Otherwise, the present value of the piano would be split between Wolfgang and Constanze.

Explanation 11—Martha's Claim to the Stock?

It is clear that the stocks were originally Stewart's separate property, since it can be assumed that they were acquired before he married Martha. The question then is whether there was a transmutation of Stewart's separate property into Martha's separate property. That type of transmutation is permitted under Family Code §852(a). Therefore, the court must determine whether the language "transfer" in Stewart's letter is sufficient to meet the requirement of "an express declaration in writing" by the spouse whose interest is adversely affected. Here, the spouse adversely affected is Stewart. Even though Stewart's letter is in writing, a court would find the word "transfer" alone to be insufficient to accomplish a transmutation. The reasoning is that it is unclear from the language itself that Stewart knew that he was giving up his interest in the stock and that he is transferring his interest in the stock to Martha as her separate property. This example is based on the case of *Marriage of Barneson*, 69 Cal. App. 4th 583, 81 Cal. Rptr. 2d 726 (1999). The Court stated that "a transmutation may be effected by means of a transfer, but a transfer is not necessarily a transmutation." *Id.* at 596. This is another indication that the express declaration requirement will be strictly applied. Please note that the court will not look beyond the language of the writing to examine Stewart's intentions regarding the stock. In the *Barneson* case, even though the Securities and Exchange Commission transfer requirements were met, that did not control the characterization of the property between the spouses.

Explanation 12 — Life and Love on Hickory Lane

The homes that Edward and Mary owned were separate property because each owned them before marriage. Concerning the home at 123 Hickory Lane, the issue is whether the deed signed by Edward and Mary is a valid transmutation. A valid transmutation requires an express declaration in writing by the spouse whose interest is adversely affected. Here, the transmutation is from Edward's separate property to community property. Edward, whose interest is adversely affected, signed the deed. The language indicates that the property will now be community property, which is sufficient under *Estate of MacDonald* to transmute the property. Thus, the property will be characterized as community property. Mary would be entitled to one-half of the property at divorce, depending on whether Edward can establish a right to reimbursement. See Chapter 4 on joint titles and reimbursement.

Concerning the home at 122 Hickory Lane, that home also started out as separate property — Mary's separate property because she owned it before marriage. The issue would be whether it remained her separate property, despite their agreement that they wanted to share both houses. The problem was that their agreement was oral. According to *Estate of MacDonald*, oral transmutations are not allowed under Family Code §852(a), and extrinsic evidence may not be relied on to show a transmutation agreement. If those rules are applied here, evidence of their oral agreement is excluded, and the home at 122 Hickory Lane remained Mary's separate property.

This example points up the inequity that can result from ignoring evidence of an oral agreement. Edward gave up his interest in 123 Hickory Lane, relying on Mary's promise to give up her interest in 122 Hickory Lane. If the *MacDonald* rules are followed, Mary, who did not carry through on their oral agreement, receives all of her separate property (122 Hickory Lane) and one-half of the community property (123 Hickory Lane). Because of the Supreme Court's strict interpretation of §852 in *Marriage of Benson*, extrinsic evidence of Mary's oral promise would be inadmissible.

The result would give Mary an unfair benefit, but §852 would not give Edward any relief. Edward's only other alternative would be to attempt to invalidate the deed that he signed based on Mary's breach of fiduciary duty. This scenario would fit into the description in the *Benson* concurrence that Mary unfairly gained a benefit from the other spouse in exchange for an orally promised transmutation that in fact had no legal effect. If a court accepted Edward's argument, the deed he signed would be invalid and the home at 123 Hickory Lane would not have been transmuted from his separate property to community property. Mary would lose the unfair benefit of the transmutation.

Explanation 13 — Hank Strikes Out

Because Jackie purchased the autographed baseball during marriage, it would be presumed to be community property. Since she could trace the purchase to funds from her inheritance, it would initially be characterized as her separate property. However, there is a question as to whether she transmuted the baseball to Hank's separate property when she gave it to him on their anniversary. Since she gave him the baseball in 2014, Family Code §852 of the transmutation statute controls. Therefore, an "express declaration in writing" is required for transmutation from Jackie's separate property to Hank's separate property. There was only the oral conversation between Jackie and Hank when she gave him the baseball, which is insufficient to constitute a valid transmutation. Additionally, the transmutation would likely not survive under the gift exception, as an autographed baseball cannot be considered a "tangible article of personal nature" under the holding in the *Neighbors* case.

The statement in Jackie's will could be considered an express declaration in writing, which would suffice to transmute the autographed baseball from Jackie's separate property to Hank's separate property. Clearly, when she drafted the will, Jackie knew that she would be recharacterizing the baseball from her separate property to Hank's. However, Family Code §853 prohibits the use of a statement in a will as admissible evidence of a transmutation in a proceeding commenced *before* the death of the person who made the will. Therefore, the statement in Jackie's will cannot be used in their divorce proceeding to show that the autographed baseball was transmuted to Hank's separate property. This makes sense because Jackie has the power to amend her will at any time before her death and would undoubtedly change it so that Hank no longer receives the baseball. In conclusion, the autographed baseball would remain Jackie's separate property because there was no "express declaration in writing."

Explanation 14 — Hank Hits a Homer

Although the agreement accompanying Jackie's trust did not use the express word "transmutation," the court in *Lund*, 174 Cal. App. 4th 40, 94 Cal. Rptr. 3d 84 (2009), declared that this language was sufficient to constitute a transmutation. When Jackie created and executed the trust, she knew and understood that she was converting all of her separate property to community property. Because the Babe Ruth autographed baseball was not sufficiently transmuted when she gave it to Hank on their anniversary, it was her separate property and was therefore transmuted to community property through the execution of the trust in 2015. Additionally, the Court in *Holtemann*, 166 Cal. App. 4th 1166, 83 Cal. Rptr. 3d 385 (2008), noted that transmutations cannot be conditional and are effective when made. As the Court pointed out, estate planning documents such as trusts differ from wills in that they become effective upon execution. Therefore, only another transmutation would convert the baseball from community property back to Jackie's separate property. If Hank wants to keep the ball, he will owe Jackie one-half of its value. Otherwise, the present value would be split evenly between Jackie and Hank.

CHAPTER 3

Evidentiary Presumptions

California community property law uses evidentiary presumptions in the characterization process. Although community property is defined as property acquired by a spouse during the marriage and separate property is defined as property owned by a spouse before marriage and property acquired during marriage by gift, devise, or descent, the definitions, by themselves, do not tell us which is preferred. It is clear from the sharing philosophy behind community property law that community property should be preferred. The courts have developed an evidentiary presumption called the *general community property presumption* that reflects the preference for community property characterization. Before going further, it is important to emphasize that in California, there are several types of community property presumptions and only one very limited separate property presumption.

THE GENERAL COMMUNITY PROPERTY PRESUMPTION

The "general" community property presumption is that property acquired during marriage is presumed to be community property. Unless the spouse who claims that the property is separate property rebuts that presumption, the presumption becomes conclusive. The conclusion is that the property is community property. At divorce, that means that community property will be divided equally. At death, if one spouse dies without a will, all the community property will go to the surviving spouse. A spouse has the right to will one-half of the community property to anyone chosen by the testator.

Before continuing, we need to review or learn a bit about evidentiary presumptions. First and foremost, presumptions are *not* evidence. That means before a presumption is applied, some facts must be proved to *raise* the presumption. Once those facts are proved, the presumption is raised or arises. Presumptions regarding community property are all rebuttable presumptions (even if rebuttal is extremely difficult!). That means that if facts are proved that are contrary to the presumption, then those facts override or, in evidence terms, *rebut* the presumption. Then those facts become the *conclusion*. If no facts are proved that are contrary to the presumption, the presumption becomes conclusive, and the facts of the presumption become the conclusion. In addition, sometimes the rebuttal must be proved by "clear and convincing" evidence rather than by the lesser standard of "preponderance" of the evidence. The spouse who tries to rebut the community property presumption is called the "separate property proponent" and carries the burden of proving facts to rebut the presumption.

Let's start with a simple illustration. Harry and Wilma, a married couple, buy a piano in 2010, using funds that Wilma inherited from her Aunt Sally. If Harry and Wilma divorce, Wilma will want to claim that the piano belongs to her. Her lawyer will ask her, "When did you buy the piano?" Wilma responds, "In 2010, about a year after we were married." Her lawyer thinks in presumption terms: The piano was acquired during marriage; therefore, it will be presumed to be community property. Proof that it was acquired during marriage will *raise* the community property presumption. That favors Harry, who could claim that it is community property because it was acquired during marriage. The next question for Wilma is, "What funds were used to buy the piano?" Wilma replies, "I received money from my Aunt Sally's estate and bought the piano soon after." Her lawyer thinks in presumption terms: Wilma, the separate property proponent, can *rebut* the community property presumption by showing that the funds used to buy the piano came from her separate property, an inheritance Wilma received during marriage. The lawyer then responds, "If we can show that the piano was bought with funds from your inheritance, it will be yours."

If the community property presumption is rebutted, the conclusion is that the piano is characterized as Wilma's separate property. If the community property presumption is not rebutted, the conclusion is that the piano is community property. This process is also an example of the tracing principle that was introduced in Chapter 1. Here, tracing to separate property funds rebuts the presumptive characterization of the piano as community property and establishes the character of property as Wilma's separate property. Tracing is an integral part of the general community property presumption and is sufficient to rebut that presumption.

Acquired or Possessed?

The previous example is a simple one and would be resolved in an attorney's office and would in all likelihood never be litigated. More complex scenarios arise, and the community property presumption can be determinative of the characterization of the property. For instance, let's say that Harry and Wilma were married in 1990, and Harry died recently without a will. While going through Harry's closet, Wilma finds a shoebox filled with cash totaling $100,000. Harry's brother claims that part of the $100,000 goes to him as Harry's separate property. Wilma claims the $100,000 is community property that belongs to her as the surviving spouse.

The problem, however, is that there is little evidence that would assist in characterizing the $100,000. Assume that Harry had handled all the couple's financial affairs while they were married and rarely discussed them with Wilma. She knows that Harry had always been a saver and that he was wealthy before they married. Also, Harry had worked hard during their marriage and had made a good salary. In this situation, the $100,000 could be either community property or separate property. If Harry had saved some of his earnings during marriage and put cash from those earnings in the shoebox, then the $100,000 would meet the definition of community property. Recall that community property is property acquired during marriage through the efforts of either spouse—Harry's earnings are community property belonging to both Harry and Wilma. If the $100,000 belonged to Harry before his marriage to Wilma or, alternatively, were rents, issues, or profits from property owned before marriage, it would meet the definition of separate property. Therefore, the definitions do not help us determine the character of the $100,000. The real problem is the *lack* of evidence of the character of the property. Harry is not there to testify about the source of the money, and neither Wilma nor Harry's brother has enough information to testify about the character of the money. In the dispute over the $100,000 between Wilma and Harry's brother, the court must characterize the funds to determine their distribution. The formulation of the general community property presumption as property *acquired* during marriage does not help, since it is unknown how and when the funds were acquired.

Very early on in community property history, the courts established a variant of the general community property presumption that handled this very problem of lack of evidence. The court in *Lynam v. Vorwerk*, 13 Cal. App. 507, 110 P. 355 (1910), held that the general community property presumption encompasses property *possessed* during marriage as well as property *acquired* during marriage. *See also Estate of Jolly*, 196 Cal. 547, 238 P. 353 (1925). Therefore, after a long marriage where there is limited evidence of the source of the funds, the general community property presumption will apply to property possessed during the marriage. In the above scenario, possession of the $100,000 at the end of the marriage will be sufficient to raise the community property presumption. This will definitely favor Wilma, the surviving spouse. In the dispute over the $100,000, the separate property proponent, Harry's brother, will carry the burden of rebutting the community property presumption. It would seem that in this scenario, Harry's brother would not be able to trace to a separate property source. Therefore, the community property presumption would be conclusive, and the conclusion would be that the $100,000 was community property. Wilma, as the surviving spouse, would be entitled to all.

Short Marriages/Burden of Proof

Two issues remain unclear concerning the general community property presumption: (1) whether the *possessed* formulation applies to short marriages where evidence can be inferred as to the source of the funds, and (2) whether the burden of rebutting the general community property presumption is "preponderance of the evidence" or "clear and convincing evidence." As to the first issue, as a practical matter, if it is possible to adduce evidence as to when the property was acquired, a wise attorney would not rely on the *possessed* formulation. As to the second issue, although several appellate courts stated that the "clear and convincing" standard is used to rebut the general community property presumption, the California Supreme Court originally held that preponderance of the evidence is sufficient to rebut that presumption. *Freese v. Hibernia Savings and Loan Society*, 139 Cal. 392, 73 P. 172 (1903). The California Supreme Court recently confirmed that the standard of proof for rebutting the general community property presumption is preponderance of the evidence. *Marriage of Valli*, 58 Cal. 4th 1396, 1400, 324 P.3d 274, 276, 171 Cal. Rptr. 3d 454, 457 (2015), *citing Marriage of Ettefagh*, 150 Cal. App. 4th 1578, 1591, 59 Cal. Rptr. 3d 419, 429 (2007).

The first issue deals with "which" property was acquired during the marriage. In the case of *Fidelity & Casualty Company v. Mahoney*, 71 Cal. App. 2d 65, 161 P.2d 944 (1945), the wife and son of Mr. Mahoney from a prior marriage both claimed the proceeds of a flight insurance policy that Mr. Mahoney had bought for $1. It was clear that the policy was bought during the marriage, but it was unclear whether the $1 used to purchase the policy was acquired before or during the marriage. The Mahoneys had been married for only two months when Mr. Mahoney's flight crashed. The trial court determined that the proceeds were separate property and thus went to the son as the named beneficiary of the policy. The appellate court agreed, stating that the wife was required to establish that the policy was acquired with community funds in order to prove that the proceeds also were community property. That seems to be incorrect. The wife should have been able to raise the community property presumption merely by showing that the policy was purchased during marriage. Then the burden would have been on the separate property proponent, the son, to trace the $1 used to purchase the policy to his father's earnings before marriage. Surely, the court had a difficult decision to make in dealing with such a tragedy—a newly married wife and a 16-year-old son from a former marriage. Yet, putting the burden of rebuttal on the community property proponent is contrary to the rules regarding the general community property presumption.

PRESUMPTION WHEN TITLE IS IN ONE SPOUSE'S NAME

So far, the property to be characterized via the general community property was untitled property. Many acquisitions during marriage are untitled. For example, home furnishings such as a piano or a painting, collections such as stamps or coins, and other collectibles such as antiques do not have a title. Obviously, cash also does not have a title. However, many acquisitions during marriage carry a title. Homes, cars, boats, airplanes, and bank accounts all have titles. It is not unusual for married couples to hold property either jointly or in one spouse's name. There are two very important principles to remember regarding characterization of property with a title: (1) Property titled in one spouse's name is treated differently from jointly titled property, and (2) title in one spouse's name does *not* mean that that property is the separate property of that spouse. The presumption that applies to property titled in one spouse's name is the *general community property presumption* that property acquired (or possessed) during marriage is presumed to be community property.

To illustrate how the general community property presumption applies, we will assume that during their marriage, Harry and Wilma buy a sailboat for $25,000. They use funds from the inheritance that Wilma received from her Aunt Sally. They also put the sailboat in Wilma's name. They have no agreement of any kind regarding the sailboat. (See Chapter 2 regarding transmutation.) In the event of a divorce, Harry would want to claim the sailboat as community property, and Wilma will want to claim it as her separate property. Looking at the situation using common sense, you would say that the sailboat is Wilma's separate property because it is in her name and she used her separate property to buy the sailboat. But, remember that the law, particularly California community property law, does not always follow common sense. The general community property presumption would apply here. Because the sailboat was acquired during marriage, the community property presumption will be raised. That favors Harry. Wilma, the separate property proponent, will have the burden of rebutting the presumption. All that is necessary to rebut the presumption is for Wilma to trace the purchase of the sailboat to her inheritance. The title will *not* control. It is the source of the funds that control.

Why? The major reason why the title does not control is that couples put the title in one spouse's name for reasons other than to determine ownership. For instance, it just might be more convenient for the couple to put the title in one spouse's name. Take the example of a community property business that is managed by one spouse. The business bank account may be in one spouse's name. Putting the title in one spouse's name does not necessarily signify that the bank account is a gift to that spouse or transmutes the business proceeds deposited into that account into the managing spouse's separate property. Another reason for ignoring the title in the characterization process is that a spouse may put the title in his or her own name without the knowledge or permission of the other spouse. In that case, allowing the title to control would go against the intentions of the other spouse. Thus, when the title is in one spouse's name, the title is not determinative of the character of the property.

Let us take another example involving the purchase of the sailboat. All the facts are the same, except the title is put in Harry's name, not Wilma's. Because Harry handled most of the couple's financial affairs, it was just more convenient to put the title in his name. They never discussed or had any agreements about the sailboat. Unfortunately, they divorce. The general community property presumption applies—the sailboat was acquired during marriage. Wilma, the separate property proponent, has the burden of rebutting the presumption by tracing to her separate property, the inheritance from Aunt Sally. If she can do so, the conclusion is that the sailboat is her separate property. The title in Harry's name neither makes it Harry's separate property nor does it have any bearing on the characterization of the property. The title is irrelevant to the characterization of the property. In our characterization scheme of FIT, when property is titled in one spouse's name, it is the *funds* that control, not the *title*. The *intentions* of the parties only control if there has been a valid transmutation. (See Chapter 2.)

The case of *Marriage of Ettefagh*, 150 Cal. App. 4th 1578, 59 Cal. Rptr. 3d 419 (1st District 2007), illustrates how the general community property presumption is applied when title is taken in one spouse's name. In *Ettefagh*, the husband, Vahid, had acquired several parcels of real estate during his marriage to Semrin. All of those at issue in this case were taken in Vahid's name. The deed to two parcels stated that Vahid was "an unmarried man," and one stated that the property was conveyed to Vahid, "a married man as his sole and separate property." *Id*. at 1581-1582, 59 Cal. Rptr. 3d at 421-422. The Court of Appeal stated, "Because the properties were acquired during the marriage . . . they are presumed to be community property . . . ." *Id*. at 1584, 59 Cal. Rptr. 3d at 423. The question in the case was whether the presumption had been rebutted by Vahid's father's testimony that he, and not Vahid, had supplied the funds that were used to buy the properties.

Those funds would then be a gift to Vahid during marriage, making the funds Vahid's separate property. Therefore, tracing to those funds would be sufficient to rebut the presumption. The Court of Appeal rejected Semrin's argument that a standard of proof higher than a preponderance of the evidence was required. Thus, the trial court's determination that the properties were Vahid's separate property was affirmed. Despite the deeds being held in Vahid's name, the property was presumed to be community property, and it was tracing to the funds that determined the character of the property.

The presumption that applies when a title is taken in one spouse's name also arose in *Marriage of Brooks and Robinson*, 169 Cal. App. 4th 176, 86 Cal. Rptr. 3d 624 (4th District 2008). In that case, the couple purchased a home. They agreed to take the title in the wife's name even though the down payment came from the husband's earnings. The deed to the home used the language "Annikawa A. Robinson, a Single Woman." The couple was advised that using such wording would facilitate financing. The wife later sold the home, and the husband tried to assert rights to the proceeds as community property.

If the Court of Appeal had followed the *Ettefagh* precedent, it would have applied the general community property presumption. Despite the deed being in Robinson's name, the title would not control since Robinson was married at the time the couple purchased the home. Then it would have been the wife's burden to show that the property was her separate property. Tracing would not have worked because the funds used to purchase the home were community property. The title would not be determinative because the language "a Single Woman" does not by itself indicate an agreement or transmutation of the community property into the wife's separate property. Therefore, the ruling should have been that the home and the proceeds were community property.

There was, however, a surprising result in the case. The Court of Appeal applied a "form of title presumption" from Evidence Code §662. According to the Court, the fact that the title was in the wife's name raised the presumption that it was her separate property. Because the husband could not rebut that presumption, the Court concluded that the husband had no community property rights to the home. It is possible that the peculiarities of the case led the Court to resolve the case against the husband and in favor of the purchaser of the home, who did not have direct knowledge of Brooks and Robinson's marriage. See Chapter 6, Management and Control of Community Property, for a fuller discussion of *Marriage of Brooks and Robinson*.

The similarities between *Ettefagh* and *Brooks and Robinson* are striking. In both cases, one spouse took title as "unmarried." The *Ettefagh* Court of Appeal applied the traditional understanding that the general community property presumption applies when the title is in one spouse's name. The *Brooks and Robinson* Court of Appeal applied the "form of title presumption," reversing the traditional interpretation and holding instead that title in one spouse's name raises a separate property presumption. In *Ettefagh*, the title was in the husband's name; in *Brooks and Robinson*, the title was in the wife's name. That difference should not be relevant. The presumption should be the same whether the title is in the husband's name or the wife's name. This is especially true since the separate property presumption regarding title in a "wife's" name was abolished in 1975. See "The Married Woman's Special Presumption," later in this chapter.

The Supreme Court in *Marriage of Valli*, 58 Cal. 4th 1396, 324 P.3d 274, 171 Cal. Rptr. 3d 454 (2014), discussed the *Brooks and Robinson* case. In *Valli*, the husband Frankie purchased a $3.75 million life insurance policy with community property funds. He designated his wife, Randy, as "owner." At the time of their divorce, the policy had a cash value of more than $365,000. The major issue was the character of the policy: Was it Randy's separate property because she was designated as the "owner"? Or was it community property because of the funds used to purchase the policy? Randy argued that the "form of title presumption" applied and that Frankie had to rebut that presumption with an agreement. Frankie argued that the general community property presumption applied and that designating Randy as "owner" was not sufficient for a transmutation of the community funds to her separate property.

Justice Chin, in his concurring opinion, stated that the "general rule is that property acquired during marriage is community property unless the preponderance of evidence establishes that a specifically enumerated statutory exemption applies to make it something else." *Id.* at 1408, 324 P.3d at 281, 171 Cal. Rptr. 3d at 463. That meant the life insurance policy was presumed to be community property, and Randy would have to rebut the presumption by showing that it was her separate property. "In my view, as in the view of all amici curiae to appear in this case—law professors and attorneys specializing in the field—the section 760 presumption [the general community property presumption] controls in characterizing property acquired during marriage in an action between spouses. Section 662 [form of title presumption] plays no role in such an action." *Id.* at 1408, 324 P.3d at 282, 171 Cal. Rptr. 3d at 463-464. There is a possibility that the "form of title presumption" from Evidence Code 662 applies in a case involving rights of a spouse and a third-party bona fide purchaser, like *Brooks and Robinson*, but not to an action between spouses. *Id.* at 1413, 324 P.3d at 285, 171 Cal. Rptr. 3d at 468. (See Chapter 6, Management and Control of Community Property.)

APPORTIONMENT

The next issue regarding the general community property presumption arises when the couple uses both community and separate funds to purchase property. Assume that Harry and Wilma buy an antique Tiffany lamp for $10,000 during their marriage. They use $6,000 from Wilma's inheritance from Aunt Sally and $4,000 from Harry's earnings. Both love the lamp. Unfortunately, they are going through divorce proceedings, and they both want the lamp.

Characterization of the lamp would start with the general community property presumption because the lamp is untitled and was acquired during their marriage. The separate property proponent, Wilma, would attempt to rebut the presumption by tracing to her inheritance. If she can show that the $6,000 used to buy the lamp was from her inheritance, she can rebut the presumption only partially. The ultimate conclusion regarding the lamp would be that it is part separate property and part community property. The portion of separate property is in direct proportion to the contribution toward the purchase price. Since $6,000 of the purchase price of $10,000 is from Wilma's separate property, then the lamp is 60% Wilma's separate property. Since $4,000 of the purchase price is from community funds, then the lamp is 40% community property. If the lamp is worth $10,000 at divorce, then Wilma would be entitled to $6,000 as her separate property and $2,000 as her one-half share of the community property. Harry would be entitled to $2,000 as his one-half share of the community property.

Apportionment is particularly important if the property has increased in value during the marriage. For instance, in our Tiffany lamp example, assume that the lamp is now worth $30,000. It has increased in value by $20,000. That increase in value is also apportioned according to the proportions of the contributions to the purchase of the lamp. In this example, the lamp is 60% Wilma's separate property and 40% community property. The increase in the value of the lamp will also be 60% Wilma's separate property and 40% community property. The $20,000 increase in value will be split: $12,000 (60% of the increase in value) as Wilma's separate property, and $8,000 (40% of the increase in value) as community property. Wilma will be entitled to $12,000 as her separate property and $4,000 as her one-half share of the community property. Harry will be entitled to $4,000 as his one-half share of the community property. Then we add the proportional original contributions to the purchase of the lamp plus the increase in value to determine how the lamp will be divided between Harry and Wilma. At divorce, Wilma will be entitled to $24,000 of the value of the lamp, and Harry will be entitled to $6,000 of the value of the lamp. There are various ways to resolve who actually retains the lamp. If Wilma wants the lamp, she can buy out Harry's share by either giving him $6,000 or another item valued at $6,000. It is also possible that they can sell the lamp and divide the proceeds according to the separate property and community property shares.

At this point, you may ask why the analysis was broken up between the initial contributions to the purchase of the lamp and the increase in value. For those who actually enjoy the calculations, you immediately recognized that the same result would be reached by dividing the value at divorce of $30,000 by 60% and 40%. The figures are the same: 60% of $30,000 is $18,000, and 40% of $30,000 is $12,000. Thus, Wilma would be entitled to $18,000 plus one-half of $12,000, which equals $24,000. Harry would be entitled to one-half of the $12,000, which equals $6,000. The reason we separated the original contributions from the increase in value is that in more complicated scenarios (such as jointly titled property) it is important to treat the original contributions separately from the increase in value. For those who do not enjoy the calculations (that's why you went to law school instead of pursuing accounting), the major message here is that when both separate property and community property are used to acquire property, the property will be apportioned according to the funds used. That concept is called pro rata apportionment.

THE MARRIED WOMAN'S SPECIAL PRESUMPTION

It must be emphasized that there is only one *separate* property presumption in California community property law. It is called the Married Woman's Special Presumption. While there is no question that married women are special, this presumption is special because it applies to very limited circumstances and is opposite to what we have learned about the general community property presumption. The presumption is that if property was acquired *prior* to January 1, 1975, by a married woman in an instrument in writing, it is presumed to be *her* separate property. Family Code §803.

Please note how limited the presumption is. First, the application of this presumption is limited to married women. Second, it is limited in time to property acquired prior to 1975. Third, it applies only to instruments in writing. Please also note how different it is from what we have learned about the general community property presumption. First, it is opposite from the general community property presumption because the presumption is that the property is the married woman's *separate* property. Second, it differs significantly because the *title* in the married woman's name raises the presumption. Third, as we will see, the presumption is rebutted not by the source of *funds* but by the *intention* of the husband. Our framework of FIT does not help in this particular instance; rather, this presumption can give you "FITs" because it is so different from what we have already learned about the general community property presumption. To understand this presumption, some explanation of community property history is necessary. Prior to 1975, management and control of the community property was in the hands of the husband alone. Equal management and control of community property went into effect as of January 1, 1975.

Therefore, let us try to think in the mind-set prior to 1975. A husband, manager and controller of the community property funds, buys some property and puts it into his wife's name. Obviously, there are various reasons why a husband would do that. On the one hand, it could be convenient for the wife to manage and control that property, and he had no intention to change the community property to her separate property. On the other hand, it could be that the husband wanted to give the property to his wife, thus changing the property from community property to her separate property. The question is, "What should the law presume when community funds are used to acquire property in the name of the wife?" The law presumes that because the husband controlled the community funds, putting the title or deed in the wife's name signified a *gift* of the community property to her. Therefore, the title or deed in the wife's name *raises* the presumption that the property is *her* separate property.

There is one similarity to the general community property presumption. The married woman's special (separate property) presumption is rebuttable. However, the rebuttal is *not* by tracing. Showing that community property funds were used to acquire the property is insufficient to show that the property is community property. Instead, it is the *intention* of the husband that controls. If he did not intend a gift or if he did not intend to change the nature of the property, then his testimony can rebut the presumption that the property is the wife's separate property.

In conclusion, the married woman's special presumption is a separate property presumption. It applies only to property titled in a wife's name prior to January 1, 1975. It can be rebutted by showing that the husband did not intend to change the community property funds into the wife's separate property.

Examples

Example 1 — Who Gets the Dividends?

Frank and Gwen married in 1970. Frank came from a wealthy family and opened a bank account in his own name soon after their marriage. In that account, which we will call the "dividend account," he deposited all the dividends he received from the stock that he owned before their marriage. By the time of the couple's recent divorce, the account contained $75,000. Does Gwen have any claim to the bank account?

Example 2 — Bank Accounts: Separate or Community?

Both Frank and Gwen have high-paying jobs. Frank is an engineer and has his own business. Gwen is an accountant and has a high-paying job with an accounting firm. During marriage, each open bank accounts in their own names in which they deposit their earnings. Note that Frank's account is a different one from his account with the dividends from his stocks. We will call these accounts Frank's business account and Gwen's earnings account. How would the bank accounts be characterized?

Example 3 — The Cabin at the Lake

In 1972, Frank uses some of the funds from his dividend account and buys a cabin near Lake Arrowhead. He puts the title in his name. The cabin cost $20,000 at that time. At the time of Frank and Gwen's recent divorce, it is worth $100,000. How would the Lake Arrowhead cabin be characterized?

Example 4 — Can Gwen Sail into the Sunset?

In 1972, Frank uses some of the funds from his business account to buy a sailboat for Gwen's birthday. He puts the title in Gwen's name and arranges to have a huge "Happy Birthday" ribbon tied around the boat. How would the sailboat be characterized?

Example 5 — Frank Uses the Dividend Account

Assume the same facts as Example 4, except that Frank uses funds from his dividend account to buy the sailboat for Gwen's birthday. How would the sailboat be characterized?

Example 6 — Who Owns the Thunderbird?

In 1973, Gwen uses funds from her earnings account to buy a Thunderbird convertible for Frank. She puts the title in Frank's name and arranges to have a huge "Happy Birthday" ribbon tied around it. Frank always kept the Thunderbird in mint condition, and it is very valuable at the time of their recent divorce. How would the Thunderbird be characterized?

Example 7 — The Chalet at Mammoth

In 1995, Gwen becomes a ski enthusiast. Frank and Gwen use funds from Frank's business account and Gwen's earnings account to buy a chalet near Mammoth Mountain. The chalet costs $100,000, and they put the title in Gwen's name. Gwen would like to claim the chalet as her separate property in their divorce. How would the chalet be characterized?

Example 8 — Frank Uses Both Accounts

Assume the same facts as in Example 7, except that $30,000 of the purchase price of the chalet is paid from Frank's dividend account, and the remaining

$70,000 is paid from Frank's business account. At divorce, the chalet is valued at $100,000. How would the chalet be characterized?

Example 9 — The Chalet Appreciates

Assume the same facts as Example 8, except at divorce the chalet is now worth $150,000.

Example 10 — Who Owns the Cards?

In 2000, Frank uses funds from his dividend account to buy a baseball card collection in an auction on eBay. The collection cost $10,000. In divorce proceedings, how will the collection be characterized?

Example 11 — Who Gets the "Mattress Money"?

Franklin and Eleanor grew up during the Great Depression. They married in 1980. Because Franklin's parents had lost all their money in a bank closure, Franklin did not believe in banks. He therefore kept his savings under his mattress. Eleanor tried to convince him that banks today were insured, but he refused to listen. Franklin recently died without a will. The "mattress money" totals $50,000. Franklin's sister Gertrude claims that money is from an inheritance that Franklin received in 1995. In a dispute over the "mattress money," how will it be characterized?

Example 12 — Franklin Dies in His Sleep

Assume the same facts as Example 11, except Franklin and Eleanor married two months ago. Also assume that one month before Franklin and Eleanor married, Franklin received an inheritance of $50,000. Franklin recently died without telling Eleanor about the $50,000 that he kept under the mattress. In a dispute over the "mattress money," how will it be characterized?

Explanations

Explanation 1 — Who Gets the Dividends?

The general community property presumption does not help Gwen here, even though the bank account was opened during their marriage and the dividends were received during marriage. The opening of the bank account during marriage would raise the general community property presumption that the bank account was acquired during marriage. However, the separate property proponent, here Frank, could easily rebut the presumption by tracing to the dividends, which are his separate property. The rents, issues, and profits of separate property are separate property. The stocks he owned before marriage are his separate property and thus the dividends from those stocks are his separate property. The conclusion is that the bank account is Frank's separate property. It is the funds in the bank account rather than the title in Frank's name that ultimately determines the character of the bank account and the funds in that account.

Explanation 2 — Bank Accounts: Separate or Community?

Both bank accounts would be considered community property. Because the bank accounts were acquired during marriage, they are presumed to be community property. The title in Frank's or Gwen's name is not determinative. The funds deposited in each bank account are Frank's and Gwen's earnings. Earnings during marriage are community property. Therefore, there is no possibility of rebutting the community property presumption. The conclusion is that the bank accounts are community property containing community property funds.

Explanation 3 — The Cabin at the Lake

The cabin was acquired during marriage; therefore, it is presumed to be community property under the general community property presumption. Frank, the separate property proponent, has the burden of rebutting the community property presumption. Here, Frank can trace to separate property funds, those funds that were the rents, issues, and profits of his stocks owned before marriage. That the cabin and the bank account are in Frank's name is not determinative of the character of the cabin. Because separate property funds were used to buy the cabin, the conclusion would be that it is Frank's separate property and it will not be divided in the divorce proceedings.

Explanation 4 — Can Gwen Sail into the Sunset?

In this example, it is significant that the sailboat was acquired in 1972 and the title put in Gwen's name. Prior to January 1, 1975, Frank was considered the controller of the community property funds. The funds in his business account are from his earnings and are therefore community property funds. Frank's using community property funds and putting the title in Gwen's name raises the special married woman's presumption that the sailboat is Gwen's separate property. The separate property presumption can be rebutted if Frank can show that he did not intend to give the sailboat to Gwen. That would be very difficult for Frank to accomplish since it seems that the sailboat was a birthday gift to Gwen. The use of community property funds does not rebut the presumption that the sailboat is Gwen's separate property. Therefore, the conclusion would be that the sailboat is Gwen's separate property, and it will not be divided in the divorce proceedings.

If you recognized that there was a "transmutation" of Frank's community property into Gwen's separate property, you are correct. However, prior to January 1, 1985, transmutations did not have to be by express declaration in writing. In a sense, Frank's putting the title in Gwen's name could show an implied agreement to change the community property into Gwen's separate property. She would not mind. The better analysis for acquisitions in the wife's name prior to 1975 is to apply the Married Woman's Special Presumption.

Explanation 5 — Frank Uses the Dividend Account

Again, it is significant that the sailboat was acquired in 1972 and that the title was put in Gwen's name. The funds used to buy the sailboat in this variation are Frank's separate property. A spouse has complete control over his or her separate property funds. The presumption here is the same: that the sailboat acquired prior to January 1, 1975, in a married woman's name is presumed to be her separate property. The rebuttal is again the same. It is Frank's intentions that control. Even though Frank could trace to the use of his separate property funds, it seems that here his intentions rather than the funds would be significant. It still seems that Frank intended a gift of the sailboat to Gwen. The gift was of his separate property to her separate property, rather than community property to her separate property. Thus, the most likely conclusion would be that the sailboat is Gwen's separate property, and it will not be divided in the divorce proceedings.

Explanation 6 — Who Owns the Thunderbird?

Prior to 1975, acquisitions in the husband's name are treated differently from acquisitions in the wife's name. The Married Woman's Special Presumption does not apply in this situation. Even though the Thunderbird was acquired prior to 1975, the title is in Frank's name, not Gwen's. The general community property presumption applies in this situation. Since the Thunderbird was acquired during marriage, Gwen could raise the community property presumption through testimony that the car was acquired during marriage. Frank, the separate property proponent, could not rebut the presumption by tracing to separate property funds because the car was bought with Gwen's earnings that are community property. Remember that the title in his name is not determinative of the character of the property when using the general community property presumption.

Is there any other way that Frank could claim that the Thunderbird is his separate property? It looks like Gwen really did intend a gift by putting the title in his name and by including the "Happy Birthday" ribbon. Frank could argue that there was a transmutation from community property to his separate property because they had an oral or implied agreement to change the character of the property. For transmutations prior to January 1, 1985, no express declaration in writing was required. Therefore, Frank would have a good chance of showing a transmutation. However, it would depend on the testimony of both parties and sometimes memories fade and are distorted by the process of divorce. Please see Chapter 2 on transmutation.

Explanation 7 — The Chalet at Mammoth

The chalet was purchased in 1995; therefore, the general community property presumption applies. The title in Gwen's name is irrelevant. It is only relevant for property in a married woman's name acquired prior to January 1, 1975. Gwen, the separate property proponent, would have the burden of rebutting the presumption by tracing to separate property funds. Here, the funds used to buy the chalet came from Frank's business account and Gwen's earnings account. Both of them have been characterized as community property containing community property funds. Therefore, Gwen could not carry her burden, and the conclusion would be that the chalet is community property. It will be divided equally at divorce.

Explanation 8 — Frank Uses Both Accounts

The chalet was purchased in 1995; therefore, the general community property presumption applies. However, in this scenario, Frank would want to claim part of the chalet as his separate property. He would be considered the separate property proponent and would carry the burden of rebutting the community property presumption. He could rebut the presumption by tracing to his dividend account. The dividend account has already been characterized as Frank's separate property because it contains the dividends from the stock he owned prior to marriage. If he can show that the funds to purchase the chalet came from that account, he will be able to rebut the presumption to the extent of $30,000. The other $70,000 used to purchase the chalet came from his business account that contained his earnings from his business and therefore is community property.

Since the purchase price of the chalet was $100,000, the conclusion would be that the chalet is 30% Frank's separate property and 70% community property. Since the value of the chalet did not change since it was purchased, Frank would be entitled to $30,000 as his separate property and $35,000 as his one-half share of the community property. Gwen would be entitled to $35,000 as her one-half share of the community property. This is an example of apportionment, where the property is characterized as part separate property and part community property. If title to the chalet had been taken as joint tenancy or in other joint form, the analysis would differ significantly. Please see Chapter 4 on joint titles. Finally, if Gwen, the ski enthusiast, wanted the chalet, she could "buy out" Frank's portion of the property or "offset" his portion of the property with other community property.

Explanation 9 — The Chalet Appreciates

In this example, the chalet has appreciated in value. The appreciation equals $50,000. Since the ski chalet is part separate property and part community property, the appreciation is apportioned accordingly. Since the result of the characterization in Example 8, the chalet was 30% Frank's separate property and 70% community property, the appreciation is 30% Frank's separate property and 70% community property. Applying those percentages to the appreciation means that Frank is entitled to $15,000 of the appreciation as his separate property (30% of $50,000 equals $15,000) and $17,500 of the appreciation as his one-half share of the community property (70% of $50,000 equals $35,000). Gwen is entitled to $17,500 as her one-half share of the community property. Frank will ultimately be entitled to $45,000 as his separate property and $52,500 as his one-half share of the community property. Gwen will ultimately be entitled to $52,500 as her one-half share of the community property.

The major message here is that the proportion of contributions to the original purchase price determines how the appreciation in the property will be apportioned. Also please note that apportionment gives the separate property contributor a share greater than a 50/50 split of the property.

Explanation 10 — Who Owns the Cards?

The baseball card collection was acquired during marriage. It is untitled property; therefore, the general community property presumption applies. However, Frank, who is the separate property proponent, can rebut the presumption by tracing to funds from his dividend account. That account has already been characterized as separate property containing separate property funds. Since Frank can rebut the community property presumption, the baseball card collection will be considered his separate property and will not be divided at divorce.

Explanation 11 — Who Gets the "Mattress Money"?

Under the California Probate Code, a surviving spouse will receive all the community property if the decedent dies without a will. A surviving spouse will receive part of the separate property of the decedent if the decedent dies without a will. Therefore, characterization of the mattress money is crucial to whether Eleanor will receive all of the $50,000 or whether Franklin's sister Gertrude will have a share of the $50,000. Because Franklin cannot testify as to the source of the funds, the formulation of the community property presumption used will most likely determine the outcome of the characterization. If a court uses the formulation that the presumption is that property acquired during the marriage is community property, Eleanor will have to prove "acquisition" during marriage to raise the community property presumption. If a court uses the formulation that the presumption is that property possessed during marriage is community property, Eleanor will only have to prove "possession" during marriage to raise the community property presumption. The "possessed" formulation clearly favors Eleanor because once she proves possession during marriage, the mattress money is then presumed to be community property. Then the separate property proponent, Gertrude, must rebut the community property presumption by tracing to Franklin's inheritance. That is difficult to do when we are dealing with cash, and it is likely that the presumption will become conclusive and the mattress money will be community property and go to Eleanor as the surviving spouse.

Explanation 12 — Franklin Dies in His Sleep

Since this is a short marriage, there is some precedent that a court will require Eleanor to prove that the $50,000 was acquired during marriage to raise the community property presumption. At this point, we can see that it is easier to show possession than acquisition. Eleanor can clearly testify that the money was under the mattress during their marriage, but she has no personal knowledge if the money was acquired during the marriage. She cannot truthfully testify that it was acquired during marriage. If a court uses the "acquired" formulation, Eleanor cannot raise the general community presumption. It would seem, in that case, the court would be free to decide that the mattress money was separate property, and it would then be split between Eleanor and Gertrude, assuming that there were no other heirs.

CHAPTER 4

Let Me Call It Mine, Yours, or Ours: The Role of Title in Characterization of Property

We started this book with the proposition that title is usually not determinative of the character of spouses' property. This was particularly true when the title to the property was in one spouse's name. Now get ready for a sea change. When the property—either a house, bank account, stock, or car—is put in *joint* title, it is treated completely differently from property put in one spouse's name. Why, you ask? Shouldn't all titled property be treated the same way? Many lawyers, professors, and students would certainly prefer that all titled property be characterized in the same way. Many would say, "Let's be consistent." Let the title control in all cases or let the funds control in all cases or let the spouses' intentions control in all cases. But that is not the way the law developed and that is not what the law is today. Therefore, we must have a separate category for characterization of property held in joint title. We even must have subcategories of titles of joint tenancy and community property.

One threshold issue is whether the joint title presumption applies to property that does not use the traditional language of joint tenancy, community property, or tenancy in common. That issue was raised in the 2015 case *Marriage of Lafkas*, 237 Cal. App. 4th 921, 188 Cal. Rptr. 3d 484 (2015). John Lafkas had owned a one-third interest in a real estate partnership before he married Jean. During their marriage, the partnership modified the agreement to add Jean to the title. The modified agreement stated the names of each partner, including husband and wife as owners of a one-third interest. When their marriage was dissolved, John claimed that the partnership interest remained his separate property because he owned it before marriage and it was never transmuted into joint title. Jean claimed that the modified agreement was a joint title subject to the joint title presumption. The trial court agreed with Jean; the Court of Appeal agreed with John. The Court of Appeal held that "when a spouse places separate property in joint title form, the transmutation requirements of section 852 must be satisfied before the joint title presumption of section 2581 applies." *Id.* at 926, 188 Cal. Rptr. 3d at 487. The language in the modified partnership agreement was not a valid transmutation from John's separate property to a joint title because "[a] valid transmutation requires more than simply naming one or both spouses as the owner in a title document." *Id.* at 940, 188 Cal. Rptr. 3d at 498. Therefore, the joint title presumption will not apply unless there has been a valid transmutation to a joint title. See Chapter 2 on transmutation.

JOINT TENANCY DEEDS AND TITLES

Let us start with joint tenancy. If you remember anything from your first-year Property course, you remember that joint tenancy has the unique feature of the right of survivorship. For married couples, if they know anything about property, they also know that joint tenancy carries with it the feature of survivorship. When they buy a house, for instance, they were often counseled by real estate agents or escrow officers to take the title in joint tenancy. At that point, we are assuming they are happily married and would want the house to pass to the surviving spouse through the mechanism of joint tenancy. The situation becomes more complicated if the spouses unfortunately divorce. The complication is that we only have two types of marital property: community property and separate property. Since joint tenancy is not denominated as community property, it must be classified initially as separate property. That does not seem to present too many problems at divorce because we know that joint tenancy is a type of property that provides that the spouses hold undivided one-half interests in the joint tenancy. Since community property is divided equally at divorce, it would seem that there should be no problem in just dividing the joint tenancy in half at divorce, with each spouse receiving one-half. If the spouses use community property to buy the house or any other purchase and hold it in joint tenancy, again the obvious solution is to divide the property in half at divorce.

The Title or the Funds?

Matters become more complex when the purchase is made with the separate property of one spouse or with part separate property and part community property. Thus begins the dilemma, "What should control—the title or the funds?" Let's start with the title. As of 1984, the Legislature determined that all joint tenancy property acquired during marriage will be presumed to be community property at divorce. Family Code §2581 (formerly Civil Code §4800.1). The next question becomes, "How to rebut that presumption?" Up to this point, based on what you learned in Chapter 3, you would probably answer, "Look at the funds used to purchase the property." Although that is perfectly logical, that answer would be *wrong*. Why? The best way to understand why the funds would not control is that when spouses take the property in joint tenancy it "is tantamount to an agreement" to hold the property jointly. *Siberell v. Siberell*, 214 Cal. 767, 7 P.2d 1003 (1932). When the spouses make an agreement to hold the property jointly, the presumption that arises can only be rebutted by another agreement. Thus when the spouses put the property in joint title, the community property presumption can *never* be rebutted by tracing to funds used to buy the property. Thus the principle here is that an agreement must always be rebutted by another agreement. Tracing to funds will not rebut the presumption that property held in joint tenancy is community property at divorce.

Let's take our imaginary couple Harry and Wilma. In 1995, Wilma receives an inheritance of $100,000 and they use that inheritance to buy a house for that amount. (These figures are obviously unrealistic—it is impossible to buy even a hovel in California for $100,000.) They put the title in joint tenancy. The house has appreciated and is now worth $350,000. They have recently separated, and Wilma goes to an attorney for advice. She asks the attorney about the house. She says, "I put in $100,000 from my inheritance to buy this house. Isn't it mine?" When the attorney finds out that the house is in joint tenancy, he explains that the house is presumed to be community property and if the presumption becomes a conclusion, community property is split evenly at divorce. He asks her if they have any agreements about the house. She says, "No, we never discussed it or put anything in writing about the house." He tells her that the house will be characterized as community property and Harry and Wilma would each receive $175,000 at divorce.

Now, let's think about how Wilma feels. She thinks that she deserves more than just half, since it was her inheritance, her separate property, that actually bought the house. In property terms, it looks like her inheritance was a gift to the community, to herself and Harry. Although we do not know what her intentions were at the time they bought the house, at the time she is seriously considering divorce, she mostly likely would not intend that her separate property is a gift. She did not realize that putting the title in joint tenancy would result in her giving her inheritance to the community. She feels, "It's my house. I bought it with my separate property." She is wrong. Many spouses do not realize the implications of putting a house or other property into joint tenancy. Property acquired during marriage held in joint tenancy will be presumed to be community property at divorce. It can only be rebutted by an agreement that the house is not held jointly and as of 1984 that agreement has to be in writing or in a clear statement in a deed or title. Family Code §2581.

Reimbursement of Separate Property

But the Legislature was not insensitive to a spouse who uses separate property funds to purchase property and holds that property in joint tenancy. In our example, Wilma's separate property investment, so to speak, in the property will be protected. As of 1984, the Legislature also provided that there is a right to reimbursement of "contributions to the acquisition of the property to the extent the party traces the contributions to a separate property source." Family Code §2640(b) (formerly Civil Code §4800.2). Since the house was purchased after 1984, if Wilma can trace to her separate property the $100,000 contribution to the acquisition of the house, she will be reimbursed without interest. The next question concerns the $250,000 appreciation of the house. Because Family Code §2640(b) states, "The amount reimbursed shall be without interest or adjustment for change in monetary values . . . ," appreciation will remain community property and will be split between Harry and Wilma. Therefore, if Wilma can trace to her separate property contribution, she will receive $100,000 as reimbursement plus one-half of the appreciation, $125,000 and Harry will receive $125,000. At divorce, Wilma will receive $225,000 and Harry will receive $125,000. Thus, the Legislature has attempted in these two statutory provisions to protect both the community and the separate property contributor to the acquisition of the property.

The Two-Step Analysis: Characterization and Reimbursement

At this point, you should be saying to yourself, "But I thought that just above you said that the funds do not control, and now you say that there is a right to reimbursement based on the funds." If you think this is confusing, you are right. Here we enter the *Alice in Wonderland* aspect of California community property law. It is "curiouser and curiouser." The best way to understand this confusion is to think of the process regarding joint tenancy as a two-step analysis: (1) characterization of the property, and (2) remedy for the separate property contributor. At Step One, characterization, we look *only* to the title and any agreements about the property. Once it has been determined that there are no agreements about the property, and the joint tenancy property is characterized as community property, then we move to Step Two, remedy for the separate property contributor. At Step One, we ignore the funds. At Step Two, the funds pop up and provide a remedy for the separate property contributor.

So far we have been dealing with couples who have no agreements regarding the joint tenancy property. Let's change the hypothetical regarding Harry and Wilma. Let's say that when Harry and Wilma buy the house, they sign a written agreement that states, "In the event of a divorce, the house at 123 Hickory Lane will be considered Wilma's separate property." If they divorce, under §2581, the house held in joint tenancy will initially be presumed to be community property. But the written agreement that the house is actually Wilma's separate property will be sufficient to rebut the community property presumption. The house will then be characterized as Wilma's separate property, and she will receive the house as hers in toto. We do not need to go to §2640(b), the reimbursement statute, for two reasons. First, the determination has been made at Step One that the house is Wilma's separate property. She will receive the entire house as her separate property, and in a sense reimbursement is included in the characterization. Second, the language of §2640(b) reinforces our understanding that reimbursement applies only at Step Two after we have characterized the house as community property in Step One. That understanding is based on the statutory language "in the division of the community estate." Because the house is her separate property and not part of the community estate, §2640(b) does not apply.

Let's say that Harry and Wilma's written agreement states, "In the event of a divorce, the house at 123 Hickory Lane will be considered part Wilma's separate property and part community property." Ordinarily, they would have to be more specific in spelling out the exact proportions of separate and community property, but here we will just use the idea that it is possible to apportion shares of the property between the separate property of one spouse and the community. Step One: Let's characterize the house. If they divorce, under §2581, the house again will initially be presumed to be community property. The written agreement characterizing the house as part separate/part community property will be sufficient to rebut the community property presumption. Do we apply Step Two reimbursement now? No. We do not go to §2640(b) because that section applies only if we characterize the house as *all* community property. Thus the house will be apportioned according to the proportions specified in the agreement. If the proportions are 30% Wilma's separate property and 70% community property, Wilma will receive 30% of the value of the property, and the community will split 70% of the value of the property. That means that Wilma will receive 65% (30% and 35%) of the value of the property, and Harry will receive 35% of the value of the property. This remedy is called apportionment. It is not unusual for couples to agree that the property will be split according to the amount of money contributed. If Wilma had contributed $30,000 of the purchase price for the house and the community had contributed $70,000, they could have agreed to apportion the house accordingly. But don't be confused. In that case, the characterization is not based on the funds themselves, but on their agreement to apportion the property according to the contributions.

Oral or Written Agreement for Rebuttal?

Until now, we have been considering only two hypothetical situations: The spouses either have no agreement about the joint tenancy property, or they have some written document that characterizes the property as something other than community property. Then the obvious question is, "What if they have an agreement about the property but that agreement is oral or implied from conduct?" Here at least we have one simple and concrete answer. As of 1984, if the property was acquired in joint tenancy, the agreement *must* be in writing. An oral or implied-from-conduct agreement will *not* rebut the presumption that joint tenancy property is presumed to be community property upon divorce. At this point, let us reiterate our "mantra" that tracing to funds can never rebut the community property presumption that arises when spouses' property is held in joint form. Therefore, if a couple came to you for advice regarding the purchase of property and were contemplating putting it in joint tenancy, you would have to tell them that the property would be characterized as community property at divorce. Furthermore, an oral agreement or their intentions as manifested by their conduct would be insufficient to rebut the community property presumption. You could also explain the right to reimbursement if separate property funds were used to purchase the property, but here the emphasis is on the strict writing requirement that applies to joint tenancy as of 1984.

Oral Agreement Prior to 1984

The next question is, "What if the property was acquired before 1984 and the couple had an oral or implied agreement?" Again, let us say that Harry and Wilma bought a house with Wilma's $100,000 separate property, but the acquisition was in 1980. They put the title in joint tenancy, and at that time they orally agreed that the house would be Wilma's separate property. The house has appreciated and is worth $350,000. They have recently separated, and Wilma goes to an attorney for advice. The first step is characterization. Here the house is in joint tenancy and again would initially be presumed to be community property at divorce. The community property presumption for single-family residences in joint tenancy was first enacted in 1965, but the community property presumption applies to all joint titles at divorce no matter when the property was acquired, per *Marriage of Heikes* (pronounced "high-kiss"), 10 Cal. 4th 1211, 1215, 899 P.2d 1349, 1351, 44 Cal. Rptr. 2d 155, 157 (1995).

Although the law is now well settled that all joint titles are presumed to be community property at divorce, for many years it was unclear whether the writing requirement for rebuttal applied to acquisitions prior to 1984. That was the first year a written agreement or a clear statement in the title or deed was required to rebut the community property presumption. The Legislature tried several times to make the writing requirement apply to all acquisitions, even those prior to 1984. The Supreme Court in *Marriage of Buol*, 39 Cal. 3d 751, 705 P.2d 354, 218 Cal. Rptr. 31 (1985), and the Courts of Appeal in a later series of cases refused to apply the writing requirement to acquisitions prior to 1984. To try to understand the controversy, let us again look at the situation through Wilma's eyes and also look at the consequences of requiring some kind of writing for acquisitions prior to 1984.

Harry and Wilma acquired the house in 1980 and orally agreed that the house was Wilma's separate property. At that time, oral agreements were permitted to rebut the community presumption at divorce. In essence, even if they were totally unaware of the law, Harry and Wilma would expect that the law as it was at the time they acquired the property would apply to their situation. As of 1984, the Legislature changed the law regarding agreements permitted to rebut the community property presumption and said, "No oral agreements allowed." Usually, when the Legislature changes the law, it applies to future events, such as acquisitions after the date the legislation becomes effective.[1] But in this case, the Legislature was trying to prevent extensive litigation over oral or implied agreements and tried to apply the law retroactively to "all proceedings" as of 1984. Therefore, if Harry and Wilma divorced in 1984 or anytime thereafter, Wilma would have been required to produce a written agreement or a clear statement in the title or deed showing that the house was her separate property.

Now let's think about Wilma's reaction if she was now considering a divorce and her attorney advised her that her oral agreement was not sufficient. She would say, "That's not fair! At the time we bought the house and made our agreement that the house was mine. It was perfectly legal to have an oral agreement, and now you want me to have an agreement in writing. I shouldn't be required to have something in writing. Just think—Harry would never agree now." The attorney would have to explain that oral agreements are not allowed. The house would be considered community

1. In 2006, the California Supreme Court held that the general rule is that the Family Code and amendments to the Family Code are retroactive. *Marriage of Fellows*, 39 Cal. 4th 179, 138 P.3d 200, 46 Cal. Rptr. 3d 49 (2006). See Chapter 2, Retroactivity of Family Code Amendments.

property, and they would split the value of the house. Each would receive $175,000. But again Wilma would protest, "That's not fair! We agreed that the house was mine, all mine. And now I lose $175,000. That's not fair!" The Supreme Court in the *Buol* case agreed with Wilma's argument and voided the Legislature's attempt to apply Civil Code §4800.1 (now Family Code §2581) retroactively to acquisitions prior to 1984. In the *Buol* case, the unfairness was even more egregious because the Legislature tried to apply the writing requirement to all cases, even those that were on appeal, as was the *Buol* case. The language of the Court overturning retroactive application of the writing requirement is couched in terms of constitutional law—that retroactive application "would substantially impair [a] vested property right without due process of law." In essence, the Court was saying that there would be "unfair surprise" if the law were applied retroactively to acquisitions prior to 1984 where there was an oral agreement that would rebut the presumption. The bottom line, after ten years of wrangling between the Legislature and the courts, is that the community property presumption can be rebutted with an oral or implied agreement if the property was acquired prior to 1984.

No Agreement Prior to 1984

This leaves one more scenario unexplained. We use the same facts of Harry and Wilma's purchase of the house in 1980, but now we assume there is no agreement of any kind about the character of the house. Thus the house would be characterized as community property at divorce. Wilma would still want to know if she will have a right to reimbursement of her separate property contribution as was also provided by the 1984 legislation, Civil Code §4800.2 (now Family Code §2640(b)). The answer is no. According to the case of *Marriage of Lucas*, 27 Cal. 3d 808, 816, 614 P.2d 285, 289, 166 Cal. Rptr. 853, 858 (1980), the Supreme Court held that a separate property contributor could receive reimbursement "only if there is an agreement between the parties to that effect." In essence, the Court viewed the separate property contribution as a gift to the community. That meant that any appreciation in the property would be split between the community. Therefore, the answer to Wilma would be that based on the *Lucas* case, she would have no right to reimbursement of her $100,000 contribution because they had no reimbursement agreement.

"Now wait," Wilma exclaims, "I thought that as of 1984, the Legislature mandated protection for my separate property contribution and that I have a right to reimbursement if I can trace to my separate property contribution." The 1984 legislation was intended to reverse the *Lucas* Court's reimbursement agreement requirement, and it was intended to apply to acquisitions prior to 1984. However, the Supreme Court would not allow retroactive application of that "about-face" in the law. Thus, the right to reimbursement "is limited by the due process clause to property acquired on or after January 1, 1984." *Marriage of Heikes,* 10 Cal. 4th at 1225, 899 P.2d 1349, 1358, 44 Cal. Rptr. 2d 155, 164. Thus, Wilma would not receive reimbursement because the acquisition of the house occurred prior to 1984.

Summary

To summarize, 1984 is a pivotal date regarding the law of joint tenancy titles and deeds at divorce. Step One is determining the character of the property. Any joint tenancy deed or title held in joint tenancy is presumed to be community property at divorce. The presumption applies no matter when the property was acquired. Rebuttal of the presumption may be by agreement *only,* not tracing to funds. If the property was acquired prior to 1984, oral or implied agreements regarding the character of the property will be sufficient to rebut the community property presumption. If the property was acquired in 1984 or thereafter, the community property presumption may be rebutted *only* by a written agreement or a clear statement in the title or deed. If there is an agreement, the property will be characterized according to the spouses' agreement. The spouses could agree that the property is the separate property of one spouse or part separate property/part community property. If there are no agreements, the joint tenancy property will be characterized as community property and split between the spouses.

Step Two is to determine if there is any right to reimbursement when there has been a separate property contribution to the acquisition of the property. Step Two is relevant only if there has been a characterization of community property at Step One. For acquisitions in 1984 or thereafter, there is a right to reimbursement based on tracing. That right is a bare right. Appreciation of the property goes to the community; it is not apportioned. For acquisitions prior to 1984, reimbursement is available to the separate property contributor *only* if there is an agreement to that effect. That agreement could be oral, implied, or written. If there is no agreement regarding reimbursement, the separate property contribution is considered a gift to the community. See the flowchart on pages 79-80.

Examples

Example 1 — The RV and JT

Harry and Wanda were married in California in 1980. In 2000, they purchased a large recreational vehicle (RV) that they wanted for traveling around the United States. The title stated that the owners were "Harry and Wanda, husband and wife, as joint tenants." They had no agreements about the RV. They paid for the RV with savings from Harry's salary and an inheritance that

Wanda had received. After a recent trip, they realized their travels through life together were at an end and separated. Wanda comes to you for advice. She wants to know what rights she has to the RV. The RV has neither appreciated nor depreciated in value. How would a California court characterize the RV? What are Wanda's rights?

Example 2 — On the Rocks at Malibu

Tom and Linda married in 1995. Tom came from a wealthy family, and a large chunk of his income came from a trust fund his parents had set up for him as a child. Tom also earned a huge salary from his job. In 1998, they bought a home in Malibu for $1 million. They paid cash, with $750,000 from Tom's trust fund and $250,000 from Tom's salary. They put the title in joint tenancy but signed an agreement that stated:

> Tom's interest in the Malibu home is in proportion to his separate property contribution of $750,000 to the purchase price of $1 million.

Tom is considering a divorce from Linda and wants to know what rights he has to the Malibu home. The home has appreciated in value. How would a California court characterize the Malibu home? How would the court divide the value of the home at divorce?

Example 3 — Tom and Linda Don't Agree

Assume the same facts as in Example 2, except that Tom and Linda have no agreements about the Malibu home. How would a California court characterize the Malibu home? What are Tom's rights regarding the home?

Example 4 — Orange County Split-Level

Gerald and Betty were married in California in 1970. In 1982, they purchased a home in Orange County for $100,000. They used $30,000 from an inheritance Betty received in 1981 and paid for the rest from Gerald's earnings during the marriage. The deed stated that the owners were "Gerald and Betty, husband and wife, as joint tenants." They have no agreements about the home. Their marriage has deteriorated, and they are considering a divorce. The house is now valued at $300,000. How would a California court characterize the house and divide it in Gerald and Betty's divorce?

Example 5 — Gerald and Betty Talk It Over

Assume the same facts as Example 4 except that Gerald and Betty have an oral agreement that the house is Betty's separate property. How will the court characterize the home and divide it in Gerald and Betty's divorce?

4. The Role of Title in Characterization of Property

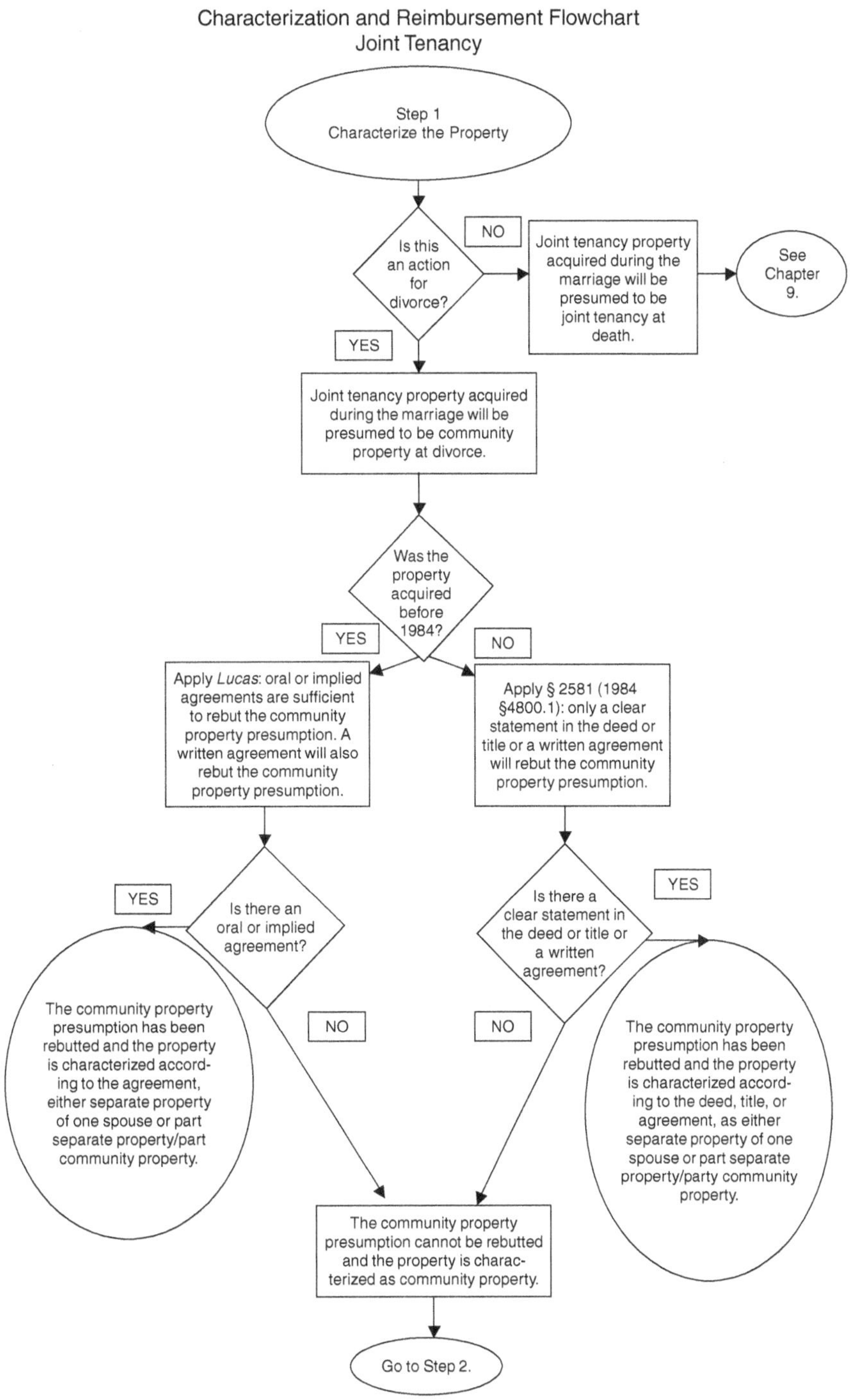

4. The Role of Title in Characterization of Property

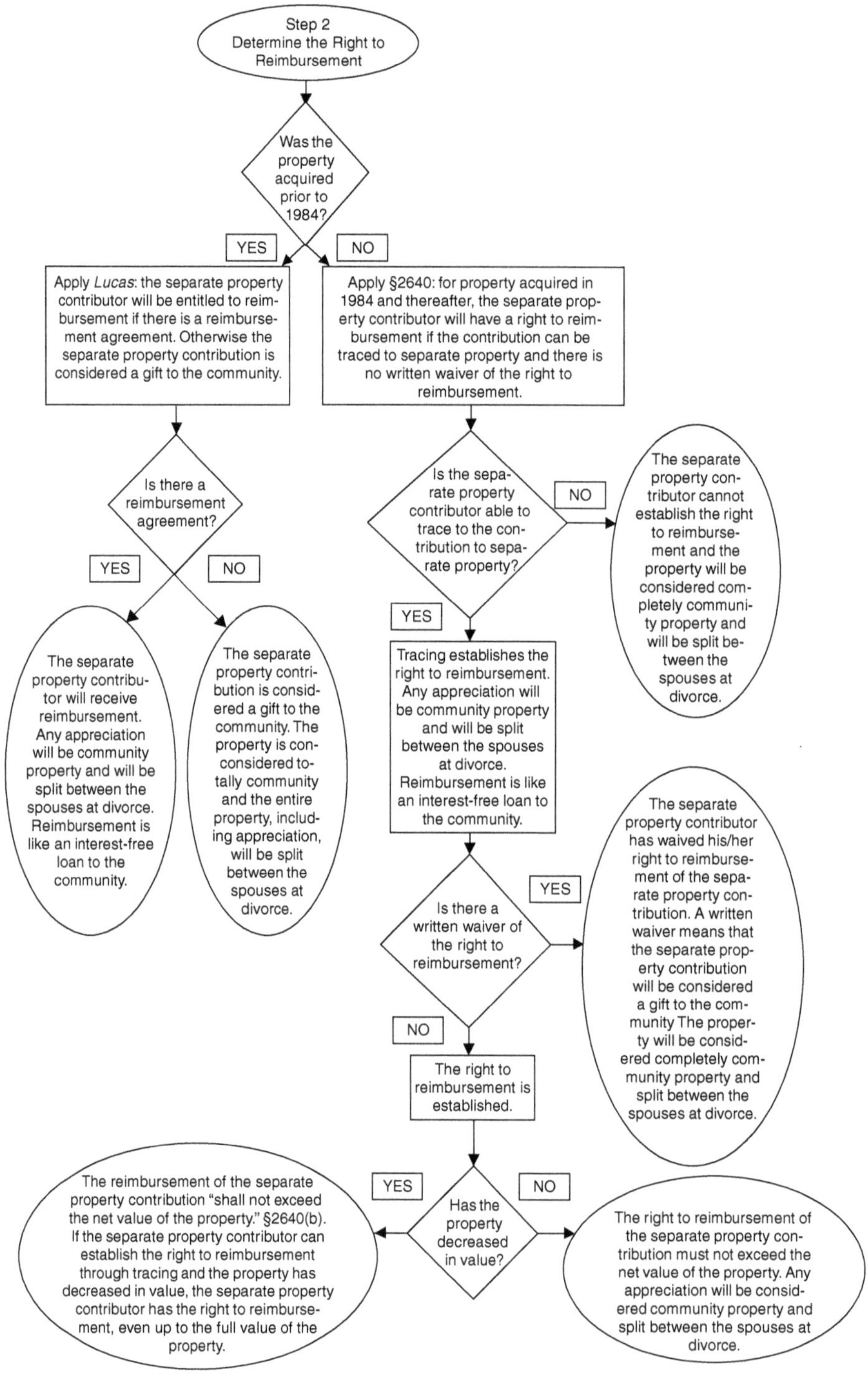

Example 6 — Did Cindy Know the Law?

Cindy married Joe in 2001 soon after she graduated from law school. Cindy's grandfather was so proud of her accomplishment that he gave her a gift of $100,000. They used that money as a down payment on a condo near the ocean. The purchase price of the condo was $500,000, and they took title as joint tenants at the suggestion of Cindy's grandfather. Joe told Cindy, "It's all due to your hard work at law school that we have this condo. If we ever split up, I think it should be yours." They discussed putting that in writing, but Cindy said, "I know and you know that the house is mine, and that is all that matters." Cindy's commitment to her job as an attorney took its toll on their marriage, and they recently separated and filed for divorce. The condo has appreciated in value and is now worth $1,000,000. At divorce, how would a California court characterize the condo? How would the court divide the condo?

Explanations

Explanation 1 — The RV and JT

The first step is to characterize the RV. At divorce, all property acquired during marriage in joint tenancy is presumed to be community property. Family Code §2581. For acquisitions in 1984 or thereafter, the presumption can be rebutted only by a written agreement or a clear statement in the deed or title. Here the RV was purchased during marriage after 1984. The community property presumption cannot be rebutted because there are no agreements of any kind regarding the character of the RV. Also, there is no statement in the title other than joint tenancy. Thus a California court would characterize the RV as community property, which would be split in half at divorce.

However, the facts also state that they used Wanda's inheritance to purchase the RV. Because at Step One we have characterized the RV as community property, Family Code §2640(b) potentially provides the separate property contributor to the acquisition of the property a right to reimbursement. Family Code §2640(b) applies to acquisitions in 1984 or thereafter. That is met here because the RV was purchased in 2000. If Wanda can trace to her separate property, she will be able to establish her right to reimbursement. She will be able to recover that amount without any additional interest in the property. The rest of the value of the RV belongs to the community and will be split between Harry and Wanda.

Explanation 2 — On the Rocks at Malibu

The Malibu home was purchased during Tom and Linda's marriage and held in joint tenancy. Tom used funds from his trust fund. The trust fund was owned before their marriage and is thus separate property. The rents, issues, and profits of separate property are separate property; therefore, any income from the trust fund would also be separate property. The agreement they signed reiterates that the $750,000 is Tom's separate property. The funds from Tom's salary are community property.

At divorce, it would be presumed to be community property. Family Code §2581. For acquisitions in 1984 or thereafter, the presumption can be rebutted by a written agreement or a clear statement in the deed or title. Here Tom and Linda have a written agreement that gives proportional interests to Tom and the community. Make sure you understand that it is the agreement, not the funds, that gives Tom a separate property interest. Tom's interest, as specified in the agreement, is 75%, and the remaining 25% belongs to the community. Thus the property is characterized as part Tom's separate property and part community property. The court will divide the property according to those proportions. The appreciation of the home will be split according to those proportions. Seventy-five percent will go to Tom, and 25% will be split between Tom and Linda.

Because at Step One the house was characterized as part separate/part community property, Family Code §2640(b) does not apply. That code section applies only if the home had been characterized as community property. Part separate/part community property does not fall within §2640(b).

Explanation 3 — Tom and Linda Don't Agree

Again, to characterize the home, we start with the community property presumption. Because there are no agreements about the home, the presumption cannot be rebutted. Even though Tom put in $750,000 of his separate property, that does not make the character of the house partially his separate property. Only a written agreement or clear statement in the deed can rebut the community property presumption. Thus the court would characterize the home as community property.

However, Tom does receive reimbursement under §2640(b). That section applies because at Step One we have characterized the home as community property. If Tom can trace to his separate property contribution of $750,000, he will receive that amount. Tom's separate property contribution is treated as a loan to the community. He gets his money back but without any accrued interest. The appreciation of the home belongs to the community and will be split between Tom and Linda. Tom does not receive 75% of the appreciation.

Explanation 4 — Orange County Split-Level

Betty's inheritance is separate property and Gerald's earnings are community property. The funds are irrelevant to Step One, characterization, when the deed or title is in joint tenancy. The home was acquired in 1982, but all joint tenancy deeds are presumed to be community property at divorce. We look only to the spouses' agreement to rebut the presumption. For acquisitions prior to 1984, oral or implied agreements are permitted. Here there are no agreements. The community property presumption cannot be rebutted. The home will be characterized as community property.

At Step Two, we ask if Betty will receive reimbursement of her separate property contribution. Even though we characterized the home as community property at Step One, Family Code §2640(b) does not apply here because it applies only to acquisitions in 1984 or thereafter. Here Gerald and Betty acquired the home in 1982. Betty could receive reimbursement under the *Lucas* case if she can prove that Gerald and she had a reimbursement agreement. That agreement could be oral or implied as well as written. Since there are no agreements here, Betty does not receive reimbursement. Her separate property contribution is considered a gift to the community. The court will split the value of the house in half—Gerald will receive $150,000 and Betty $150,000.

Explanation 5—Gerald and Betty Talk It Over

At Step One, characterization, the community property presumption applies, but here the question is whether it can be rebutted by an oral agreement. The answer is yes. For acquisitions prior to 1984 in joint tenancy, oral (or implied) agreements are permitted to rebut the community property presumption, according to the *Buol* and *Heikes* cases. Here, Gerald and Betty's agreement is that the home is Betty's separate property. Again note that the funds used to buy the home are irrelevant at this stage. Even though Betty put in only $30,000 from her separate property, the entire house is her separate property because of their agreement. When there is a joint tenancy, it is the agreement that controls at the characterization step, not the funds.

Step Two, reimbursement, is not relevant here because the entire home is Betty's separate property. Family Code §2640(b) does not apply because the acquisition was before 1984. Even if you somehow thought that section was retroactive (it is not!), it would not apply because at Step One, the characterization was Betty's separate property not community property.

Explanation 6—Did Cindy Know the Law?

Step One requires characterization of the condo. The condo was acquired during Cindy and Joe's marriage and the title was taken in joint tenancy. At divorce, joint titles are presumed to be community property; therefore, the condo is presumed to be community property. The question here is whether the community property presumption can be rebutted. For acquisitions of property in 1984 and thereafter, a written statement in the deed or written agreement is required to rebut the presumption. Family Code §2581. The only agreement that Cindy and Joe have appears to be an oral agreement that the condo is Cindy's separate property. However, Cindy should have paid better attention in her community property class and learned that an oral agreement will not rebut the community property presumption if the property was acquired during marriage in 1984 or thereafter in joint tenancy. Thus, unfortunately for Cindy, the condo would be characterized as community property.

Cindy is not entirely out of luck. At Step Two, she will be able to claim a right to reimbursement of her separate property contribution to the purchase of the condo. Since the condo was characterized as community property at Step One, we move to an analysis under Family Code §2640(b). At divorce, §2640(b) applies to acquisitions in 1984 or thereafter. For Cindy to succeed in establishing a right to reimbursement, she must be able to trace to a separate property contribution to the condo. "Contributions to the acquisition of the property" include down payments. Here, the $100,000 gift from Cindy's grandfather that was used for the down payment on the condo is Cindy's separate property. If she received it before she married Joe, then it is separate property because she owned it before marriage. If she received it during marriage, it is still her separate property because it was a gift to Cindy. Thus, Cindy could demonstrate her right to reimbursement unless there was a "written waiver" of that right. No facts indicate that Cindy waived her right to reimbursement. Therefore, Cindy would be able to establish her right to reimbursement of $100,000. Because the condo would be characterized as community property, Cindy and Joe would split the appreciation of the condo.

COMMUNITY PROPERTY DEEDS AND TITLES

Up to this point, we have been discussing deeds and titles that are held in joint tenancy. The focus of the Legislature in 1984 was on joint tenancy because the majority of litigation over joint titles focused on joint tenancy. However, it is also possible for married couples to choose to hold their houses, cars, or stocks in community property deeds or titles. If you have mastered the complexities of joint tenancy, there are only a few differences regarding community property deeds and titles.

Let us first review the basics of joint titles. Joint title includes not only title taken in joint tenancy, but also community property title, tenancy in common, and any joint form. If a couple holds property jointly, the property is presumed to be community property at divorce. So far, so good, you say, that makes sense—a community property deed or title will be presumed to be community property. The murkier questions are (1) how the presumption will be rebutted, and (2) whether there will be a right to reimbursement if there is a separate property contribution to the property. Again we see that we have a two-step analysis. At Step One, the answer is that the community property presumption can be rebutted by an agreement that the property is not community property. Even though the deed or title states the property is community property, the spouses can agree that the property is one spouse's separate property or part separate/part community property. If there is no agreement that rebuts the community property presumption, then the property is characterized as community property at divorce. At Step Two, once the property has been characterized as community property, if there was a separate property contribution to the property, the right to reimbursement depends on WHEN the property was acquired. If the property was acquired in 1984 or thereafter, there is a right to reimbursement based on tracing. Appreciation is split between the community. If the property was acquired prior to 1984, the right to reimbursement can be established only by agreement. Absent a reimbursement agreement, the separate property contribution is considered a gift to the community.

The 1987 Amendments

Step One, characterization, is more complicated regarding community property deeds and titles, again thanks to the California Legislature. When the Legislature enacted the 1984 Civil Code §4800.1, called the Anti-*Lucas* legislation, they focused exclusively on joint tenancy deeds and titles. They omitted any mention of community property or any other joint deeds or titles. So arose an anomalous situation—joint tenancy became a more secure form of community property than was a community property title. Let's explain. Both a joint tenancy title and a community property title are presumed to be community property at divorce. So far, it seems that both forms of titles would be treated the same. But wait! We must consider how to rebut that community property presumption. As of 1984, a joint tenancy title required something in writing to rebut the presumption. Because community property deeds and titles were omitted from the 1984 legislation, prior law continued to operate. Under that law, a community property title could be rebutted by an oral or implied agreement. Thus, as of 1984, it was harder to rebut the community property presumption if the deed or title was in joint tenancy because of the writing requirement, than if the deed or title was in community property. Therefore, at that time, to ensure that the property would be considered community property at divorce, it was preferable to put the property in joint tenancy rather than in community property title. Incredible!

Let's look at an example to illustrate. Again assume that our hypothetical couple, Harry and Wilma, buy a house for $100,000 in 1984, and the deed states that the house is "community property." They have an oral agreement that the house is Wilma's separate property. They unfortunately are considering divorce. If the house were in joint tenancy, the oral agreement would *not* rebut the community property presumption at divorce. As of 1984, either a written agreement or clear statement in the deed or title is required to rebut the community property presumption that applies to joint tenancy. But the law regarding community property deeds and titles continued to allow rebuttal by an oral or implied agreement. Therefore, in this case, the house would be characterized as Wilma's separate property based on their oral agreement. If the house were in joint tenancy, it would be characterized as community property because there was nothing in writing to rebut the presumption. Thus, until the Legislature noticed this error, to make sure that property would be considered community property at divorce, it would have been wise to hold property as joint tenancy rather than as community property. The illogic of that time was that joint tenancy would be characterized as community property at divorce; a community property title or deed may or may not have been characterized as community property at divorce.

This anomaly was noticed. And the Legislature, presumably with some red faces, amended §4800.1 (now Family Code §2581) in 1987 to include all property "in joint form, including property held in tenancy in common, joint tenancy, tenancy by the entirety, or as community property." However, that did not fully correct the problem. What about deeds and titles that were put in community property form between 1984 and 1987? As we know, the type of rebuttal of the community property presumption depends on *when* the property was acquired. For joint tenancy, oral or implied agreements can rebut the presumption for acquisitions up until 1984, the effective date of the joint tenancy legislation. Consistency then requires that, for community property deeds and titles, oral or implied agreements can rebut the presumption up until 1987, the effective date of the amendments regarding all joint titles. That is the easy and most logical way to analyze this peculiar time period.

Let us now take Harry and Wilma's acquisition of the house and move it forward to 1987, the year the joint title amendments became effective. The deed states that the house is "community property." They have an oral agreement that the house is Wilma's separate property. They unfortunately are considering divorce. Their lawyer would tell them that an oral agreement would not rebut the community property presumption that arises from the community property deed. The house would be characterized as community property.

Two Sets of Rules?

This scenario brings up an even "curiouser" situation. Although oral agreements are allowed to rebut the community property presumption for acquisitions up until 1987, the right to reimbursement of separate property contributions based on tracing applies to acquisitions in 1984 or thereafter. So let us add to the above scenario the fact that Harry and Wilma used $100,000 of Wilma's separate property to buy the house. At Step One, the funds used to buy the house are irrelevant; only an agreement can rebut the community property presumption. Here the agreement was oral. As of 1987, an oral agreement would not rebut the community property presumption and the characterization of the house is community property. At Step Two, because the house was acquired after 1984, the effective date of §4800.2 (now Family Code §2640(b)), Wilma will have a right to reimbursement if she can trace to her separate property contribution. Hopefully, it becomes clear again why we must separate into two steps, characterization and reimbursement. Especially with community property deeds and titles, depending on the date of acquisition, one set of rules applies to characterization and another set of rules applies to reimbursement rights.

So far we have assumed that up until 1987 oral agreements are permitted to rebut the community property presumption when there is a community property deed or title. However, there is a possibility that oral agreements are allowed only up until 1985. The reason is that the transmutation statute, Family Code §§850-853, became effective on January 1, 1985. As of 1985, transmutations of real or personal property are "not valid unless made in writing by an express declaration." Family Code §852(a). Let's take our Harry and Wilma example and move the date they acquired the house to 1985. Again they have an oral agreement that the house is Wilma's separate property. We could say that that oral agreement is essentially a transmutation of community property to separate property of one spouse, which is covered by Family Code §850(a). Thus we could also say that the rebuttal of the community property presumption must also be in writing. Clearly the Legislature was moving toward strict writing requirements, as seen in the 1984 §4800.1 regarding joint tenancies and the 1985 transmutation statute. The counterargument is that the transmutation statute says nothing about rebuttal of presumptions and was not intended to cover community property deeds and titles. The specific writing requirement for community property deeds and titles was not addressed until 1987 with the amendments to §4800.1. Thus the prior law permitting oral agreements for rebuttal should apply until 1987.

There is an even more enigmatic phrase in the transmutation statute. It states in §852(d): "Nothing in this section [the express declaration in writing requirement] affects the law governing characterization of property in which separate property and community property are commingled or *otherwise combined.*" (Emphasis added.) Under our understanding of Step One characterization, we certainly know that using separate and community property funds has nothing to do with the characterizing of the property once the spouses put the title in joint form. Therefore, it seems that "combining" funds would be irrelevant at the characterization step. Let's again analyze Harry and Wilma's acquisition of their house in 1985. The deed states that the house is community property. They use part separate property and part community property to buy the house and they have an oral agreement that the house is Wilma's separate property. If we disregard the transmutation statute, the house would be presumed to be community property, rebuttable by oral agreement up until 1987. Because there is an oral agreement that the house is Wilma's separate property, the house would be characterized as her separate property. Neat and simple. If the transmutation statute applies, it is much more complicated. As of 1985, the agreement transmuting the property would have to be an express declaration in writing. Therefore, the oral agreement would not be sufficient to be that express declaration and therefore it would not rebut the community property presumption. But under §852(d), separate property and community property were "combined" to purchase the house, and it seems that the express declaration requirement would not apply and the oral agreement would rebut the community property presumption. It is unclear what the Legislature intended here, and in this author's opinion, the transmutation statute should not apply when we have another whole body of law specifically dealing with joint titles at divorce. See the flowchart on pages 89-90.

Examples

Example 7 — Does George Get the Cherry Trees?

George and Martha were married in California in 1990. George came from a wealthy family. When his father died in 1995, George received an inheritance, which he used to buy a cherry orchard near Fresno. Their tax advisor suggested that it would be a good idea to put the deed to the orchard in "community property." In the deed was the following language: "George and Martha, husband and wife, as community property." At that time they orally agreed that the orchard was George's separate property. George and Martha unfortunately have recently separated. George comes to you for advice. He wants to know what rights he has to the cherry orchard. How would a California court characterize the orchard? What are George's rights to the orchard?

Example 8 — George and Martha Don't Agree

Assume the same facts as in Example 7, except that George and Martha have no agreements about the orchard. How would a California court characterize the orchard? What are George's rights to the orchard?

4. The Role of Title in Characterization of Property

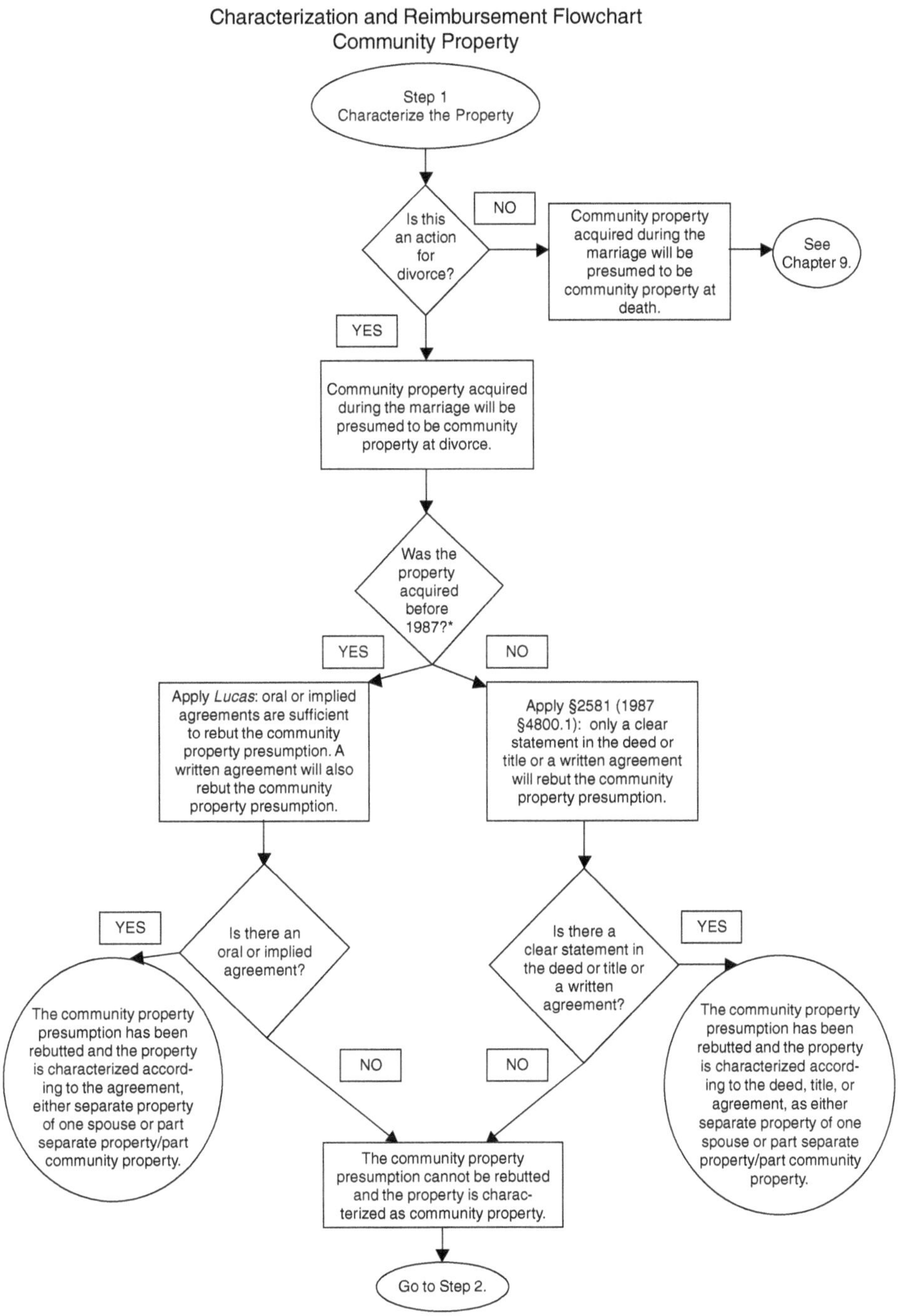

*There is a possibility that *Lucas*, which allows rebuttal by oral or implied agreements, applied only until January 1, 1985, when all transmutations had to be by express declaration in writing.

4. The Role of Title in Characterization of Property

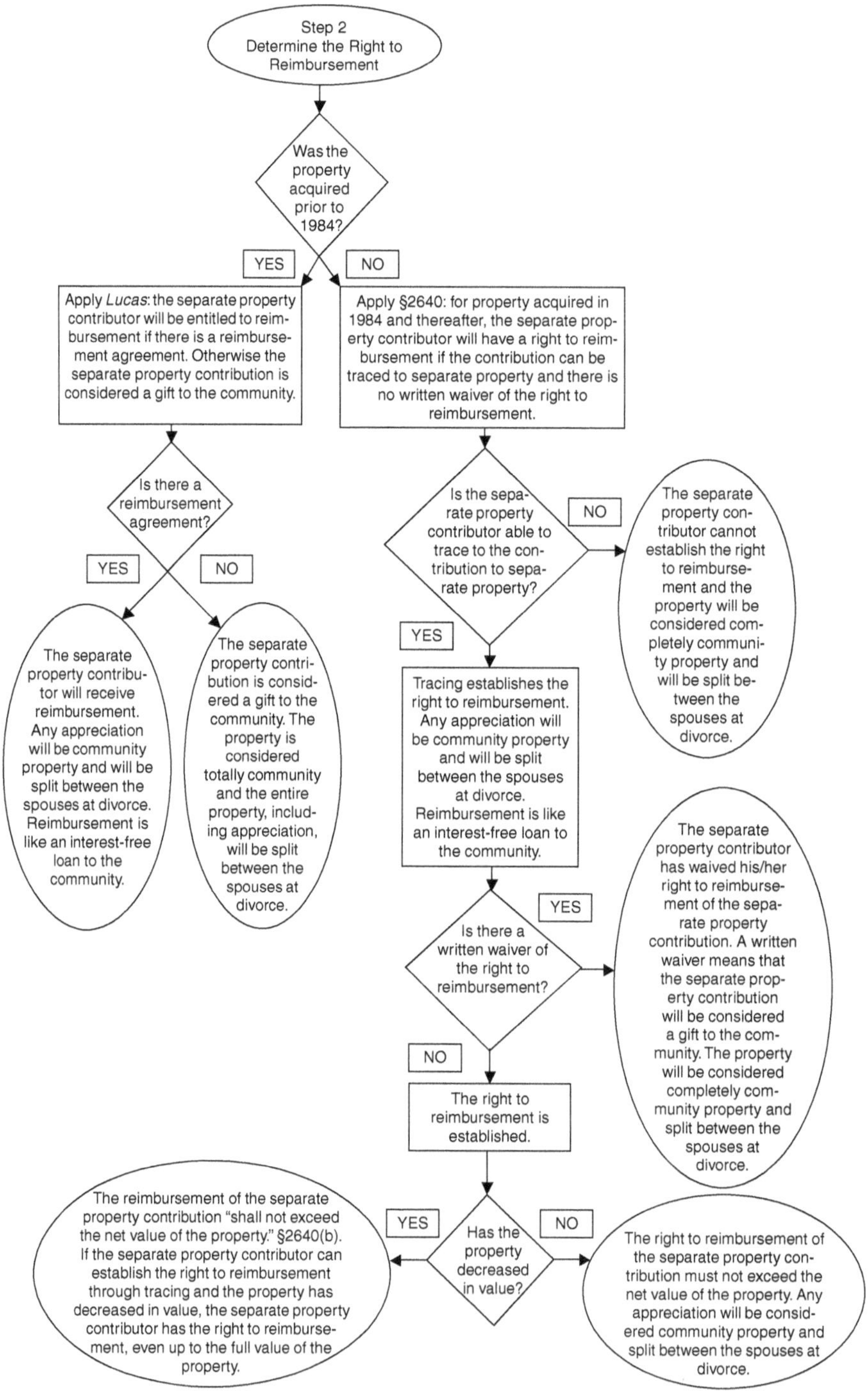

Example 9—George and Martha Agree in Writing

Assume the same facts as in Example 7, except that George and Martha have a written agreement that the orchard is George's separate property. How would a California court characterize the orchard? What are George's rights to the orchard?

Example 10—Do Abe and Mary Split the Log Cabin?

Abe and Mary were married in California in 1980. In 1987, they bought a rustic cottage near Big Bear using earnings they accumulated during their marriage. The deed to the cottage stated that the owners were "Abe and Mary, husband and wife, as community property." Because Abe was considerably older than Mary and he was concerned about her financial security, they orally agreed at the time they purchased the cottage that it should be her separate property. Unfortunately, the age difference has had an effect on their marriage, and Mary is considering leaving Abe. She comes to you for advice. She wants to know if the cottage would be hers if they divorce. How would a California court characterize the cottage? What are Mary's rights to the cottage?

Example 11—They Bought the Cabin in 1984

Assume the same facts as in Example 10, except that the cottage was purchased in 1984. How would a California court characterize the cottage? What are Mary's rights to the cottage?

Example 12—They Bought the Cabin in 1985

Assume the same facts as in Example 10, except that the cottage was purchased in 1985. How would a California court characterize the cottage? What are Mary's rights to the cottage?

Explanations

Explanation 7—Does George Get the Cherry Trees?

The first step is to characterize the orchard. At divorce, all property acquired during marriage in joint form, including community property, is presumed to be community property. Family Code §2581. For a community property deed acquired in 1987 or thereafter, the presumption can be rebutted only by a written agreement or a clear statement in the deed or title. Here the orchard was acquired during marriage in 1995, which is after 1987. The community property presumption cannot be rebutted by an oral agreement. There is no clear statement in the deed specifying that the orchard is anything other than community property. Thus a California court would characterize the orchard as community property, which would ordinarily be split in half at divorce.

However, the facts also state that George used his inheritance, separate property, to purchase the orchard. Because at Step One, the orchard was characterized as community property, Family Code §2640(b) provides a right to reimbursement to the separate property contributor to the acquisition of the property. Family Code §2640(b) applies to acquisitions in 1984 or thereafter. That is met because the orchard was acquired in 1995. If George can trace to his inheritance, he will be able to establish his right to reimbursement. He will be able to recover that amount. If the orchard appreciated in value, that value belongs to the community and will be split between George and Martha.

Explanation 8 — George and Martha Don't Agree

Because there are no agreements about the orchard, the community property presumption at divorce that arises from the title becomes the conclusion re characterization. Thus the orchard will be characterized as community property.

Still, because separate property was used to purchase the orchard, George will have a right to reimbursement if he can trace to those funds. Again any appreciation belongs to the community.

Explanation 9 — George and Martha Agree in Writing

The first step is again characterization. Although the orchard is presumed to be community property at divorce because the deed states it is "community property," the couple's written agreement is sufficient to rebut the presumption. Therefore, the orchard will be characterized according to their agreement, and the court will characterize the orchard as George's separate property.

There is no need to discuss a "right to reimbursement." The orchard belongs to George as his separate property. In addition, Family Code §2640(b), the reimbursement statute, only applies to the "community estate," and the orchard is not part of that estate.

Explanation 10 — Do Abe and Mary Split the Log Cabin?

The first step is characterization. Since the deed to the cottage states it is held as community property, the cottage is presumed to be community property at divorce. Because the cottage was purchased in 1987, the year the amendments regarding all joint titles became effective, the writing requirement for rebuttal would apply here. In order for Mary to establish that the cottage was her separate property, she would need a written agreement or a clear statement in the deed to that effect. She has only an oral agreement. That would not rebut the community property presumption; the court would characterize the cottage as community property, and it would be split in half at divorce.

Neither Abe nor Mary would have any reimbursement rights. Although the characterization at Step One is that the cottage is community property, Family Code §2640(b) allows reimbursement for separate property contributions only. Here the cottage was purchased with their earnings, which are community property.

Explanation 11 — They Bought the Cabin in 1984

At the characterization step, the important question is whether Abe and Mary's oral agreement will rebut the community property presumption. Here the crucial fact is the date they acquired the cottage and agreed that it was Mary's separate property. Since that occurred before the effective date of the 1987 §4800.1 (now Family Code §2581), their oral agreement could rebut the community property presumption. Therefore, the court will characterize the cottage as Mary's separate property. Mary will receive the cottage as her separate property.

If you answered that the oral agreement would not rebut the community property presumption, you probably had the year 1984 stuck in your mind. That date is important for two reasons. First, it is the effective date of the writing requirement for rebuttal of the community property presumption that applies to joint *tenancy* deeds and titles. Second, it is the effective date of the reimbursement statute. But neither applies here. The effective date of the writing requirement for rebuttal of the community property presumption that applies to *community property* deeds is 1987. The reimbursement statute does not apply because the characterization here is Mary's separate property not community property. In addition, there are no separate property contributions to the acquisition of the property since community funds were used to purchase the cottage.

Explanation 12 — They Bought the Cabin in 1985

The answer will be the same. The assumption being made is that oral agreements can rebut the community property presumption arising from a community property deed up until the effective date of the 1987 §4800.1 (now Family Code §2581). Thus the cottage would be Mary's separate property.

The only caveat here is whether the transmutation statute, Family Code §852(a), would require an "express declaration in writing" to rebut the community property presumption. That statute applies to all *transmutations* as of 1985. If a court would apply that statute, Abe and Mary's oral agreement would not rebut the community property presumption. In that case, the court would characterize the cottage as community property. Although it is unlikely that a court will apply the transmutation statute to joint titles, it could happen especially if the court thinks that would result in a more equitable division of property.

COMMUNITY PROPERTY WITH RIGHT OF SURVIVORSHIP

Community property with right of survivorship, also known as survivorship community property, is a new type of joint title in California. As of July 1, 2001, a husband and wife may hold title as community property with right of survivorship. This title is created when "expressly declared in the transfer document" that the title is community property with right of survivorship. Civil Code §682.1. There is no explanation of the exact requirements of the "transfer document." The statute seems to envision the scenario where couples will take existing joint tenancy or community property and "transfer" it to community property with right of survivorship. A court would likely focus on the "expressly declared" language if the property is designated in some document other than a "transfer document." For instance, a title or deed could be deemed to be the required "transfer document." It is noteworthy that this provision is placed in the Civil Code and tracks the same language for creating a joint tenancy. Civil Code §683. It is most likely that any document claiming to create community property with right of survivorship would need those exact words to create survivorship community property.

Survivorship community property combines the qualities of community property and joint tenancy. If the marriage ends in divorce, the property will be treated as community property. If the marriage ends in death, the property will be treated as joint tenancy, and the surviving spouse gains the property by right of survivorship. Let us consider our hypothetical couple, Harry and Wilma. Assume Harry and Wilma will soon reach retirement age and they seek financial advice concerning their property. In 2003, they consult an attorney who notices that they hold much of their property in joint tenancy. Wilma is concerned because she has heard many stories of how retirement sometimes destroys long-term marriages. Also she is concerned about Harry, whose health has begun to deteriorate. She asks questions concerning how their joint tenancy would be treated at divorce and at death. The attorney explains that there is a new type of joint property that would cover both her concerns. He suggests that they transfer their joint tenancy property into survivorship community property that would be treated like community property during marriage and at divorce and would be treated like joint tenancy at death. Their attorney creates the transfer document in which their property is listed and is expressly declared to be community property with right of survivorship and they sign it. Their property would then become survivorship community property.

If Harry and Wilma divorce, the right of survivorship will be inapplicable and the property will be treated as community property, and each will be entitled to one-half of the property. If Harry dies, the entire property will pass to Wilma via the right of survivorship. Similarly, if Wilma dies first, the entire property will pass to Harry via right of survivorship. How survivorship community property is treated at death is explained in Chapter 9.

Examples

Example 13 — Alex and Natasha Buy a Home

Alex and Natasha are immigrants from the former Soviet Union. They arrived in California several years ago and have become U.S. citizens. They married in 1996. Their distaste for communism and its property system has turned into admiration for capitalism and our property system. After they married, they started a business in Los Angeles, and by 2002, they saved enough money to purchase a home. Their friend Sergei, who is an attorney, suggested that they should hold the title in community property with right of survivorship. They trusted Sergei so much that they took his advice, and the deed expressly stated that the home was community property with right of survivorship. They have recently initiated divorce proceedings. How would a California court characterize and divide the home?

Example 14 — Natasha Buys Stock

In 2003, Natasha received an inheritance of $5,000 from her Uncle Boris. Natasha took the $5,000 and invested in stock in a corporation that was reviving the cartoon series *Rocky and Bullwinkle*. Remembering Sergei's advice, she asks that the title of the stock state that it belongs to Alex and Natasha, husband and wife, as "community property with right of survivorship." The cartoon series was a great success, and the stock has tripled in value. If Alex and Natasha divorce, how would a court characterize and divide the stock?

Explanations

Explanation 13 — Alex and Natasha Buy a Home

Since the home was purchased after the effective date of Civil Code §682.1 — July 1, 2001 — community property with right of survivorship is an available form of joint title. We start with the premise that community property with right of survivorship will be treated like community property at divorce. We would have to assume that the title stating the property was "community property with right of survivorship" would be sufficient to meet the "expressly declared" requirements of Civil Code §682.1. A court would have to consider the title a "transfer document" that created community property with right of survivorship.

At divorce, the home would be treated as community property, and the right of survivorship would be inapplicable because they are seeking a divorce. Since the home was purchased during marriage and the deed specifies that it is community property, Step One characterization applies. The home will be presumed to be community property under the presumption found in Family Code §2581. That presumption can be rebutted by a statement in the deed or a written agreement that the home is other than community property. There is no evidence here that Alex and Natasha had anything in writing concerning the character of the home. Thus the home would be characterized as community property.

Under Step Two, it would be necessary to determine if either spouse has a right to reimbursement of separate property funds. §2640(b). Since the home was purchased with savings from the business they started during marriage, those savings would be considered community property. Since the home is community property and there is no reimbursement, the home would be split between the spouses at divorce. This analysis should be very familiar to you—survivorship community property will be treated like any other joint title at divorce.

Explanation 14—Natasha Buys Stock

Again, the stock was purchased after the effective date of §682.1—July 1, 2001—so this type of title was available to Natasha. If the title was sufficient to create survivorship community property, the analysis is the same as any community property title. At Step One, under §2581, community property titles are presumed to be community property. Rebuttal is by a statement in the title or a written agreement. Here there is nothing in writing other than the title itself, therefore the stock would be characterized as community property.

At Step Two, Natasha would have a right to reimbursement under §2640(b) if she can trace the stock purchase to her inheritance from Uncle Boris. An inheritance during marriage is considered separate property, and §2640(b) establishes a right to reimbursement of separate property contributions to the acquisition of community property. The increase in value of the stock will be considered community property and split between Alex and Natasha.

Again we see the "survivorship" part of the title is not applicable at divorce.

TENANCY IN COMMON

The form of property designated as "tenancy in common" is very uncommon between spouses in California. If spouses know about any type of property, it is joint tenancy. To a person without legal training, the two seem very similar. A person would ask, "Aren't 'common' and 'joint' the same idea? Aren't they both joint titles?" The answer would be they are the *same* in that they mean that more than one person is sharing ownership of the property, but they are *different* in that the people sharing ownership have different rights.

Tenancy in common and joint tenancy do not FIT comfortably with community property law. Under California community property law, there are only two categories of marital property, community and separate property. Under those categories, if a type of property is not community property, it is separate property. It is obvious that property acquired during marriage held in tenancy in common or joint tenancy cannot also be community property based on the title alone.

In California, prior to the enactment of joint title legislation, the presumption followed the title. Tenancy in common and joint tenancy were presumed to be tenancy in common or joint tenancy and were in essence separate property, unless the spouses agreed otherwise. But yet we must remember that under our FIT concept, title is not the ultimate determinant of the character of the property. By this stage in this chapter, hopefully, it is obvious that because tenancy in common is a "joint title" and because it is specifically listed in §2581 as of January 1, 1987, tenancy in common, like joint tenancy, will be presumed to be community property at divorce. Therefore, the analysis that applies at divorce will, in most situations, result in tenancy in common property being treated as community property. In that respect, tenancy in common title is identical to joint tenancy.

The differences between tenancy in common and joint tenancy arise in other situations. First, the people owning property in tenancy in common can have equal or unequal interests. For instance, if Alice and Bob own partnership property in tenancy in common, they could each have a one-half interest in the partnership property. But let's say that Alice provided three-quarters of the funds for the partnership property and Bob only provided one-quarter of the funds for the partnership property. They could specify that their interests in the tenancy in common are three-quarters Alice's interest and one-quarter Bob's interest. Joint tenants have equal, undivided interests in the property. If Alice and Bob own the partnership property in joint tenancy, they have one-half interests in the property, even if they have invested unequal amounts in the property.

Second, at death, tenancy in common and joint tenancy differ significantly. Joint tenancy carries with it the right of survivorship; tenancy in common does not. For purposes of this discussion, let's say Alice and Bob own the partnership property in equal shares. If the partnership property is held in joint tenancy and Alice dies, Bob automatically receives the partnership property via the right of survivorship. The entire partnership becomes Bob's property. If the partnership property is held in tenancy in common and Alice dies, Bob has a right to only his interest, one-half of the property. Alice's one-half belongs to her heirs if she dies without a will. Alice may will her one-half interest in the partnership property to anyone she wishes. If she wanted Bob to receive her one-half interest, she would have to specify that in her will.

Finally, the ability to deal with tenancy in common and joint tenancy property also differs. In particular, if one joint tenant assigns or sells his interest in the property, the joint tenancy is "severed" and the joint tenancy is transformed into a tenancy in common. This feature of joint tenancy is particularly important when one spouse dies in the midst of divorce proceedings. If the joint tenancy is not severed, the survivor receives the entire property via the right of survivorship. If the joint tenancy is severed and becomes tenancy in common, the decedent's share goes to his or her heirs via intestacy law or by will to whomever he or she specifies. It is highly doubtful that a divorcing spouse would want the other spouse to receive the entire property in the event of death. This particular issue is pertinent to joint tenancy at death, which is discussed in Chapter 9.

Examples

Example 15 — Bill and Hillary Move to California

Bill and Hillary, both attorneys, moved from New York to California in 2003 after they retired. They had gone to law school in the East, and their knowledge of community property law was nil. They bought a houseboat and wanted to spend their time quietly reading and fishing. Throughout their married life they took title to their property in tenancy in common. Without consulting with anyone, they followed their usual pattern and put the title to the houseboat in tenancy in common. They used $50,000 that Hillary received as an inheritance after they moved to California to buy the houseboat. The houseboat turned out not to provide the idyllic life they hoped. They are filing for divorce. Hillary decided she should consult a lawyer concerning her rights to the houseboat.

Example 16 — Allan and Barbara's Business Venture

Allan and Barbara attended college and graduate school together. They both received master's degrees in business and married soon after. As a graduation and wedding gift, Allan's family gave him a gift of $10,000; Barbara's family gave her a gift of $30,000. They decided to combine the gifts and invest in a business venture. They bought a small store that sold personalized gifts. Because of the difference in the amounts that they invested, they consulted an attorney who suggested that they could protect their differing investments by specifying in the deed that the store was held in tenancy in common, with Allan having a one-quarter share and Barbara having a three-quarter share. They went ahead with that plan. The store was a success, but their marriage was not, and they are filing for divorce. How would the court characterize and divide the store in Allan and Barbara's divorce?

Explanations

Explanation 15 — Bill and Hillary Move to California

Tenancy in common is a form of joint title that must be characterized at Step One. At divorce, a joint title is presumed to be community property under §2581. That presumption can be rebutted but only by a statement in the title or deed or a written agreement. Because the facts do not indicate that they have anything in writing to rebut the community property presumption, the houseboat will be characterized as community property.

At Step Two, Hillary will be entitled to reimbursement of separate property contributions to the acquisition of community property if she can trace to separate property funds. Hillary received the inheritance while in California, and in California inheritances received during marriage are separate property. Assuming that she can prove that her inheritance was used to purchase the houseboat, she will establish her right to reimbursement. If the houseboat has appreciated in value, that appreciation will be split between Bill and Hillary.

Explanation 16 — Allan and Barbara's Business Venture

At Step One characterization, we examine the title. Allan and Barbara's store is held in tenancy in common, and they have specified their respective interests in the deed. At divorce, because tenancy in common is a joint title, it is presumed to be community property under §2581. A statement in the deed can rebut the community property presumption. Here we have that situation. The statement in the deed shows that Allan and Barbara did not want the store to be treated as community property. Instead they specified that the store was part Allan's separate property and part Barbara's separate property. Allan's interest is one-quarter of the property; Barbara's interest is three-quarters of the property. Therefore, the community property presumption will be rebutted, and the store will be characterized as Allan and Barbara's separate property.

At Step Two, we do not go to §2640(b) because the store was not characterized as community property at Step One. Instead, the court will divide the store, one-quarter to Allan and three-quarters to Barbara. The appreciation in the store will be divided in proportion to those interests.

SPOTLIGHT ON REIMBURSEMENT

Once a joint title has been characterized as community property and there was a separate property contribution to the acquisition of the property, Family Code §2640(b) (formerly Civil Code §4800.2) provides a right to reimbursement based on tracing. Those are the basics of the reimbursement right mandated for acquisitions of property in 1984 or thereafter. However, there are several sections of §2640 that we have not yet explained. First, the statutory definition of "contributions to the acquisition of the property" includes certain contributions and excludes others. In all prior examples, the separate property contributions were funds used to *purchase* the property in question. The statute's definition of contributions is broader and includes down payments, payments for improvements, and payments to reduce the principal of a loan used to finance the purchase or improvement of the property. Excluded from the definition of contributions are payments of interest on a loan and payments for maintenance, insurance on, or taxation of the property. Family Code §2640(a). Those payments that are excluded are viewed as "expenses" rather than "contributions to the acquisition of the property." Generally, expenses are not considered reimbursable.

Second, Family Code §2640(b) provides that the right to reimbursement can be waived in writing. For instance, if a spouse wants to make a gift to the community of the separate property contribution, she can sign a "written waiver of the right to reimbursement" or "a writing that has the effect of a waiver." Even though many spouses may view a separate property contribution as a gift at the time when the spouses choose to hold the property as joint tenancy or community property, it is doubtful that any spouse would sign a written waiver once the consequences are explained to them. Certainly they would not at the time they are contemplating divorce. The consequences are that they would not receive reimbursement of their separate property contribution upon divorce.

Third, Family Code §2640(b) provides that "the amount reimbursed . . . shall not exceed the net value of the property at the time of division." That section of the statute is directed to the possibility that the property may decrease in value. It is evident that some contributions, like down payments and improvements, contemplate that the spouses will acquire real property. The real estate market in California has almost always resulted in appreciation rather than depreciation, thus rendering this section of little use. However, the statute is not limited to real property, and it is clear that personal property such as stock can be acquired by using one spouse's separate property funds. Most relevant is the decrease in the value of stock purchased by many Californians during the 1990s. Where property has decreased in value, §2640(b) will allow the separate property contributor to recoup whatever value is left at the time of division.

For instance, let's assume our hypothetical couple, Harry and Wilma, bought stock in XYZ Corporation in 1995 for $10,000. To purchase the XYZ stock, Harry sold some stock in ABC Corporation he owned before they were married. They put the title to the XYZ stock in joint tenancy. In 1998, the stock was worth $50,000. After the stock market bubble burst, Harry and Wilma's dream marriage bubble also burst, and they are considering divorce. The XYZ stock is now worth $5,000. If Harry consults a lawyer concerning the divorce, he will learn that the joint tenancy stock will be presumed to be community property at divorce, and if they have no agreement about the character of the stock, it will be characterized as community property. He will also find out that §2640 provides him with a right to reimbursement if he can trace to his separate property. The proceeds of ABC stock owned before their marriage are considered his separate property and therefore he would receive $5,000 as reimbursement. Because §2640 states that the amount shall not exceed the net value of the property at the time of division, he will not be reimbursed for the entire $10,000 separate property contribution.

One of the thorniest issues concerning §2640 reimbursements is the application of its provisions to acquisitions of property prior to 1984. After many years of uncertainty, the California Supreme Court has clearly stated that "the applicability of that requirement is limited by the due process clause to property *acquired* on or after January 1, 1984" (emphasis added). *Marriage of Heikes,* 10 Cal. 4th 1211, 1225, 899 P.2d 1349, 1358, 44 Cal. Rptr. 2d 155, 164 (1995). One problem arises when the "acquisition" is prior to 1984, but the separate property contribution to the property is made in 1984 or later. Should the law at the date of acquisition control, or should the law at the date of the separate property contribution control? Let's say Harry and Wilma buy a motel in 1983 with community property funds and put the title in community property. They have no agreements about the motel. In 1984, they use some of Harry's earnings from before their marriage to improve the motel. If they divorce, it is clear that the motel will be characterized as community property. The major question would be whether Harry can receive reimbursement for the improvements made to the motel. We will assume that he can trace to those earnings that are separate property because they were earned before their marriage. If we take the language of the Supreme Court literally, §2640 does not apply and the law at the date they "acquired" the motel will control, that is, the purchase date of 1983. That law is that a separate property contribution is a gift to the community unless there is a reimbursement agreement, and here the facts state they have no agreement.

Should the language of the Supreme Court be taken literally? Harry would not think so if he were involved in divorce proceedings. He would think that he should be reimbursed since he made his "contribution to the acquisition of the property" in 1984, after the effective date of the statute, and he could assume that the law at that time should control. If he had consulted with a lawyer before he made the contribution, the law was still unsettled concerning application of §2640 (then Civil Code §4800.2), and certainly the Legislature tried (albeit unsuccessfully) to apply the reimbursement right to acquisitions prior to the effective date of the statute.

What is the solution? In most cases, the answer is clear. Most litigated cases involve a situation where a down payment is made or a purchase is made with separate property funds. In those cases, the date of the "acquisition" of the property and date of the separate property contribution are contemporaneous. Then clearly the relevant date would be the purchase date. In cases where improvements are made with separate property funds some time after the purchase of the property, it would be possible to interpret "acquisition" as "transaction" and apply the law at the date the separate property contribution was made. The rationale would be that at the time of the contribution, a spouse could be expected to check what the law was at that date. Thus applying that law would not result in any "unfair surprise" and violate due process. Yet it is also clear that family law attorneys sought a bright-line rule, and the Supreme Court obliged in the *Heikes* case. The courts may want to stick to such a rule for clarity's sake. In that case "acquisition" would include only the original purchase or transfer and disregard later transactions that contribute separate property funds when determining the date of "acquisition."

Examples

Example 17 — George's True Love Is Sailing

George and Barbara met in San Diego in 1980. They married soon after. George was extremely wealthy and loved sailing, and the couple bought a yacht in 1985 using George's separate property funds. The title to the yacht was put in joint tenancy, and the couple had no agreements about the yacht. The yacht cost $50,000 but was a bit run-down. He added a cabin that cost $15,000, also expended from his separate property funds. George spent more of his separate property to have the yacht sanded and painted red, white, and blue. That cost approximately $10,000. George purchased insurance on the yacht, which cost about $1,500 a year. Unfortunately, Barbara was a real landlubber, and their marriage is on the rocks. If they divorce, how would a California court characterize the yacht? Would George have any right to reimbursement for the funds expended on the yacht?

Example 18 — The Quake That Caused the Break

Franklin and Eleanor were married in California and have lived in Los Angeles for many years. Eleanor had a trust fund that her parents set up for her as a child. It increased in value over the years, and there was a substantial amount of cash in the fund. As the couple reached retirement age, Eleanor decided she wanted to live in Palm Springs. She found the air clear and the desert beautiful. In 1998, they bought a condo there for $250,000 using funds from Eleanor's trust fund. They put the title in joint tenancy on the advice of the realtor and never discussed the character of the property or had any agreements about it. Franklin detested the desert heat and missed city life. A 7.0-magnitude earthquake seriously damaged the condo, which is now valued at $50,000. Their marriage was also affected by the quake, and Franklin has vowed never to return to Palm Springs. Eleanor consults you about the possibility of divorce. She wants to know what rights she has to the condo.

Example 19—The Lot and the Cottage

Norm and Rose married in 1976. At that time, Norm owned a lot in Santa Barbara. Soon after their marriage, he conveyed the lot to himself and Rose as joint tenants. The lot was worth $25,000 at the time of the conveyance. In 1987, Norm hired a construction company to build a small cottage on the lot. It cost $200,000 and was completed that year. He used his separate property funds to pay for the construction of the cottage. They have no agreements concerning the lot or the cottage. Unfortunately, Norm and Rose have separated. Norm comes to you for advice about his rights to the lot and the cottage. You should assume the deed to the cottage is also joint tenancy and the cottage is an improvement to the lot. Who owns the lot? The cottage? Does Norm have any rights to reimbursement?

Explanations

Explanation 17—George's True Love Is Sailing

Step One, characterization, depends on the title and whether there are any agreements between the spouses regarding the character of the yacht. Under Family Code §2581 (formerly Civil Code §4800.1), joint tenancy is presumed to be community property at divorce. Since there are no agreements or anything else in writing concerning the character of the yacht, a California court will characterize the yacht as community property.

Because the yacht was "acquired" in 1985 after the effective date of Family Code §2640(b) (formerly Civil Code §4800.2), George has a right to reimbursement to separate property contributions to the acquisition of the yacht. If he can trace to his separate property funds, he will be reimbursed for the funds expended to purchase the yacht, $50,000. The addition of the cabin would most likely be considered an "improvement," and he would be reimbursed for that. The $10,000 sanding and painting of the yacht would most likely be considered "maintenance," and he would not be reimbursed for that. Separate property contributions for insurance are specifically excluded from the definition of contributions to the acquisition of property, and thus the $1,500 a year would not be reimbursed.

Explanation 18—The Quake That Caused the Break

The condo held in joint tenancy will be presumed to be community property at divorce under Family Code §2581. Because there are no agreements or anything else in writing, it will be characterized as community property. However, Family Code §2640(b) gives Eleanor a right to reimbursement of her separate property funds if she can trace to them. Since the trust fund was set up when she was a child, it would be considered her separate property, and any rents, issues, or profits from the trust fund would also be her separate property. Therefore, we will assume that she can trace to them. She will receive $50,000 only because §2640(b) mandates that the amount reimbursed shall not exceed the value of the property at the time of division. Even though she actually contributed $250,000 of her separate property funds to the acquisition of the condo, she will bear the loss from the earthquake. So even though the condo is characterized as community property, in this case Eleanor will receive the total value if the couple divorces.

Explanation 19—The Lot and the Cottage

The first question is characterization of the lot and the cottage. At Step One, we look only at the deed and any agreements concerning the lot and the cottage. The lot was "acquired" by Norm and Rose at the time that Norm conveyed it to himself and Rose as joint tenants. Ordinarily, we think of "acquisition" as purchase, but it is clear that it has a broader meaning—conveyance to the spouses is also included. Therefore the lot was "acquired" during their marriage and thus will be presumed to be community property at divorce, unless there is an agreement to the contrary. Because the acquisition was before 1984, the agreement can be oral or implied as well as written. Here there is no agreement, so the lot will be characterized as community property. Even though the cottage was built in 1987 and thus acquired then, still the community property presumption could not be rebutted because there is no agreement at all about the cottage.

Still Norm would want to know if he would receive reimbursement for his separate property contributions to the property. Here there are two contributions: (1) the original value of the lot, his separate property, because it was owned before marriage, and (2) the improvement of the lot by building the cottage with his separate property funds. If we use the law as of the date of the original acquisition by the community, 1976, then both the value of the lot and the separate property funds used to build the cottage are gifts to the community, absent a reimbursement agreement. There are no agreements here, thus Norm will not receive reimbursement. The total value of the lot and cottage will be split in half at divorce. If we use the law of the date of the improvement as the date of "acquisition," 1987, then the separate property funds used to build the cottage would be reimbursed to Norm based on tracing. As of 1984, the Legislature provided that right to reimbursement for separate property "contributions to the acquisition of the property." Those contributions included payments for improvements.

Perhaps we can now see the complications of using the date of the contribution to determine which law will apply. There could have been several contributions to the lot during Norm and Rose's marriage. It would be exceedingly complex to apply different laws to different transactions concerning the same property. Norm, however, might not mind the complexity if it resulted in reimbursement of $200,000. At present, there is no case law on this particular problem, and the Supreme Court opted for a clear rule that indicates that the law at the time of the original acquisition will apply. Bottom line: For acquisitions of property prior to 1984, there is no right to reimbursement absent a reimbursement agreement. For acquisitions of property in 1984 and thereafter, there is a right to reimbursement based on tracing. At present, "acquisitions" of property include purchases and transfers during marriage but contributions of separate property for improvements made to the acquired property are not considered "acquisitions."

IMPROVEMENTS: SELFISH OR SELFLESS?

So far, we have discussed reimbursement only with respect to separate property contributions to community property. Under Family Code §2640, there is a right to reimbursement for various types of separate property contributions based on tracing. One type of contribution is for "improvements" to community property. What exactly is an improvement? The best way to define an improvement is to take some examples. For instance, a couple buys a home and decides to put in a swimming pool. Or the couple adds a family room and two bedrooms to their existing home. Or the couple owns land and builds a cottage on the land. All of those would be considered improvements. One aspect of improvements is that they are "attached" to the existing property and really cannot be sold separately from the property itself. Therefore, there are really only two alternatives for determining rights to the improvement: (1) Consider the improvement a gift, or (2) permit reimbursement of the funds used for the improvement. Using funds for an improvement would not ordinarily result in an ownership interest in the property.

The scenario regarding improvements becomes complicated when the property improved is separate property of one spouse and the funds used are community property or separate property of the other spouse. Three different situations may arise:

1. One spouse uses his or her separate property funds to improve the other spouse's separate property.
2. A spouse uses community funds to improve the other spouse's separate property.
3. A spouse uses community funds to improve his or her own separate property.

When a couple is married, although they may have some awareness that some funds are separate property and some funds are community property, very often they do not differentiate when they make improvements to property. However, when the couple divorces, suddenly one spouse thinks it unfair that the other spouse will be entitled to separate property that has been *improved* without any recognition of the contribution made by the community or made by the other spouse's separate property funds. Therefore, the courts have been faced with how to sort out these disputes over improvements.

Separate Property Funds Improve Other Spouse's Separate Property

Let us consider our hypothetical couple Harry and Wilma. The first scenario involves one spouse using separate property funds to improve the separate property of the other spouse. In our case, Wilma inherits a home near Palm Springs. Harry receives a gift from his parents of $20,000. Harry and Wilma decide that the home near Palm Springs would be much nicer if they added a swimming pool. They go ahead and add the pool using Harry's $20,000. If they divorce, it is clear that the swimming pool is considered an improvement to Wilma's separate property. The question is whether Harry has gained an interest in the separate property by contributing his $20,000 separate property or whether he has a right to reimbursement of the $20,000. Up until January 1, 2005, Harry had neither an interest nor a right to reimbursement. Prior law provided that when one spouse used separate property funds to improve the other spouse's separate property, that contribution would be presumed to be a gift. That presumption could be rebutted—with evidence that the separate property was not a gift. *Dunn v. Mullan*, 211 Cal. 583, 589, 296 P.604, 607 (1931). The rationale was that a spouse has management and control of his or her separate property funds. When that spouse chose to use separate property funds to improve the other spouse's separate property, it was a "selfless" act and did not gain that spouse an interest in the other spouse's separate property nor did it merit reimbursement. The choice to use those funds was deemed a gift unless there was proof to the contrary.

The law changed as of January 1, 2005, and Harry would have a right to reimbursement of his separate property contribution to improve Wilma's separate property. The Legislature added a new section to Family Code §2640, which covers reimbursement of "contributions to the acquisition of property." §2640(a). Those contributions include payments for improvements. The new section, Family Code §2640(c), gives a right to reimbursement "for the party's separate party contributions to the acquisition of property of the other spouse's separate property estate during marriage." It would seem obvious that Harry would have to show that the funds he contributed came from separate property, the gift from his parents. The section also provides that there would be no reimbursement if there was a written waiver or there was a transmutation in writing. If Wilma could show that Harry waived his right in writing or Harry transmuted his separate property to Wilma's separate property, then Harry would lose his right to reimbursement.

This new section provides consistency regarding reimbursement of contributions to improvements to property. Under §2640(b), there is a right to reimbursement of separate property funds contributed to improvements to community property. Under §2640(c) there is a right to reimbursement of separate property funds contributed to improvements to the separate property of the other spouse. This section is also consistent with the case law that now provides a right to reimbursement of community property funds to the community when used to improve the separate property of either spouse.

The only question remaining is whether §2640(c) will be applied retroactively to separate property contributions for improvements made prior to the effective date of the statute, January 1, 2005. Retroactivity of amendments to the Family Code is controlled by §4, as interpreted by the California Supreme Court in *Marriage of Fellows*, 39 Cal. 4th 179, 138 P.3d 200, 46 Cal. Rptr. 3d 49 (2006). Under §4(c), "as a general rule, future changes to the Family Code apply retroactively." *Id.* at 188, 138 P.3d at 204, 46 Cal. Rptr. 3d at 54. There is an exception to retroactive application of an amendment if it impairs a vested property right without due process, which was codified, according to the Supreme Court, in §4(h). *Id.* at 189, 138 P.3d at 205, 46 Cal. 3d at 56.

In our hypothetical, §2640(c) changed prior law from a presumption of a gift of separate property funds to a right to reimbursement of the separate property funds. The Legislature was silent about retroactivity of this change, but under *Fellows*, §4 provides that all amendments to the Family

Code that change the prior law are retroactive. Therefore, the only question would be one of due process. It is possible that the Supreme Court will consider that such a dramatic change in the law should only be applied prospectively, as was the case with §2640(b). In the *Heikes* case, the Supreme Court stated that reimbursement of separate property contributions to community property applied only to property acquired on or after the effective date. See "Spotlight on Reimbursement" in this chapter. The Supreme Court may decide similarly that reimbursement of separate property contributions to the separate property of the other spouse will apply only to acquisitions or contributions made on or after the effective date of January 1, 2005. In that case, the prior law of a gift presumption would apply to the Harry and Wilma scenario.

Community Property Funds Improve Other Spouse's Separate Property

The use of community funds to improve separate property is more problematic. The law regarding use of community funds developed in the era before January 1, 1975, when the husband was the sole manager of the community property funds. Let us go back in time and imagine that the scenario regarding the Palm Springs home occurred when Harry was the sole manager of the community property. Let us also assume that Harry chose to use $20,000 of community funds to add the swimming pool to Wilma's home. Here, one spouse is using community funds to improve the other spouse's separate property. If we use the gift rationale, Harry chose to use community funds; therefore, this would be viewed as a "selfless" act and would be presumed to be a gift to the other spouse unless rebutted by an agreement to reimburse.

In *Marriage of Warren*, 28 Cal. App. 3d 777, 104 Cal. Rptr. 860 (1972), the husband used $38,000 of community property funds to improve the wife's separate property. Unfortunately, when the couple divorced, the value of the improvement was only almost $34,000. The trial court found that neither the husband nor the wife had intended a gift to the wife. The court then ordered reimbursement to the community of the lower amount. The husband appealed. The Court of Appeal reviewed the law regarding community property contributions to separate property. When the husband as manager used community funds to improve his wife's separate property, there is no right to reimbursement. "The rationale is that since the husband is the manager of the community, his use of it to improve the wife's separate property, in the absence of an agreement to reimburse, constitutes a presumed gift." *Id.* at 781, 104 Cal. Rptr. at 862. In *Warren*, because neither party intended a gift, the presumption was rebutted and the community did have a right to reimbursement. On the issue of the amount of reimbursement, the Court of Appeal opted for the amount of the community funds used, $38,000, not the value of the building, $34,000. In conclusion, the traditional rule was when the husband as manager uses community funds to improve the wife's separate property, those funds are presumed to be a gift to the community, absent an agreement to reimburse.

Fast-forward to 1975, when equal management and control becomes effective. Does the same rule apply when the wife as manager uses community funds to improve the husband's separate property? The rationale would be the same no matter whether the husband or the wife was manager of the community property funds. The choice to use those funds represents a gift, a "selfless" act, and should be presumed a gift absent an agreement to the contrary. In *Marriage of Frick*, 181 Cal. App. 3d 997, 1019-1020, 226 Cal. Rptr. 766, 779 (1986), the Court of Appeal considered the issue and stated:

> Beginning in 1975, both spouses were granted equal management and control of the community real property and personal property, with limited exceptions. . . . However, we do not believe that this change in the law should alter the basic principles. . . . Indeed, we believe the effect of this change should be to place each spouse in the same position as the husband was before 1975.

Fast-forward to 2001, when courts began to question the underlying rationale of the gift presumption. In *Marriage of Wolfe*, 91 Cal. App. 4th 962, 110 Cal. Rptr. 2d 921 (3d Dist. 2001), the trial court had ordered reimbursement to the community of $15,000 used to pay taxes and to improve separate property belonging to the husband, Phillip. Phillip appealed based on the gift presumption. The wife, Joyce, challenged the rationale supporting the gift presumption. The Court of Appeal agreed with Joyce and opted to discard the gift presumption: "We agree there is no logical basis for denying a spouse reimbursement for a community-funded improvement to the other spouse's separate property." *Id.* at 967, 110 Cal. Rptr. 2d at 924. The Court recognized that spouses rarely contemplate dissolution of their marriage when they decide to improve one spouse's separate property with community funds. According to the Court, "it is fanciful to suppose that a spouse would wish the divorcing partner to walk away from the marriage with property enriched by an infusion of community funds and with no obligation to reimburse. The presumption is simply not grounded in human nature or experience." *Id.* at 971, 110 Cal. Rptr. 2d at 928. Although the Court also pointed to changes in several other policies in community property law, the best basis for discarding the gift presumption is that most couples who divorce would anticipate reimbursement in this situation. The Court of Appeal concluded that Joyce was entitled to one-half of the community funds expended on the improvements. Two other District Courts of Appeal have adopted the *Wolfe* rationale. *Marriage of Allen*, 96 Cal. App. 4th 497, 116 Cal. Rptr. 2d 887 (2d Dist. 2002), *Bono v. Clark*, 103 Cal. App. 4th 1409, 128 Cal. Rptr. 2d 31 (6th Dist. 2002).

In conclusion, the traditional rule is that use of community property funds to improve the other spouse's separate property is presumed to be a gift, absent an agreement to the contrary. Under *Marriage of Wolfe* and other recent cases, use of community funds to improve the other spouse's separate property creates instead a right to reimbursement to the community without interest. If you have by now concluded that California community property is hopelessly inconsistent and has differing rules for every situation, there is a glimmer of consistency here. Note that the *Wolfe* rationale is actually consistent with Family Code §2640(b), which reversed the gift presumption when separate property funds are used to improve community property. When separate property is used to improve community property, the separate property contributor also has a right to reimbursement.

Traditional Rule:

Community property→Other spouse's separate property = Gift presumption absent an agreement

Wolfe Rule:

Community property→Other spouse's separate property = Right to reimbursement to the community

Family Code §2640(b):

Separate property→Community property = Right to reimbursement to separate property contributor

Community Property Funds Improve His or Her Own Separate Property

Again, we have to return to the time when the rules regarding improvements were developed, prior to 1975, when the husband was manager of the community funds. Back to Harry and Wilma. Let us say that Harry owns a home in Palm Springs as his separate property, and he uses community funds to add a swimming pool. Let us also assume that Harry does this without discussing it with Wilma. What is your reaction? What is Wilma's reaction? Is it, "Harry, how selfish you are! How dare you take *our* money and use it for *your* property?" If Harry and Wilma's marriage continues happily ever after, Harry using community funds for his Palm Springs home may pose no problem, but if their marriage ends in divorce, Wilma will feel the community has suffered a loss and Harry has reaped a gain. Put in legal terms, "if the husband expends community funds, without the consent of his wife, for the improvement of his separate property, the community is entitled to reimbursement." *Marriage of Jafeman*, 29 Cal. App. 3d 244, 256, 105 Cal. Rptr. 483, 491 (1972). "It is reasoned that when the husband exercises this power so as to effect the improvement of his separate property, recoupment by the community is necessary in order to avoid constructive fraud against the wife." *Id.* at 256, 105 Cal. Rptr. at 491. If, however, the wife consented to the use of the community funds, then the community is not entitled to reimbursement.

In *Marriage of Jafeman*, the wife, Mary, thought the home was their community property. However, the Court determined that it was actually separate property belonging to the husband, Edward. Although it was clear that Edward used community funds to improve the home, it was unclear that Mary consented to the use of those funds for the improvement. Therefore, the Court of Appeal remanded on the question of consent. If Mary did not consent, then the community was entitled to reimbursement, and Mary would be entitled to one-half of those funds.

Again, we must ask if this rule survives the 1975 equal management and control provisions. Simply put, "Can a wife be equally as selfish as a husband?" The Court of Appeal in *Marriage of Frick* thought so: "If either spouse appropriates community funds for his or her own benefit, *without the consent of the other spouse*, the community should be reimbursed. Even if in theory both spouses have an equal right to management and control, if one spouse acts in his or her self interest to the detriment of the community interest, the community should be entitled to restitution." *Marriage of Frick*, 181 Cal. App. 3d at 1019-1020, 226 Cal. Rptr. at 779. Thus the same rule regarding reimbursement applies today. If we update our Harry and Wilma scenario, the community would be entitled to reimbursement unless Wilma had consented to Harry's use of the funds. If they never discussed the use of the community funds, the community would be entitled to reimbursement, and Wilma would receive one-half of those funds.

However, both the *Jafeman* and *Frick* cases were decided prior to enactment of Family Code §2640(c) and the *Wolfe* case. Arguably, the *Jafeman* and *Frick* holdings are inconsistent with those more recent developments. The *Jafeman* and *Frick* rules allow for reimbursement of one-half of community property funds if a spouse used community property to improve his or her separate property without the consent of the other spouse. Yet both §2640(c) and *Wolfe* are based on the reasoning that a spouse in every case would expect reimbursement of either separate property funds or one-half of the community property funds expended to improve the other spouse's separate property. Even if the spouse consented at the time the funds were used for the improvement, there would still be an expectation of reimbursement at divorce. Should the final scenario follow this more recent trend?

Let's change the original hypothetical so that Wilma did know and did consent to Harry's use of community property funds to add the swimming pool to his separate property home. Despite that consent, at divorce she would feel that she deserves reimbursement of one-half of the community property funds. In essence, that is the *Wolfe* scenario. Applying the *Wolfe* Court's rationale, there is "no logical basis for denying a spouse reimbursement for a community-funded improvement to the other spouse's separate property." *Wolfe*, 91 Cal. App. 4th at 967, 110 Cal. Rptr. 2d at 924. Knowledge and consent would be irrelevant to whether the community has a right to reimbursement. It seems that the trend represented by §2640(c) and *Wolfe* would result in a court ruling that there is an absolute right to reimbursement of one-half of the community property funds even if the spouse consented. Then all three scenarios regarding improvements would be consistent. If there was failure to disclose or failure to secure consent, such failure could lead to a separate claim for breach of fiduciary duty. See "Fiduciary Duty" in Chapter 6.

Amount of Reimbursement

Up until now, we have assumed that the amount of reimbursement was limited to the actual expenditure of funds. In *Marriage of Warren*, the Court of Appeal directed that the amount expended was the correct amount to be reimbursed. In that case, however, the amount expended was greater than the value added by the improvement. In fact, the improvement did not result in any additional value. The Court of Appeal in *Warren* noted that when a husband (spouse) attempts to improve his own land with community funds, the injured wife (spouse) "is entitled to either the amount expended or the value added—whichever is greater, so that there will be no benefit from the breach of trust. . . ." *Marriage of Warren*, 28 Cal. App. 3d at 782, 104 Cal. Rptr. at 863-864.

In our Harry and Wilma scenario, Harry used $20,000 of community funds to add a swimming pool to his Palm Springs home. Assume it can be determined that the swimming pool added approximately $50,000 to the value of the home. Should the community be entitled to $20,000 or $50,000? Since the rationale of the rule is to prevent Harry from using community funds for his own self-interest, then the value added by the improvement would be the correct figure to use. It makes sense that the community should benefit from the appreciation that can be attributed to the improvement.

Examples

Example 20 — Upscale in Beverly Hills?

Hilliard and Billie were married in California in 2003. Prior to their marriage, Hilliard owned a farm valued at $1,000,000. Shortly after their marriage, Hilliard sold the farm and deposited the proceeds of the sale in the bank. Around the same time, Billie received a $5,000,000 inheritance, which she used to buy a run-down apartment building in Beverly Hills. Hilliard is considering using $500,000 of the farm sale proceeds to remodel Billie's apartment building. Hilliard and Billie come to you for advice. They want to know if Hilliard gains an ownership interest in the property by contributing the $500,000. Also they want to know what would happen in the event they divorce.

Example 21 — Down on the Farm in Fresno?

Frank and Fran were married in California in 1990. In 1999, Frank inherited a farm near Fresno from his parents that was valued at $1,000,000. The farm was quite run-down, but it had a vineyard that Frank was advised could become very productive and profitable with some attention. He talked it over with Fran, who handled all their finances. Fran thought it was worthwhile to invest some of their savings from their earnings in upgrading the vineyard. They spent about $300,000 on installing a drip irrigation system and upgrading the vineyard. In about three years, the vineyard was producing quality grapes that were producing fine wine. The farm and vineyard are now valued at $3,000,000, mainly due to the vineyard. Unfortunately, Frank has been drinking too much wine, and Fran is considering a divorce. She is quite concerned about her rights to the farm and the vineyard, particularly the $300,000 that was invested in the vineyard. She comes to you for advice. Explain what she may receive if they divorce.

Example 22 — Fraud on the Farm in Fresno?

Assume the same facts as Example 21, except Frank uses the $300,000 of their savings from their earnings without consulting with Fran. When Fran finds out, she is very upset and is considering a divorce. She comes to you for advice. Explain what her rights are if they divorce.

Example 23 — What if Fran Consents?

Assume the same facts as in Example 21, except that Frank managed all the finances. He talked it over with Fran, who thought it was a good idea that he take some of the savings from their earnings to invest in upgrading the vineyard. When Fran is considering divorce, she comes to you for advice about her rights to the $300,000.

Explanations

Explanation 20 — Upscale in Beverly Hills?

First, it is important to characterize the property improved and the funds used for the improvement. Hilliard's farm is separate property because he owned it prior to marriage. The proceeds from the sale of the farm are also separate property as the rents, issues, and profits from separate property are also separate property. Billie's inheritance is her separate property because inheritances during marriage are separate property. The apartment building acquired with her inheritance would also be her separate property.

Hilliard wanted to know if he would obtain an ownership interest in the property by contributing to an improvement. The answer is no. Improvements are "attached" to the property itself, and an ownership interest is not created. The apartment is Billie's separate property, and improvements to that property are also her separate property.

In the event of divorce, it depends on whether the new Family Code §2640(c) applies to this scenario or whether the prior law applies. Under the law prior to January 1, 2005, if Hilliard chooses to use $500,000 of his separate property to remodel Billie's separate property apartment building, that contribution to improve her separate property will be presumed to be a gift. That presumption can be rebutted by an agreement for reimbursement. If Billie is willing to sign such an agreement, upon divorce, Hilliard would be entitled to reimbursement of his $500,000 investment. Therefore, the $500,000 separate property contribution would be a loan to Billie.

Under the new Family Law Code §2640(c), Hilliard would have a right to reimbursement of his $500,000 separate property contribution to improve Billie's separate property apartment building. If Billie could show that Hilliard had signed a waiver of his right to reimbursement, then that $500,000 would still be considered a gift to Billie. Under §2640(c), the only other way Billie could show that Hilliard was not entitled to reimbursement would be to show a transmutation of his separate property funds to her separate property.

That would lead to Billie's due process argument that §2640(c) should not be applied retroactively to separate property acquisitions made prior to January 1, 2005, the effective date of the statute. If both Billie's acquisition of the apartment house and Hilliard's separate property funds occurred prior to 2005, Billie would have a good argument that the amendment should not apply to their case. She would be able to argue that she relied on the law as it was prior to 2005 when there was no reimbursement absent a reimbursement agreement. Because the law changed so dramatically, she could not comply with the new requirements of a written waiver. Her argument would be based on the *Heikes* case where the Supreme Court refused to apply the right to reimbursement in §2640(b) retroactively.

Considering the *Fellows* case, there is a good possibility that §2640(c) will apply retroactively to property acquired prior to 2005. In this scenario, Billie acquired the apartment house before 2005, but Hilliard is considering making his separate property contribution for improvements after 2005. The argument is that the date of the contribution should control application of §2640(c). Hilliard and Billie should be aware of the new requirements of §2640(c) and cannot rely on the law as it was prior to 2005. Hilliard should know that he has a right to reimbursement. Billie should know how to avoid reimbursing Hilliard in the event of a divorce. If §2640(c) applies, she will need to obtain a written waiver of his right to reimbursement or consider a writing that will transmute Hilliard's funds into her separate property. They may even consider a writing that will transmute Billie's apartment into community property or some other form of shared property. See Chapter 2 on transmutation and this chapter on joint titles.

Explanation 21 — Down on the Farm in Fresno?

According to the traditional rule, Fran will receive nothing for the improvements to the vineyard. Again, it is important to characterize the property and the funds used for the improvement. Here the farm is Frank's separate property because it was an inheritance. The funds used for the irrigation system and upgrading the vineyard were community property since those funds were earned during marriage. Fran was the managing spouse who used community funds to improve Frank's separate property. A contribution of community property funds used for an improvement is presumed to be a gift. If there was an agreement to reimburse the community, then Fran would be entitled to one-half of the amount reimbursed. Here there is no reimbursement agreement, so the community funds would be considered a gift to Frank.

According to *Marriage of Wolfe* and other recent cases, in the event of divorce, the community should have a right to reimbursement. The rationale is that when Fran used the community funds, she did not anticipate divorce. If she had thought about it, she probably would have expected reimbursement. To match the expectations of most couples, community property contributions to separate property of one spouse should result in reimbursement. In a sense, the community has lent those funds to the spouse who has separate property. If a trial court follows *Wolfe,* the community would be entitled to reimbursement of the $300,000 community funds. Fran would receive one-half of the amount, $150,000.

In this case, the farm and the vineyard have appreciated in value from the initial valuation of $1 million to $3 million. Fran might argue that the increase in value was due to the improvements made to the vineyard; therefore, she may think she is entitled to share in that appreciation. In *Marriage of Wolfe,* the wife did not claim a right to a share of the appreciation due to the community contribution to the property. In this situation where the managing spouse has agreed or consented to use the community property funds for the improvement, the present rule is that reimbursement is the proper remedy. However, it is possible to argue that the community should share in the appreciation, at least in that portion that can be attributed to the improvement.

Explanation 22—Fraud on the Farm in Fresno?

It is clear that Frank and Fran have the right to manage the community property funds. However, Frank is using the community property funds to improve his own separate property. He did not consult with Fran; therefore, he did not seek her consent or agreement. Frank's use of those funds for his own benefit is viewed as a breach of fiduciary duty. In that situation, the presumption is that the community will be reimbursed for the community funds used for the improvement. If the spouse consented to the use of the funds, there would be no reimbursement under the traditional rule. Fran did not consent, so Fran would have a right to one-half of the reimbursed community funds.

There is a question of whether the amount reimbursed should be more than the actual funds expended on the improvement. Here, $300,000 was spent on the improvement of the vineyard. The farm had appreciated by $2 million. In *Marriage of Warren*, the Court of Appeal stated that "the injured wife is entitled to either the amount expended or the value added—whichever is greater, so that there will be no benefit from the breach of trust. . . ." In that case, however, the amount expended on the improvement was *more* than the value of the property. In our case, the amount expended on the improvement was *less* than the value of the property. If the remedy is a penalty for Frank's actions, it is possible that a court could choose the "greater amount" for reimbursement. That means the community could share in the appreciation due to the improvements to the vineyard, and Fran would be entitled to a one-half share of the $2 million appreciation. She would be entitled to $1 million. Frank would suffer a severe penalty for his using community property funds for his own benefit. It is unclear if a court would be willing to assess such a penalty in the situation where Fran would be able to at least recoup $150,000, one-half of the amount expended.

Explanation 23—What if Fran Consents?

Here Frank took community property funds to improve his separate property. The ruling in *Jafeman* and *Frick* was that there is no right to reimbursement to the community if the other spouse consented to the use of those funds. Their discussion indicates that Fran approved of the use of the community funds, and such approval would be construed as consent. Under the traditional rule, she would not be entitled to reimbursement of one-half of the community funds. However, that result is arguably inconsistent with the *Wolfe* rule. Even if the couple agreed to use the community funds to improve the other spouse's separate property, the expectation at divorce would still be reimbursement to the community. Applying the *Wolfe* rule to this scenario would give that Fran the right to reimbursement of one-half of the community funds.

CHAPTER 5

The Tangible and the Intangible: Classification of Specific Types of Property

COMMINGLED BANK ACCOUNTS

One characterization problem concerns the character of property acquired with funds from an account where community and separate funds have been "commingled." *Commingling* is a term of art that refers to the situation where both community property and separate property funds have been deposited into a bank account. There are special rules that apply when tracing to funds in those accounts. First, we will examine accounts that are in one spouse's name. Accounts that are held jointly will be explained at the end of this section. Second, we will examine special rules that assist in the characterization of property acquired with funds from a commingled account.

Family Expense Presumptions: Community Property First

The special rules deal with tracing to funds that are used for family expenses. Family expenses differ from acquisitions. For instance, funds expended for food, rent, vacations, and medical and dental care are for family expenses. Food, rent, vacations, and medical and dental care are "consumed" and do not result in acquisition of property that would ultimately be divided at divorce or death. The rules concerning family expenses are:

1. Available community property funds are presumed to be used to pay for family expenses. Separate property funds are deemed to be used for family expenses *only* when community funds are exhausted.
2. When separate property funds are used to pay for family expenses, the separate estate has no right to reimbursement unless the parties have agreed to reimbursement.

The rationale for these rules is the duty of the spouses to provide support for each other during marriage. Since the spouses make up the "community," it is logical that family expenses, even though they may benefit only one spouse, should be paid first from community property funds. If there are no community property funds, there is still an obligation of support. Therefore, it is also logical that a spouse who has separate property funds would be responsible to pay for family expenses. The "no reimbursement absent an agreement" rule also makes sense. In property terms, the "no reimbursement rule" could mean that the spouse with separate property funds is making a gift of those funds to the community. The underpinning for that rule is that the obligation of support is incumbent on each spouse regardless of the source of the funds. However, freedom of contract principles also permit spouses to agree to structure their relationship to require reimbursement of separate property funds used for family expenses. Such agreements are presumably exceedingly rare.

Let's apply these family expense rules to our hypothetical couple Harry and Wilma. When they marry, Harry's checking account contains $1,000 from his last paycheck. Because that money was earned before marriage, that $1,000 is separate property. At the end of their first month of marriage, Harry deposits a paycheck of $1,500. That paycheck represents his earnings during marriage. Those earnings are community property. Aha! Depositing that paycheck into the account in Harry's name that contains separate property funds results in *commingling*! Think of it as dead presidents mingling in the bank vault. Assuming that no checks have been written from that account, there is now $2,500 in Harry's checking account, $1,000 separate property and $1,500 community property.

In their second month of marriage, Harry and Wilma take a trip to Ireland. The entire trip costs $2,000, and Harry pays for it from his checking account. Under our family expense rules, it is clear that a trip to Ireland is an expense, not an acquisition. No property was acquired (just bills and maybe some photographs and mementos of the trip). According to the first family expense rule, community property funds are presumed to be used for family expenses. Since there was $1,500 of community property funds in Harry's checking account, that $1,500 is presumed to have been used to pay for the trip. Once that $1,500 of community property funds is gone, or "exhausted," then only separate property funds remained in the account.

The remaining $500 used for the trip to Ireland came from Harry's separate property funds. Under the second rule of no reimbursement, Harry cannot claim reimbursement from the community or from Wilma's separate property unless they had an agreement that he would be reimbursed. At the end of the second month of their marriage, Harry deposits another paycheck into the checking account. Again we have commingling. There is still $500 of separate property funds in Harry's checking account, and the new paycheck adds $1,500 of community property funds to Harry's account.

The next issue concerns property purchased from Harry's account. Let's say that Harry receives an inheritance of $10,000 from his Uncle Max. He puts the entire amount, which is considered separate property, into his checking account. At that point, his checking account contains $10,500 of separate property funds and $1,500 of community property funds. Harry then pays bills for medical expenses that equal $2,000. Under our family expense presumption, available community property funds are used to pay for family expenses. Therefore, the $1,500 of community property funds is used to pay for the medical expenses. Since the community funds are now used up or "exhausted," the remainder of the $2,000 medical expense paid from Harry's account is deemed to have come from his separate property funds. Harry has no right to be reimbursed for the expenditure of his separate property funds for a family expense. Once that expense is paid for, the only funds remaining in Harry's checking account are his separate property funds. At that point in time, Harry buys a vintage car for $10,000 and puts the title in his name. If Harry and Wilma divorce, Harry wants to claim that the car is his separate property. And if he can prove the facts as stated above, he will succeed.

Presumptions and Tracing Rules

The analysis, however, depends on application of the general community property presumption and special rules for tracing to commingled bank accounts. First, the general community property presumption applies because the car was acquired during marriage. That would favor Wilma, and the burden is on Harry, the separate property proponent, to rebut the presumption by tracing to his separate property. The title in his name is not determinative.

Exhaustion Method: *See v. See*

Second, there are special rules for tracing to a commingled bank account. The primary rule for tracing is derived from the California Supreme Court case of *See v. See*, 64 Cal. 2d 778, 415 P.2d 776, 51 Cal. Rptr. 888 (1966). The Court held that the separate property proponent can rebut the community property presumption if, at the time of acquisition, all community income was exhausted by family expenses. Then clearly the property must have been purchased with separate property funds. This type of tracing is called the *Exhaustion Method*.

In our hypothetical situation, Harry could show that at the time the car was purchased, all the community funds were exhausted, having been used for family expenses. Therefore, the only funds in the account were separate property funds. However, think about the situation. What if Harry purchased the car 20 years ago? Would it be easy for him to show that at the time he purchased the car there were no community property funds in the account? The *See* Court was not too sympathetic to a spouse who commingles community and separate property funds. When that spouse makes the choice to commingle funds, that spouse "assumes the burden of keeping records adequate to establish the balance of community income and expenditures at the time an asset is acquired." *Id.* at 784, 415 P.2d at 780, 51 Cal. Rptr. at 892. The Court recognized that a spouse who wants to ensure that separate property will remain separate could easily keep a bank account for separate property funds and a completely different bank account for community property funds. Thus commingling clearly favors community ownership of property purchased from a commingled account.

The husband in the *See* case, Laurance, argued that he should be able to show that an excess of community expenses over community income over the entire length of the marriage was sufficient to show that all property acquired during the marriage was his separate property. The marriage was one where most of the wealth was based on Laurance's separate property, but Laurance did receive a salary that he commingled with his separate property. The Court rejected Laurance's argument, which is called *Total Recapitulation*. The main basis for rejecting the theory was that there would be no clear way to establish character of property until the marriage was over and then determine that some of the property was acquired with community funds. The Court clearly stated that it is the time of acquisition that controls; the character of property is not left in limbo until the end of the marriage.

However, the Court seemed to leave open one "loophole." It stated, "Only when, through no fault of the [spouse], it is not possible to ascertain the balance of income and expenditures at the time property was acquired, can recapitulation of the total community expenses and income throughout the marriage be used to establish the character of property." *Id.* at 783, 415 P.2d at 780, 51 Cal. Rptr. at 892. We can think of possible scenarios where the spouse would not be able to know exactly what income and expenditures there were at the time of acquisition, such as a fire or earthquake destroying the records. However, it seems that it would be equally hard to totally recapitulate all community expenses and income throughout the marriage. Perhaps the Court was thinking of the situation in the *See* case itself, where the community income was exceedingly small and the separate property was exceedingly large. Yet the *See* case stands for the proposition that the Exhaustion Method is clearly the preferred method for tracing to a commingled fund.

Direct Tracing Method: *Marriage of Mix/Estate of Murphy*

The California Supreme Court revisited the tracing to a commingled account issue in the case of *Marriage of Mix*, 14 Cal. 3d 604, 536 P.2d 479, 122 Cal. Rptr. 79 (1975). (A law professor did not think of that name!) The Court approved another method of tracing called *Direct Tracing*. It is the method preferred by the separate property proponent because it does not require exhaustion of community property funds. When both types of funds are in a bank account, under the Direct Tracing Method, the separate property proponent need only show that separate property funds were in the account and the separate property proponent intended to use the separate property funds to acquire the property in question.

To illustrate the differences between the Exhaustion and Direct Tracing methods, let's return to our hypothetical Harry and Wilma scenario and change the facts only slightly. Harry receives the $10,000 inheritance, his separate property, and puts it into his checking account. Before he purchases the vintage car, he also deposits community property funds that total $4,000. Then he purchases the vintage car. The car is presumed to be community property. Under the Exhaustion Method, Harry cannot trace to the separate property funds because the $4,000 of community property funds were still in the account—they had not been "exhausted." Therefore, since those funds were not used for family expenses, under the Exhaustion Method, they were used to acquire the car. Thus the car is only part separate property, the part that Harry can trace to separate property after the community funds are exhausted. The car was purchased with $4,000 community funds and $6,000 separate property funds. Harry could only claim that part of the car was purchased with his separate property funds.

Under the Direct Tracing Method, Harry would be allowed to prove that (1) separate property funds of $10,000 were available at the time of acquisition, and (2) he intended to use those funds to purchase the car as his separate property. Under that method, if Harry could prove availability of his separate property funds and intent to use those funds, he would rebut the community property presumption, and the car would be his separate property. The Direct Tracing Method clearly favors the separate property proponent. However, this method has been criticized and very strictly applied in later cases, leaving a doubt about the level of acceptance of the Direct Tracing Method in commingling cases.

Keeping Adequate Records

The California Supreme Court once again took up the issue of commingling and tracing the very next year after deciding *Marriage of Mix*. The case arose after the death of Mr. Murphy. *Estate of Murphy*, 15 Cal. 3d 907, 544 P.2d 956, 126 Cal. Rptr. 820 (1976). Mr. Murphy's legatees claimed that certain property was acquired from Mr. Murphy's separate property. The question in the case was whether the legatees, the separate property proponents, had adequately rebutted the community property presumption. It was clear that the Exhaustion Method would not have worked, because there had always been community property available in the commingled account. Therefore, the Direct Tracing Method was the only way for the legatees to succeed.

The Supreme Court reaffirmed that the Direct Tracing Method could be used to rebut the community property presumption; however, it tightened the requirements for succeeding under that method. Even though the legatees could show that separate property funds were available at the time the property was acquired, that was not sufficient, according to the Court. The Court stated that "Evidence which merely establishes the availability of separate funds on particular dates without showing any disposition of the funds is not sufficient proof of tracing to overcome the presumption in favor of community property." *Id.* at 918, 544 P.2d at 964, 126 Cal. Rptr. at 828. Thus, the Court added this requirement of "showing disposition of the funds." Showing disposition of the funds would be particularly difficult without producing documentary evidence and testimony to show that separate property funds were used to acquire the property.

The Court was also not receptive to the legatees' argument that the burden on the separate property proponent in a death case should be relaxed, because the spouse who commingled was unavailable to testify regarding the acquisition of the disputed property. The Court was unwilling to bend the rules where a spouse chooses to commingle property. The burden upon the spouse who commingles separate and community property funds is a heavy one. The burden is "not simply that of presenting proof at the time of litigation but also one of keeping adequate records." *Id.* at 919, 544 P.2d at 965, 126 Cal. Rptr. at 829. The *Murphy* case stands for the proposition that the commingling rules apply at death as well as divorce. More importantly, it can be viewed as the Supreme Court retreating from the ease of using the Direct Tracing Method, as exemplified by the Mix case.

The lower courts got that message. In *Marriage of Frick*, 181 Cal. App. 3d 997, 226 Cal. Rptr. 766 (1986), Jerome Frick relied on the Direct Tracing Method to argue that he used separate property funds to pay off an encumbrance on property he owned before marriage. The problem was that he had commingled his salary with his separate property income. He argued that he met his burden of rebutting the community property presumption by showing that he received a specific amount of separate property each month that he deposited into his commingled account, and he paid a specific amount every month to make payments on the encumbrance. He was also available to testify that he intended to use his separate property funds for those payments. Yet he failed to meet the burden because of inadequate records. According to the Court, the evidence was insufficient to give a full picture of the activity in the account at the time he made the payments—the Court was "left in the dark." *Id.* at 1011, 226 Cal. Rptr. at 773. Therefore, Jerome's testimony was insufficient without additional documentary evidence of all the activity in the account at the time the payments were made. Contemporaneous deposits and payments and his testimony of his intent to use only separate property funds were insufficient to meet his burden of rebutting the community property presumption. The requirements for Direct Tracing are exceedingly difficult to meet after *Murphy* and *Frick*. It is clear that a spouse who commingles must be advised that the chances are great that any acquisitions from a commingled account will be considered community property. A sign could be created: Commingle—Danger Ahead!

Joint Bank Accounts

One troubling question concerns a bank account that is jointly titled rather than in one spouse's name. Does the title control or do the funds in the account control? If the title controls, putting the bank account in joint title would mean that the funds in the account are presumed to be community property and cannot be rebutted by tracing but only by a written agreement or statement in the title. (See Chapter 4.) If the funds control, a separate property proponent could trace to separate property either under the Exhaustion or Direct Tracing method. The Legislature opted for a special provision regarding joint bank accounts: At divorce, the contributions to bank accounts of married persons are presumed to be community property and can be rebutted by tracing to separate property. Probate Code §5305. In our Harry and Wilma scenario, even if the bank account was in both their names, Harry would be able to use tracing to try to rebut the community property presumption.

Examples

Example 1 — Merrill Marries Lynch: Commingling Begins

Merrill had always loved the stock market. Even as a young girl, she liked to read the *Wall Street Journal*. When she was a teenager, she used her birthday money and allowance to buy shares in a new company called Microsoft. By the time Merrill married Lynch, her holdings in Microsoft were worth $10,000. She also had bought other stock before their marriage. She received monthly income from that stock totaling $1,000. Merrill also had trained as a stock analyst and had a salary of about $5,000 a month. She had one bank account in her name, and she deposited both her stock income and her salary into that account.

At the time of their marriage, Merrill's bank account had a balance of $20,000. Merrill paid for their honeymoon trip from that account. The trip cost about $7,000. During their marriage, Merrill planned to put her stock income and her salary into that account. Their food and entertainment expenses were approximately $2,000 that month. Merrill spent $1,000 that month for clothing. At the end of the first month of their marriage, Merrill deposited $1,000 of her stock income and her $5,000 paycheck into her account. In the second month after they married, Merrill bought stock in a biotech firm called Genetics, Inc. The stock cost $5,000. The stock was put in her name. It has increased in value. If Merrill and Lynch divorce, how would the court characterize the stock?

Example 2 — Merrill Pays the Architect: Family Expense?

Assume that in the second month after Merrill and Lynch were married and before Merrill bought stock in Genetics, Inc., they hired an architect to design a home for them. The architect required a retainer of $5,000. Merrill gave the architect a check for $5,000 from her account. Soon after, in that same month, she bought the Genetics, Inc., stock. If Merrill and Lynch divorce, how would the court characterize the stock?

Example 3 — The Check Is for $3,000

Assume the facts are the same as in Example 2, except the check to the architect was for $3,000. If Merrill and Lynch divorce, how would the court characterize the stock?

Example 4 — Merrill Asks for Advice

Merrill comes to you for advice before she gets married. How would you advise her about setting up her bank accounts?

Explanations

Explanation 1 — Merrill Marries Lynch: Commingling Begins

The stock was acquired during their marriage; therefore, it would be presumed to be community property. The general community property presumption applies. The separate property proponent, here Merrill, would have the burden of rebutting the presumption by tracing to her separate property funds. Remember that the title in her name is not determinative, and we will assume they had no agreements about the stock. The problem with rebutting the presumption is that the funds came from a commingled account. The account is considered commingled, because Merrill deposited her salary into her account. The salary she earned during the marriage is community property. The salary she earned before the marriage was her separate property. The stock owned before marriage is her separate property. Any income from that stock is considered her separate property because the "rents, issues, and profits" of separate property are separate property.

To succeed in rebutting the community property presumption, the burden is on Merrill, and it is also her burden to keep adequate records. We will assume she could produce records showing what went into the account and the expenditures from the account. At the time of marriage, the account contained $20,000. All of those funds were her separate property. Additional funds were put into the account at the end of their first month of marriage: $1,000 from her stock income and $5,000 from her salary. The stock income was her separate property, and the $5,000 was community property. The expenditures from the account during their first month of marriage included:

1. Honeymoon trip: $7,000
2. Food and entertainment: $2,000
3. Clothing: $1,000

These expenses would be in the category of family expenses, because they did not result in any property that would be divisible at divorce. Although it is clear that the trip and food and entertainment did not result in any property acquisitions, clothing is tangible property. It is possible that a very expensive item of clothing could be considered an acquisition, but ordinarily purchase of clothing would be considered an expense rather than an acquisition. All those expenses were paid from Merrill's account during the first month of marriage. Since only Merrill's separate property was in the account at that time, all were paid from her separate property. Merrill cannot claim reimbursement from the community absent an agreement. Food and clothing are certainly part of the obligation of support, and the honeymoon trip would be considered in property terms as a gift to the community.

Therefore, at the end of the first month of marriage, Merrill's account had been reduced to $10,000 in separate property.

Merrill then deposited her stock income and her salary into the account. The stock income was still her separate property, but her salary, which was earned during the first month of their marriage, was community property. At that point, Merrill has commingled! When property is acquired using funds from a commingled account, the general community property presumption applies. Merrill must use one of the two tracing methods, Exhaustion or Direct Tracing, to rebut the presumption. When Merrill bought the stock, the amount of separate property funds had increased to $11,000 ($1,000 from the stock income added to the $10,000 remaining in the account), and the amount of community property in the account was $5,000 (her salary).

The Court in the *See* case clearly stated that the character of property is determined at the time of acquisition. Under the Exhaustion Method, Merrill would have to prove that, at the time of acquisition, there was no community property in her commingled account. That would show that the Genetics, Inc., stock was bought with her separate property only. Because $5,000 of community property was deposited into her account before she bought the Genetics, Inc., stock, she could not show that the $5,000 was exhausted at the time of the acquisition. Therefore, she could not rebut the presumption that the Genetics, Inc., stock was community property, and the stock and any increase in value would be split 50/50 at divorce.

Because utilizing the Exhaustion Method would fail, Merrill would argue that the court should use the Direct Tracing Method. Whenever community property and separate property funds are available, the Direct Tracing Method is the only possibility for the separate property proponent to claim that an acquisition from a commingled fund is separate property. The requirements of that method are (1) availability of separate funds, and (2) the intent of the separate property proponent to use those funds. Even though the California Supreme Court approved this method in the *Mix* case, later cases have strictly applied those requirements. For instance, availability of separate property funds may require showing all the expenditures from the account and exactly when they were made and what funds were used for each expenditure. *See Marriage of Frick*, 181 Cal. App. 3d 997, 226 Cal. Rptr. 766 (1986). The requirement of record keeping on the spouse who commingles is indeed a heavy one. *See Estate of Murphy*, 15 Cal. 3d 907, 544 P.2d 956, 126 Cal. Rptr. 820 (1976).

In Merrill's case, she may be able to meet the requirements of the Direct Tracing Method. The amount of separate property funds was $11,000, and the amount of community property funds was $5,000. It is clear that separate property funds were available. She would also testify that she intended to use those funds to buy the Genetics, Inc., stock. However, it would be difficult to show which funds were used to buy the stock. It is particularly damaging in this case that the amount of the purchase of the stock was exactly the same amount as her salary deposit. The more stringent requirements would also demand that Merrill show all expenditures from that account and what exactly they were for. If the divorce occurred many years after their marriage, it is doubtful that those records would exist, and a court could decide that Merrill's testimony about which funds were used was insufficient to rebut the presumption. Since the presumption favors community property and commingling is a choice a spouse makes, a court may be unwilling to find that the stock is Merrill's separate property.

Explanation 2 — Merrill Pays the Architect: Family Expense?

At the end of the first month, Merrill's account has $11,000 in separate property funds and $5,000 in community property funds. Please see Explanation 1. Merrill's payment to the architect is considered a family expense and under the family expense presumption will be presumed to come from community property funds. Therefore, the only funds left in Merrill's account are separate property. Assuming that she bought the Genetics, Inc., stock before she deposited any more community funds, she would be able to meet the requirements of the Exhaustion Method: At the time she acquired the stock, there were no community funds in the account, and the only funds that could have been used to acquire the stock were separate property funds. Thus Merrill would be able to rebut the community property presumption, and the stock would be characterized as her separate property. It would belong to her at divorce.

Explanation 3 — The Check Is for $3,000

In this example, Merrill's check to the architect has reduced the community property funds in her account by $3,000. At the time of the purchase of the Genetics, Inc., stock, $2,000 in community property funds still remain in the account as well as $11,000 in separate property funds. The purchase of the Genetics, Inc., stock cost $5,000. Under the Exhaustion Method, community property funds were available to pay for only part of the Genetics, Inc., stock, $2,000 of the $5,000 purchase price. The remaining $3,000 of the $5,000 purchase price had to come from separate property funds, since community property funds were at that point exhausted. Thus, under this method, Merrill could rebut the community property presumption by showing that $3,000 of the purchase was made with separate property funds.

The court would then characterize the stock as part community and part separate property and apportion the stock accordingly. To do the figures, the stock would be two-fifths (40%) community property and three-fifths (60%) Merrill's separate property. If the stock had not appreciated in value, Merrill would receive $3,000 as her separate property and $1,000 as one-half of the community property. Lynch would receive $1,000 as one-half of the community property. If the stock had appreciated by the time they divorced, the appreciation would also be split proportionally according to the separate property and community property funds.

Explanation 4 — Merrill Asks for Advice

The pitfalls of commingling should now be obvious. The best advice for Merrill to avoid complications upon divorce would be to keep separate accounts for her stock income and her salary. It would be best to explain the consequences of commingling: Without excellent records showing what each transaction was for and from which funds they came, acquisitions from a commingled account would most likely be characterized as community property. To keep separate property funds and community property funds in separate accounts would be the best way to protect Merrill's acquisitions as her separate property.

COMMUNITY BUSINESSES, PROFESSIONAL PRACTICES, AND GOODWILL

Often, spouses own their own businesses and professional practices, or interests in a business or professional corporation or partnership. To the extent that these property interests are acquired during the marriage, they are community property. At divorce, a community business or practice has to be valued by the court. The value of a business or professional entity is the sum of its parts — the assets that comprise it. Most of these assets are tangible items: real estate, equipment, inventory, office furnishings, bank deposits, etc. Community businesses have intangible assets as well. One common intangible asset that many businesses and practices have is "goodwill."

What Is Goodwill?

The goodwill of an entity is an asset that is a valuable property interest, which accounts for, in the words of the California Legislature, "the expectation of continued public patronage." Business & Professions Code §14100. It is a value that we place on the probability that an establishment will continue to exist and be successful.

The following example will illustrate why the intangible notion of "goodwill" has value. Assume that spouses have owned and operated a dry-cleaning business for the past 15 years. Over the years, they have built up a reputation of quality dry cleaning, and they are widely patronized. In fact, for the past five years, their net profits have been above $250,000 annually. They own their building and equipment outright, all of which is worth approximately $150,000. Last week, however, they received a firm offer of $500,000 to purchase the business.

The reason the offeror would want to pay over three times the value of the tangible assets to purchase the business is because of the expectation that the business will continue to be a moneymaker. If net profits remained constant, the purchaser would recoup the original investment in two years; after that, the net profits would be the return on the investment. The value that the purchaser is willing to pay above the actual, tangible value of the business is the value of the "goodwill" of the business. In our scenario, the offeror believes the goodwill of the dry-cleaning business to be $350,000.

Defining goodwill as "the expectation of continuing public patronage" is somewhat incomplete. Many definitions for goodwill have been promulgated over the years. In *In Re Lyons*, 27 Cal. App. 2d 293, 297-298, 81 P.2d 190, 193 (1938), the Court of Appeal defined goodwill as "the advantage or benefit which is acquired by an establishment beyond the mere value of the capital stock, funds or property therein, in the consequence of the general public patronage and encouragement it receives from constant or habitual customers, on account of its local position, or common celebrity, or reputation for skill or affluence, or punctuality, or from other accidental circumstances, or necessities, or even from ancient partialities or prejudices. . . . It is the probability that the business will continue in the future as in the past, adding to the profits of the going concern and contributing to the means of meeting its engagements as they come in." (*Id.*, quoting J. Story, *Commentaries on the Law of Partnerships* (6th ed. 1868) §99, and *Bell v. Ellis*, 33 Cal. 620, 625 (1867).) Whatever its definition, "[g]oodwill is property of an intangible nature and is a thing of value." *Marriage of Foster*, 42 Cal. App. 3d 577, 582, 117 Cal. Rptr. 49, 52 (1974).

California community property law recognizes goodwill in the context of businesses and professional practices. Conceptually, business goodwill is the easiest type of goodwill to understand; and in practice, it is the easiest to value. All types of businesses, from a print shop to a construction company to a restaurant, can have goodwill.

Professionals, such as doctors and lawyers, can also develop "goodwill" of the same nature as that of a business. In *Mueller v. Mueller*, 144 Cal. App. 2d 245, 251, 301 P.2d 90, 95 (1956), the Court of Appeal noted that "[w]here a person acquires a reputation for skill and learning in a particular profession, as for instance, in that of a lawyer, a physician, or an editor, he often creates an intangible but valuable property by winning the confidence of his patrons and securing immunity from successful competition for their business, and it would seem to be well settled that this is a species of good will which may be the subject of transfer." Thus, "[i]n a divorce case it is well established that the goodwill of a husband's professional practice . . . is taken into consideration in determining the community property award to the wife." *Marriage of Foster*, 42 Cal. App. 3d at 582, 117 Cal. Rptr. at 52. Professional goodwill is not recognized in all community property states. Texas, for example, has rejected the notion. *Nail v. Nail*, 486 S.W.2d 761 (Tex. 1976).

Until the *McTiernan v. Dubrow* case, 133 Cal. App. 4th 1090, 35 Cal. Rptr. 3d 287 (2005), *rev. denied*, Jan. 25, 2006, the California courts had not addressed the issue of whether there is "celebrity goodwill." The notion of celebrity goodwill is similar to professional goodwill. As a celebrity earns a "reputation" for being entertaining, he or she accumulates a fan base that regularly goes to see the movies or purchases the records. Just like the professional, the celebrity has an "expectation of continued public patronage," which might likewise be considered goodwill.

In the *McTiernan* case, the trial court found that successful motion picture director John McTiernan (of *Die Hard* and *The Hunt for Red October* fame) had goodwill in his "business." Because that goodwill had been accumulated during his marriage to Donna Dubrow, it was community property and it was valued at $1.5 million. The trial court considered that the profession of a motion picture director who has achieved exceptional success in his field is "similar to that of an attorney, physician, dentist, accountant, editor, architect, or any other professional . . . ." *Id.* at 1094, 35 Cal. Rptr. 3d at 290.

The Court of Appeal disagreed, reasoning that a "business" cannot be defined to include "a person doing business." *Id.* at 1096, 35 Cal. Rptr. 3d at 291-292. A business "refers to a professional, commercial or industrial enterprise with assets" and excludes "natural persons." *Id.* at 1098, 35 Cal. Rptr. 3d at 293. Even though Mr. McTiernan has "elite professional status," shorthand for his exceptional "earning capacity and professional reputation," *he* is not a "business." *Id.* at 1102, 35 Cal. Rptr. 3d at 287. To further support its conclusion, the Court noted that his professional standing is "entirely personal to him" and he cannot sell or transfer that standing to anyone else. That is what distinguishes a "celebrity" from other professionals who can transfer their practices to others. *Id.* at 1100-1101, 35 Cal. Rptr. 3d at 295. Thus an individual who would be considered a "celebrity" has no goodwill unless that person has a practice similar to an attorney, physician, dentist, or accountant. *Id.* at 1101, 35 Cal. Rptr. 3d at 295. In *Marriage of Finby*, 222 Cal. App. 4th 977, 166 Cal. Rptr 3d 305 (2013), the "book of business" belonging to the wife, Rhonda, was considered a "valuable asset," which was based not only on her high standing as a financial advisor in the securities industry but also on her being a licensed professional.

The Court of Appeal decision included a concurrence and a dissent on the issue of goodwill. Justice Boland, in his concurrence, agreed that Mr. McTiernan's work as a motion picture director is not a business or professional practice that generates goodwill. The underlying reason is that his "business" is nontransferable. "Whatever we may call it—talent, occupation, livelihood or profession—the creative processes of a movie director, like that of any other artist, cannot be bought, sold or given away, and therefore does not fit within any recognized definition of property." *Id.* at 1112-1113, 35 Cal. Rptr. 3d at 304. He distinguished cases involving physicians because they involved medical practices, which could be bought and sold. *Id.* at 1113, 35 Cal. Rptr. 3d at 304-305. Dissenting Justice Cooper criticized the majority for applying "restrictive concepts that disregard established family law precedent." *Id.* at 1115, 35 Cal. Rptr. 3d at 306. He challenged the majority definition of business and the conclusion that a business cannot attach to an individual: "Any professional who independently practices his or her profession, for profit—be it lawyer, doctor, computer consultant, or film director—thereby conducts a business . . . [and] generated goodwill while practicing their professions." *Id.* at 1116-1117, 35 Cal. Rptr. 3d at 307-308. The established family law precedent that the majority disregarded included decisions involving professional individuals who worked at home and had no office, employees, or commercial location. On the issue of transferability, he concluded that the same statute used by the majority settles the issue as a matter of law: "The goodwill of a business is property and is transferable." *Id.* at 1117, 35 Cal. Rptr. 3d at 308.

For the present, the *McTiernan* case stands for the proposition that individuals like Mr. McTiernan—for instance, artists, entertainers, or athletes who command high compensation—are not considered to have professional practices to which goodwill attaches. Thus, in California, celebrity goodwill is not property divisible at divorce. Professional goodwill remains a distinct category that has been limited to those professionals who have commercial or professional practices.

How to Value Goodwill?

The value of goodwill is a question of fact that must be determined by the court at divorce. There are many ways to value goodwill, most of which are acceptable in court. "The courts have not laid down rigid and unvarying rules for the determination of the value of goodwill, but have indicated that each case must be determined on its own facts and circumstances . . . ." *Marriage of Foster*, 42 Cal. App. 3d at 583, 117 Cal. Rptr. at 53. "[A] proper means of arriving at the value of . . . goodwill contemplates any legitimate method of evaluation . . . ." *Id.* at 584, 117 Cal. Rptr. at 54.

At divorce, both husband and wife present evidence on the value of goodwill, usually consisting of expert testimony. Experts employ a wide variety of methods of evaluating goodwill. Common methods include a "market value" analysis, where the expert looks at what a willing buyer would pay in cash for the community business if it were sold at the time of separation or divorce. Also common are capitalization methods that look at the net income of a professional practice for one year, subtract from it what a reasonable salary would be for a professional of comparable experience, and multiply by a multiplier of some value. Different methods arrive at different values for the same goodwill. Sometimes, experts conduct several evaluations using different methods and present to the court a range of possible values or an average value.

Though many methods of valuation are utilized in practice and accepted in court, there is an important prohibition: "[G]oodwill may not be valued by any method that takes into account the post-marital efforts of either spouse." *Id.* at 584, 117 Cal. Rptr. at 54. "Since the philosophy of the community property system is that a community interest may be acquired only during the time of the marriage, it would then be inconsistent with that philosophy to assign to any community interest the value of the post-marital efforts of either spouse." *Marriage of Fortier*, 34 Cal. App. 3d 384, 388, 109 Cal. Rptr. 915, 918 (1973).

Thus, any method of valuing goodwill based in any way on the earnings or projected earnings of a spouse after separation or divorce is prohibited. Indeed, those earnings are separate property, not goodwill. "It must be recognized that the value of the goodwill must exist *at the time* of the dissolution. That value is *separate and apart* from the expectations of the spouse's future earnings." *Id.* at 388, 109 Cal. Rptr. at 918, emphasis added.

Examples

Example 5 — How Much Do Tacos Cost?

Tacos "Linda Tapatia" is a well-patronized taco stand that has been in business for 35 years in Pasadena. It is wholly owned by Mr. Zavala, a widower. Mr. Zavala founded the place and used to be a cook there, but he has not worked there for the past 15 years. Its assets consist of $45,000 worth of real property and fixtures and $10,000 worth of supplies and equipment, yet it generates $150,000 a year in profit. The entity has no liabilities.

Mr. Zavala has decided to move back to his hometown of Guadalajara, Mexico, and is accepting offers to purchase Tacos "Linda Tapatia."

a. If you wanted to buy the business, how much would you offer Mr. Zavala? More than $55,000? If so, why? If you were Mr. Zavala, how much would you sell Tacos "Linda Tapatia" for?

b. Why might Tacos "Linda Tapatia" be worth more than $55,000?

Example 6 — Who Can Figure?

Henry and Wendy were married in Sunnyvale in 1985. At the time, Henry was an accountant with H&R Block. In 1990, Henry decided he wanted to open his own financial services office. He purchased a small office building, furniture, and equipment, and opened up for business. In his first full year of operation, he generated only $20,000 in profit. His business, though, grew by word of mouth and reputation. His revenues steadily increased over the past 11 years. Last year, he made $250,000 in profit.

Wendy soon became distressed at Henry's increasing hours, and recently she filed for dissolution of their marriage. Part of the community property, as determined by the court, included $300,000, which the court characterized as the "goodwill" of Henry's practice. This figure was derived from Wendy's expert witness, who testified that that was the value of Henry's goodwill. Henry presented no evidence about the value of his goodwill, instead contending that his goodwill was not community property.

a. Is Henry right? Why or why not? b. Assume that Wendy's expert gave the following testimony:

> In figuring out what Henry's goodwill is, I looked at the amount of revenue his operation generated last year, and I subtracted the amount of salary that an accountant of equivalent experience would make in a year from that figure. Then I multiplied that amount by a multiplier of 4.

What methodology of valuation is seen here? Was it proper for the court to accept the expert's valuation of goodwill?

c. Assume that Wendy's expert gave the following testimony:

> In figuring out what Henry's goodwill is, I projected what Henry's earnings are going to be over the next five years. I think he is going to make $10,000 more each year.

Was it proper for the court to accept the expert's valuation of goodwill?

Example 7 — How to Value a Hot Spot?

Hank and Winona were married in Eureka in 1978. In 1985, they moved to San Clemente and purchased a small, run-down nightclub. Winona managed the nightclub while Hank stayed home and raised their two children. Over the years, she has turned it around, and it has become the beach cities' hot spot. It currently generates $150,000 a year in profit.

One night last spring, Hank found Winona getting friendly with the piano player. He immediately filed for dissolution of their marriage. At trial, Hank and Winona stipulated that the nightclub's tangible assets were worth $250,000. Hank called an expert, who testified that the goodwill of the nightclub was worth an additional $250,000. Hank's expert based his valuation on a variety of considerations, which included, among other things, market competition analysis, projected city growth, and a variety of technical economic indicators for which the outlook was positive. Winona's expert testified that in his opinion the nightclub's goodwill was worth $100,000, even though he admitted he had never evaluated a nightclub before.

What is the value of the nightclub's goodwill? Would a court be abusing its discretion in finding the value to be $75,000 or $100,000, as Wendy's evidence suggests? What about $250,000, like Hank's expert suggests? What about a middle ground?

Example 8 — Harry's Does Surgery on Goodwill

Harry and Wilma have been married since 1987. Harry is a cosmetic surgeon. In 1990, he opened a partnership in the Silicon Valley with three colleagues from medical school. The partnership has been successful from the beginning; Harry's interest in the partnership generates about $350,000 in profits annually.

Harry and Wilma have decided to part ways. In the dissolution proceeding, Wilma presented expert witness testimony that the value of Harry's interest in the partnership was $500,000, $400,000 of which constitutes Harry's interest in the goodwill of the partnership. Wilma's expert employed a capitalization method of valuation. Harry presented no expert testimony and instead offered into evidence a certified copy of his partnership agreement. A clause in the agreement stated:

> Should a partner, for whatever reason, cease to practice in the partnership, the other partners shall purchase the leaving partner's interest in the partnership. The purchase price for that interest shall be the reasonable value of all tangible assets, including financial assets, plus the additional sum of two weeks' worth of average receipts, which shall constitute payment for the leaving partner's interest in the goodwill.

Harry contends that if he had left the partnership on the date of separation, he would only have been entitled to a $100,000 payment for tangible assets and $25,000 for goodwill. He contends that as a matter of law, the court must find this to be the community's interest in the partnership. Is Harry right? Is the court limited to adopting as conclusive Harry's contractual withdrawal rights?

Example 9 — Does Herb Need Legal Support?

Herb and Wanda are the best of friends and the worst of marital partners. They have decided to get a divorce after six years of marriage. When they were married, Herb began a legal support services business, which, on account of his hard work and personality, has grown immensely. The business nets $200,000 per year in annual revenue.

Herb and Wanda have stipulated that the business has a value of $200,000 and that $100,000 of that figure constitutes Herb's "goodwill." Herb contends, however, that the value should be reduced by $75,000, since in the event that he sold the business, he would be required to give a covenant not to compete. Wanda, on the other hand, contends that the value should be increased by $50,000, which would be the amount of consideration Herb would receive for the covenant not to compete. Who is right? Herb? Wanda? Neither? How should the court value the goodwill of Herb's business?

Example 10—Winnie Is Not Amused

When Hal and Winnie were married, Hal was a struggling comedian on the stand-up circuit. Winnie was a nurse and supported them when Hal was trying to make it big. Five years ago, Hal got a lucky break when he was cast in a supporting role in a Mel Brooks flick. He was a riot and carried the otherwise corny movie to box office success. Since then, Hal has worked on many successful movies and often plays the leading role. He is also a regular on late night shows, as well as still doing stand-up comedy at large venues. Hal's net earnings for the past three years have been $2 million, $6 million, and $15 million, respectively.

Winnie decided this year that she no longer wants to be an entertainer's wife. She has come to you to see about filing for a divorce, and she wants to know what property rights she has in Hal's fame. She thinks that since she "supported" the family when he was "still a deadbeat," she should "own" a "piece of his stardom." Is Winnie right? Advise Winnie on her property rights at divorce.

Explanations

Explanation 5—How Much Do Tacos Cost?

a. Tacos "Linda Tapatia" seems like a great business, and it is probably easy to run. There is already an established clientele. Assuming that you get the recipes and all of the suppliers will continue to supply your food, the patronage will probably stay intact. Since the real property is owned, there is no rent to pay. There are no liabilities. Assuming that you are a good boss, the current workers probably will stay on. For all these and many more reasons, it would probably be a stable and lucrative investment. It might be worth it to offer Mr. Zavala upwards of $300,000 and maybe more for the business if you plan on keeping it long term. Granted, this value is more than five times the value of the tangible assets. However, if things keep going the way they are, you will recoup your investment within two years, and everything that you earn from that point on will be purely profit. Indeed, it is likely that Mr. Zavala will expect more money than just the value of the tangible assets of the business for the same reasons that you are willing to offer Mr. Zavala *more* than the business is worth in tangible assets.

b. Tacos "Linda Tapatia" is worth more than its $55,000 tangible asset value because it has "goodwill." Goodwill is an asset that causes the value of a business or a professional practice to be more than the actual value of its tangible assets. Justice Story defined it long ago as the "advantage or benefit, which is acquired by an establishment, beyond the mere value of the capital stock, funds, or property employed therein, in consequence of general public patronage and encouragement, which it receives from constant or habitual customers, on account of its local position, or common celebrity, or reputation for skill or affluence . . . ." (J. Story, *Commentaries on the Law of Partnerships* (6th ed. 1868) §99, at 170.) Also, the California Business and Professions Code §14100 defines it as "the expectation of continued public patronage." Goodwill in the context of Tacos "Linda Tapatia" is exactly that: the expectation (indeed, probability) that the customers are going to keep coming, and revenues are going to keep generating. Clearly, Tacos "Linda Tapatia" has goodwill and thus is worth much more than its place and equipment.

Explanation 6 — Who Can Figure?

a. Henry is wrong. The value of his *professional* goodwill is a property interest, which, to the extent that it was developed during the marriage, is community property. Indeed, according to *Mueller v. Mueller*, "goodwill . . . exists in a professional practice or in a business which is founded upon personal skill or reputation. Where a person acquires a reputation for skill and learning in a particular profession, as, for instance, in that of a lawyer, a physician, or an editor, he often creates an intangible but valuable property by winning the confidence of his patrons and securing immunity from successful competition for their business." Thus, the value of Henry's goodwill is divisible community property.

b. Wendy's expert is applying a *capitalization* method of valuing goodwill, which was recognized as valid in *Marriage of Foster*. The idea of capitalization is to take "into account past earnings and project these into the present value of the goodwill." There is no abuse of discretion where goodwill is valued according to capitalization by ascertaining the average net income over a period of years, subtracting the portion allocable to salary, and by capitalizing the difference over a period of four years.

c. We can see in this testimony that Wendy's expert is basing his valuation of goodwill on what Henry's future earnings are projected to be. This is not a proper method of valuing goodwill, and a court would be abusing its discretion to base its findings on this testimony. In *Marriage of Fortier*, the Court reasoned that it would be "inconsistent with that philosophy [of community property] to assign to any community interest the value of the post-marital efforts of either spouse. It must be recognized that *the value of the goodwill must exist [as a property interest] at the time of the dissolution*. That value is separate and apart from the expectation of the spouses' future earnings," which are the separate property of the earning spouse, since they are not earned during the marriage. Effectively, the court would be awarding Wendy a portion of Henry's future earnings, which are his separate property, since they are earned after their marriage. This would be improper.

Explanation 7 — How to Value a Hot Spot?

The value of the nightclub's goodwill could be *anything*! As succinctly stated in *Marriage of Foster*, "it is 'always just somebody's opinion.'" There are many ways to value goodwill. "The courts have not laid down rigid and unvarying rules for the determination of the value of goodwill, but have indicated that each case must be determined on its own facts and circumstances and the evidence must be such that as legitimately establishes value."

Given that there are no set rules for valuing goodwill, and given that valuation turns on the facts and circumstances of each individual case, trial courts are given "broad latitude" in establishing the value of goodwill. *Marriage of Lopez*, 38 Cal. App. 3d 93, 109, 113 Cal. Rptr. 915, 918 (1974). Appellate courts defer to trial court rulings, applying only an abuse of discretion standard of review. As stated in *Marriage of Fortier*, "The problem . . . is not whether some formula which was suggested but not accepted by the court could have been accepted as a proper means of arriving at the value of goodwill, but rather: Was the formula which the court applied a proper one, and is there evidence to support the court's decision." Often, trial courts are faced with a wife who says value is established by "x," and a husband who says value is established by "y." Whichever way the court goes is probably OK, provided that there is evidence to support the conclusion. The court in this case would probably not be abusing its discretion by adopting Winona's expert's opinion. Also, a court would not be abusing its discretion by adopting Hank's expert's testimony. However, a court may be abusing its discretion by picking a middle ground without giving a reason for that decision. For instance, the Court of Appeal in *Marriage of Hargrave*, 136 Cal. App. 3d 346, 354, 209 Cal. Rptr. 764, 769 (1985), rejected a trial court's valuation of goodwill where "there appears to be no discernible reason for the choice." As long as there is evidence and reason in the court's decision, it is proper.

Explanation 8 — Harry's Does Surgery on Goodwill

If the court considered Harry's contractual withdrawal rights, without more, it would probably be abusing its discretion. When determining the community property interest in the partnership, we consider the worth of that interest as a "going business," and *not* the price that the partners get to pay to buy each other out. This is because "[t]he asset being divided in the proceeding [is] the husband's interest in the partnership, not his contractual withdrawal rights." *Marriage of Slater*, 100 Cal. App. 3d 241, 245, 160 Cal. Rptr. 686, 688 (1979); see also *Marriage of Lopez*, 38 Cal. App. 3d 93, 109, 113 Cal. Rptr. 58, 68 (1974) ("where the issue is raised in a marital dissolution action, the trial court must make a specific finding as to the existence and value of the 'goodwill' of the professional business *as a going concern* whether related to that of a sole practitioner, a professional partnership or a professional corporation" (emphasis added)).

"The value of the contractual withdrawal right *may provide a basis* for ascertaining the value of the community property interest [citation]; however, it does not preclude a consideration of other facts." *Marriage of Slater*, 100 Cal. App. 3d at 246-247, 160 Cal. Rptr. 686, 689. In *Slater*, the trial court abused its discretion by looking only to the contractual withdrawal rights of the professional spouse and not to any other factors. Likewise, it will probably be necessary here to consider facts other than a buyout agreement price to ascertain the value of the interest "as a going concern."

Explanation 9 — Does Herb Need Legal Support?

Neither Herb nor Wanda is correct in asserting that the value of the goodwill should be reduced or increased by the value of the covenant not to compete. "Establishing a value for a future covenant not to compete, separate from the value of the business goodwill itself, is entirely too speculative. Once having made an equal division of community property, the court is not required to speculate about what either or both of the spouses may possibly do with his or her equal share and therefore to engraft on the division further adjustments reflecting situations based on theory rather than fact." *Marriage of Czapar*, 232 Cal. App. 3d 1308, 1315-1316, 285 Cal. Rptr. 479, 482 (1991).

The court should accept the parties stipulated values of the business and goodwill as final. Then, if Herb sells his business at some point in the future, it will be a decision affecting his separate property. The consideration he receives for a covenant not to compete will be his separate property. This is because Wanda will already have been "bought out" of the business, so to speak, when she received the value of her half of the community property upon divorce. Moreover, as acknowledged in *Marriage of Czapar*, 232 Cal. App. 3d at 1315, 285 Cal. Rptr. at 482, there are "any number of scenarios . . . in which a sale or transfer of the business would not require such a covenant or in which the covenant would not have the value which the court placed on it." An example of that situation would be when Herb retires, or becomes incapacitated and cannot work anyway. On the one hand, it would be unfair to Herb, in this instance, if the court awarded Wilma more community property after increasing the value of the goodwill by the hypothetical covenant's consideration. On the other hand, if the court were to reduce the value of the goodwill by the value of the covenant, and Herb ended up selling the business without creating such a covenant, Herb would be receiving a windfall. Courts are generally not in the business of setting values and basing awards on property interests that might not even exist.

Explanation 10—Winnie Is Not Amused

Winnie is wrong. In *McTiernan v. Dubrow*, 133 Cal. App. 4th 1090, 35 Cal. Rptr. 3d 287 (2005), the Court of Appeal defined "business" that would generate goodwill to exclude a "person doing business." To generate goodwill, a business must include a "professional, commercial or industrial enterprise with assets." *Id.* at 1096, 35 Cal. Rptr. 3d at 290. The Court distinguished a person like Hal who has exceptional earning capacity and professional reputation from professionals who have a professional practice. Therefore, artists, entertainers, and athletes would not have goodwill, while attorneys, physicians, dentists, and accountants would. The Court explained that talented individuals do not have an asset that can be sold or transferred—it is personal to them. On the other hand, a professional with a practice can sell or transfer that practice. Hal would fall into the category of talented individual who does not have a professional practice. Therefore, there would be no goodwill in his "celebrity" status.

There was a vigorous dissent in the *McTiernan* case. Justice Cooper differed on the definition of a business, explaining that a person like Hal is a professional who practices his profession and thus generates goodwill. The business, according to Justice Cooper, is not dependent on having an office, employees, or a commercial location. That definition of goodwill is based on past cases. For instance, an attorney who worked at home on criminal appeals had goodwill. Also a computer consultant had goodwill even though he had no office or employees. If a court accepted that viewpoint, Winnie might have a chance to receive a portion of Hal's goodwill as a professional entertainer. Because Winnie's argument is based on a dissent, it may be a better strategy for her to try to work out a property settlement with Hal. Since the millions earned during their marriage are community property, Winnie would have a right to one-half of those earnings. To avoid the possibility of litigation, Hal may agree to a settlement.

EDUCATIONAL DEGREES

The Debate

One major issue in community property law is how to classify intangible property. When a married student pursues higher education, such as a medical degree, a law degree, or an advanced business degree, is that degree the separate property of the degree holder spouse or is that degree community property? The debate is particularly interesting to law students who are in the process of working toward their degrees and who are married or who are contemplating marriage. Most states that have considered the issue have concluded that educational or professional degrees are not property or community property.

Although the degree is certainly acquired during marriage, which would presumptively put it in the category of community property, the debate revolves around the issue of whether it is really divisible property. A degree is valuable, as it enhances the earning capacity of the degree holder. If other intangible property like unvested pension rights and goodwill are considered property, then so too should an educational degree be considered property. However, courts have been convinced by the argument that an educational degree is personal to the holder and therefore cannot be considered divisible property. The reason is that the degree cannot be sold, transferred, or assigned to anyone else. It cannot be inherited. No one can use that degree other than the person who attains it. Thus they conclude that an educational degree is not divisible property and therefore cannot be subject to division at dissolution.

Even if it were considered property, an educational degree is extremely difficult to value. Also significant is the rationale that valuation of enhanced earning power will involve post-dissolution earnings that are clearly separate property. These reasons have swayed the vast majority of courts to conclude that an educational degree is not property or that it is the separate property of the spouse who attained the degree.

The Problem

However, there is a still a dissolution scenario involving an educational degree that reeks of unfairness. It often happens that a married couple decides that one spouse should strive to attain an advanced degree. Both view the degree as a ticket to greater earnings and a better standard of living. They sacrifice. The student spouse spends many long hours studying. The supporting spouse works to keep the economic community afloat and, in some cases, sacrifices his/her own educational goals for the student spouse. Sometimes the stress of school and economic difficulties results in divorce. At the end of the educational process, the student spouse receives the degree, and, unfortunately, the supporting spouse receives a divorce decree. That spouse feels cheated. The courts and legislatures have struggled with how to remedy the inequity to the supporting spouse.

The Solution

In California, the courts have long held that a professional degree, such as a law or medical degree, is not community property divisible at divorce. In many cases involving divorce, the professional spouse has already enhanced her earning capacity, and the couple has accumulated significant community property. Thus, any inequity can be remedied by dividing the couple's community property. In addition, spousal support is sometimes available to the nonprofessional spouse. Those remedies do not work in the problem scenario because (1) the couple has not had a chance to accumulate significant community property, and (2) the supporting spouse has usually been working and therefore is probably ineligible for spousal support.

In California, Family Code §2641 provides a partial remedy for the problem scenario. Although the student spouse receives the educational degree, a loan incurred during marriage for education is assigned for payment to the student spouse. With the diploma goes the debt. The primary remedy for the supporting spouse is "reimbursement of community contributions." Along with assignment of the loan to the student spouse without offset, reimbursement is the exclusive remedy. However, the attainment of a degree and the efforts of the spouse who supported the student spouse may also be considered in the awarding of spousal support. Family Code §4320(b).

Who Receives the Reimbursement?

The first question that arises under the statute is, "Who receives the reimbursement?" It is clear that it is the *community* that receives reimbursement. That means that any reimbursement is split between the spouses at divorce. The second question is, "How are community contributions defined?" "Community contributions to education or training" include payments from community or quasi-community property for payment for education or training or repayment of a loan incurred for education or training. Those payments include direct payments for tuition, fees, books, supplies, and transportation. They may also include any special living expenses related to the education experience itself, but do not include ordinary living expenses, because they are incurred regardless of whether one spouse is attending school, staying home, or working. The next question is, "How is the reimbursement calculated?" The amount reimbursed includes interest at the legal rate, starting from the end of the calendar year in which the contributions were made.

This limited reimbursement remedy is even further limited by an "unjust" provision. The statute provides that reimbursement and assignment of the loan may be reduced or modified if unjust. The major reason for reducing the reimbursement is when the community has "substantially benefited" from the education, training, or loan incurred. There is a rebuttable presumption that the community has substantially benefited from community contributions made more than ten years before commencement of the proceeding. This presumption addresses the situation where the spouses have already accumulated significant community property, and thus there is no need to reimburse the community for the contributions made to education or training. There is also the contrary presumption that the community had not substantially benefited from community contributions made less than ten years before the commencement of the proceeding. That presumption addresses the problem scenario where the couple divorces soon after the student spouse receives the educational degree, and there is little or no community property to divide.

Loan Incurred Prior to Marriage

As mentioned at the beginning of this part of the chapter, it is not uncommon for a person to attain an educational degree and then marry. Add to that scenario that the educational degree is financed with a student loan, and community funds are used to repay that loan. Under Family Code §2641(a), community contributions include "payments made with community property . . . for repayment of a loan for education or training." Under Family Code §2641(b)(1), the community shall be reimbursed for those contributions. This exact scenario occurred in the case of *Marriage of Weiner*, 105 Cal. App. 4th 235, 129 Cal. Rptr. 2d 288 (2003).

Michael Weiner graduated from medical school in 1991. In 1993, he married Kelly Ann. They separated in 1999. During their marriage, they paid more than $12,000 on Michael's loans incurred during medical school. Although the trial court found that Michael was required to reimburse Kelly for one-half of the medical loan payments made during marriage, the trial court did not base that decision on Family Code §2641, because it concluded that §2641 did not govern premarital educational loans.

The Court of Appeal disagreed. The language of the statute and the history and intent of the statute supported the conclusion that reimbursement included payments for premarital educational loans. "By its terms application of the statute is governed solely by whether community funds were used to pay for the education, even if the education took place before marriage." *Id.* at 239, 129 Cal. Rptr. 2d at 291. According to the Court of Appeal, the statute was intended to correct the inequity that arises when the community contributes financial support to the education but does not share in the benefits of that education. "The potential inequity the statute was designed to remedy arises even if the education itself occurred long before the marriage." *Id.* at 240, 129 Cal. Rptr. 2d at 291. Therefore, the reimbursement remedy provided in the statute did govern community contributions made to repay a premarital educational loan.

Another issue regarding premarital loans for education was not addressed in the *Weiner* case, and that is the assignment of the educational loan. If a balance on the loan remains, how is that loan assigned? Family Code §2641(d) provides that "reimbursement and assignment" is the exclusive remedy regarding educational loans. The Family Code section dealing with division of debts states that "educational loans shall be assigned pursuant to Section 2641." Family Code §2627. Cross-referencing is terrific, except there is a slight problem. Although the reimbursement remedy has now been held to apply to premarital educational loans, Family Code §2641(b)(2) is limited to assignment of loans *incurred* during marriage. Have no fear! This problem is easily solved by reference to another Family Code section concerning debts incurred before marriage. Family Code §2621 provides that "[d]ebts incurred by either spouse before the date of marriage shall be confirmed without offset to the spouse who incurred the debt." If Michael Weiner still had a balance owing on his debt from medical school, it was all his.

The bottom line here is that reimbursement applies to community contributions during marriage that repay an educational loan incurred prior to marriage. Assignment of a premarital loan will also be to the student spouse who incurred the loan, based not on §2641 but on the division of debt under §2621. Please see Chapter 8 on division of debts upon divorce.

Education: Enhancement of Earning Capacity

The reimbursement remedy provided in Family Code §2641 is for "community property contributions to education or training that *substantially enhances the earning capacity* of the party." It is possible that a person could seek education or training for a different purpose other than enhancing earning capacity. For instance, let us take our hypothetical couple, Harry and Wilma. In this scenario, we will assume that Harry and Wilma were both successful in their professions. Harry is a physician and Wilma is a psychologist. They never had children, and by age 50, they had saved enough from their earnings to live comfortably. They decided to retire and enjoy life. Harry had always loved reading and felt that he had missed out on pursuing an advanced degree in English literature. After they retired, he enrolled in a master's of arts program at the University of South California. He received the degree in two years and tuition was $50,000. The tuition was paid from Harry and Wilma's savings from their earnings. He also became romantically involved with one of his professors, and now Harry and Wilma have separated. Wilma seeks reimbursement for the community contributions of the tuition for Harry's degree.

The contributions that were made to Harry's tuition are clearly community property and are potentially reimbursable. However, this particular scenario is not the inequity that Family Code §2641 was intended to remedy. Family Code §2641(b)(1) does not provide reimbursement for any and all education or training. The limitation is that the education or training must substantially enhance the earning capacity of the spouse seeking the education. In our scenario, Harry sought the degree for his love of English literature not to substantially enhance his earning capacity. Plus such a degree would not substantially enhance his earning capacity. Therefore, the education is beyond the parameters of the reimbursement remedy. Wilma therefore is out of luck. The community contribution, therefore, is a gift to Harry. Presumably Wilma and Harry have substantial assets accumulated during their marriage and Wilma will receive her share of all their community property.

That scenario is rather clear-cut, but there are scenarios that are ambiguous. For instance, let us take the couple Jeffrey and Katherine. Jeffrey was a police officer in the Costa Mesa Police Department and Katherine worked as a registered nurse. Jeffrey enrolled in law school at night. While in law school, he continued working as a police officer. He had no plans to take the bar exam and become an attorney. He also felt that he had wasted his time in college, and he wanted to go to law school to further his education, not for financial gain. Katherine and Jeffrey separated while he has still in law school. Jeffrey had financed law school with a student loan and with their earnings. The community contributions to tuition and other educational expenses were over $12,000. Katherine sought reimbursement for the community contributions.

In the actual case based on these facts, *Marriage of Graham*, 109 Cal. App. 4th 1321, 135 Cal. Rptr. 2d 685 (2003), the issue was whether Jeffrey's education was one that "substantially enhanced" his earning capacity. The trial court concluded that it did not, and the Court of Appeal affirmed that conclusion. The Court reasoned that the enhancement of Jeffrey's earning capacity was questionable at that stage of Jeffrey's education, and it was too speculative "to try to figure out whether he is going to make more money in the future, and he may or he may not." *Id.* at 1326, 135 Cal. Rptr. 2d at

688. The test used by the Court is a subjective one: Did this spouse pursue the education or training to substantially enhance his or her earning capacity? Therefore, a student spouse can defeat community reimbursement by testifying that the degree was sought for reasons other than enhancing earning capacity. It should be noted, however, that Jeffrey accepted responsibility for the student loan undertaken to finance his education.

In *Graham*, Katherine had proposed that the Court declare a law degree substantially enhances the earning capacity "as a matter of law." *Id*. The Court rejected that proposition, noting what the trial court had said: "A law degree is not a ticket to prosperity. Some people are very good at it and make money, and other people become disillusioned and they don't make any money . . . It may happen, it may not . . . ." *Id*. That comment seems to impose an additional requirement: that the earning capacity actually is enhanced by the education. That goes beyond an inquiry into whether the student's purpose was to enhance his or her earning capacity by pursuing an educational degree. It seems wiser to limit the inquiry to the student's purpose and allow the section dealing with modification of reimbursement control whether or not the educational degree has resulted in an actual benefit to the community.

Marriage of Graham stands for the proposition that the issue of whether the education or training substantially enhances the earning capacity of the student spouse will be determined on a case-by-case basis. Even though most people pursue an advanced degree to increase their opportunities for better-paying jobs, unless the particular student pursues a degree for that purpose, and it seems that the increase in earning capacity is actualized, the education will not even qualify for the reimbursement remedy. That interpretation of Family Code §2641(b)(1) could increase litigation over the intentions of each student spouse and severely limit the already limited reimbursement remedy.

Examples

Example 11 — Does Wilma Share Harry's J.D.?

Harry and Wilma married in 1979. Harry then entered law school. Harry graduated in 1982 and began practicing in Los Angeles. Tuition for law school was $10,000. (Don't laugh; everything was cheaper then!) GI educational benefits paid $5,000 of that amount. Harry took a loan for $2,000, and the remaining $3,000 was paid from Wilma's earnings. The loan was paid off in 1983 with Harry and Wilma's earnings. Wilma worked until 1984, when she became a full-time homemaker who took care of the couple's three children. Harry and Wilma separated recently. Harry's law practice has assets of $200,000, and his salary is $100,000 a year. What are Wilma's rights upon dissolution of their marriage?

Example 12 — Does Wanda Share Henry's M.D.?

Henry and Wanda married in 1999. Henry then entered medical school. Henry not only wanted to help people; he also thought that a medical degree would help provide a secure income. He graduated in 2005, and the couple moved to Oregon for his internship. Tuition for medical school was $60,000 (a bit more realistic!). Henry took a loan for $40,000, and the remaining $20,000 was paid from Wanda's earnings. Their move to Oregon cost $2,000. They stayed in Oregon until Henry finished his residency in 2009. Wanda worked full-time during that period but took a year off from 2007 to 2008 to care for their baby. When she returned to work, they incurred child care expenses of $6,000. They returned to California in 2010, and Henry took a high-paying job with a successful medical practice. They have recently separated. What are Wanda's rights upon dissolution of their marriage?

Example 13 — Will Bill Succeed?

Bill and Melinda met while they were both enrolled at Cal Tech. He majored in computer science and received his degree in 2007. He graduated with high honors and was voted "most likely to succeed" by his class. Bill's parents paid for half of his tuition, and he took a student loan for the remaining $50,000. Melinda also graduated from Cal Tech with high honors. She had attended Cal Tech with full scholarships. Bill and Melinda married two weeks after graduation. A high-tech company immediately hired Melinda. Bill started his own computer software company, which immediately started to show a profit. They used Melinda's salary to pay back part of Bill's student loan. They have recently separated, and Melinda comes to you for advice. At the time they separated, the balance on the loan was $20,000. She wants to know what rights she has to the payments she made from her salary. Advise.

Example 14 — Mary Jane Takes a Leap to Higher Education

When Peter and Mary Jane were married, they were both idealists. Peter works as a journalist doing investigative reporting and also moonlights for the San Bernardino Police Department. He feels that it is his duty to fight crime and evil. Mary Jane has always loved children and is a teacher in the San Bernardino public schools. Mary Jane already has a master's degree in education, but she thought that she could advance her career and make a greater contribution if she had an additional degree in special education. Peter and Mary Jane lived very frugally and saved for five years so that Mary Jane could pursue that special education degree. Mary Jane applied and was accepted to a special education program. She devoted two years to the degree and used their savings of $10,000 to pay for her tuition. Mary Jane also took a student loan for $15,000 to cover the remainder of the educational expenses. Mary Jane continued to work long hours at school, both teaching and studying. Peter has begun disappearing and reappearing at very odd hours. Mary Jane has begun to doubt his commitment to fight crime and evil and his commitment to their marriage. Soon after Mary Jane received her degree, they separated. She has found that there are no jobs for special education teachers at this time due to a glut of special education teachers. She comes to you for advice about how a court will assign the student loan and the savings spent on her tuition. Advise.

Explanations

Explanation 11 — Does Wilma Share Harry's J.D.?

First, we look at the payments made for Harry's education. They include $5,000 from a GI benefit, $3,000 that was paid from Wilma's earnings, and $2,000 that was paid from Harry's and Wilma's earnings. Those items must be classified as either separate or community contributions. Since the GI benefits were probably earned before Harry and Wilma married, they would be classified as separate property and not reimbursable under Family Code §2641. The $3,000 loan repayment and the $2,000 tuition payment are from spouses' earnings and are classified as community property. They are thus eligible for reimbursement to the community. Next, we determine the amount to be reimbursed to the community. Interest at the legal rate from the end of the calendar year in which the contributions were made will be added to the $5,000. Here the loan was paid in 1983, and tuition was most likely paid by 1982. Therefore, reimbursement to the community would be $5,000 plus interest at the legal rate. At divorce, the community splits the reimbursed amount, and Wilma would receive one-half.

However, Harry could argue that Wilma does not even deserve that small amount. He would argue that because the community has substantially benefited from the community contributions to his education, the reimbursed amount should be reduced (probably to zero!). He could raise the presumption by showing that the contributions were made in 1982 and 1983, clearly more than ten years before commencement of the dissolution proceedings. Wilma would not be able to rebut the presumption, because Harry's community property law practice, which is valued at $200,000, shows that the community has benefited from Harry's law degree. That practice would be an asset that is divided equally at divorce. In addition, Wilma, who worked during Harry's attainment of the law degree and is a full-time homemaker, would probably receive spousal support. This hypothetical shows that Family Code §2641 is directed specifically at the problem scenario. The statutory remedy is very limited, when the degree was earned many years prior to the divorce and the couple has significant community property.

Explanation 12—Does Wanda Share Henry's M.D.?

It is clear that a professional degree is not community property divisible at divorce. However, the statutory remedy was aimed at this particular scenario, where a couple seeks a divorce soon after the completion of the education and training. Here Henry's medical degree and training were for the purpose of substantially enhancing his earning capacity. First, he sought the degree to "provide a secure income," and second, it seems that his earning capacity was in fact enhanced because he took a "high-paying job." Therefore, it is possible that Wanda will be able to benefit from the statutory remedy in Family Code §2641.

Here, the scenario involves both a loan and community contributions to Henry's educational degree. Assuming that the loan has not been paid, the $40,000 loan will be assigned to Henry under Family Code §2641. Additional examples concerning the loan can be found in Chapter 8. The $20,000 from Wilma's earnings that paid for Henry's tuition is community property and thus subject to reimbursement to the community plus interest. It can be assumed that the $2,000 in moving expenses was paid from community funds. The question can be raised whether this is a contribution to Henry's education or training. Although Henry finished his educational degree before their move, a credible argument can be made that his internship is a requirement of his medical training, and expenses incurred as part of the training are reimbursable. These payments for moving expenses are special living expenses that relate to the educational experience itself and are not ordinary living expenses. The $6,000 child care expenses are questionable. Even though Henry's residency might also be considered part of his medical training, the child care expenses are likely to be considered ordinary living expenses that a couple with a child would incur. A weak argument could be made that if Henry was not a medical resident, he could have taken care of their baby and thus not incurred child care expenses. However, with most couples today in the work force, child care expenses are likely to be considered ordinary living expenses that are not reimbursable.

The $20,000 tuition payment and the $2,000 payment for moving expenses would be considered community contributions to Henry's education. The community would be reimbursed for $22,000 plus interest. That means that Henry and Wanda would each receive $11,000 and one-half of the interest as calculated. Remember that even though the tuition payments came from Wanda's earnings, they are community in character, and it is the community that is reimbursed under the statute. This seems to cushion the blow for Henry, who will be assigned the loan, and is some consolation to Wanda, who will not be sharing in Henry's enhanced earning capacity.

It is doubtful that either Henry or Wanda can argue an injustice, because the presumption applicable here is that the community has not substantially benefited from community contributions made less than ten years before the commencement of the proceedings. Here the contributions were made between 1999 and 2005. Although Henry and Wanda both earned salaries while Henry was an intern and resident, it is doubtful that they were able to accumulate any significant community property even though Henry has a high-paying job. Because Wanda worked throughout her marriage, except for the year she took off to care for their baby, it is unlikely that she will be eligible to receive spousal support. The statutory remedy provides some monetary solace for Wanda's disappointment in not sharing in the fruits of Henry's education.

Explanation 13 — Will Bill Succeed?

Although there are no specific facts regarding why Bill sought his educational degree, a court could find that it is a degree that in this case has substantially enhanced Bill's earning capacity. The company that he started has already started to show a profit. Therefore, there is a good possibility that Melinda could benefit from the statutory remedy in Family Code §2641. Community contributions to education and training include "payments made with community property . . . for repayment of a loan for education or training." Family Code §2641(a). Therefore, the community will be reimbursed for those payments. Here, Melinda's salary is considered community property, and $30,000 of her salary repaid Bill's student loan. The community is entitled to reimbursement, and Melinda would be entitled to $15,000 plus interest as calculated.

Two questions arise concerning the loan, because Bill incurred the loan *prior* to their marriage. The issues involve (1) reimbursement of community contributions and (2) assignment of the loan. Community property contributions to repayment of an educational loan can be reimbursed, even if the loan was incurred prior to marriage, according to *Marriage of Weiner*, 105 Cal. App. 3d 235, 129 Cal. Rptr. 2d 288 (2003). The second issue presents a slight problem, since Family Code §2641(b)(2) refers to loans "incurred during marriage" and specifies that those loans "shall be assigned for payment by the party [student spouse]." Since this loan was not incurred *during* their marriage, who will be responsible for the loan? Common sense tells us that Bill should be assigned the loan. Common sense in this case is correct. The part of the Family Code dealing with division of debts at dissolution of marriage provides that "debts incurred by either spouse before the date of marriage shall be confirmed without offset to the spouse who incurred the debt." Family Code §2621. More extensive treatment of division of debts is found in Chapter 8.

Explanation 14—Mary Jane Takes a Leap to Higher Education

The first issue would be whether the education Mary Jane pursued is eligible for the reimbursement remedy. The education must be one that "substantially enhances the earning capacity" of the student spouse. According to the *Graham* case, that issue is decided on a case-by-case basis, focusing mainly on the reason the student spouse pursued the education. Mary Jane pursued the special education degree to enhance her earning capacity. So from Mary Jane's point of view, that was why she wanted the degree. If the court adopts the rationale that Mary Jane's purpose in pursuing the degree controls, then she would have a right to one-half of the community contributions to her tuition, $5,000.

However, both the statutory language and the *Graham* Court seem to indicate that the education or training must *actually* enhance the earning capacity. It must not be "speculative." Here it is clear that the special education degree did not at the present time enhance her earning capacity. The jobs for special education teachers are limited, and she is still in the same position she was before she attained the degree. On the one hand, because her education did not actually enhance her earning capacity, then her reason for pursuing the degree may not be sufficient to consider the education one that substantially enhances her earning capacity. On the other hand, if jobs in the field of special education do materialize in the future, Mary Jane would be qualified for those jobs. She could argue that the education has enhanced her earning *capacity*, but that potential earning capacity has not yet been actualized. It is not easy to predict whether the education meets the criterion of one that substantially enhances the earning capacity of the student spouse. If the court takes the view that the education must actually enhance earning capacity of the student spouse, it will be much more difficult to qualify for the reimbursement remedy.

This scenario underlines that the remedy is for the community—both spouses. In prior hypothetical scenarios, it was the supporting spouse who sought the remedy of reimbursement. Here the student spouse who is left with a degree that at the present time has no economic value is trying to recoup some of the expenses. It is questionable how a court will view that spouse. Perhaps the attitude would be that a spouse who makes a wrong decision about the economic advantage of the degree has no right to complain later about the expense of the education.

Even if Mary Jane is not eligible for the reimbursement remedy, Family Code §2641(b)(2) mandates that Mary Jane be assigned the student loan. Family Code §2641(b)(2) states that the loan for the education "shall be assigned for payment by the party [student spouse]." Mary Jane seems to have a degree that has not actually enhanced her earning capacity, yet she ends up owing a substantial amount of money. Where are truth and justice and the American Way?

Now go back and reread Family Code §2641(c)(1). Please note that both the reimbursement and *assignment* "shall be reduced or modified to the extent circumstances render such a disposition unjust." Here, even if Mary Jane is not eligible for the reimbursement remedy, because the education is not one that substantially enhanced her earning capacity, there is an argument that it would be unjust to assign the entire loan to her. It would seem that a sympathetic court has the discretion to modify the assignment of the loan and split the amount owed between Peter and Mary Jane. Would such an argument fly? Peter would argue strongly against that outcome. Mary Jane has the education, which has intrinsic value. After their divorce, Mary Jane will have the special education degree and may be able to benefit in the future from that education. Peter will not benefit from that degree at all. Therefore, he should not be saddled with that debt. He would argue that the educational benefit belongs to Mary Jane and so should the obligation for the loan that financed that education. The clear language of the statute would probably support Peter.

PENSIONS

Often a couple has limited assets when only one spouse works outside the home: a home, two cars, and the pension of the spouse who works outside the home. At divorce, the spouse who worked outside the home will feel entitled to that pension and is unwilling to share the pension with the other spouse. The spouse who stayed at home will feel that it is unfair for the spouse who worked outside the home to walk away from the marriage with both earning capacity and the fruits of the earnings—the pension.

Pension Vocabulary

The courts struggled with how to deal with pensions, especially when they were still an intangible right that ripened into tangible dollars only upon retirement. It is necessary to define the vocabulary used to describe pensions before explaining the rights to pensions at divorce. It would seem that everyone knows what a pension is, but legally it is not so easy to define. Is it "deferred compensation"? Is it "savings for retirement"? Is it a "fringe benefit"? Is it "insurance against income loss due to retirement"?

If you answered "yes" to all of the above, you are correct. A pension can be defined as deferred compensation. Earnings or payment for work can be deferred until a certain date such as retirement. Therefore, if compensation is earned during marriage but paid at a later date, that type of pension would be considered community property and be divisible at divorce. A pension can also be looked at as savings for retirement. If a worker took part of her salary each month and put it in a savings account for the purpose of having money at retirement, that is also similar to a pension. Taking money from earnings for payment later can also be considered community property if earned during marriage. Under that definition, retirement savings are also subject to division at divorce. A pension is also considered a fringe benefit if an employer pays part of that pension. That is a very broad definition, because many fringe benefits such as health insurance paid by an employer would not be considered property divisible at divorce. However, if a pension benefit is offered by an employer as an inducement to become an employee, it could be viewed as compensation that may be divisible at divorce. The last definition, insurance against income loss due to retirement, is based on the idea that a pension replaces earnings once an employee no longer is working. This is comparable to disability benefits that replace earnings when an employee can no longer work due to a disability. Under that definition, it is possible to argue that the pension should belong to the worker, because that worker is no longer working. In conclusion, there are many ways to define a pension but most include the concept that "if earned during marriage, a pension is considered community property divisible at divorce."

Vested/Unvested Pensions: *Marriage of Brown*

Additional terms are also necessary to understand the law regarding pensions. It is important to learn the difference between a "vested" and an "unvested" pension and what it means for a pension to "mature." Many pensions require a period of employment before the pension "vests." If an employee leaves her employment before the pension "vests," there are no rights accruing from the pension. In other words, the employee must work for some period of time before gaining any pension rights. In the landmark case of *Marriage of Brown*, 15 Cal. 3d 838, 544 P.2d 561, 126 Cal. Rptr. 633 (1976), the California Supreme Court defined the term "vested" as "a pension right which survives the discharge or voluntary termination of the employee." Clearly, vested pension rights, if earned during marriage, are community property that are subject to division at divorce.

There is a possibility that an unvested pension may never vest, for example, if the employee quits or is fired before the pension vests. There is also the possibility that an employee may divorce prior to the pension vesting. That was the issue in the *Brown* case. By the time Gloria and Robert Brown separated, Robert had accumulated only 72 of the 78 "points" necessary for the vesting of his pension. Thus, his pension was an "unvested" pension. He had no absolute rights to the pension. If he had been discharged from his employment, he would have forfeited his pension rights. Prior law had described an unvested pension as a "mere expectancy," because there was a possibility that the pension would never vest. The *Brown* Court redefined an unvested pension as a "contingent interest in property." This definition only helps slightly, since an unvested pension is still contingent upon continued employment. But the Court distinguished the two by saying that an expectancy does not rise to the level of any "interest," but a contingent interest is still a "right," even if it is a contingent right.

That distinction is rather unsatisfying. The real point of the *Brown* case is that characterizing an unvested pension as a "mere expectancy" would "result in an inequitable division of community assets." *Id.* at 847, 544 P.2d at 566, 126 Cal. Rptr. at 638. Robert Brown had worked for 24 years and was two years away from his pension vesting at the time of the couple's separation. According to the Court, if the mere expectancy definition of the pension was used, those 24 years of community effort would "escape division by the court as a community asset." *Id.* at 847, 544 P.2d at 566, 126 Cal. Rptr. at 638. If the unvested pension escaped division, then that would violate the "fundamental principle that property attributable to community earnings must be divided equally when the community is dissolved." *Id.* Gloria would be deprived of what the Court considered her fair share of the community efforts if the pension were not considered community property divisible at divorce. Thus the *Brown* Court overruled prior precedent and declared that pension rights, "whether vested or not vested, comprise a property interest of the community and that the [spouse] may properly share in it." *Id.*

Matured/Unmatured Pensions: *Marriage of Gillmore*

Even though a pension has vested, meaning that an employee has a right to it even if the employment may terminate, it may not yet have matured. A pension has matured when it provides an unconditional right to immediate payment. Usually, a pension matures when an employee reaches the eligible age for retirement. However, an employee may decide to continue working even though the employee is eligible to retire. For instance, take the example of Vera and Earl Gillmore. Earl became eligible to retire soon after the couple's marriage was dissolved. Because he was young and healthy, Earl decided to continue to work rather than retire. Vera requested that the court order Earl to pay her share of the pension benefits even though Earl had not retired and was not planning to retire. Earl's pension was both vested and had matured so there was no doubt that Vera had a right to the pension as community property. The question was whether she had a right to it immediately. The California Supreme Court, in *Marriage of Gillmore*, 29 Cal. 3d 418,

629 P.2d 1, 174 Cal. Rptr. 493 (1981), answered that she did. The Court recognized that Earl was in control of when he would retire. It is clear that Earl could try to deprive Vera of her community property rights by choosing not to retire. The Court held that "It is 'settled principle that one spouse cannot, by invoking a condition wholly with his control, defeat the community interest of the other spouse.'" *Id.* at 423, 629 P.2d at 4, 174 Cal. Rptr. at 496. Thus, the trial court was ordered to distribute to Vera her share of Earl's retirement benefits. Earl would be required to pay Vera her share until he retired. Also Vera's share becomes "fixed" and does not increase as Earl's pension rights increase. Vera does, however, share in cost of living increases added to Earl's pension rights. *Marriage of Castle*, 186 Cal. App. 3d 206, 216, 225 Cal. Rptr. 382, 388 (1986).

Enhanced Retirement Benefits: *Marriage of Green*

The question of how to characterize additional retirement benefits offered to an employee has presented difficulties for the courts. The most recent case presents both clear facts and a clear answer. That case is *Marriage of Green*, 56 Cal. 4th 1130, 302 P.3d 562, 158 Cal. Rptr. 3d 247 (2013). Husband Timothy served in the military and became employed as a firefighter before he married Julie. His employer, the Fire Authority, participated in CalPERS, the state retirement system. CalPERS gave Timothy the right to buy additional credit toward his retirement benefits based on his military service. That additional credit was purchased with community funds.

The issue in the couple's divorce was whether the additional credit for Timothy's military service was separate or community property. The trial court held that the military service credit was Timothy's separate property and ordered that Timothy pay Julie one-half of the payments made with community funds toward the purchase of the additional credit. The trial court's decision regarding the character of the military service credit was based on timing: The military service occurred before he was married. The Court of Appeal reversed based on the funds: The military service credits were paid for with community funds during the marriage. The Supreme Court quoted from *Marriage of Lehman*, 18 Cal. 4th 169, 183, 955 P.2d 451, 74 Cal. Rptr. 2d 825 (1998), explaining, "What is determinative is the single concrete fact of time. To the extent—and only to the extent—that an employee spouse accrues a right to property during marriage before separation, the property in question is a community asset." *Marriage of Green*, 56 Cal. 4th at 1135, 302 P.3d at 565, 158 Cal. Rptr. 3d at 251. The rule, therefore, is that enhanced retirement benefits "are characterized in accordance with the employee's marital status at the time the service were rendered: i.e., the benefits are community to the extent attributable to employment during marriage." *Id.* at 1138, 302 P.3d at 567, 158 Cal. Rptr. 3d at 253. Because Timothy's military service was before the marriage, the military service credit was his separate property. Thus timing of the service that leads to the enhanced retirement benefits is crucial to determining the character of the additional benefit. Also, the Court upheld the trial court's reimbursement of one-half of the community funds used to purchase the additional service credit.

Justice Werdegar, in her concurring opinion, noted that Timothy served in the military and was employed as a firefighter before he married Julie. She raised the "more difficult question" of how to characterize the additional service credit "if the parties had married before husband began working as a local firefighter." *Id.* at 1143, 302 P.3d at 571, 158 Cal. Rptr. 3d at 257. The difficulty is that the employee has no right to any pension benefits until he becomes employed. If Timothy had been married when he was employed as a firefighter, "should the credits' characterization be governed by the employee's marital status when he *earned* them through his military service, or by his marital status when he *acquired a property right* to obtain them by virtue of employment . . .?" *Id.* On the one hand, the marital status at the time of the military service can potentially lead to fair results by apportioning the credit for time before and after marriage. On the other hand, using the time employment begins as the determinative date would lead the additional credit to be characterized as community property. Justice Werdegar left the question open since, in this case, both the service credit and the employment occurred prior to the marriage.

Disability Benefits

The issue regarding characterization of pensions is more complicated when the employee spouse is disabled and then retires. Disability benefits serve two purposes: (1) to compensate for the personal suffering caused by the disability, and (2) to compensate for the loss of earnings resulting from the disability. When an employee spouse continues working until retirement, even after becoming disabled, then the retirement benefits may not be solely for personal suffering and loss of earnings. The retirement benefits may accrue because the spouse "earned" them. Thinking in community property terms, we can see the complication. "Personal suffering" and "loss of earnings attributable to the disability" fall on the disabled spouse alone and thus could be considered his or her separate property. If an employee spouse continues working, the time and effort that results in retirement benefits would be considered community property. How then is a court to characterize and divide benefits that a spouse receives that are both "disability" and "retirement" benefits?

Marriage of Stenquist

The major case that addressed these issues was *Marriage of Stenquist*, 21 Cal. 3d 779, 582 P.2d 96, 148 Cal. Rptr. 9 (1978). Like many cases on this topic, the husband served in the military and was injured. The Stenquists married in 1950 after the husband had been in the Army for six years. In 1953, he suffered an injury that left him 80% disabled. Yet he continued to serve in the military until he retired in 1970. Upon retirement, he was entitled to choose regular retirement pay or disability pay. Retirement pay was paid at the rate of 65% of his basic pay; disability pay was paid at the rate of 75% of his basic pay. He began to receive the higher disability pay.

In 1974, the husband sought a divorce. The trial court apportioned his disability pay. The first apportionment was by time: The pension rights attributable to the time before he married were considered his separate property. The second apportionment was by type of benefit: The pension rights attributable to his disability were considered his separate property; the pension rights attributable to ordinary pension rights earned during marriage were considered community property. The community property was divided equally between the spouses. The husband appealed, arguing that the entire pay was his separate property. He lost.

The California Supreme Court used two rationales to support its decision to affirm the trial court. First, the Court recognized that the spouse's power to elect "disability" pay over "retirement" pay had the potential to defeat the community interest in the pension. Characterizing disability pay as separate property "would violate the settled principle that one spouse cannot, by invoking a condition wholly within his control, defeat the community interest of the other spouse." *Id.* at 786, 582 P.2d at 100, 148 Cal. Rptr. at 13. Second, the Court noted that the label "disability" was a misleading label. "Disability" pay "is primarily to compensate the disabled veteran for 'the loss of earnings resulting from his compelled premature military retirement and from diminished ability to compete in the civilian job market' and secondarily to compensate him for the personal suffering caused by the disability." *Id.* at 787, 582 P.2d at 101, 148 Cal. Rptr. at 14. In this case, the husband's benefits were partially for those reasons and partially "retirement" pay based on his length of service and his rank in the military. Therefore, the trial court was correct in allocating only the "additional" pay attributable to the husband's disability as his separate property. The Court approved the formula in *Marriage of Mueller*, 70 Cal. App. 3d 66, 71, 137 Cal. Rptr. 129, 132 (1977): "only the net amount thus received over and above what would have been received as retirement benefits constitutes compensation for personal anguish and loss of earning capacity, and is, thus, the employee spouse's separate property. The amount received in lieu of matured retirement benefits remains community property subject to division on dissolution." *Stenquist*, 21 Cal. 3d at 788, 582 P.2d at 101, 148 Cal. Rptr. at 14. Thus the apportionment of benefits is not only by time—before marriage/during marriage—but also by type of benefit—retirement/disability.

It is important to note that federal law preempts community property law for many federally authorized benefits. For instance, pension benefits of railway workers are owned by the retired worker rather than treated as community property. *Hisquierdo v. Hisquierdo*, 439 U.S. 572 (1979). Military retirement benefits, however, are treated according to state law, except for disability pay. Thus, disability pay elected instead of retirement pay is controlled by federal law. *Mansell v. Mansell*, 490 U.S. 581 (1989).

Marriage of Saslow/Elfmont

Although most disability cases arose in the context of the military services, more recent cases have involved the private sector when a spouse purchased disability insurance. Again, apportionments by time and type of benefit were major determinants of the character of the disability benefit. The first major case that addressed this issue was *Marriage of Saslow*, 40 Cal. 3d 848, 710 P.2d 346, 221 Cal. Rptr. 546 (1985). The husband had purchased disability policies with community funds and, during the marriage, became disabled. A few years after he began collecting benefits, he and his wife divorced. The question was whether the disability benefits were the husband's separate property or community property. The Supreme Court struggled with applying the *Stenquist* analysis to the private sector. It was unclear how to apportion the benefits between community property and separate property. Because the policies were purchased with community funds, the benefits could be considered community property. Because the purpose of the policies was to provide the disabled spouse with lost earnings caused by the disability, the benefits could be separate property. Because the husband, a physician, did not have a retirement or pension plan, the disability policies seemed to serve both purposes.

The Supreme Court acknowledged the difficulty of determining whether disability insurance was also to serve as retirement income. How should a trial court know? The Court held that the spouses' intent controlled. If the spouses intended that the disability insurance was to replace lost earnings resulting from the disability, the benefits would be considered separate property. If the spouses intended that the disability insurance was intended to replace retirement income, then the benefits would be considered community property and split between the spouses. This uneasy balance of spouses' intent resulted in increased difficulty in the next major case, *Marriage of Elfmont*, 9 Cal. 4th 1026, 891 P.2d 136, 39 Cal. Rptr. 2d 590 (1995).

Marriage of Elfmont also involved a physician who had purchased disability insurance during marriage with community funds. The factual difference from *Saslow* was that the husband did not begin to receive disability payments until about two years after the couple's dissolution proceedings commenced. Therefore, the payments after the couple separated were made with his earnings, which were separate property. Although the trial court determined that the disability benefits were community property, that determination was reversed on appeal. The determining factor, according to the Supreme Court majority opinion, was that the husband renewed the disability policies after separation with separate property funds and that at that time the husband did not intend to provide the community with retirement income. *Id.* at 1032, 891 P.2d at 140, 39 Cal. Rptr. 2d at 595.

The Supreme Court was not unanimous. Justice Baxter concurred that the disability benefits were the husband's separate property, but he believed that *Saslow* was wrongly decided and should be overruled. His point was that the analogy to military pensions was faulty: Disability insurance is solely to replace lost earnings, because the insured is disabled. Thus, disability benefits from disability insurance would, according to Justice Baxter, replace lost earnings of the disabled spouse, and trying to determine whether some of those benefits are for retirement "simply makes no sense." *Id.* at 1037, 891 P.2d at 144, 39 Cal. Rptr. at 598. Chief Justice George (then Associate Justice) concurred and dissented. He concurred that the husband's benefits were his separate property, but he thought that there should be some remedy for the community because the "right to renew" the disability policies had been acquired with community funds during marriage. His remedy was to reimburse the community for the value at separation of the community's contractual right to renew the disability policies. *Id.* at 1038, 891 P.2d at 145, 39 Cal. Rptr. at 599. Justice Kennard, in dissent, took a completely different tack. She supported *Saslow*'s rationale and would have applied it to this case. Thus, to the extent that the spouses intended the disability policies to provide for retirement income, "the policy proceeds are community property, in an amount proportional to the percentage of the policy premiums paid for with community funds." *Id.* at 1044, 891 P.2d at 149, 39 Cal. Rptr. at 603.

The lower courts (and we who are trying to master this area of community property law) are left to deal with several views of disability benefits. In this one case, *Marriage of Elfmont*, we can see several concepts articulated. The first is that of the majority, where the timing and the funds are paramount: acquisitions after separation with separate property funds are characterized as separate property. The second is that even if there is a characterization as separate property, there should be reimbursement of community funds. The third is that property should be apportioned according to the proportion of funds invested, resulting in property that is part separate/ part community property.

The most recent case addressing the issue of private disability benefits followed the *Elfmont* majority view based on the timing of the purchase of the benefits and the funds used. *Marriage of Rossin*, 172 Cal. App. 4th 725, 91 Cal. Rptr. 3d 427 (2009). In *Rossin*, the wife, who was a pediatrician, purchased a private disability policy about nine years before her marriage. She became disabled about three years before her marriage and began to receive benefits. Once she was disabled, no further premium payments were required. After she married, she continued to receive the benefits. In the divorce proceedings, the husband claimed part of the benefits since they were received during marriage. The trial court, relying on *Saslow*, determined that the benefits were community property.

The Court of Appeal reversed and followed the reasoning of the *Elfmont* majority. The Court concluded that the disability benefits paid during marriage were her separate property, because she acquired the right to those benefits prior to the marriage without any contribution from the community. The policy was acquired prior to the marriage using her earnings that were separate property. She started to receive the benefits before the marriage. Thus, the timing and funds were essential: "The pivotal factor is the time of acquisition of the right to the benefits; a secondary consideration here is the source of the funds for acquisition." *Id.* at 735, 91 Cal. Rptr. 3d at 434.

The Court considered *Rossin* to be an issue of first impression because the rights to the disability benefits were acquired prior to marriage. However, *Rossin* follows the trend that the most significant fact is when the private disability policy was acquired and benefits paid. In *Saslow*, the benefits were purchased and received during marriage; in *Elfmont*, the benefits were purchased and received after separation; in *Rossin*, the benefits were purchased and received before marriage. It seems that the courts are developing rules based on tracing to characterize private disability benefits. The most difficult issue remains: how to characterize those purchased and received during marriage.

Severance Pay/Early Retirement Benefits

Severance Pay

Let's again visit with our hypothetical couple Harry and Wilma. Harry comes home from work at ABC Company with a very sad face. Wilma sees him and asks, "What happened at work today?" Harry replies, "Everyone is getting younger! I am worried about my job. With downsizing and the downturn in the economy, I do not feel very secure." The following week when Harry comes home, his face is even sadder. He explains to Wilma, "There is good news and bad news." He starts with the bad news—Harry was terminated.

Then comes the good news—Harry was offered a "severance" package that equaled one year's salary. This scenario occurred while Harry and Wilma were still married.

If Harry was terminated and received that severance package after Harry and Wilma separated, there could be an issue of whether it was community property or Harry's separate property. It is clear that community property includes employment benefits earned *during* marriage; it is also clear that separate property includes employment benefits earned *before* marriage and *after* separation. But timing is not the only determinant. As we have seen, even during marriage, disability benefits that accrue while a spouse is employed can be considered separate property of the disabled spouse. The characterization of many employment benefits, therefore, is determined not only by timing but by categorizing them either as pension benefits or disability benefits. If the employee spouse earns the benefits during marriage, those benefits are community property. If the benefits instead compensate for loss of future earnings and diminished earning capacity after separation, the benefits are separate property. Severance pay is similar to disability benefits; therefore, in Harry's case, if paid after Harry and Wilma separated, it would be considered Harry's separate property.

In *Marriage of Wright*, 140 Cal. App. 3d 342, 189 Cal. Rptr. 336 (1983), the Court of Appeal considered the characterization of "termination pay." The husband worked for San Joaquin Hospital Corporation. After he separated from his wife, he was terminated and received a lump sum of over $24,000 as termination pay. The employer knew that the husband would have difficulty securing another job due to the threats of his wife and father-in-law to "ruin him financially, professionally, and personally." During divorce proceedings, the wife claimed that the termination payment was based on services the husband rendered during marriage and thus was community property. The husband argued that the termination payment was his separate property because he received it after separation.

According to the Court of Appeal, the primary issue was characterization rather than timing. Because the termination pay was similar to disability benefits, it would be characterized as separate property. "The purpose underlying the separate property treatment of both [disability benefits and termination pay] is compensation for future loss of earnings, not payment for services previously performed." *Id.* at 344, 189 Cal. Rptr. at 337. Since the employer recognized that the husband would encounter difficulty in securing employment in the future after separating from his wife, the termination pay was his separate property.

In conclusion, employment-related benefits are characterized by analogy. If the benefits can be characterized as "earned" by the employee spouse, then the benefits will be community property if earned during marriage. Therefore, retirement benefits, even if received after separation, will be community property. If the benefits can be characterized as "replacing" future earnings, then the benefits will be separate property if received after separation. Since benefits like severance pay replace future earnings and are not tied to employee's earnings during marriage, they would be separate property.

Early Retirement Benefits

Let's return to Harry and Wilma. Let's say that Harry and Wilma separate and Harry continues to work at ABC Company. In the judgment of dissolution of their marriage, the court determines that Harry's retirement benefits are community property to the extent earned during marriage. The court retains jurisdiction to divide Harry's retirement benefits once Harry retires. After several years, ABC Company offers Harry an "early retirement package," which means that ABC Company will increase Harry's monthly retirement payment if he retires early. In our case, let's say that the early retirement benefit would increase Harry's monthly retirement payment by $700 per month.

The question then is whether this additional payment is community property or Harry's separate property. Because Harry will be entitled to and will receive the additional payment many years after he is divorced from Wilma, he thinks the $700 is his separate property. Because the early retirement benefit arose after separation, really after divorce, he will argue that it is his separate property. All that is true, but Wilma will argue that characterization is the main issue. Even though the entitlement and payment arose after separation and divorce, Harry had the right to receive the additional payment because it was "earned" during marriage, at least to some extent. Who is correct? According to the California Supreme Court, Wilma is correct.

In *Marriage of Lehman*, 18 Cal. 4th 169, 955 P.2d 451, 74 Cal. Rptr 2d 825 (1998), Jack and Marietta Lehman were haggling over Jack's "retirement benefits as enhanced." Jack and Marietta had divorced in 1977, but Jack had continued to work at Pacific Gas and Electric Company (PG&E) until 1995. Rather than terminate employees, PG&E offered "enhanced" retirement benefits to those employees who took early retirement. Jack took advantage of the offer and the "enhancement" amounted to approximately $700 added to his retirement benefit. Although it was agreed that Jack's retirement benefits were community property, the dispute revolved around the "enhancement." Jack claimed it was his separate property; Marietta claimed it was community property. The Supreme Court agreed with Marietta.

The main basis for characterizing the enhancement as community property is that the enhancement "derives" from retirement benefits earned during marriage. The Supreme Court stated the connection in several ways. For instance, the Court explained that "the right to retirement that accrues, at least in part, during marriage before separation, *underlies* any right to an enhancement." *Id.* at 179-180, 955 P.2d at 456, 74 Cal. Rptr. 2d at 829. The Court also noted, "Once he or she has accrued a right to retirement benefits, at least in part, during marriage before separation, the retirement benefits themselves are *stamped* a community asset from then on." *Id.* at 183, 955 P.2d at 459, 74 Cal. Rptr. 2d at 833. The Court bolstered its characterization by referring to the enhancement as "a *modification* of an asset not creation of a new one." *Id.* at 184, 955 P.2d at 459,74 Cal. 2d at 833. Because the enhancement could be tied to the retirement benefits earned at least in part during marriage, the enhancement was characterized as community property.

Jack argued that the enhancement was earned after separation and was in essence "severance" pay. The Court rejected the argument. First, the enhancement was termed "retirement benefits as enhanced," not severance pay. Second, the nature of the enhancement differed from severance pay, because severance pay cannot be tied to a benefit earned during marriage. The Court pointed out that in the severance cases Joe relied on, "the employee spouse had not previously accrued any right to the [benefit] whatsoever." *Id.* at 186, 955 P.2d at 461, 74 Cal. Rptr. 2d at 835. Justices Baxter and Chin were not convinced by this distinction. In Jack's case, the enhancement benefit was not tied to retirement benefits accrued during marriage. Jack's rights to the enhancement "stemmed from a separate contract between the employee and the employer, offered and accepted after the marriage ended for reasons unrelated to the former community's efforts." *Id.* at 197, 955 P.2d at 468, 76 Cal. Rptr. at 842 (Baxter, J. and Chin, J. dissenting). The enhancement was for the purpose of encouraging Jack to retire early—a reason unrelated to Jack's community efforts. Thus, the enhancement benefit could be characterized as akin to severance pay and therefore Joe's separate property.

These distinctions are not always crystal clear. The key to analysis is to remember the two categories: retirement benefits as one, and disability/ severance pay as the other. If the type of employment benefits can be tied to community efforts during marriage, it will be characterized as community property. If the benefit serves a purpose other than rewarding employment during marriage, it would not derive from employment and could then be characterized as separate property.

Examples

Example 15 — Edgar Needs to Work

Edgar and Diane married in 1990. In 1995, Edgar began working for Big Business, Inc. They recently separated. At that time, Edgar's pension had vested and was valued at $200,000. Edgar is not eligible to retire for another five years. He has no plan to retire until he is eligible. Diane has never worked outside the home and is now going to school to become a paralegal. At dissolution, what rights does Diane have in Edgar's pension?

Example 16—Edgar Wants to Work

Assume that the facts are the same as in Example 15, except that Edgar was eligible to retire from Big Business, Inc., in 2012, but decided to continue working. His retirement benefits are valued at $1,400 a month. What rights does Diane have in his pension?

Example 17—Edgar Isn't Vested Yet

Assume that the facts are the same as Example 15, except that Edgar's pension has not vested at the time that the couple separated. What rights does Diane have to Edgar's pension? If Edgar quits his job, will that have any effect on Diane's rights?

Example 18—Carol Worked, Married Bert, Then Retired

Bert and Carol were married in 1995. Carol had been working at ABC Insurance Company since 1990. Her pension vested in 2013, and she was able to retire in 2014. Her monthly pension is $1,000 a month. Unfortunately, the couple has separated. What rights does Bert have to Carol's pension?

Example 19—GI Joe Retires

Joe and Barbie married in 1995. At that time, Joe had been in the military for five years. After an additional 15 years in the military, Joe retired. In 2010, he began receiving his monthly pension benefits of $1,000 a month. Unfortunately, Joe and Barbie have separated. Assuming that military pensions are community property when earned during marriage, what rights does Barbie have to Joe's pension?

Example 20—GI Joe Is Injured and Then Retires

Joe and Barbie married in 1990, and then Joe joined the Army. He was injured while on active duty in 1995. He was given a desk job and continued to serve in the Army until he became eligible for retirement. He elected to start receiving disability pay of $1,500 a month. If Joe had retired without electing to receive disability pay, his retirement pay would have been $1,000 a month. Unfortunately, Joe and Barbie have recently separated. What rights does Barbie have to Joe's disability pay?

Example 21 — GI Joe Becomes Dr. Joe

Joe served in the Army during the Vietnam War. When he was discharged from the Army in 1975, he attended medical school and became a surgeon. He married Barbie soon after he set up his medical practice. He was successful and had a comfortable income. When one of his colleagues suffered a heart attack at age 50, he decided that he needed insurance in case he became disabled. He bought a disability policy that would provide him with $5,000 a month if he became totally disabled. The disability policy was purchased with community funds. In 2000, he was diagnosed with Parkinson's disease. He was no longer able to operate and had to abandon his medical practice. He began receiving the full disability benefits of $5,000 a month. Barbie faithfully cared for Joe since he became disabled, but Joe now seeks a divorce. What rights does Barbie have to the disability benefits?

Example 22 — Barbie Splits

Assume that the facts are the same as Example 21, except Joe and Barbie separate three years before Joe is diagnosed with Parkinson's disease. After they separate, Joe continues to pay for the disability policy from his earnings. Barbie thinks that she has a right to some of the $5,000 that Joe is receiving, because for many years community funds paid for the policy. Is she correct?

Example 23 — Meredith Is Depressed

In 2010, Meredith, who was a pediatrician, purchased a private disability insurance policy in case she became disabled and unable to work. In 2006, she was diagnosed with severe depression and had to leave the practice of medicine. That same year she began to receive full disability benefits of $6,000 a month, and she continues to receive those payments. Her policy provided that she no longer had to pay premiums once she was declared disabled.

In 2014, she met Derek and as a result they were married. Recently, Meredith's depression has become more severe, and as a result they are seeking a divorce. Derek claims that he is entitled to a portion of the disability benefits because the benefits were received during marriage and actually allowed Meredith to have retirement income. Meredith claims that the disability benefits are her separate property because she acquired the rights to them prior to marriage without any contribution from the community. Who is correct?

Example 24 — Lost and Gone Forever

Paul and Clementine, who lived in Northern California, were high school sweethearts. Soon after graduation, they married. They were both hired by the Bunyan Timber Company (BTC). Clementine worked in the billing office, and Paul worked in the logging division. BTC sent Paul all over the United States to cut timber, but mainly he worked cutting down redwoods in California. Paul worked for several years for BTC. Their marriage suffered because he was away so often. Paul and Clementine separated. After his separation, things went from bad to worse for Paul. Because of the expansion of Redwood National Park, he lost his job. However, he did receive some compensation from BTC because he lost his job. BTC did not offer a pension plan for its employees. The compensation Paul received was called "replacement pay" and was equal to six months' salary. BTC explained that it recognized his service with the company and knew that he would have difficulty finding another job. Clementine claims that she has a right to part of the replacement pay. Is she right?

Example 25 — Injured and Out

Rudy graduated from University of Notre Dame as a star on the football team. After graduation, he married Susie. He felt honored and excited to be drafted to play for the San Diego Chargers. The contract that he signed was negotiated by the Players Association and had generous provisions regarding severance pay. The amount of severance pay was based on the number of player's years in the National Football League. For about five years, Rudy sat on the bench and never played in a Chargers' game. In his sixth year on the team, at training camp, he was injured to the point that he could no longer play football. When Susie left him and filed for divorce, he became severely depressed. After their separation, Rudy received his severance pay, according to the contract provisions. Susie is claiming that she has a right to the severance pay. Is she right?

Example 26 — Merged and Purged

Shelly and Tex were married several years when Shelly landed a job at Big Oil Company. She enjoyed her work there and was an excellent employee. Unfortunately, her marriage with Tex had run dry and they separated. Soon after they separated, she was informed that the division where she worked was going to merge with another division. The likelihood was that after about two or three years her job would be eliminated. Big Oil offered all those employees affected by the merger the option of a severance allowance or continuing in their job until the merger was complete. The amount of the severance allowance was computed based on years of service and was in addition to regular pension benefits. Shelly chose the severance allowance. Tex is claiming a right to part of the severance allowance. Is he right?

Explanations

Explanation 15 — Edgar Needs to Work

Edgar's pension is vested but has not yet matured. It will mature when Edgar is eligible to retire in another five years. A vested pension, even though it has not matured, is considered community property divisible at divorce if the pension was earned during marriage. It is clear that it was earned during marriage, since Edgar was already married when he started working at Big Business, Inc. Therefore, Diane is entitled to one-half of the value of the pension at the time of divorce. Since the pension is valued at $100,000, she is entitled to $50,000.

There are various ways of ensuring that Diane receives her share of Edgar's pension. The court could value the pension and order Edgar to pay Diane a lump sum or award Diane other community property equal to her share of the pension. Another option would be to use the present valuation of the pension, and Edgar could pay Diane in installments over a period of time. It is also possible to award Diane 50% of the pension and the court to reserve jurisdiction over the case until Edgar retires and then Diane would receive 50% of the pension proceeds. If Edgar and Diane have a contentious divorce, the best option is to settle Diane's share at the time of divorce so that the couple can make a clean break and do not have to deal with each other after their marriage is dissolved.

Explanation 16 — Edgar Wants to Work

According to the *Gillmore* case, Diane is entitled to her share of Edgar's pension even if Edgar continues working. Edgar's pension is a vested pension that has matured. He has chosen to work instead of retiring. If he had retired, he would have received $1,400 a month; that amount would be considered community property, because it was earned during marriage. Edgar cannot choose to continue working for the purpose of defeating Diane's right to one-half of his pension benefits. That would be considered invoking a condition wholly within his control to defeat the community interest. The court would order Edgar to pay Diane her one-half of the community interest in retirement until Edgar retires. After he retires, she will continue to receive that "fixed" share.

Explanation 17 — Edgar Isn't Vested Yet

Edgar's pension is an unvested pension. He has not met Big Business, Inc.'s requirements for the pension to vest. If he quits his job, any rights to his pension terminate. Even though the pension is unvested, it is still community property, because during marriage he was working at Big Business, Inc. That period of community effort, even though contingent on his continued employment at Big Business, Inc., is credited to the community. Therefore, Edgar's pension is community property that is divisible at divorce. Diane is entitled to one-half of the value of his pension at the time of divorce.

It is not unusual for parties to a divorce to take actions that are ill conceived at best. For instance, there is no question that Edgar has the right to quit his job at Big Business, Inc. He might do that for spite, thinking that he could affect Diane's rights to his pension. Some might say that action would be "cutting off his nose to spite his face." After all, he would lose any potential pension rights he might have as well. The *Gillmore* Court's statement that a spouse cannot invoke a condition wholly within the spouse's control to defeat the community interest applies if Edgar would quit his job. Diane would still be entitled to one-half of the value of his pension at the time of divorce.

Explanation 18—Carol Worked, Married Bert, Then Retired

Carol's pension is an example of a pension that has matured, and she has begun receiving pension benefits. A pension that is acquired with community effort during marriage is considered community property divisible at divorce. Here the issue is that Carol was working at ABC Insurance Company for five years *before* she was married. Therefore, the part of the pension that is attributable to that time is separate property. Only the part of the pension that is attributable to community effort is community property. This is an example of *apportionment*. Here the apportionment is by time. The time period for Carol's pension to vest was 20 years. Of those 20 years, 5 were before marriage and 15 were during marriage. Therefore, one-quarter of Carol's pension (5 years divided by 20 years) is her separate property and three-quarters (15 years divided by 20 years) is community property. Carol will receive one-quarter of her monthly pension as her separate property ($250). Bert and Carol will split the three-quarters of Carol's monthly pension: Bert will receive $375 and Carol will receive $375 (one-half of $750).

Explanation 19—GI Joe Retires

Because part of Joe's military pension benefits were earned during marriage, that part will be considered community property and split between Joe and Barbie. Joe retired from the military after 20 years, but for the first 5 years of his military service, he was not married to Barbie. The military pension that was earned during that period would be Joe's separate property. Therefore, part of his pension benefits is his separate property.

We determine the proportions of separate and community property according to time married divided by time in the military. Before marriage would yield a percentage of 25% (5 years divided by 20 years). During marriage would yield a percentage of 75% (15 years divided by 20 years).

Joe's monthly pension benefits are $1,000, thus $250 is Joe's separate property, and $750 is community property. Joe and Barbie will split the community share. Joe will receive $625 ($250 as his separate property and one-half of $750, $375). Barbie will receive $375 (one-half of $750).

Explanation 20—GI Joe Is Injured and Then Retires

This example is the scenario in *Marriage of Stenquist*. There is no apportionment based on time, because Joe was married when he served in the Army. All benefits were earned while he and Barbie were married. However, Joe will argue that the disability pay is for his personal suffering from the disability and his loss of earnings because of the disability and therefore should be considered his separate property. Barbie will argue that because he continued working that his disability pay is based on his length of service, and that is community property. Both are right, but the result is not all separate property or all community property. *Stenquist* held that only the portion of the benefits that could be attributed to his disability would be his separate property; "disability" pay that could be attributed to ordinary pension rights earned during marriage would be community property. *See Mansell v. Mansell*, 490 U.S. 581 (1989).

According to these facts, the additional $500 per month that Joe receives can be attributed to disability and is thus his separate property. The $1,000 that he would have received as retirement pay would be considered community property, because it was earned during his marriage to Barbie. Therefore, Joe will receive $1,000 a month ($500 as his separate property and $500 as one-half of community property). Barbie will receive $500 a month (one-half of community property).

Explanation 21—GI Joe Becomes Dr. Joe

This scenario highlights the difficulty of the characterization process when disability benefits are paid during marriage, and then there is a divorce. It is clear that Joe needs the disability benefits, because he no longer can practice his profession, and those benefits serve as replacement for post-dissolution earnings that are separate property. It is also clear that community funds were used to purchase the disability policy, so under basic characterization principles, the policy and the proceeds would be community property. The Supreme Court in *Saslow* applied the military disability/retirement analysis to disability insurance benefits. The Court generally favored the disabled spouse, but if the spouses intended for the disability insurance to serve as retirement income, then the benefits could be considered community property.

In this case, the facts show that Joe's intention was that the policy was needed in case he became disabled. There is no indication that he and Barbie ever discussed the purpose of the policy. If the court found that the intention was that the policy serve as disability benefits, those benefits would be Joe's separate property. In our FIT analysis, we see that in this case, the *Saslow* Court opted for the *Intentions* of the parties rather than the *Funds* to control the characterization of the disability benefits.

Explanation 22 — Barbie Splits

This example tracks the *Elfmont* case. In that case, the important fact was that the *Funds* used to purchase the policy were separate property. The use of those funds and the timing of the actual purchase of the policies indicated that the husband's *Intention* was not to provide retirement benefits. In Joe and Barbie's case, a similar argument would support Joe's contention that the disability benefits are his separate property.

Barbie's arguments would have to be based on the concurrences and dissents in *Elfmont*. Her strongest argument would be based on Justice Kennard's dissent that because during their marriage the disability policies were intended to provide retirement income and were paid with community funds, the benefits should be apportioned according to the contributions of community and separate property. Even under Justice Kennard's dissent, Barbie must show that the parties intended that the disability benefits were at least in part to serve as a substitute for retirement income. If Barbie could not convince a court to accept Justice Kennard's dissent, her next argument would be based on now-Chief Justice George's concurrence and dissent. She would have to concede that Joe's disability benefits are his separate property but that the community should receive reimbursement of the value of the contractual right to renew the policy that enabled Joe to ultimately receive the benefits. Barbie should avoid Justice Baxter's ideas; they favor Joe. Disability policies are for disability and are not a replacement for retirement income. In conclusion, Barbie is wrong under the majority opinion in *Elfmont*.

Explanation 23 — Meredith Is Depressed

Meredith is correct. This example mirrors the scenario in *Marriage of Rossin*, where the wife purchased and started receiving disability benefits prior to marriage. Meredith purchased the disability policy before marriage. Therefore, the funds used were separate property. Also, she stopped paying premiums once she became disabled, which occurred prior to the marriage, so Derek is precluded from arguing that community funds were used to pay for part of the policy.

Derek's argument is based on the trial court's reasoning in *Rossin* and the reasoning of the *Saslow* case. That argument is that disability benefits received during marriage are community property if the spouses intend that they function as retirement income rather than as a replacement for lost earnings. The Court of Appeal in *Rossin* was clear that the timing and type of funds used to purchase the disability policy controlled, not the intended function of the disability benefits. The Court of Appeal avoided dealing with the thorny issue of the purpose of the disability benefits by using a tracing method to determine the character of the property. If all the facts had occurred during marriage, the Court of Appeal would have faced a more difficult decision, which in *Saslow* was determined based on the intentions of the spouses.

Explanation 24 — Lost and Gone Forever

Clementine is wrong. Her argument is she had a right to the replacement pay because it is exactly that—pay. Because it stems from Paul's employment with BTC, it is community property even though Paul received it after they separated. Paul will argue that he received it after their separation and therefore it is his separate property. The court will decide the issue based on characterization. Paul's strongest argument is that the replacement pay is like severance pay. The purpose of the replacement pay is to recognize the difficulty he will face trying to find new work in the timber industry. This argument is bolstered because BTC provided no pension plan and therefore the replacement pay was not derived from his work prior to separation from Clementine. A court would most likely side with Paul, based on the reasoning of *Marriage of Wright*. Since the replacement pay replaced future earnings and was not payment for work done for BTC, it would be considered his separate property. This hypothetical scenario is similar to *Marriage of Flockhart*, 119 Cal. App. 3d 240, 173 Cal. Rptr. 818 (1981).

Explanation 25 — Injured and Out

Maybe. Susie's first argument is that it does not matter that the Rudy's benefit is called severance pay and that he received it after they separated. Her second argument is that the benefit derives from Rudy's employment contract and is based on his years of service to the San Diego Chargers during marriage. Thus, the severance pay is in actuality a retirement benefit. Rudy's first response is that the benefit he received is called severance pay in the contract. His second argument is that the severance pay is intended to replace lost earnings suffered by those injured in the sport of football. Therefore, the severance pay is like disability benefits and is Rudy's separate property.

If the court accepts Susie's argument, then the severance pay will be considered community property. If the court accepts Rudy's argument, then the severance pay will be considered his separate property. On somewhat similar facts, the Court of Appeal in *Marriage of Horn*, 181 Cal. App. 3d 540,

226 Cal. Rptr. 666 (1986), held that a contractual right determined by years of service was a form of deferred compensation, making the severance pay a pension benefit and therefore community property. According to the Court, even though the payments were intended to help players in their transition from football to other employment, the severance pay was still community property. *Id.* at 549-550, 226 Cal. Rptr. at 672.

Explanation 26 — Merged and Purged

Maybe. Tex's first argument is that it does not matter that Shelly's benefit is called a severance allowance and that it was received after they separated. His second argument is that the allowance derives from her employment with Big Oil. He supports that argument with the fact that the allowance is calculated based on her years of service. The severance allowance is an additional pension benefit and therefore community property.

Susie will argue that the severance allowance is truly severance pay, because it is offered because of the loss of her job through the merger. It is meant to replace lost earnings in the future and is thus severance pay. Also, since the allowance is not considered part of her pension benefits, it is a separate contract made with the employer and therefore is not a retirement benefit deriving from her employment during marriage. The dissenting justices in *Marriage of Lehman* took that position. If the court accepts her arguments, the severance allowance would be her separate property. On somewhat similar facts, the Court of Appeal in *Marriage of Lawson*, 208 Cal. App. 3d 466, 256 Cal. Rptr. 283 (1989), determined that the severance allowance was separate property. The severance allowance was "a voluntary noncontractual payment made by the employer . . . intended as future replacement compensation for long-term employees pursuing new jobs or professions." *Id.* at 454, 256 Cal. Rptr. at 288.

SEPARATE PROPERTY BUSINESSES

Let us review the basics of separate property ownership. If a spouse owns property prior to marriage or receives property via gift or inheritance during marriage, that property is the spouse's separate property. Also, any rents, issues, and profits of that property are separate property. Therefore, if a spouse owns a business prior to marriage or starts a business during marriage using funds received from a gift or inheritance, then that business is separate property. According to our principles, the rents, issues, and profits of that property are also separate property. So, you say, "Thank you, that is the end of this section of the book." Not so fast!

In the situation where there is a long marriage and the major portion of the wealth comes from the separate property of one spouse, the other spouse may feel that he or she is deserving of part of the wealth accumulated from that separate property. The basis for that "feeling" is partially that after a long marriage, it seems inequitable for one spouse to walk away with all the wealth. The basis for that "feeling" is not only equity, but also the principle that effort during marriage is attributed to the community. Thus the effort that the spouse owning the separate property expended on that separate property is really "community" effort. Expending efforts on separate property does not change the nature of the property. However, if those efforts resulted in increasing the value of the property, that increase in value should be attributed to the community, and both spouses would then share in that increase in value. The spouse owning the separate property probably does not feel that way: "I came in with this wealth or inherited this wealth, and it is all mine."

The Formulas: *Pereira/Van Camp*

To accommodate the ownership interest of the separate property spouse and the share that the community may have in the increase in value of the business, two differing formulas apply. If the increase in value can be attributed to community effort, then the *Pereira* approach is used. If the increase in value is attributed to something other than community effort, the *Van Camp* approach is used. The *Pereira* approach is derived from an early case, *Pereira v. Pereira*, 156 Cal. 1, 103 P. 488 (1909), and apportions the profits of a separate property business by allocating a "fair return" on the separate property investment and allocating any "excess to the community property." The *Van Camp* approach, derived from a later case, *Van Camp v. Van Camp*, 53 Cal. App. 17, 199 P. 885 (1921), determines the "reasonable value" of the spouse's services and allocates that as community property and the remainder is separate property. Before looking at the formulas in more detail, remember that the *Pereira* approach usually favors the community, and the *Van Camp* approach usually favors the separate property owner.

Now let's explain how it works. Let's take our hypothetical couple, Harry and Wilma, and assume that Wilma owned a business before they married called Beautiful Beads. She sold all types of beads and made necklaces and bracelets to meet special orders. She started the business as a hobby and eventually opened a small shop that employed only one employee. After she married Harry, she designed a bracelet using crystal beads. It was an instant hit, and Wilma received thousands of orders for her special design. Because of that design, Wilma's business tripled in value. When they divorce, Harry claims that he should share in the increase in value in Wilma's business.

It is obvious that Wilma's business is her separate property because she owned the business before they married. However, during the marriage, Wilma's design of the bracelet was community effort, and therefore any profits attributable to that effort belong to the community, both Harry and Wilma. To accommodate both Wilma's separate property interest and the community effort, the *Pereira* approach allocates something to both. For Wilma's separate property interest, *Pereira* says that Wilma deserves some of the increase in value—it is as if she had taken her separate property and put it in a bank instead of having it invested in a separate property business. She deserves a "reasonable rate of return" on that investment as her separate property. That "reasonable rate of return" is considered the "rate of legal interest," which is 10% unless a different rate is proven appropriate. The community interest is anything over that reasonable rate of return. Since Wilma's business tripled in value due to her efforts, the community will have a greater share in that value. Wilma will keep the business as her separate property, plus the reasonable rate of return, plus her one-half share of the community interest. Although Wilma receives all that, Harry does have his one-half share in the success of Wilma's business that can be attributed to community effort.

Let's take the same scenario, except that it is not Wilma's design that causes the increase in her business. Instead, there is a fashion fad that uses a certain type of bead that Wilma happens to stock in her store. The business does increase in value, but the increase is attributable not to Wilma's efforts but to an economic circumstance. In that case, the courts are instructed to use the *Van Camp* approach. In that case, the community does deserve whatever can be attributed to community effort, but that effort is looked at in a different way. In this approach, it is assumed that Wilma's community efforts were rewarded if she received a salary. In a small business, especially a sole proprietorship, the owner does not always receive a salary but instead draws out money as needed or if available. If Wilma did receive a salary, then that is considered what the community deserved from the separate property business. If Wilma did not receive a salary, then the courts will use the reasonable salary that someone in Wilma's position would have received. The *Van Camp* approach also subtracts the community expenses from the community income to calculate the community share of the profits from the separate property business. If all the income was spent during the marriage, the remainder is all separate property that belongs to Wilma. If Harry and Wilma lived frugally, and their expenses were less than their income, then the community will split whatever remains. In most cases, there will be little to attribute to the community, and under the *Van Camp* approach, the separate property owner will receive the bulk of the increase in value as separate property.

Which Approach to Use?

One of the most contentious issues facing the trial court in these situations is which approach to use, the *Pereira* or *Van Camp* approach. We assumed in the first hypothetical that Wilma's design of the bracelet was attributable to her efforts (community), and in the second, that the fashion fad was attributable to an economic circumstance (not community). The facts are not always so clear. In *Gilmore v. Gilmore*, 45 Cal. 2d 142, 287 P.2d 769 (1955), the husband owned three car dealerships before he married. They married in 1946, and the divorce was instituted in 1952. During that time, the dealerships' value increased from about $182,000 to about $786,000. He also received salaries ranging from about $22,000 to about $67,000 during the marriage. The trial court applied the *Van Camp* approach and allocated to the community the salaries the husband received. The trial court also concluded that all that income was spent on community expenses during the marriage, and therefore the community had received its share of the increase attributable to the separate property business. Therefore, the community received its share and all the increase in value in the dealerships belonged to the husband as his separate property.

On appeal, the wife argued that the trial court should have applied the *Pereira* approach. That would have meant that the husband should have received a reasonable rate of return on his $182,000, and anything remaining should have gone to the community. If a reasonable rate of return of 7% were used, that would have resulted in $12,740 a year. Since they were married six years, that would have meant that $76,440 would have been attributed to the husband's separate property, and the remainder would have gone to the community. It would have meant that $527,560, the increase in value less the husband's separate property share, would have gone to the community share, and the wife would have received $263,780. Thus we can see that the choice of formula is significant. Under *Van Camp*, the wife receives nothing other than what was expended during the marriage; under *Pereira*, the wife receives a very large sum.

To resolve the issue of which formula to apply, the court determined why the business increased in value. In the *Gilmore* case, the major factor in determining to use the *Van Camp* formula was that in the period after World War II, there was "a tremendous increase in automobile business." Therefore, it was market conditions that caused the increase in value, not the husband's efforts. It is difficult to imagine a car dealer, here the separate property owner, arguing, "It wasn't *me*!" That's exactly the kind of evidence that was presented in the case: The dealerships employed workers who "were capable of carrying on the businesses unassisted" and that the husband "worked short hours and took many extended vacations." However, it is equally difficult to imagine the wife, who was filing for divorce, to argue that her ex-husband was "absolutely terrific" and that the dealerships increased in value because of his efforts. The Supreme Court upheld the trial court's use of the *Van Camp* approach. Beyond the actual evidence in the *Gilmore* case, there was a short marriage and a large salary for the times. Therefore, the equities of applying the *Pereira* formula were not so compelling.

It is usual that a court will use only one formula, *Pereira* or *Van Camp*, when a separate property business has increased in value. In *Marriage of Brandes*, 239 Cal. App. 4th 1461, 192 Cal. Rptr. 3d 1 (2015) (*denial of rehearing* Sept. 9, 2015) (*petition for review denied* Nov. 24, 2015), the trial court used a hybrid approach in allocating the increased value of husband Charles's separate property investment business, BIP. Between 1986 and 1991, BIP's increased value was attributed to Charles's personal efforts; therefore, the *Pereira* approach applied. Between 1992 and 2004, when BIP's managed assets increased in value from $213 million to $85 billion, the increased value was attributed to factors other than Charles's personal efforts; therefore, the *Van Camp* approach applied. Under the *Pereira* approach, the community's interest was over $3.6 million. Under the *Van Camp* approach, the community was not entitled to any additional funds because "the community had already been substantially compensated for his services. . . ." *Id.* at 1470, 192 Cal. Rptr. 3d at 7-8. Despite wife Linda's arguments for a much larger share of BIP's increased value, the Court of Appeal held that the trial court's approach was "considered and fair." *Id.* at 1478, 192 Cal. Rptr. 3d at 14. Thus, according to *Brandes*, courts may use a hybrid *Pereira/Van Camp* approach when allocating the increased value of a separate property business between the separate property owner and the community.

Examples

Example 27 — Who Owns Tofu Toots?

After Ben and Geraldine married, Ben received a $100,000 inheritance from his grandfather. Ben had always liked ice cream but was also worried about his weight and health. He read several articles about how Americans were increasingly becoming obese. He decided that there would be a market for delicious ice cream and that health-conscious customers would appreciate low-calorie ice cream made from healthy ingredients. He researched the area and consulted with food scientists, who helped him develop a delicious frozen dessert made from tofu. He used his $100,000 inheritance to start a small business manufacturing Tofu Toots. Ben spent long hours supervising every aspect of the business. Once Tofu Toots made it onto the market, it was an immediate hit. Its delicious flavor and health value spread by word of mouth, and Ben's business was very successful. Unfortunately, his marriage has not fared so well, and he and Geraldine have instituted divorce proceedings. His business is now valued at $500,000. How would the court characterize the business? How would the increase in value be allocated?

Example 28 — It Was Geraldine's Idea

Assume the same facts as Example 26, except that it was Geraldine's idea to start the business, and she was the one who did the research and developed the delicious frozen dessert. Also assume that she worked the long hours supervising every aspect of the business. How would the court characterize the business? How would the increase in value be allocated?

Example 29 — It Was Ben's Salary

Assume the same facts as Example 26, except that Ben started the business from funds he saved from his salary. Also, at the time Ben and Geraldine separated, the business is worth $100,000. However, during their separation but before the trial, the business increases in value to $500,000. Also assume that the court has determined that the increase in value was due to an article in a respected health journal explaining the benefits of Tofu Toots. How would the court characterize the business? How would the court allocate the increase in value?

Explanations

Explanation 27 — Who Owns Tofu Toots?

Ben's business is his separate property, even though it was "acquired" during marriage and therefore presumed to be community property. Ben, the separate property proponent, would be able to trace the inception of the business to his inheritance, which is his separate property. Therefore, the business is his separate property, and any rents, issues, and profits from the business would be separate property. Ben would argue that the increase in value is also his separate property.

The major issue would be which formula, *Pereira* or *Van Camp*, should the court use to allocate the increase in value. Geraldine would be arguing that it was Ben's efforts (community) that caused the increase in value, and therefore *Pereira* should be used. To bolster her argument, she would present evidence that it was Ben's idea and his research that led to the development of Tofu Toots. She could also point to the long hours he spent. Those facts all support the argument that it was community effort that caused the increase in value, and therefore the community should benefit from the effort that occurred during marriage. Ben would argue *Van Camp* should apply. He would support that argument by saying that it was the increasing health concerns of the general populace and the interest in health food that led to the increase in value of the business. His long hours were compensated by either his receiving a salary or by his drawing money from the business. In this line of argument, the increase in value resulted from factors other than his efforts; therefore, the increase in value should go to the business itself, which is Ben's separate property.

If the court decides to use the *Pereira* approach, Ben would receive a "reasonable rate of return" on his initial investment of $100,000. Using 7 percent, that would mean $7,000 a year. Assuming that the period in question was ten years, $70,000 would be attributed to Ben's separate property. That would be deducted from the $400,000 increase in value, and the remaining $330,000 would go to the community and be split between Ben and Geraldine. Geraldine would then receive $165,000, one-half of the amount allocated to the community. Ben would receive $335,000: $70,000 of the increase in value as his separate property, $165,000 as his one-half share of the community property, and $100,000 as his initial separate property investment. Please note here that community expenses are not deducted from what is attributed to the community under the *Pereira* formula. The reason is that under this formula, all community expenses have been actually paid, and there is still this large increase in value in the business left to divide.

If the court uses the *Van Camp* formula, it is necessary to determine two items: (1) Ben's actual salary or the reasonable value of his services in a comparable business and (2) the community expenses while the business was owned. Neither of these figures is provided in the example. Let us assume some figures to illustrate how the *Van Camp* formula works. Let's say that the reasonable value of the services of a person in a small manufacturing business such as Ben's is $50,000 a year. Also let's say that Ben and Geraldine lived frugally and only spent an average of $40,000 a year on their expenses. If the period in question was ten years, the court would calculate the community income as $500,000 and would deduct $400,000 in community expenses to yield the community's share as $100,000. Of that community share, Geraldine would receive $50,000. The remainder of the increase in value would go to Ben, and he would receive $450,000: $50,000 as his one-half share of the community property and $400,000 as his separate property share.

If, however, Ben and Geraldine spent $50,000 or more on their community expenses, there would be no community share at all. That would mean that the community had benefited by either a salary or by attributing the reasonable value of Ben's services to the community. Under *Pereira*, Geraldine would receive $165,000, and under *Van Camp*, she would receive $50,000 or less. Hopefully, this analysis has illustrated how *Pereira* favors the community (and thus the *spouse* of the separate property owner) and how *Van Camp* favors the separate property owner (by assuming that the *spouse* of the separate property owner has benefited by living off the separate property profits).

Explanation 28 — It Was Geraldine's Idea

The business would still be characterized as Ben's separate property. It is the funds that are used to start the business that determine the character, and here it was Ben's inheritance that started the business. Geraldine's efforts in working in Ben's separate property business would be considered community efforts, just as Ben's efforts in the business could be considered community efforts. Here, however, a court may be more sympathetic toward the community and thus lean toward using the *Pereira* approach, which would give Geraldine a greater share of the increase in value.

Explanation 29 — It Was Ben's Salary

It is clear that the business is community property. It was acquired during the marriage using community property funds. The salary earned during marriage by either spouse is considered community property. Ben's savings from those earnings are community property. The thorny question concerns the increase in value during separation. We know that the rents, issues, and profits of separate property are separate property, and the rents, issues, and profits of community property are community property. The obvious answer then would be that the increase in value is community property. However, there is the question of "when" does the community end as determining the character of income? The answer is that the determinative date is "separation." After the spouses have separated, earnings of a spouse become his or her separate property. Please see Chapter 8 for a more extensive discussion of how "separation" is determined.

If a community business increases in value after the date of separation, the courts are instructed to use what is called *reverse Pereira/Van Camp*. *See Marriage of Imperato*, 45 Cal. App. 3d 432, 119 Cal. Rptr. 590 (1975). If the increase in value can be attributed to a spouse's efforts during separation, that effort is considered *separate* effort, and the increase in value would be considered separate property. If the increase in value can be attributed to other factors, such as economic circumstances, then the increase in value is considered community property. In our scenario, Ben would try to argue that the increase in value was due to his efforts, perhaps meeting with a reporter for the health journal. Because that occurred during separation, it was his efforts, and during separation those efforts (and the earnings from them) are his separate property. Geraldine would argue that the business increased in value due to the article in the respected journal, not Ben's efforts. On these facts, Geraldine would have the better argument, and the increase in value would belong to the community.

CREDIT ACQUISITIONS

Credit is ubiquitous today. Buy a car on credit. Purchase a home with a mortgage loan. Start a business with a business loan. Advertisements for loans on television and radio abound; applications for credit cards arrive daily in the mail. It is not surprising that married couples acquire property on credit. When a married couple acquires an asset on credit during marriage and then later divorces, the characterization and remedies regarding that asset are prime targets for litigation.

Intent of Seller/Lender Test

We start with our basic understanding of the characterization process, the general community property presumption. Property acquired by either spouse during marriage is presumed to be community property. A car acquired in one spouse's name is presumed to be community property. A home acquired in one spouse's name is presumed to be community property. A business acquired during marriage is presumed to be community property. So far, so good.

The general community property presumption is rebutted by tracing to separate property funds. However, when property is acquired on *credit* during the marriage, the separate property proponent must trace by using the intent of the lender. The characterization of property acquired on credit is determined by whether the lender's intent was to rely upon the purchaser's separate property or community property for repayment of the loan. When the lender relied on community assets for repayment of the loan, the community property presumption is not rebutted, and the property will be characterized as community property.

Let's start with the scenario that was involved in two major California cases that established the test for characterization of credit acquisitions. In both cases, the acquisition concerned a business that was started during marriage. The first was a California Supreme Court case, *Gudelj v. Gudelj*, 41 Cal. 2d 202, 259 P.2d 656, that was decided in 1953. The second was a Court of Appeal case, *Marriage of Grinius*, 166 Cal. App. 3d 1179, 212 Cal. Rptr. 803, that was decided in 1985.

The California Supreme Court and the Court of Appeal used different variations of the intent of the lender test. According to the California Supreme Court in *Gudelj*, if there is no evidence showing that the lender or seller "primarily" relied on the purchaser's separate property in extending the credit, the community property presumption stands. The Court of Appeal in *Grinius* held the community property presumption may be rebutted by showing the lender intended to rely "solely" upon a spouse's separate property. It is not clear whether courts will follow the "primarily" language of the earlier Supreme Court case or the "solely" language of the later Court of Appeal case.

The *Gudelj* case involved husband John's interest in a cleaning business that was purchased during marriage. John paid for part of the business with cash and part with a note. The cash was determined to be John's separate property; the question was whether the note was also his separate property. In *Grinius*, the couple Victor and Joyce started a restaurant business with funds borrowed from a bank and the Small Business Administration (SBA). Even though the business was considered community property, there was a question about the restaurant real property that was in Victor's name and that he claimed to be his separate property.

Both cases started where we would start: The interest in the cleaning business and the restaurant real property, even though acquired through credit, were presumed to be community property. The presumption that property acquired on credit during marriage is community property is rebuttable. The separate property proponent has the burden of rebutting the presumption by tracing. When tracing to borrowed funds, "the character of property acquired by a sale upon credit is determined according to the intent of the seller to rely upon the separate property of the purchaser or upon a community asset." *Gudelj*, 41 Cal. 2d at 210, 259 P.2d at 661. If the seller "primarily" relied on the purchaser's separate property, then the community property presumption would be rebutted and the asset would be characterized as separate property. *Id.* at 210, 259 P.2d at 661.

In the *Gudelj* case, there was no testimony as to the intent of the seller. However, there was some evidence regarding the purchase of the interest in the cleaning business. Shortly before buying that interest, John received some cash that arguably was his separate property. Also, John had failed in previous cleaning businesses. He argued that it could be inferred that the seller must have relied on his separate property in selling him the interest on credit and not on his personal ability and capacity. His personal ability and capacity would be considered community in character, hardly an "asset" in John's case. However, the court decided that without evidence that the seller had actually known of John's separate property and his business failures, John's rebuttal failed. Thus, we learn that it is the seller or lender's intent that controls whether the community property presumption can be rebutted.

We also learn a seller or lender can rely on a community asset—namely, the purchaser's or borrower's creditworthiness. In John's case, he portrayed himself as not being creditworthy because of prior business failures. What does "creditworthiness" mean? A seller or lender who extends credit usually will look at many factors, including past business success, which indicates ability to repay debts and reputation for repaying debts. In other words, a seller or lender may rely on many factors in extending credit: (1) simply having separate property and/or (2) having earning ability, which would be a community asset. Under the *Gudelj* test, the seller or lender must have relied *primarily* on the spouse's separate property for the separate property proponent to succeed in rebutting the community property presumption. John failed to rebut the community property presumption regarding the note, and the note was therefore characterized as community property. Since part of the cleaning business was purchased with John's separate property cash, that part was John's separate property. Since the note was characterized as community property, that part was community property. Therefore, the interest in the cleaning business was apportioned: part John's separate property and part community property.

Primarily or Solely Is the Test?

In *Grinius*, the restaurant real property was purchased with loan funds. Victor argued that those funds were separate property, and thus the community property presumption was rebutted. The Court of Appeal, speaking 32 years after the Supreme Court in the *Gudelj* case, restated what the Court called the "intent of lender" test. Based on an examination of cases that determined why credit was extended to a borrower, the Court concluded that the characterization in all those cases depended on evidence that the lender relied *solely* on separate property. Thus, the Court restated the test: The community property presumption "may be overcome by showing the lender intended to rely solely upon a spouse's separate property and did in fact do so." *Grinius*, 166 Cal. App. 3d at 1187, 212 Cal. Rptr. at 808. The Court concluded that there was no showing that the lender had relied solely on Victor's separate property.

The Court looked at the circumstances that surrounded the loans that were used to set up the restaurant business. The real property in question was used as collateral for the loan, which means that if the loan was not paid, the property could be sold to repay the loan. That could not be used as evidence of the lender's intent, because the character of the property was neither separate nor community property at the time the loan was extended. John pointed to the conditions for receiving the SBA loan and argued that those conditions indicated that the SBA relied on his separate property in extending the loan to purchase the restaurant real property. Several of the conditions were based on the ability of the community to repay and to manage the restaurant business itself. According to the Court, that evidence demonstrated that the SBA did not rely solely on Victor's separate property; thus, Victor failed to rebut the presumption. Even if Victor could have shown that the SBA had *primarily* relied on his separate property as well as community assets (the *Gudelj* test), he would have failed to rebut the presumption, because, under the *Grinius* formulation, the SBA had to *solely* rely on his separate property. Thus the restaurant real property was characterized as community property that would be divided equally at divorce.

To summarize, the more recent test regarding credit acquisitions, even though from a Court of Appeal decision, requires that to rebut the community property presumption, the separate property proponent must show that a seller or lender relied solely on separate property in selling the property on credit or in lending the funds to purchase the property. If the seller or lender relied on both, the separate property proponent fails, and the property will be characterized as community property. Here we see that the presumption and its rebuttal favor a finding that a credit acquisition during marriage will be considered community property.

Separate Property Loan/Community Property Repayment

California courts have dealt with one complex yet common scenario involving credit acquisitions. The scenario arises where a person acquires property prior to marriage on credit. Then that person marries. During the marriage, community property is used to pay back the loan on the property. In the event of divorce, the issue is whether the community property contributions represent acquisition of an interest in the property or merely will provide a right to reimbursement of the community funds used to pay back the loan. Acquiring an interest in the property means that the property will be apportioned part separate property/part community property, giving the community a share in any increase in the property's value. Reimbursement means that the community will receive the funds used to reduce the loan but no share in any increase in the property's value. In this type of scenario, the spouse who owned the property before marriage would argue that the community does not acquire any interest in the property by providing funds to reduce the loan. The other spouse would argue that the community has acquired part of the property by providing funds to reduce the loan. The answer is that the community gains an interest in the property. Details of how to calculate that formula are discussed below.

A secondary issue arises in this scenario, because payments on a loan, particularly a mortgage loan, include both principal and interest, and in some cases, also taxes and insurance. Another factor is that each payment on a mortgage loan is allocated between principal and interest and amortized over the life of the loan. That means that at the beginning of a mortgage loan, the greatest percentage of the payment is for interest, and the smallest percentage is for principal. At the end of a mortgage loan, the allocation will have shifted so that the greatest percentage of the payment is for principal, and the smallest percentage is for interest. The reasons for this allocation are twofold: (1) The lender receives the majority of the interest on the mortgage loan at the beginning of the repayment period, and (2) the borrower will usually be able to use the interest portion of the payment as an income tax deduction. Because of this allocation, any payments of principal will be small in the early years of a mortgage loan. If only payments of principal are considered in determining the community's interest in the property, the community would gain a very small interest in the property. If both principal and interest payments are considered in determining the community's interest in the property, the community would gain a much larger interest in the property. The spouse who purchased the property before marriage would argue that only principal payments should be considered. The other spouse would argue that both principal and interest payments should be considered. Please note that we are using the word "interest" in two different ways: (1) payments of "interest" charged by the lender of the loan, and (2) acquisition by the community of an "interest" in the property.

Marriage of Moore

Let's now turn to the major case that decided these issues, *Marriage of Moore*, 28 Cal. 3d 366, 618 P.2d 208, 168 Cal. Rptr. 662 (1980). The Court stated the issue as follows:

> The principal issue to be decided in this case is the proper method of calculating the interest obtained by the community as a result of payments made during marriage on the indebtedness secured by a deed of trust on a residence which had been purchased by one of the parties before marriage.

Id. at 369-370, 618 P.2d at 209, 168 Cal. Rptr. at 663.

Lydie Moore had bought a house about eight months before she married David. She took the title in her name alone, as a single woman. She purchased the house for approximately $57,000 and made a down payment of approximately $17,000. She secured a mortgage loan to purchase the house. Prior to marriage, Lydie made payments on the loan, and the principal had been reduced by approximately $250.

At this point, let us stop and try to characterize the house itself and the loan used to purchase the house. Lydie purchased the house before marriage; therefore, it would be characterized as her separate property. The loan would also be characterized as her separate property, because it was acquired prior to marriage. Since Lydie was then unmarried, the lender must have been relying on *her* credit and *her* ability to repay the loan when deciding to grant the loan. Lydie's creditworthiness would be her separate property because creditworthiness before marriage is considered separate in character. Also, the principal payments would be separate property even if they came from her earnings—earnings prior to marriage are separate property. So our conclusion so far is that the house and the loan are Lydie's separate property.

David and Lydie lived in the house during their marriage until they separated almost ten years later. While they were married, they made payments on the loan from community funds, and the loan principal was reduced by almost $6,000. Also, the house had appreciated in value; the market value of the house was determined to be $160,000. If the house was considered to be Lydie's separate property in its entirety, then Lydie would have been entitled to all of the increase in the house's value. If the community acquired an interest in the property via the community funds that reduced the principal of the loan, the community would have some proportional share in the increase in the house's value. David and Lydie would each be entitled to one-half of the community share in the increase in value.

David argued that the community acquired an interest. Both the trial court and the California Supreme Court in *Moore* accepted that argument. That was the easy part. The more difficult issues involved how to calculate the community's interest and also whether interest payments on the loan and taxes would be considered in the calculation as well as the payments of principal on the loan. The trial court accepted a calculation of the community's interest in the property that favored David. That community interest was calculated using a ratio: the ratio that community funds bore to the total funds that reduced the principal of the loan. Lydie's separate interest was calculated by the ratio that separate funds bore to the total funds that reduced the principal of the loan. In this case, the principal had been reduced by almost $24,000, $6,000 attributed to the community funds and $18,000 attributed to Lydie's separate funds—the down payment and principal payments she made before marriage and after separation. Therefore, under the trial court's calculation, the community had an interest in the property of 25% ($6,000/$24,000), and Lydie had a separate property interest of 75% in the property ($18,000/$24,000). That percentage was then multiplied by the value of the property after deducting the amount owed to the bank. The community interest was $32,000 and Lydie's separate property interest was $94,000 of the $126,000 that remained after deducting the loan balance. David would receive one-half of the community interest, $16,000; Lydie would receive the other half, $16,000, plus her separate property interest, $94,000.

Although the calculation favored David, the trial court rejected David's argument that the payments of interest and taxes should be included in the calculation of the community interest. David appealed that part of the decision. The appeal was unsuccessful. He even received a surprise when the Supreme Court modified the method for calculating the community interest in the property. The case that he relied on to support his argument that the payments of interest and taxes should be included in the calculation of the community also stated that the community interest would be "only to the extent and in proportion that the *purchase price* is contributed by the community." *Id.* at 371, 618 P.2d at 210, 168 Cal. Rptr. at 664, citing to *Vieux v.Vieux*, 80 Cal.App. 222, 229, 251 P. 640, 643 (1926). The trial court, therefore, incorrectly formulated the ratios. The ratios are calculated based on the ratios of funds to the *purchase price*, not to the *total reduction of payments of principal*. Therefore, the calculations according to the Supreme Court yielded a much smaller community interest. The $6,000 community funds yielded a community interest of a bit more than 10% ($6,000/$57,000) and Lydie's separate interest of almost 90% ($51,000/$57,000). The $51,000 figure was reached by attributing to Lydie the down payment of $17,000 plus the $40,000 loan, and then subtracting the $6,000 of community funds. Thus, under these calculations, the community interest was almost $17,000, and Lydie's separate property interest was $110,000.[1] The result was much less favorable to David. Under these calculations, David would receive one-half of the community interest, $8,500, and Lydie would receive $118,500, her separate property interest, $110,000, plus the other one-half of the community interest. The Court noted in *Moore* that the trial court erred, because it ignored the loan itself, which was Lydie's separate property. Under the Supreme Court's formula, the community interest was greatly reduced, and Lydie's interest greatly increased. The Supreme Court's formula is the one that is used to calculate the interests in property acquired before marriage on credit with community property funds used to reduce the principal of the loan. The calculations are included to illustrate the difference the formula makes. For those students who like doing the math, great! For those students who find doing the math difficult (that is why you went to law school, isn't it?), most professors are more concerned that you understand the concepts rather than calculate the actual figures correctly.

The Supreme Court's reasoning for rejecting David's argument regarding the interest and taxes was solidly based. Even though the Court conceded that the interest and taxes paid from community funds were a substantial amount, those payments were deemed expenses, not acquisitions of property. Under that reasoning, payments for insurance on the house would also be considered an expense. They are not an "investment" in the property and cannot be included in the calculation of the community's interest in the property.

David's appeal was based on the interest and taxes argument, and he lost on appeal. But he received another surprise. Because Lydie did not appeal the trial court's calculation of the community interest, the Supreme Court did not reverse that part of the judgment. In the future, however, the calculation

---

1. The Supreme Court corrected the trial court's calculations of the value of the house and reached the above final figures.

of the community and separate interests would be the ratio the separate/community contributions that reduce principal bear to the purchase price: SP funds/purchase price and CP funds/purchase price. That ratio will produce a percentage that is the share to be attributed to the community and the separate property spouse. That ratio will be multiplied by the amount of appreciation. That figure will be added to the community funds and the separate property funds, respectively. The resulting community interest will be split between the spouses. The separate property spouse will receive the separate interest plus one-half of the community interest. The other spouse will receive the other half of the community interest.

The major points that should be remembered from *Moore* are:

1. Community funds paid to reduce the principal on a separate loan will result in the community obtaining a proportional interest in the property according to the formula established by the Supreme Court in the *Moore* case.
2. Community funds paid for interest on the separate loan and for taxes and insurance will not be included in the calculation of the community interest in the property.

Marriage of Marsden

An even more complex scenario arises when a person purchases property before marriage on credit and then marries, and community funds are used to pay back the loan. The scenario becomes more complex when the marriage comes some years after the purchase of the property. During the time between the purchase and the marriage, payments are made that reduce the principal of the loan, and the property increases in value. Then during marriage, community funds are used to reduce the principal of the loan, and the increase in value of the property is even greater. Then the couple divorces. In that case, how does a court calculate the separate property and community interests in that property?

Let's modify the David and Lydie scenario. Lydie bought a house in 1995. She took title in her name, as a single woman. The purchase price is $100,000 and she made a down payment of $20,000. She secured a mortgage loan for the remaining $80,000. Between 1995 and 2000, she made payments on the loan that reduced the principal to $70,000. Also, the house appreciated in value to $200,000. In 2000, she married David. At that point in time, the house and the loan would be considered her separate property. Also, the payments made to reduce the principal on the loan are her separate property, and the increase in value of $100,000 is her separate property because both occurred before marriage. After their marriage, payments to reduce the principal were made from community funds. At the time David and Lydie divorce, payments from community funds of

$20,000 have reduced the principal on the loan to $50,000. Also the house has appreciated in value to $500,000.

The Court in *Marriage of Marsden*, 130 Cal. App. 3d 426, 181 Cal. Rptr. 910 (1982) dealt with this scenario. The Court applied the *Moore* formula. Clearly, Lydie's separate property interest included all the contributions to reduce the loan and the increase in value of the property before marriage. To calculate the community interest, the Court used the ratio that the amount of community funds bore to the purchase price to calculate the community interest. That was $20,000/$100,000 or 20%. Then that figure was multiplied by the increase in value during marriage. That would be 20% of $300,000. That equals $60,000. Thus the community interest would be the community funds that reduced the principal ($20,000) plus the community share in the appreciation ($60,000). That total of $80,000 would be split between David and Lydie. David would receive $40,000, and the rest would belong to Lydie. (Of course, we cannot forget that the bank will still be owed whatever remains on the mortgage loan.) Clearly, the greatest contribution to the purchase of the house was Lydie's initial down payment of $20,000 and the payments before marriage of $10,000 and her share of the community funds. Because the house is considered essentially her separate property, the community will always have a comparatively small interest in the property.

An argument was made in *Marriage of Frick*, 181 Cal. App. 3d 997, 226 Cal. Rptr. 766 (1986), that the *Marsden* analysis should be modified. The husband, Jerome, was in the same situation as in our modified David and Lydie scenario. He argued that the Court should calculate the separate and community interests using the fair market value of the property at marriage rather than the initial purchase price. In our modified David and Lydie scenario, the fair market value at marriage was $200,000 and the purchase price was $100,000. Let's see how that would change the community interest based on community funds of $20,000 that reduced the principal of the loan during marriage. The ratio using the fair market value at marriage would be $20,000/$200,000 (10%); the ratio using the purchase price would be $20,000/$100,000 (20%). It is obvious that using Jerome's formula would decrease the community interest and increase his interest.

The Court of Appeal rejected Jerome's argument based on fairness. The "purchase price" ratio certainly produces a greater interest for the community. That means that the spouse who is not the owner of the property will have a greater share in the appreciation during the marriage. The Court stuck to "the method of computation that has historically been followed in this state and we believe is the appropriate one. To do as Jerome asks would give him *double* credit for premarital appreciation in the value of this property." *Id.* at 1009, 226 Cal. Rptr. at 771. What the Court meant is that Jerome would receive the benefit of the premarital appreciation both as his outright and in the calculation of the interests during marriage. That did not seem fair.

In addition, the Court reaffirmed that the ratio used in apportioning the separate and community interests is based on the purchase price and not on any other figure.

Do Time and Title Change the Outcome?

The major factor in characterizing the house involved in the David and Lydie scenario is that Lydie purchased it before marriage. As a way of reviewing the presumptions presented in Chapters 3 and 4, let us assume that the house in question was purchased during David and Lydie's marriage instead of before their marriage. We will assume Lydie purchased the house in 1966 for $100,000, and the title was in her name. We will also assume that the $20,000 down payment came from her separate property, her earnings before marriage. She also obtained a mortgage loan for $80,000. If David and Lydie divorce, the Married Woman's Special Presumption applies, because the house was acquired in a married woman's name before January 1, 1975. The presumption is that the house is Lydie's separate property. Remember that this is our only *separate property* presumption. Ordinarily, the source of the funds will not rebut that presumption. But here the funds used for the down payment were her separate property, and we will assume that the loan was also obtained based on her separate property. Those facts support the separate property presumption rather than rebut the presumption. That favors Lydie. The burden would be on David to rebut the separate property presumption. It is possible to rebut the presumption by showing either an agreement that the house was community property or that David did not intend that the house was separate property when the title was put in Lydie's name. We do not have any facts supporting that argument, so under the Married Woman's Special Presumption, the conclusion would be that the house is Lydie's separate property.

If the timing was different, and the house was purchased in 1975 or thereafter in Lydie's name, the analysis would also be different. The general community property presumption applies when property is acquired during marriage, and the title is in one spouse's name. Thus the house would be presumed to be community property, and the burden would be on Lydie to rebut that presumption by tracing to separate property funds. Assuming that she could trace to her down payment of $20,000 that came from separate property funds, at least 20% of the property would be her separate property. The other question is whether the mortgage loan would be considered her separate property. The mortgage loan would also be presumed to be community property, and under the *Grinius* test, which is extremely difficult for the separate property proponent to meet, the loan would be community property. Thus, 80% of the property would be considered community property. The house would then be considered part separate property/part community property, and any increase in value in the property would be apportioned 20% separate property and 80% community property.

Finally, what if the house was purchased after they married, and the title was taken in joint form, for instance, joint tenancy? Let us first assume that the purchase occurred in 1984 or thereafter. At divorce, Step One is characterization. The house would be presumed to be community property under Family Code §2581. That presumption can be rebutted only by a statement in the deed or title or by a written agreement. Since we have no facts regarding anything in writing, the conclusion would be that the house would be community property. Please note that we do not have a separate analysis of the character of the loan—the characterization of the house includes the loan when the title is taken in joint form. Since the house was characterized as community property at Step One, at Step Two, Family Code §2640 applies, and Lydie will claim a right to reimbursement of the $20,000 down payment made from her separate funds. Assuming she can trace to those funds, she will receive reimbursement, but any appreciation in value will be community property and split between the spouses.

However, if the house was purchased *prior* to 1984, and David and Lydie have no agreements, the analysis will be slightly different. Again the house will be presumed to be community property—the presumption in Family Code §2581 is retroactive. However, the presumption can be rebutted by an oral or implied agreement for joint tenancy property acquired prior to 1984. Because David and Lydie had no agreements, the community property presumption becomes the conclusion. The remaining question is whether Lydie can claim reimbursement of the $20,000 separate property down payment. Under *Lucas*, a right to reimbursement can be established only by a reimbursement agreement. Here there are no agreements and Lydie's down payment is considered a gift to the community. The house is community property in its entirety and would be split in half at divorce. Because there is a mortgage loan, the amount remaining on the loan would have to be deducted from the amount the community would split.

If you were able to analyze these scenarios, you have the presumptions and time periods straight. It is complicated but not impossible to master! If you had trouble with these scenarios, go back and review Chapters 3 and 4.

Examples

Example 30—Wood We Carve Rare Rabbits Equally?

Harvey and Beatrice Potter were married many years. Harvey was skilled at wood carving; his specialty was small rabbits in many different poses. He was very successful, and he sold his creations to many toy companies. Beatrice worked at a gift shop for many years. After Harvey received an inheritance of $20,000 from his father, they decided that they should combine their expertise and open their own shop. They applied for a business loan from their local bank where they had savings and checking accounts for over ten years. They received an $80,000 business loan from that bank. They used Harvey's inheritance and the business loan to start a business called Rare Rabbits. Initially, the business was a success, but it seems that working together put a strain on their marriage. Harvey believes that the business is his separate property because he invested his inheritance in the business. Beatrice believes that the business belongs to both of them and should be considered community property.

Harvey consults an attorney who investigates and finds that the bank officer who approved the business loan is willing to testify if the case goes to trial. In a deposition, the bank officer explains that the loan was made primarily based on Harvey's personal credit but also on his willingness to invest his separate property in the business. If Harvey and Beatrice divorce, how will the loan be characterized? How will the business be characterized and divided? You should assume that the business has neither increased nor decreased in value.

Example 31 — Love Pops Under Low-Carb Craze

When Orville met Jolly, he thought that she was the woman of his dreams. They met at a Food Expo at the popcorn exhibit, where they were both sampling the many varied and fancy popcorns. They married soon after their meeting and continued their love for all sorts of popcorn. With the recent craze for low-carb diets, Orville thought it would be a good idea to buy a farm and plant a new variety of low-carb corn that could be made into low-carb popcorn.

Before Orville and Jolly married, Orville had invested in commercial real estate and owned several parcels of land in Riverside County. He became interested in some farmland in Fresno County and purchased a 70-acre parcel of land for developing the specialized corn. The purchase of land was financed by a bank loan. The bank had demanded that one of his parcels of land in Riverside County be given as security for the loan, even though Orville had excellent credit and always repaid his loans on time. The 70-acre parcel was held in Orville's name, and the loan was also in his name.

Unfortunately, Orville and Jolly's marriage was not the dream that Orville envisioned, and he is considering a divorce. Would the 70-acre parcel be considered Orville's separate property?

Example 32 — The Princess Moves to Hollywood

Their romance sounded like a Hollywood script. In fact, Brian and Trish met while they were both on location for a film. Trish, an unknown in Hollywood, was cast as a princess locked away in the highest room of a tall tower. Only true love could set her free. For years she waited. Finally, Brian who played the role of a young brave knight came to her rescue. Reality almost imitated fantasy. She loved the damsel-in-distress role, and he loved being the bold knight rescuer; needless to say, they were a perfect match. They married immediately. Brian had been in many films prior to their marriage and had accumulated a large treasure. He lived near Hollywood. Because they heard most princesses live in Hollywood, they hoped to live happily ever after there. They soon found a castle-like home in the hills for $900,000. Brian took title to the house on Drury Lane in his name alone. Since the film with Brian was Trish's first starring role, she had no savings and many debts. Brian came to the rescue again and used $180,000 of his treasure as a down payment on the house. They obtained a loan for the rest of the purchase price.

Within a few years several movie stars bought houses on Drury Lane, causing the value of the neighborhood to skyrocket. Tourists with maps to the stars' homes were causing traffic on Drury Lane. Brian finally had enough and wanted to move. Trish refused, and that was the end of the romance. They recently filed for divorce. The house is worth an astonishing $2,700,000. The balance remaining on the loan is $432,000. The loan had been repaid from their earnings during marriage. How would the court characterize the house and the loan? Also how would the court calculate Brian's share of the house and Trish's share of the house?

Example 33 — Truffle Hunting

Tamara and Kevin met while at the annual Garlic Festival in Pomona. Tamara was in culinary school and just crazy about food. Kevin was just crazy about Tamara. A few months after they met, Tamara went to live in the Quercy region of France to hunt the elusive black truffle. Kevin had a business remodeling houses. He bought a house in Pomona in 1992 and took title in his name alone, since clearly he was unmarried at the time. The purchase price of the house was $600,000. He made a down payment of $120,000 and obtained a loan for the remaining $480,000. Kevin fixed up the house beautifully in a French country style in hopes of wooing Tamara to come back to California. Tired of waiting, Kevin flew to France and proposed to Tamara. In 1994, they married. At the time of marriage, the fair market value of the house was $650,000, and the loan balance was $440,000. When Tamara saw the house, she loved it so much that she forgot all about her dream of finding truffles. As time went on, Tamara became well known for her culinary abilities and received an offer to host *Tamara Live* on cable television. She accepted. The time constraints and dedication both had to their jobs eventually led to their separation. At divorce, the house was worth $900,000, and the balance on the loan was only $200,000. All loan payments during marriage were made from Kevin's earnings. How would you characterize the house and the loan? How would the house be apportioned between Kevin and Tamara?

Explanations

Explanation 30 — Wood We Carve Rare Rabbits Equally?

Since the Rare Rabbits business was acquired during Harvey and Beatrice's marriage, it will be presumed to be community property. Harvey, the separate property proponent, will have the burden of rebutting the presumption by tracing to separate property funds. If he can show that the $20,000 investment came from his separate property, the inheritance during marriage, that percentage of the original investment of $100,000 would be considered his separate property. That means that 20% of the business is Harvey's separate property.

The characterization of the remaining 80% of the business depends on how the business loan is characterized. The *Gudelj* rule states that the intent of the seller/lender is what controls. The *Gudelj* rule also states that if the lender relied primarily on separate property, then the loan would be separate property. The *Grinius* rule states that if the lender relied solely on separate property, then the loan would be separate property. Harvey loses under either rule. The loan officer would testify that the loan was based on Harvey's personal credit. Personal credit of a married person is *not* separate property; creditworthiness of either spouse is considered to be community in character. Even though the loan officer did base the bank's decision partially on Harvey's separate property investment, that basis clearly does not meet the *Gudelj* "primarily" rule or the stricter *Grinius* "solely" rule. Harvey could not rebut the community property presumption, and the loan would be characterized as community property. The percentage of the business that was based on the loan would be community property. In this scenario, that means that 80% of the business is community property, which would be split between Harvey and Beatrice. The lawyer would then advise Harvey that he would receive 20% of the business as his separate property and the 40%, which is one-half of the 80% that is community property.

Explanation 31 — Love Pops Under Low-Carb Craze

Again we start with the community property presumption, because the 70-acre parcel was purchased during marriage. That presumption is rebutted by tracing to separate property funds. You might have thought that his name on the deed and on the loan would have been sufficient to rebut the presumption. But remember under our FIT analysis, the title in one spouse's name does not control.

Here, the tracing to funds leads us to the loan that Orville obtained to purchase the 70-acre parcel. Therefore, it is necessary to characterize the loan to determine if the 70-acre parcel is Orville's separate property. Because the intent of the lender controls, the outcome will depend on the bank's intent in loaning Orville the money to purchase the parcel. At this point, the outcome is unclear. Orville hopes that the bank's testimony would support his argument that the bank granted the loan because some of his separate property was required as security. If the bank granted the loan because of his personal creditworthiness, which is considered a community asset, he will have difficulty rebutting the presumption. If the bank granted the loan based on both his separate property and his personal creditworthiness, again he will have difficulty rebutting the presumption. If the bank granted the loan solely based on Orville's separate property, then he could rebut the community property presumption based on either the *Gudelj* (primarily) rule or on the *Grinius* (solely) rule.

If the bank granted the loan based only on his personal creditworthiness, he could not rebut the community property presumption based on either rule. If the bank granted the loan based on both, under the *Gudelj* (primarily) rule, Orville's rebuttal would depend on which the bank primarily relied on—if the separate property, Orville can rebut; if his personal creditworthiness, he cannot. Under the *Grinius* (solely) rule, Orville cannot succeed, because obviously the bank did not rely solely on his separate property.

Under the more recent *Grinius* rule, it is exceedingly difficult to rebut the community property presumption. If Orville wanted to ensure that the property was his separate property, the best way to ensure that would be to secure an agreement from Jolly that the 70-acre parcel was his separate property, in accordance with the transmutation statute. See Chapter 2.

Explanation 32—The Princess Moves to Hollywood

The house was acquired during marriage in Brian's name alone. It is first necessary to characterize the house. The general community property presumption applies when property acquired during marriage is untitled or in one spouse's name. The title in Brian's name is not determinative. That presumption can be rebutted by tracing to separate property funds. Brian can trace the down payment to his separate property, because it came from the treasure he earned before marriage. The loan will also be presumed to be community property, because it was acquired during marriage. Brian will argue that the lender was relying on his separate property in granting the loan. There is no evidence to suggest the lender's intent, therefore the general presumption stands, and the loan is characterized as community property. The initial loan amount was $720,000. The loan was reduced by $288,000 during marriage. They used their earnings to pay down the loan, and the balance remaining is $432,000. The loan and the payments reducing the balance are community property.

To determine Brian's and the community's interests in the house, we use the *Moore* formula. Brian's separate property interest in the house is determined by dividing his separate property contribution by the purchase price of the house. Brian's only separate property contribution to the house is the $180,000 down payment ($180,000/$900,000 = 20%). Brian has a 20% separate property interest in the house. The community's interest in the house is determined the same way by dividing the community's contribution by the purchase price. Here both the loan and the repayments on the loan are community property contributions. Therefore, the community property contribution to the house was $720,000. When divided by the purchase price of $900,000, we come out with an 80% community property percent interest ($720,000/$900,000 = 80%).

Appreciation to the house is calculated by subtracting the purchase price of the house of $900,000 from the fair market value at divorce of $2,700,000. The appreciation to the house is $1,800,000. Next we need to determine both Brian's separate property share of the appreciation and the community's share of the appreciation. To determine Brian's separate property appreciation, his 20% interest is multiplied by the amount the house appreciated, $1,800,000. Brian's separate property appreciation is $360,000. Since the community's percentage interest is 80%, use that number and multiply it by the amount the house appreciated. The community property's appreciation is $1,440,000.

At divorce, Brian will be entitled to his separate property contribution to the down payment of $180,000 and his separate property interest in the appreciation of $360,000. Thus Brian's separate property interest in the house on Drury Lane is $540,000. Brian is also entitled to one-half of the community's interest in the house. Because the loan is characterized as community property and is the bulk of the total purchase price, the community has a much larger interest compared to Brian's separate property interest. The community interest is calculated in the same manner as Brian's separate property interest. The amount of the loan of $720,000 is added to the community property share of the appreciation of $1,440,000, totaling $2,160,000. Brian's one-half share of the community property is $1,080,000.

Brian will get his separate property interest of $540,000 plus one-half of the community property, $1,080,000, which totals $1,620,000. Trish receives one-half of the community property, $1,080,000. While $1,080,000 may not be enough for the princess to buy another house on Drury Lane, it might be enough for her to buy herself a castle elsewhere.

Let us not forget that the balance of $432,000 is owed to the bank. That amount will also be considered community property and will have to be paid or deducted equally from Brian and Trish's totals. This example illustrates the importance of characterizing the loan as community property, even though the down payment was from Brian's separate property. Because the community property is the larger percentage of the property, the proportional share of the appreciation will also be larger.

Explanation 33 — Truffle Hunting

This example is similar to Example 31 in that the title was taken in one spouse's name. The crucial difference here is that the house was acquired *before* marriage. The loan was also obtained *before* marriage. In that case, the house and the loan will be characterized as Kevin's separate property. Therefore, the major questions are: (1) What is the community's interest in the house, since part of the loan was paid with community funds; and (2) how to apportion the appreciation, since some appreciation occurred before marriage and some during marriage? To answer these questions, we use the *Moore/Marsden* formulas.

At the time Kevin and Tamara married, the house had appreciated from \$600,000 to \$650,000. That appreciation of \$50,000 occurred before marriage and therefore is Kevin's separate property. That is the easy part.

Next we need to calculate the community's interest in the house. The only community contributions to Kevin's separate property house were the community payments to reduce the loan balance. At marriage, the balance on the loan was \$440,000, and at divorce it was \$200,000. The community contribution was \$240,000. According to the *Marsden* Court, the community's interest is determined by dividing the community contribution by the purchase price of the house (\$240,000/\$600,000 = 40%).

The community is entitled to its share of the appreciation that occurred during marriage. When they married, the house had appreciated to \$650,000. During their marriage, the house appreciated to \$900,000. Appreciation during marriage was \$250,000. We have already calculated the community's interest to be 40%, and therefore the community is entitled to 40% of the appreciation (40% of \$250,000 = \$100,000).

At divorce, the community's interest includes both the payments made from community property to reduce the loan (\$240,000) and the share of appreciation during marriage (\$100,000). The total community interest would be \$340,000. Thus, Tamara will be entitled to one-half of the community share, which would be \$170,000. Kevin will be entitled to the rest: one-half of the community share (\$170,000) and the remaining \$560,000. The total Kevin would receive would be \$730,000, and Tamara will only get \$170,000. Although Kevin's portion is much larger than Tamara's portion, the loan that remains to be paid also was characterized as Kevin's separate property and will be his responsibility. This example again illustrates the importance of the characterization of the loan. The community's share is so low, because it is credited with only the community payments that reduce the loan. However, the community does gain a proportional share of the appreciation rather than simply reimbursement.

Some people are better able to understand the formulas step-by-step. Therefore the steps in the formulas for Examples 31 and 32 are presented here.

Moore/Marsden Apportionment Formulas

	Example 31	Example 32
Gather the Data		
Purchase price (PP)	$900,000	$600,000
Down payment	$180,000 (SP)	$120,000 (SP)
Loan amount	$720,000 (CP)	$480,000 (SP)
Fair market value (FMV) of the house at divorce	$2,700,000	$900,000
FMV when married		$650,000
Appreciation before married		$50,000 (SP)
Balance to be paid on loan	$432,000	$200,000
SP payments on loan before married		$40,000
CP payments on loan during marriage	$288,000	$240,000
Figure Out the Separate Property and Community Property Interests		
Community interest: CP contribution/PP	$720,000/$900,000 = 80%	$240,000/$600,000 = 40%
Separate property interest: SP contribution/PP	$180,000/$900,000 = 20%	$360,000/$600,000 = 40%
Figure Out the Amount of Appreciation		
FMV–PP	$2,700,000–$900,000 = $1,800,000	$900,000–$650,000 = $250,000
Calculate the CP and SP Interests in the Appreciation (APPN)		
CP interest: CP% × APPN	80% of $1,800,000 = $1,440,000	40% of $250,000 = $100,000
SP interest: SP% × APPN	20% of $1,800,000 = $360,000	60% of $250,000 = $150,000

	Example 31	Example 32
Calculate Total of CP and SP Interests		
Total CP interest: CP contributions + CP appreciation	$720,000 + $1,440,000 = $2,160,000	$240,000 + $100,000 = $340,000
Total SP interest: SP contributions + SP appreciation	$180,000 + $360,000 = $540,000	$360,000 + $200,000* = $560,000
Calculate Each Spouse's Share		
One-half of total CP interest	One-half of $2,160,000 = $1,080,000	One-half of $340,000 = $170,000
One-half of total CP interest total SP interest	$1,080,000 + $540,000 = $1,620,000	$170,000 + $560,000 = $730,000
Pay the Bank		
Subtract from CP or SP interest	$432,000 (CP)	$200,000 (SP)

* Includes $50,000 SP APPN before marriage

CHAPTER 6

Who Has the Power? Management and Control of Community Property

California law provides that the spouses have "equal" management and control over community property. Family Code §1100(a) states that "either spouse has the management and control of the community personal property . . . with like absolute power of disposition, other then testamentary, as the spouse has of the separate estate of the spouse." The equal management and control regime became effective January 1, 1975, and is retroactive to property acquired prior to that date. Before 1975, management and control of community personal property was under the husband's control, except for a wife's uncommingled community property earnings. Major decisions regarding community property real property had required joinder of the spouses since 1917. Family Code §1102.

COMMUNITY PERSONAL PROPERTY

Please note that "either" spouse has management and control of community personal property. That means that theoretically either spouse can control the earnings of the working spouse. Before hailing "equality of the spouses," let us examine the significant limitations on "equal" management and control. First, California Financial Code §851 limits access to bank accounts in one spouse's name to that spouse. If Harry puts his earnings in a bank account in his own name, Wilma will not have access to that bank account. Even if she takes her marriage certificate to the bank and explains to the teller that under California law she is an equal owner and manager and controller of community property, the teller will refuse her access to Harry's account. So, practically, Harry has control over his earnings if they are in an account in his name. Clearly, if Wilma did the same, she would control her earnings, and Harry would be refused access to her account. If Wilma wanted to force the issue, she could obtain a court order that her name be added to Harry's account. Family Code §1101(c). However, it is questionable whether their marriage would be in such good shape if Wilma must resort to court action to enforce her equal management and control rights.

There are several other exceptions to the equal management and control scheme found in Family Code §1100(a). Two major ones, gifts to third parties and community businesses, will be treated separately. The other exception requires written consent before a spouse sells, conveys, or encumbers community personal property used as the "family dwelling, or the furniture, furnishings, or fittings of the home, or the clothing or wearing apparel of the other spouse or minor children which is community personal property." Family Code §1100(c). For instance, let's say Wilma obtained a loan and used the furniture in their home as collateral. Wilma defaulted on the loan, and the creditor carted off the furniture. In that case, the encumbrance on the furniture would be void and the creditor would have to return the furniture, because Harry did not give his written consent. *See Matthews v. Hamburger*, 36 Cal. App. 2d 182, 97 P.2d 465 (1939).

Finally, there is a general duty regarding the community personal property that "each spouse shall act in good faith with respect to the other spouse in the management and control of the community property . . . ." Family Code §1100(e). What exactly that duty encompasses is not crystal clear and will be discussed in the section concerning fiduciary duty.

Gifts

One major limitation on management and control of community personal property concerns gifts. Family Code §1100(b) prohibits gifts or disposal of community personal property for less than fair and reasonable value unless the other spouse has given written consent. Originally passed in 1891 as a measure to limit a husband's complete control over community property, it survives today under the regime of equal management and control. The intent of the 1891 statute was to prevent a husband from giving away most of the community's wealth and thus leaving a wife without any means of support upon divorce or the husband's death. It is important to note here that the section does not cover gifts between the spouses—that is covered by the transmutation statute, which allows a spouse to transmute separate property to community property and vice versa.

Questions immediately arise concerning the statute. What happens if a spouse violates the mandate of the statute and gives away community personal property without the consent of the other spouse? The short answer is that during the marriage, the nonconsenting spouse has the right either to ratify the gift or to revoke the gift and sue to recover all the property for the community. After the death of the donor spouse, the nonconsenting spouse has the right to ratify the gift or to void the gift up to one-half the value of the gift. These principles were established in the 1916 case of *Spreckels v. Spreckels*, 172 Cal. 775, 158 P. 537 (1916). The Spreckels' family feud originally concerned a gift of stock that sugar magnate Claus Spreckels had given to his youngest son Rudolph. When Rudolph fell out of favor with his father, Claus tried to revoke that gift based on the 1891 gift statute. Claus argued that the gift was void, because he had not obtained his wife's written consent. That argument failed, because the written consent statute was not applied retroactively to community property acquired prior to the date of the statute. *Spreckels v. Spreckels*, 116 Cal. 339, 48 P. 228 (1897). Claus then gave almost $26 million to elder sons John and Adolph and nothing to his younger children Gus, Rudolph, and Emma. At the time of Claus's death, his fortune had been reduced to about $10 million because of the San Francisco earthquake. The younger children sued, challenging Claus's gifts to the older sons. The lawsuit became complicated when Anna, Claus's wife, died in the midst of the proceedings. The irony was that the younger children challenged Claus's later gifts based on the same written consent statute.

The major issue in the 1916 *Spreckels* case concerned a wife's rights if a husband gave a gift without her written consent. The Supreme Court held that the husband's gift was not void, but voidable after the husband's death. The Court then considered whether the wife Anna had ratified the gifts in her will. She had. Therefore, the Court considered the gifts to be valid. For the complete background on the 1891 gift statute and the contentious legal battles of this wealthy and famous San Francisco family, see Charlotte K. Goldberg, *A Cauldron of Anger: The Spreckels Family and Reform of California Community Property Law*, 12 Western Legal History 242 (1999).

Another major issue regarding gifts is "who can be sued" to recover the gifts made without the other spouse's consent. In another case involving the rich and famous, *Fields v. Michael*, 91 Cal. App. 2d 443, 205 P.2d 402 (1949), W.C. Fields had given away gifts totaling $482,450 to various people. It was clear that he did not obtain his wife's consent. The problem was that the people who had received the gifts had mostly "used up and dissipated" the gifts. Therefore, the question was whether Fields' wife had a remedy against her husband's estate and not just against the recipients of the gifts. The Court held that "a wife whose community property rights have been violated . . . is entitled to pursue whatever course is best calculated to give her effective relief." *Id.* at 448, 205 P.2d at 406. Thus the wife was entitled to sue the husband's estate for the gifts made without her consent.

Finally, another major issue is whether the community personal property transferred to the third party was really a gift or whether it was given in return for fair and valuable consideration. The present statutory phrase is "for less than fair and reasonable value." Family Code §1100(b). For instance, in *Estate of Bray*, 230 Cal. App. 2d 136, 40 Cal. Rptr. 750 (1964), the wife of Walter Bray questioned accounts and bonds that were in the name of Walter and his son from a former marriage. The son claimed the accounts and bonds as surviving joint tenant. The wife claimed that the money in the accounts and used to buy the bonds was a gift given without her written consent. The son's argument was that the money was given in return for services rendered by the son, who worked in his father's business. The most damaging fact to the son's argument was that during the entire time Walter was putting money into the bank accounts and buying the bonds, his son never knew about them. The son had also received a salary while working for his father. The court therefore concluded that there was not enough evidence to show that the bank accounts and bonds were for services rendered. Instead they were gifts, and the wife was entitled to half of those gifts made without her written consent.

Community Businesses

Family Code §1100(d) gives "primary" management and control to "a spouse who is operating or managing a business or an interest in a business that is all or substantially all community personal property." That means that the managing spouse "may act alone in all transactions." However, the managing spouse must give "prior written notice to the other spouse" for major actions such as "sale, lease, exchange, encumbrance or other disposition of all or substantially all of the personal property used in the operation of the business." Still, if the managing spouse fails to give that prior written notice, the validity of the transaction will not be adversely affected. A spouse's recourse for that failure is found in Family Code §1101, which lists the possible remedies such as breach of fiduciary duty and the ordering of an accounting.

Let's say that Wilma started a mobile pet grooming business using community funds. She purchased three vans and equipped them for grooming dogs and cats. She had several employees. Harry was pleased that she had started this business. Since he was extremely allergic to animals, he would not even come near the vans. The mobile pet grooming business is clearly community property, owned by both Harry and Wilma. Under the general management and control provisions, either Harry or Wilma has management and control. Under the "primary" management provision, Wilma, who operates the business, may act alone in all transactions. There is no problem with Wilma purchasing the van, expending money in equipping them, hiring employees, and running the business. She need not consult Harry in making business decisions.

If Wilma receives an offer to sell her business, including the vans, she must give prior written notice to Harry that she is planning to sell the business. If she goes ahead and sells the business without giving that notice, the sale will still be valid. If Harry is displeased with the sale after the fact, he could go to court and file a claim for breach of fiduciary duty or request an accounting. Harry's displeasure with the sale may not rise to the level of a breach of fiduciary duty, and the thought of suing for an accounting or for breach of fiduciary duty during marriage would most likely have extremely detrimental effects on their marriage.

It seems that the primary management provision gives almost complete power to the managing spouse. How does this square with "equal" management and control? The policy supporting giving such power to the managing spouse is to facilitate business transactions. A spouse may want to include the other spouse in business decisions made in a community property business, but that is not mandated. Under the "primary" management provisions, the managing spouse needs freedom to run the business without interference from the other spouse. Yet the Legislature, through the mandatory written notice provision, is encouraging communication on major decisions regarding a community property business. But note that the mandatory written notice provision does *not* require joinder or consent of the other spouse in these decisions. The primary decision-making authority is in the managing spouse.

Fiduciary Duty

So far we have learned that "either" spouse has management and control of the community personal property, subject to the exceptions explained above. When a spouse undertakes that management and control, what is the responsibility the spouse owes to the other spouse when managing that community property? Family Code §1100(e) provides that "each spouse shall act . . . in accordance with the general rules governing fiduciary relationships . . . ." Therefore, this section and the general description of spousal duties in Family Code §721 provides that a spouse owes the other spouse a "fiduciary duty." That duty is not easy to define. With regard to community personal property, Family Code §1100(e) explains that the duty includes full disclosure and full access to information about assets and debts of the community, upon request. It is clear that the Legislature is trying to encourage open communication between the spouses regarding their community assets and debts.

Sharing information about community assets and debts is a laudable goal, but it has always been thought that the duty owed to the other spouse goes beyond sharing information and rises to the level of "fiduciary." That duty is stated in Family Code §721: "[A] husband and wife are subject to the general rules governing fiduciary relations which control the actions of persons occupying confidential relations with each other." So it is necessary to understand what duty a "confidential relationship" imposes. The duty is described as a duty of "the highest good faith and fair dealing." Neither spouse "shall take unfair advantage of the other." Each is subject to "the same rights and duties of nonmarital business partners." Still, we do not know what those phrases mean. In Family Code §721, we are referred to various sections of the Corporations Code which define duties owed by business partners and find three specific duties:

1. Access at all times to any books kept regarding a transaction for inspection and copying
2. Rendering upon request true and full information of all things affecting any transaction which concerns the community property
3. Accounting to the spouse, and holding as trustee, any benefit or profit derived from a transaction by one spouse without the consent of the other spouse which concerns community property

Again we see the first two specific duties concern communication of information regarding community property. The third indicates that a spouse should be responsible for benefits or profits in order to protect and answer to the other spouse regarding transactions.

Regarding the duty to communicate information about community property, there is ambiguity about whether the spouse must disclose the information only "upon request" or must disclose the information "without demand." Both §721 and §1100(e) include the term "upon request." The ambiguity occurred when in 2002, the Legislature revised §721 and incorporated by reference certain Corporations Code sections. One of those sections, Corporations Code §16403, changed the prior Corporations Code §15020. The prior section required disclosure "upon demand"; the new section requires disclosure "without demand." Corporations Code §16403(c)(1).

This change was at issue in the case of *Marriage of Walker*, 138 Cal. App. 4th 1408, 42 Cal. Rptr. 3d 325 (2006). During their marriage, the husband Robert was not interested in managing their financial affairs and therefore, wife Lynn handled all their family finances, including IRA stock and bank accounts. To meet their family expenses, over a period of five years, she withdrew a total of $69,000 from the accounts. The withdrawals also incurred small tax penalties. She never hid the withdrawals or tax penalties from him nor did he ever ask about them. The trial court found she breached her fiduciary duty to Robert by failing to inform him of the depletion of the IRA accounts and the tax penalties. The trial court awarded Robert over $71,000, the amount withdrawn plus the tax penalties.[1]

The issue on appeal was whether to apply the change in §721 that referred to the new Corporations Code §16403. If the new requirement applied, Lynn had a duty to disclose "without demand." If the prior section applied, Lynn had a duty to disclose only "on demand." The Court of Appeal held that this new duty should not be applied retroactively and therefore Lynn had no duty to disclose unless Robert had made a demand. "To penalize Wife now for breach of a statutory spousal duty that did not exist during the parties' marriage would disrupt the repose that should follow the actions she undertook in accordance with the established customs and practices of their marriage and which were intended to serve their marital community, not her personally."[2] *Marriage of Walker*, 138 Cal. App. 4th at 1428, 42 Cal. Rptr. 3d at 340.

If the same facts occurred after the effective date of the changes to §721, in 2003 or thereafter, then the result presumably would be different and the wife would have breached her duty to disclose. Corporations Code §16403(c)(1) imposes a duty on partners to furnish "without demand, any information concerning the partnership's business and affairs reasonably required for the proper exercise of the partners' rights and duties under the partnership agreement . . . ." This seems to trump the specific Family Code sections of §721 and §1100(e) that mandate disclosure about assets and transactions concerning community property, upon request. It is difficult to reconcile the ambiguity regarding the issue of "request" or "demand." However, recent Court of Appeal decisions indicate that the courts view the duty to disclose as an important aspect of spousal fiduciary duties.

In *Marriage of Fossum*, 192 Cal. App. 4th 336, 121 Cal. Rptr. 3d 195 (2011), and *Marriage of Margulis*, 198 Cal. App. 4th 1252, 130 Cal. Rptr. 3d 327 (2011), the Courts of Appeal strictly applied the duty to disclose. In the *Fossum* case, in Spring 2002, wife Sandra failed to disclose to her husband

1. It should be noted that the amount awarded for breach of fiduciary duty should have been only 50% of the total amount. Family Code §1101(g). The award of the total amount would have been appropriate if wife Lynn had been guilty of oppression, fraud, or malice. Family Code §1101(h). That did not seem to be the case in *Walker*.

2. In 2006, the California Supreme Court held that the general rule is that the Family Code and amendments to the Family Code are retroactive. *Marriage of Fellows*, 39 Cal. 4th 179, 138 P.3d 200, 46 Cal. Rptr. 3d 49 (2006). Despite this change of the general rule, the rule in *Marriage of Walker* would still hold because a court could find that applying the new Corporations Code section retroactively would violate due process. See Chapter 2, Retroactivity of Family Code Amendments.

Edward a $24,000 cash advance on a credit card that she used to purchase a horse trailer and a car for her son. The trial court found that Sandra had violated her fiduciary duty and ordered Sandra to reimburse Edward for one-half of the charged amount of $12,000, but did not award attorney's fees under Family Code §1101(g). On appeal, the Court of Appeal affirmed the $12,000 and held that an award of attorney's fees is mandated under §1101(g). The Court did not address the retroactivity issue so it is assumed that this Court applied the duty to disclose "without demand" to failures to disclose that occurred prior to January 1, 2003.

The *Margulis* case dealt with investment accounts that seemed to have disappeared during the couple's postseparation period of 12 years. Husband Alan had managed the couple's finances during their 33-year marriage. After they separated in 1996, Alan moved to Chicago and continued to manage the extensive community investments. In 2002, wife Elaine filed a petition for dissolution of their marriage. Alan did not respond to the petition until 2007. Neither her petition nor his response included the extent of the marital property. During settlement conferences, Elaine identified assets under Alan's control of almost $901,000. Alan identified their home as their only remaining asset. At trial, the most contentious issue was several investment accounts managed by Alan. After separation, the assets in those accounts seemed to be missing. The trial court found that Alan breached his fiduciary duty owed to Elaine "to maintain proper records of all community assets" that he managed and controlled. Alan was ordered to pay Elaine $20,000 in sanctions and $30,000 as a share of her attorney's fees. *Marriage of Margulis*, 198 Cal. 4th at 1265, 130 Cal. Rptr. 3d at 336.

The Court of Appeal discussed the "duty to disclose" and described it as "an affirmative and broad obligation . . . that continue[s] to bind spouses after separation until final distribution of assets." *Id.* at 1269-1270, 130 Cal. Rptr. 3d at 339-340. Thus, the Court concluded that "in a trial where community assets are missing, these statutory duties of disclosure and accounting serve to shift the burden of proof on missing assets to the managing spouse." *Id.* at 1271, 130 Cal. Rptr. 3d at 340. Based on this assessment of the duty of disclosure and the burden of proof, the Court of Appeal remanded to "retry the issue of Alan's alleged breach of fiduciary duties and revisit the question of the appropriate statutory remedies for any breach of duty it finds." *Id.* at 1283, 130 Cal. Rptr. 3d at 350.

These cases show that not only is the duty to disclose found in §16403(c)(1) applied retroactively to events occurring prior to January 1, 2003, but that failure to disclose assets will become a focal point of divorce litigation.

It is not easy to understand what is the duty one spouse owes to the other in managing the community property. Corporations Code §16404(c), listed in Family Code §721, explains that a partner's duty of care is "limited to refraining from engaging in grossly negligent or reckless conduct, intentional misconduct, or a knowing violation of the law." "Ordinary" negligence is excluded from the list. This is in line with the earlier case of *Marriage of Shultz*, 105 Cal. App. 3d 846, 164 Cal. Rptr. 653 (1980), where a spouse's negligence was not considered a "deliberate misappropriation" of community property. In that case, the husband had failed to contest a debt owed by the community. The debt was not divided equally, and the husband appealed the additional share of the debt that was awarded to him. The Court stated that a fiduciary would be liable for gross mishandling of community financial affairs, which would be tantamount to fraud, but negligence would not. Under that reasoning, negligence would not be considered a breach of the duty of care a spouse owes to the other spouse when managing community property.

The case of *Marriage of Duffy*, 91 Cal. App. 4th 923, 111 Cal. Rptr. 2d 160 (2001) seemed to be a case of "gross mishandling" or "gross negligence or reckless conduct." The husband in the case, Vincent, took his entire IRA brokerage account, almost $500,000, and invested it in five technology stocks in 1995. The stocks were very volatile and declined in value to $261,483 by May 1998. The Court of Appeal considered whether Vincent violated a "duty of care" in investing the community personal property in those stocks. After surveying the history of the fiduciary duty statutes, the Court concluded that "a spouse generally is not bound by the Prudent Investor Rule and does not owe to the other spouse the duty of care one business partner owes to another." *Id.* at 940, 111 Cal. Rptr. 2d at 172-173. Thus, because Vincent owed no duty of care; no duty of care was violated. The Court based its conclusion that there was no duty of care on the legislative omission of the language "but not limited to" from the listing of spousal duties in Family Code §721. Therefore, only the three specific duties listed there encompassed a spouse's duty of care.

In response to the *Duffy* decision, the Legislature in 2002 inserted that language—not limited to—into Family Code §721 and stated its intent "to abrogate the ruling" in *Marriage of Duffy*. Therefore, under the present statute, Vincent's decision to invest the couple's entire IRA brokerage account in highly volatile technology stocks would be considered "gross mishandling" or "grossly negligent or reckless conduct." This would be considered a violation of a spouse's fiduciary duty under Family Code §721 that refers to Corporations Code §16404(c)'s nonmarital business partner's duty of care.

However, Professor Grace Ganz Blumberg supported the *Duffy* decision and a less-stringent duty of care. She pointed out that the position of a spouse differs from a trustee. A spouse acts for both herself and her spouse, while a trustee acts only for the beneficiary. The spouse therefore would be going against her own self-interest by acting imprudently. Thus, Professor Blumberg concluded that a spouse should not be held to the "prudent investor" rule of a nonmarital business partner. California Family Law Monthly 287 (October 2001). It remains to be seen whether future courts will consider a risky investment that results in a loss to be a violation of a spouse's fiduciary duty. Most probably the answer will depend on whether a court will view a spouse's conduct as simply negligent or grossly negligent.

The duty of care found in Corporations Code §16404(c) also includes "intentional misconduct or a knowing violation of the law." In *Marriage of Beltran*, 183 Cal. App. 3d 292, 227 Cal. Rptr. 924 (1986), the husband had forfeited his community military pension because of his criminal conviction. Similarly, in *Marriage of Stitt*, 147 Cal. App. 3d 579, 195 Cal. Rptr. 172 (1983), the wife had incurred attorney's fees to defend against embezzlement charges. Both involved intentional misconduct or knowing violation of the law and would be considered a breach of a spouse's fiduciary duty.

It is also important to understand what it means in Family Code §721 that "neither shall take any unfair advantage of the other." A situation that could result in one spouse taking unfair advantage of the other is when both community and separate property funds are available for investment. For instance, in *Marriage of Lucero*, 118 Cal. App. 3d 836, 173 Cal. Rptr. 680 (1981), the husband used separate property funds rather than community funds to reinstate a community pension. By using separate property funds, the wife would have been deprived of her share of the pension. Use of the separate property funds would be considered taking unfair advantage of the other spouse and thus a breach of the fiduciary duty. On the other hand, in *Somps v. Somps*, 250 Cal. App. 2d 328, 58 Cal. Rptr. 304 (1967), the husband used separate property funds instead of community funds to buy investment realty. That was not considered taking undue advantage nor a breach of fiduciary duty. When both types of funds are available, it seems a spouse has a choice of which funds to use when making an investment. However, if the use of separate funds represents an attempt to deprive the other spouse of an interest in a community investment like a pension or employment opportunity, that action differs from a simple choice of which funds to invest.

The meaning of taking "unfair advantage of the other" has been fleshed out in cases involving interspousal transactions regarding real property. In *Marriage of Delaney*, 111 Cal. App. 4th 991, 4 Cal. Rptr. 3d 378 (2003), the husband Steven executed a grant deed conveying his separate property residence to himself and his wife Linda Sue as joint tenants. In divorce proceedings, Steven claimed that Linda Sue took unfair advantage of him when he executed the grant deed. In *Marriage of Mathews*, 133 Cal. App. 4th 624, 35 Cal. Rptr. 3d 1 (2005), the wife Yatsuko executed a quitclaim deed conveying her community property interest in their residence to her husband Todd as his separate property. In divorce proceedings, Yatsuko claimed that Todd took unfair advantage of her when she executed the quitclaim deed. Because the transmutation statute, Family Code §852, requires that the documents control and extrinsic evidence is prohibited, the deeds in both cases would represent valid transmutations. See Chapter 2 on transmutation.

However, the deeds could be challenged based on violation of the fiduciary duty found in Family Code §721. The Court of Appeal established in *Marriage of Haines*, 33 Cal. App. 4th 277, 297, 39 Cal. Rptr. 2d 673, 686 (1995), that "a rebuttable presumption of undue influence arises when one spouse obtains an advantage over another in a community property transaction." To rebut the presumption, the advantaged spouse must show that the deed in question was "freely and voluntarily made and with a full knowledge of the facts, and with a complete understanding of the effect of the transfer." *Id.* at 296, 39 Cal. Rptr. 2d at 685. In the *Delaney* case, Linda Sue gained an advantage when the residence was transmuted from Steven's separate property to joint tenancy. In the *Mathews* case, Todd gained an advantage when the residence was transmuted from community property to Todd's separate property. Under *Haines*, once a spouse is advantaged by an interspousal transaction, the presumption of undue influence arises, and the advantaged spouse must show that the disadvantaged spouse knew, understood, and voluntarily signed the deed.

In *Delaney*, Linda Sue could not rebut the presumption. Steven suffered from cognitive impairments and had entrusted all marital financial and legal matters to Linda Sue. Linda Sue was experienced in financial and legal matters and Steven signed the deed transferring his interest to joint tenancy without questioning her instruction that it was necessary. Thus the grant deed was a product of undue influence. The grant deed was void and the residence remained Steven's separate property. So we see that even though the document would withstand scrutiny based on the transmutation statute, it was void because it was procured by undue influence.

In *Mathews*, Todd was able to rebut the presumption. Even though Yatsuko's first language was Japanese, she was fluent in English. Also she managed the marital household financial affairs and her own investment accounts. Yatsuko agreed to sign the deed as it was the only way to obtain a lower interest rate on the mortgage. There was no pressure from Todd. She understood the reasons for the deed and "made a conscious decision to sign the deed." *Matthews*, 133 Cal. App. 4th at 632, 35 Cal. Rptr. 3d at 6. There was enough evidence to establish that Todd had rebutted the presumption of undue influence. Therefore, although the quitclaim deed advantaged Todd, he did not take unfair advantage of Yatsuko and the residence was his separate property.

A different scenario regarding "unfair advantage" was addressed in *Marriage of Fossum*, 192 Cal. App. 4th 336, 121 Cal. Rptr. 3d 195 (2011) (discussed above relating to duty to disclose). The Fossums purchased a home during their marriage. In 1994, to obtain a favorable interest rate, the home was purchased in husband Edward's name. Later, the deed was changed to both his name and wife Sandra's name. In 1998, when refinancing the home, the plan was to follow the same procedure. However, Edward never quitclaimed the home back to both their names. The trial court found that the home was community property. Edward appealed, arguing that the deed showing the home was his separate property should control and that he did not take unfair advantage of Sandra.

There was no question that the deed was a valid transmutation, using the language as his "sole and separate property." Because Edward was advantaged by the transaction, the presumption of "undue influence" arose and he was required to show that he did not take unfair advantage of her. Although it was clear that Sandra signed the quitclaim deed freely and voluntarily and understood the import of the deed, the Court found that Edward had not rebutted the presumption of undue influence. To do so, the Court of Appeal expanded the meaning of unfair advantage to cover this situation. Because Edward failed to fulfill his promise to use the same procedure that they had used before, "Edward abused his position as Sandra's fiduciary and confidant, and failed to deal with his spouse in the highest good faith." *Id.* at 345, 121 Cal. Rptr. 3d at 203. Therefore, the Court of Appeal upheld the finding that the home was community property. Thus, failure to carry out a promise would be a basis for overturning a deed transmuting the property. This case shows that the suggestion of the Supreme Court in *Marriage of Benson* has now been adopted in *Marriage of Fossum*. *Marriage of Benson* is discussed in Chapter 2 regarding transmutation.

In conclusion, the claim of breach of fiduciary duty presents an avenue for overturning interspousal transactions that advantage one spouse. The issue is whether that advantage is "unfair to the other."

COMMUNITY REAL PROPERTY

Equal management and control also applies to community real property. That means that "either spouse has the management and control of the community real property. . . ." Family Code §1102(a). However, "both spouses must join in executing any instrument by which that community real property or any interest therein . . . is sold, conveyed, or encumbered." Joinder is also required for leases of community real property for "longer than a period of one year." Family Code §1102(a). Regarding major real property transactions, "equal" means that both spouses must participate in those decisions. When the title to community real property is held in the names of both spouses and indicates that they are married, it would be obvious to any purchaser or lender that both spouses must participate in the transaction. It is not obvious when the community real property is held in one spouse's name. In that case, there is a "triangle" of interests involved. In this triangle there are three parties—the conniving spouse, the innocent spouse, and the innocent purchaser or lender.

Assume that Harry and Wilma own community real property, but the title is in Harry's name. Harry meets Bob Buyer while he is at a business meeting, and Bob tells Harry that he wants to invest in real property. Harry, who is swamped with debts, sells the community real property to Bob. Harry does not tell Wilma about the sale to Bob, and Harry does not tell Bob that he is married. Bob has no way of telling that the property is community property, because the title is in Harry's name. Harry subsequently disappears—he has gone to Bermuda and has spent all the money from the sale. Soon after the sale, Wilma finds out what Harry did, and she consults an attorney. If the sale is valid, Bob will keep the property. Wilma feels cheated—by Harry and by the law—if Bob retains the property. But Bob also is innocent; he is a bona fide purchaser who had no way of knowing that Harry was even married. How can a court balance the interests of these two innocent parties?

Family Code §1102(c)(2) creates a presumption of validity of the sale if the purchaser in good faith did not know about the marriage of the spouse who sold the property. In this case, Bob would be that good faith purchaser. Yet the main requirement of §1102(a) is that Wilma "join" in that sale, and she did not. Wilma has a right to "void" the instrument that Harry executed without her. Thus Bob would have no right to the property. The community, as represented by Wilma, would own the property. That is fair to Wilma, whose statutory right to join in the sale of community real property was violated. But it seems more unfair to Bob. After all, presumably Bob paid for the property but has neither the money nor the property. However, the community received the money and also retains the property. In this scenario, the Court of Appeal required that the community repay the purchase price to the bona fide purchaser. *Mark v. Title Guaranty & Trust Co.*, 122 Cal. App. 301, 9 P.2d 839 (1932). Although Harry took the money, and it is unclear that Wilma would have the funds to repay Bob, the Court of Appeal noted "the difficulty of protecting the expectancy of the innocent wife and at the same time of safeguarding the rights of innocent purchasers." *Id.* at 311, 9 P.2d at 843. Clearly, Wilma has to "pay" for Harry's wrongdoing. However, if the property has appreciated in value, the community benefits from that increase in value and may be able to borrow the money needed to pay Bob. It is left to you to decide what is fair.

The triangle scenario was presented to the Court of Appeal in *Marriage of Brooks and Robinson*, 169 Cal. App. 4th 176, 86 Cal. Rptr. 3d 624 (2008). The parties in that case, Brooks and Robinson, were married in 1997. In 2000, they purchased a home, using Brooks' earnings as a down payment.

They agreed that the home should be held in Robinson's name to assist them in obtaining financing. The deed stated that the home was owned by "Annikawa A. Robinson, a Single Woman." In 2005, the home was in the process of foreclosure and the couple separated, with Brooks remaining in the home and Robinson moving out. Enter Executive Capital Group (ECG), a company that is in the business of buying properties in the process of foreclosure. There was conflicting testimony about ECG's knowledge of Brooks and Robinson's marriage, but it was clear that Robinson sold the home to ECG for $142,000. After the sale and after Brooks filed for divorce, ECG learned of their marriage and Brooks learned about the sale of the home.

Brooks sought to have the trial court declare that there was a community property interest in the home and that the sale of the home to ECG was invalid. The trial court resolved the matter by finding that, despite murky facts, ECG was a bona fide purchaser with no knowledge that Brooks and Robinson were married. If the case had ended there, the trial court could have resolved the dispute between Brooks and Robinson over the proceeds of the sale. However, the case against ECG continued.

Without assistance of counsel, Brooks appealed, arguing that ECG had a duty to inquire as to his interest in the property since they knew he was living in the home. The Court of Appeal also resolved the case in favor of ECG—not by confirming that ECG was a bona fide purchaser, but instead by finding that Brooks did not have an interest in the home. The Court's analysis regarding the character of the home is questionable. The issue depended on the presumptions regarding the title. According to the Court, if the title in "Robinson's name, a single woman," raises the "form of title presumption," then the home would be presumed to be her separate property. Then it would be up to Brooks to rebut the presumption by clear and convincing evidence that the home was community property. On the other hand, if the general community property presumption applied, it would be up to ECG or Robinson to prove that the home was Robinson's separate property. The Court chose to apply the "form of title presumption" and concluded that Brooks could not show clear and convincing evidence that Brooks and Robinson had agreed that the home was community property. Because Brooks had no interest in the home, his claims failed and Robinson's sale to ECG was declared valid.

If this case is limited to the facts of a "triangle" scenario, perhaps it will stand as a valid precedent for an action "between one of the spouses and a third party bona fide purchaser." *Marriage of Valli*, 58 Cal. 4th 1396, 1413, 324 P.3d 274, 285, 171 Cal. Rptr. 3d 454, 468 (2014) (Concurring Opinion). However, if the *Brooks and Robinson* Court's understanding of title presumptions is applied more generally, it overturns prior law that applies when title is taken in one spouse's name. According to the Court, in Brooks' brief on the issue, he "*concedes* that when Robinson took title to the property solely in her name, a presumption arose that the property was Robinson's separate property." *Brooks and Robinson*, 169 Cal. App. 4th at 186, 86 Cal. Rptr. 3d at 631 (emphasis added). That "concession" is contrary to community property law. The presumption that title in the wife's name raises a separate property presumption was abolished in 1975. See "The Married Woman's Special Presumption" in Chapter 3.

If the dispute had been between Brooks and Robinson, the correct presumption would be that the title in one spouse's name is community property, and it is up to the separate property proponent to prove that the property is separate property. The view that the "form of title presumption" found in Evidence Code §662 does not apply in disputes between spouses was confirmed in *Marriage of Valli*. *Id.* In this scenario, it is doubtful that the facts support the position that the home was Robinson's separate property. There could be no tracing to separate property funds because Brooks' employment earnings, which were community property, were used for the down payment and Robinson did not contribute any funds. There was no agreement between Brooks and Robinson that the title signified a change from community property to her separate property. The only testimony was that the title was taken in the name of Robinson, as "a single woman," to facilitate financing of the property.

The Court of Appeal stated that the transmutation statute did not apply because the purchase of the home was an initial acquisition of property from a third person and not an interspousal transaction. The Supreme Court rejected this statement in 2014 in *Marriage of Valli*. *Id.* at 1405, 324 P.3d at 280, 171 Cal. Rptr. 3d at 461 (Majority Opinion). Application of the transmutation statute would show that the title in Robinson's name did not result in the home becoming Robinson's separate property. The title "a single woman" would not be sufficient to qualify as an "express declaration in writing." To meet the "express declaration" criterion, Brooks, who would be adversely affected, would have to know that he was giving up his community property rights when the deed was put in his wife's name. See "Transmutation: 1985 to the Present" in Chapter 2. However, the Court acknowledged that the "form of title" is significant when it quoted from the State Bar regarding a proposed transmutation statute: "'When property, for example, is taken in the name of a wife as her sole and separate property, it is the intent of the parties that it be so treated.'" *Id.* at 189, 86 Cal. Rptr. 3d at 634. The language "as her sole and separate property" differs significantly from the language "a single woman." If the deed had stated "Robinson, as her separate property," Brooks would have known that he would be giving up his community property rights in the home.

The *Brooks and Robinson* Court probably reached the right conclusion in ruling that the sale to ECG was valid. However, its analysis regarding the applicable presumption when the title is in the wife's name and its statement regarding the application of the transmutation statute are contrary to present law. Therefore, the case is a questionable precedent.

The triangle scenario becomes more complex when community real property is "encumbered." In that case, one spouse borrows money. The transaction involves two parts: the loan and the security for the loan. The loan creates a debt, and the security for the loan creates a security interest in the real property. When the loan is for a large sum, the lender requires that security interest, in the event that the debt is not paid. If the loan is not paid, the lender can obtain a judgment for the loan amount, and that judgment can be recorded as a lien on the property. Add to this scenario that one spouse borrows the money and executes an instrument creating the security interest in the community real property. That violates §1102(a), because the other spouse did not join in the encumbrance. That happened in *Lezine v. Security Pacific Financial Services, Inc.*, 14 Cal. 4th 56, 925 P.2d 1002, 58 Cal. Rptr. 2d 76 (1996).

But it was even worse. The innocent spouse Gloria filed for divorce after learning that her husband Henry borrowed large sums of money and gave the lender a secured interest in their community property home. She was successful at trial in voiding the encumbrance, but the trial court awarded Security Pacific a money judgment for the debt that Henry incurred. This follows the reasoning of *Mark*: The community receives the property back, because the encumbrance (sale) is void, but the community still owes the debt (the proceeds of the purchase). What was worse in this case was that although Gloria received the home as her separate property, Security Pacific had already recorded the judgment that created a lien on the home. So Gloria was "stuck" with the loan that Henry incurred.

This was a difficult case for the California Supreme Court, because it recognized that "our holding may nullify in substantial part the relief afforded under former section 5127 [Family Code §1102] when the unilateral transfer is a security interest for the repayment of the debt." *Lezine*, 14 Cal. App. 4th at 73, 925 P.2d at 1012, 58 Cal. Rptr. 2d at 86. Yet the holding was consistent with *Mark* and tried to balance the interests of two innocent parties. The Court also questioned which innocent party was in a better position to protect against the conniving spouse's deception—the lender or the spouse. Even though the lender dealt with the conniving spouse and could assess the spouse's marital status, the lender was provided more protection than was an innocent spouse who was totally deceived. The Court left open the possibility that the trial court could reallocate the spouses' community property to account for the resulting inequity. *Id.* at 75, 95 P.2d at 1014, 58 Cal. Rptr. at 88.

Two other aspects of Family Code §1102 are noteworthy: the one-year statute of limitations found in §1102(d) and the special section regarding encumbrances for reasonable attorney's fees found in §1102(e). The one-year limitation period gives an innocent spouse one year to file an action to avoid a unilateral transfer of community real property in violation of the joinder provision. That limitation period applies only to "bona fide transferees with no knowledge of the marriage relation who have no reason to suspect another signature is necessary." *Boyd v. Blanton*, 149 Cal. App. 3d 987, 993, 197 Cal. Rptr. 190, 194 (1983).

Family Code §1102(e), the attorney's fees section, ensures that a spouse will be able to seek adequate representation in dissolution proceedings and other similar situations. A spouse may encumber his or her interest "to pay reasonable attorney's fees in order to retain or maintain legal counsel. . . ." Please note that this section applies only to each spouse's interest, which means that the spouse may encumber only one-half of the community real property to pay those fees.

In conclusion, the equal management and control provisions regarding community real property require joint spousal decisions for major transactions and aim to protect both an innocent spouse and an innocent third party from unilateral actions by a conniving spouse.

RESTRAINTS DURING DIVORCE PROCEEDINGS

Once the spouses begin living separate and apart, their earnings become their separate property. Also, once the spouses begin living separate and apart, the community property is not liable for most debts incurred during that time period. However, the fiduciary duty found in Family Code §721 does not end when the spouses separate. The fiduciary duty continues until the "date of distribution of the community or quasi-community asset or liability in question." Family Code §2102. It is important that spouses understand that the duty continues until that time. In fact, Family Code §2040 provides that when divorce proceedings are initiated, the "summons shall contain a temporary restraining order." The temporary restraining order (TRO) prohibits the spouses from "transferring, encumbering, hypothecating, concealing, or in any way disposing of any property, real or personal, whether community, quasi-community, or separate, without the written consent of the other party or an order of court . . . ." This clearly limits spousal management and control of all property either community or separate. But there are exceptions.

The major exceptions are (1) in the usual course of business and (2) for the necessities of life. Family Code §2040(2). In addition, there is an exception for "extraordinary expenditures." For those expenditures, a spouse must notify the other spouse of any "proposed" extraordinary expenditure at least five days before incurring such an expenditure and account to the court for all extraordinary expenditures. Attorneys are protected because the TRO does not preclude a party from using community, quasi-community, or separate property to pay attorney's fees and costs.

What then can a spouse do during divorce proceedings with the community property or his or her separate property? Let us say that spouses Robert and Shirley own real property in joint tenancy. They initiate divorce proceedings, and the TRO goes into effect. After that, Robert severs the joint tenancy. And then while the divorce proceedings are pending, Robert dies. If the severance is ineffective because it violates the TRO, Shirley takes the property as surviving joint tenant. If the severance is effective, one-half of the property goes to Robert's estate, and Robert's son would inherit his interest according to Robert's will. The question in the actual case, *Estate of Mitchell*, 76 Cal. App. 4th 1378, 91 Cal. Rptr. 2d 192 (1999), was whether Robert's severance was a "transfer" of property in violation of the TRO. The Court of Appeal also considered whether the severance "disposed" of the property in violation of the TRO. The Court held that the severance was neither a transfer nor a disposition of property. It was not a transfer, because a transfer requires a transfer from one person to a different person. Because the severance resulted in both Robert and Shirley still having an undivided half-interest, there was no transfer. "[N]o right, title, or interest in the property moved from anyone to anyone else." *Id.* at 1390, 91 Cal. Rptr. 2d at 200.

The Court of Appeal also commented on the argument that the severance was a disposition of property, because it "disposed" of Shirley's right of survivorship. Although the right of survivorship is an incident of an interest in property, the Court did not consider that right of survivorship to be "property." Instead the Court considered it a "mere expectancy." According to the Court, the absolute right to sever the joint tenancy demonstrates that the right of survivorship is "at best only an expectancy." Thus, the severance only affected an expectancy not property, and therefore the TRO was not violated. Stepping back from the reasoning of the Court, it is obvious that the Court was struggling to uphold the severance based on the circumstances of the case. Robert died in the midst of a divorce. His action of severing the joint tenancy showed his intention that someone other than his soon-to-be ex-wife should receive all of his share of their jointly held property. Finding that the severance did not violate the TRO carried out his intention. In addition, if Robert and Shirley's marriage had been dissolved by the Court instead of by Robert's death, most likely the joint tenancy property would have been considered community property that would have been divided equally. Thus, under the Court of Appeal's ruling, Shirley would receive the same amount of property as if the spouses had been divorced. Although the legal reasoning seemed to stretch the plain meaning of "transfer" and "disposing," arguably the Court reached the correct conclusion.

The *McTiernan v. Dubrow* case, 133 Cal. App. 4th 1090, 35 Cal. Rptr. 3d 287 (2005), is noteworthy for its holding on "celebrity goodwill." See Chapter 5 on goodwill. In addition, the Court of Appeal addressed John McTiernan's violation of the TRO that is in effect during divorce proceedings. John had sold some community property stocks without informing his wife or the court of the stock sale. He was short of cash and used the proceeds to pay community expenses. Between the time of sale and the time of trial, the stock's market price increased substantially. Although the trial court found that the stock sale was not malicious, his action violated the TRO. The trial court awarded his wife Donna Dubrow her share of the lost profits. McTiernan appealed that award, arguing that he had not violated the TRO because his sale fell into one of the exceptions in §2040. Alternatively, he argued that the award was a form of punitive damages, unauthorized and inappropriate for his "technical violation" of the TRO. *Id.* at 1103, 35 Cal. Rptr. 3d at 297.

The Court of Appeal rejected both arguments. The sale was not within the usual course of business or the necessities of life exceptions in §2040. Moreover, the Court held that the violation could be labeled "a square one" violation and the remedy was not a form of punitive damages. In fact, the Court noted that the remedy paralleled the remedy for breach of fiduciary duty in Family Code §1101(f) [*sic*], referring to nonmalicious breaches. *Id.* Family Code §1101(g) allows an award of 50% of any asset undisclosed or transferred in breach of the fiduciary duty. The *McTiernan* case stands for the proposition that violations of the TRO, even if not malicious, will be treated like a breach of fiduciary duty.

In *Marriage of Rossi*, 90 Cal. App. 4th 34, 108 Cal. Rptr. 2d 270 (2001), the wife Denise concealed from her husband Thomas that she had won the California Lottery. When Thomas found out, he claimed that Denise had breached her fiduciary duty. The major question before the Court of Appeal was whether the award of all the concealed lottery winnings to Thomas was the proper remedy for the breach of fiduciary duty. The *Rossi* case was the first to discuss the remedy found in Family Code §1101(h) for breach of fiduciary duty. That section states:

> Remedies for the breach of the fiduciary duty by one spouse, as set forth in Sections 721 and 1100, when the breach falls within the ambit of Section 3294 of the Civil Code [oppression, fraud, or malice] shall include, but not be limited to, an award to the other spouse of 100 percent, or an amount equal to 100 percent, of any asset undisclosed or transferred in breach of the fiduciary duty.

Once the Court concluded that Denise had acted with fraud, Thomas was entitled under §1101(h) to all the lottery winnings. The Court of Appeal explained that the "strong language" serves the important purpose of ensuring full disclosure of all assets. "A failure to make such disclosure is properly subject to the severe sanction of section 1101, subdivision (h)." *Id.* at 42, 108 Cal. Rptr. 2d at 277. The Court of Appeal was unsympathetic to Denise's argument that her concealment of the lottery winnings was justified because of Thomas's conduct. She claimed he was physically and mentally abusive in addition to having gambling and money mismanagement problems. Denise's intentional concealment of the lottery winnings outweighed that argument—the trial court did not find Denise credible, and the Court of Appeal did not think Thomas's conduct justified concealing the lottery winnings. Perhaps the case represents a stern warning to spouses who attempt to conceal assets. It is better to reveal community assets and split them at divorce than to risk the loss of the entire asset if found out.

REMEDIES

A spouse has a fiduciary duty when managing community property. What are the remedies available if that duty is breached? Family Code §1101 lists the possible remedies for breach of the fiduciary duty. The breach of fiduciary duty must involve impairment of the claimant's interest in the community estate. Family Code §1101(a). Remedies include a court-ordered accounting or a court order to add a name to the community property held in one spouse's name. §1101(b) and (c). These remedies are available during marriage or at divorce or upon death of a spouse. §1101(f). The newest remedies are found in §1101(g) and (h). Both sections allow a court to award more than half of the asset. A claim for breach of fiduciary duty means that there are potential damages that can eclipse equal division of community property. For instance, under §1101(g), a remedy for breach of fiduciary duty "shall include, but not be limited to" an award to 50% of an undisclosed or transferred asset *plus* attorney's fees and costs. Under §1101(h), the remedy for breach of fiduciary duty, which amounts to oppression, fraud, or malice, "shall include, but not be limited to" an award of 100% of an undisclosed or transferred asset. These provisions in actuality provide for "tort" damages resulting from the breach of fiduciary duty. The question is whether attorneys will start routinely claiming breach of fiduciary duty for conduct during marriage and once the spouses live separate and apart.

Another statutory provision has long been available if a spouse has "deliberately misappropriated" community property. Family Code §2602. The statutory language gives the court discretion to assess an additional award from or an offset against existing property. The provision has lacked "teeth," because most often the courts have deducted the amount deliberately misappropriated from the offending spouse's share rather than awarding additional property to the innocent spouse. A case in point is *Williams v. Williams*, 14 Cal. App. 3d 560, 92 Cal. Rptr. 385 (1971). The case was decided prior to equal management and control and the remedies available under Family Code §1101(g) and (h). It is an illustration of how a court would ordinarily treat a "deliberate misappropriation." As divorce became imminent, the husband withdrew approximately $110,000 from bank and stock accounts. If we assume that all the other community property totaled $200,000, the Court would divide that $200,000 equally with $100,000 going to each spouse. The wife in *Williams* argued that that was not equal division, because she did not receive a share of the $110,000 that she claimed was community property. If we assume that the $110,000 was community property and was "deliberately misappropriated," the Court had the discretion to award her more than $55,000, which would have been her one-half share. The Court of Appeal concluded that the husband would obtain an unfair advantage "if he is not required to . . . reimburse the wife for her share of any of the community property not shown to have been used for community purposes." *Id.* at 567, 92 Cal. Rptr. at 388. Thus the penalty for taking that money was simply to reimburse the wife for $55,000, which means in the final distribution of the community estate, the wife would receive $155,000 and the husband $45,000, which takes into account the $110,000 that the husband had misappropriated.

Let's analyze the same facts under the remedies provided in §1101(g) and (h). Assuming that the Court finds that the husband breached his fiduciary duty by transferring the asset (the $110,000), the wife would again receive "an amount equal to 50 percent" plus attorney's fees and court costs under §1101(g). That is already more than she would receive under the misappropriation statute. If the Court finds that the breach of fiduciary duty included fraud, the wife would receive "an amount equal to 100 percent" under §1101(h). The remedies in §1101(g) and (h) penalize a spouse who transfers an asset to a much greater extent than the misappropriation statute. Clearly, attorneys will be encouraged to sue for breach of fiduciary duty as well as deliberate misappropriation with the prospect of recovering more than the one-half share of property undisclosed or transferred in breach of the fiduciary duty.

Examples

Example 1 — Should Daisy Rely on Abner?

Abner and Daisy have been married for 16 years. During that time, Abner kept his earnings in a bank account in his own name. Daisy comes to you to complain that she does not know anything about their financial situation, and Abner has refused to tell her. He says, "Don't worry, I'll take care of everything." Advise Daisy.

Example 2 — A Trip to New Zealand?

John and Abigail both have high-paying jobs. They decide at the beginning of their marriage that they will take $100 a month from each of their salaries and put them in separate savings accounts in their names. After two years, each has a savings account of $2,400. John wants to take their savings and spend two weeks in New Zealand. Abigail wants to take their savings and invest it in a mutual fund. You are good friends with John. He wants you to help resolve this impasse with Abigail. He asks you about his legal rights. Advise.

Example 3 — Abigail's Risky Investment

John asks you another question about their financial situation. Abigail received a $10,000 inheritance from her Uncle George. She wanted to use the inheritance and invest in a bioengineering company that is developing gene therapy. John thought the investment was very risky and asked her not to invest in the company. She did so anyway. Advise.

Example 4 — Abigail's Investment Fails

Abigail received a $10,000 bonus from her employer. She took that money and also invested it in the bioengineering company without telling John. The gene therapy that the company was working on caused many serious side effects. Abigail's investment in the company has been wiped out. When John finds out, he is very upset and consults you for advice. Did Abigail breach her fiduciary duty? What remedies could John pursue if she did?

Example 5 — False Teeth for Dogs and Cats?

John received a $10,000 bonus from his employer, and he took the money and gave it to his brother. His brother is a veterinarian and started a company to manufacture false teeth for dogs and cats. John received shares in his brother's company. Because of problems with production of the false teeth, John's brother's company failed, and the stock is worthless. John had told Abigail about how he planned to use his bonus, and she objected, but John went ahead anyway. Did John breach his fiduciary duty? What remedies could Abigail pursue if he did?

Example 6 — Financing Leads to Failure

Ron and Martha bought a house in Gendora taking title in Ron's name only "as his separate property." Because Martha had a poor credit history, their loan broker suggested that they could qualify for a better interest rate if the home were taken in Ron's name. The broker also told them that they could add Martha's name back onto the title within 45 days of the close of escrow.

Ron said he would do that. For that reason, Martha signed the quitclaim deed freely and voluntarily. She trusted that Ron would add her name to the title, but he never did. Martha recently filed for divorce and is now claiming that the house is community property and that Ron breached his fiduciary duty. How will a California court decide?

Example 7 — The Art Collection Disappears

Henri and Mattie were married for many years. Over the years they had purchased an art collection of silk screens by many famous artists. The art collection had been purchased with community property funds. About two years ago, Henri started acting strangely. Mattie noticed that many of the pieces of their art collection were disappearing. Henri told her that he had loaned them to a small museum that his friend had opened. Recently, Henri disappeared and was found dead from a drug overdose. The pieces from the art collection had not been loaned to a museum but had been sold to drug dealers in exchange for drugs. The missing pieces of the art collection were worth $50,000. Henri's will left his share of the community property to his brother Vincent. Mattie thinks that she should have some right to recover the $50,000 that disappeared. Advise.

Example 8 — Avis Sells Out

Soon after the September 11, 2001, terrorist attack, Avis and Boris took their community property savings and started an Airport Car Service (ACS). They bought a fleet of cars and hired several drivers. Boris did the driving, and Avis did the bookkeeping. Boris became bored with driving back and forth to the airport and got a job working at an auto dealership. Avis then handled ACS herself. The business prospered until the cost of gasoline and a downturn in air travel began eating into ACS's profits. Avis received an offer to sell the business. She told Boris about the offer, and he said that they should think it over. The buyer pressured Avis by giving her two weeks to decide, or he would withdraw the offer. Boris was unsure about whether they should sell. Avis finally went ahead and sold ACS before Boris made up his mind. They essentially broke even on their original investment. Boris was furious, because Avis acted without his consent. Boris thinks it was a mistake, and that Avis could have gotten a much better price. He comes to you for advice. He wants to know if he can void the sale and if he has any remedies under the law.

Example 9 — Avis Checks Out

Avis and Boris's marriage has deteriorated, and they have separated. The proceeds of the sale of ACS are in a bank account that is in both Avis's and Boris's names. Boris files a petition for dissolution of their marriage, and the summons that is served on Avis contains the TRO that explains that the spouses are prohibited from "transferring, encumbering, hypothecating, concealing or in any way disposing of any property, real or personal, whether community, quasi-community, or separate without the written consent of the other party or an order of court . . . ." After receiving the summons, Avis writes three checks from that account. The first is to pay the rent on the apartment she now lives in, the second is for a retainer for an attorney to represent her in the dissolution proceedings, and the third is for her tuition in school to become a paralegal. The last check was for $3,000 and leaves about $1,000 in their account. Boris then writes a check from the bank account for $2,000 to cover legal fees. The bank returns the check marked "insufficient funds." Boris is embarrassed, and his attorney is not too pleased. Boris finds out about the checks that Avis wrote. Did Avis violate the TRO? Did she breach her fiduciary duty?

Example 10 — Get Out of Jail Free?

Ira Iron met Terry Thimble at a Monopoly tournament. Their love of the game led to their marriage. Ira worked at a large real estate company and was very successful. Over the years, they purchased several pieces of property with funds from Ira's earnings. Their favorite was an estate that they called Park Place. The title was in Ira's name. Recently, Ira was arrested for illegal gambling, as he had arranged betting pools on Monopoly tournaments. He borrowed money to post bail and executed a deed of trust on Park Place to secure the loan. He neglected to mention to the bail bond company that he was married. Soon after Ira was released from jail, he disappeared. Terry has not heard from him and is most distraught. Even worse, Terry found out about the deed of trust on Park Place when the bail bond company contacted her and threatened to foreclose. She comes to you for advice. Advise.

Example 11 — Terry Hires an Attorney

Terry decides to file dissolution proceedings against Ira. During their marriage, they had purchased another parcel of property called Marvin Gardens. Since Terry exhausted all their savings in fighting the bail bond company, she wants to be able to borrow against Marvin Gardens to pay her attorney in the dissolution. Can she execute a deed of trust on Marvin Gardens in favor of her attorney?

Example 12 — Terry Rents the Beach Cottage

Terry also needs to raise cash to pay for her everyday expenses. She seeks to rent a beach cottage on Pacific Avenue that is community real property. She finds a couple that want to spend six months in California, and they sign a lease to that effect. Is that lease valid?

Explanations

Explanation 1—Should Daisy Rely on Abner?

Abner's earnings are community property, and Abner and Daisy are considered owners of the community property. Under Family Code §1100(a), "either" spouse has management and control of the community personal property. Therefore, Abner has the power to control the community funds. Abner has done nothing wrong by putting his earnings in a bank account in his own name. That does not change the character of those earnings. However, under Financial Code §851, Daisy will be refused access to that account.

Daisy does not seem to want access to the bank account; she wants to have knowledge of their financial situation. Under Family Code §§721 and 1100(e), Abner has a duty to fully disclose assets and transactions regarding the community property "upon request." According to *Walker*, Abner has a duty to disclose information even "without demand." Corporations Code §16403(c)(1). Therefore, the first step would be to explain to Daisy her rights under the statute and suggest that she ask Abner again to disclose information about their financial situation, at least concerning community property. Daisy could be made aware of her other rights under Family Code §1101. The problem is that the remedies provided there require court action. Daisy has a right to request that the court order an accounting of the property and/or order that Daisy's name be added to Abner's account. If Daisy's marriage is reasonably stable, it seems unwise for her to go to Abner and threaten court action. It is doubtful that Daisy has a claim for breach of fiduciary duty, because §1101(a) states that "A spouse has a claim against the other spouse for any breach of the fiduciary duty that results in impairment to the claimant's one-half interest in the community estate . . . ." Even if Abner has breached the disclosure requirement, it is questionable whether Daisy's one-half interest in the community estate has been impaired. So it seems that the management and control provisions regarding disclosure are not so easy to "enforce" in an ongoing, stable marriage. It is clear that the provisions are meant to encourage sharing of financial information regarding community personal property, but it is also clear that disclosure cannot always be obtained, and court action is not the optimum remedy. The bottom line is to inform Daisy of her rights but explain that she should try to encourage Abner to explain without jeopardizing their marital relationship. The "law" cannot solve every marital problem.

Explanation 2—A Trip to New Zealand?

You explain that John and Abigail's earnings are community property. Once they decided to put part of their earnings in separate accounts, that did not change the character of their earnings, but it did influence their "equal" management and control rights. John has no access to Abigail's account, and Abigail has no access to John's account. Financial Code §851. Each has management and control of the community personal property, but they have different ideas regarding what to do with that property. Even though John could request that a court add his name to Abigail's account and vice versa, that does not seem to address the impasse they have reached over how to spend their community property. Neither John's suggestion that they travel nor Abigail's suggestion that they invest in a mutual fund would be considered a breach of the fiduciary duty. Neither transaction would be considered "gross negligence" or "reckless conduct" that would be a breach of fiduciary duty. Under these circumstances, John and Abigail have the right to manage and control the community property as they wish. They need to work out their differences regarding their attitude to their savings. Again the "law" cannot resolve all marital differences.

Explanation 3 — Abigail's Risky Investment

Abigail's inheritance was her separate property. She has exclusive management and control over her separate property. She need not consult with John. She has no legal duty to account how she invests her separate property. She bears the risk of the investment. There is no fiduciary duty of a spouse to account or even disclose what she does with her separate property. The management and control provisions concern community property, not a spouse's separate property.

Explanation 4 — Abigail's Investment Fails

"Either" spouse has management and control of the community personal property. Abigail's bonus from her employer would in most cases be considered community property. She has every right to invest the community personal property. John, if he knew about the bonus and had access to the bonus, would also have the right to invest the community personal property. Here Abigail invested the money without telling John. Both Family Code §721 and 1100(e) premise the disclosure "upon request." "Request" was also an issue in the *Duffy* case, 91 Cal. App. 4th 923, 111 Cal. Rptr. 2d 160. The Court of Appeal reversed the trial court finding of breach of fiduciary duty of full disclosure because there was "no evidence, substantial or insubstantial, that Patricia Duffy ever sought information . . . ." *Id.* at 933, 111 Cal. Rptr. 2d 167. Thus, since John did not request information about Abigail's investment, she had no duty to disclose how she was going to invest the $10,000 bonus.

If the investment occurred in 2003 or thereafter, the *Walker* case held that disclosure is required "without demand." Corporations Code §16403(c)(1). That means that Abigail breached her duty to disclose and would probably be liable for at least 50% of the lost investment. The other question is whether Abigail had a duty to invest wisely. In *Duffy*, the husband had invested only in risky technology stock that later lost its value. That is analogous to Abigail's investment in one stock that would be considered risky. The Legislature intended to "abrogate" *Duffy* when it added language to Family Code §721 that the duties owed to a spouse are "not limited to" those enumerated. If Abigail's conduct is considered "grossly negligent or reckless" under Corporations Code §16404(c), then she has violated her fiduciary duty. Under that rationale, John would have a claim for breach under Family Code §1101(a), because Abigail's breach has resulted in an impairment of his one-half interest in the community estate. The remedy for John is found in §1101(g), which provides that he could be awarded an amount equal to 50% of any asset "transferred in breach of the fiduciary duty" plus attorney's fees and court costs. It is possible for John to bring a claim for breach of fiduciary duty while they are still married, but it is unclear whether John wants to sue his wife during their marriage. Money problems often lead to a marriage breakup, but that is a question that John would have to consider if he would want to pursue a lawsuit for the loss of the $10,000 bonus.

Explanation 5 — False Teeth for Dogs and Cats?

John has management and control of the community personal property. The bonus from his employer would be considered community property. There is no problem with disclosure, since Abigail knew what John planned to do with the money. Her disapproval does not limit John's management and control rights — either spouse has the right to manage and control the community personal property.

One question may arise. Was the money John "gave" to his brother a gift? Under Family Code §1100(b), "a spouse may not make a gift of community personal property, or dispose of community personal property for less than fair and reasonable value, without the written consent of the other spouse." John himself would have no right to recoup a "gift," but Abigail could attempt to argue that the money given to John's brother was a "gift," even though it was in the form of an investment. Since John received what turned out to be worthless stock for his "investment," he did not receive "fair and reasonable" value. That the money was given to a family member does suggest that it could be construed as a gift. If a court found that the money to John's brother was a gift, Abigail would have a right either to ratify the gift or void the gift and seek return of the entire gift during marriage. It is doubtful, however, that a court would find that the money was a gift rather than an investment.

If the $10,000 was an investment, the remaining question would be whether this would be a breach of the fiduciary duty. The analysis would be similar to Explanation 4 concerning Abigail's investment in the bioengineering company and would depend on whether John's investment was "grossly negligent or reckless." Since John told Abigail about the investment, he did not breach the duty to disclose.

Explanation 6 — Financing Leads to Failure

It is likely that a court will find that the house is community property and that Ron breached his fiduciary duty. Although the title in Ron's name as his separate property and Martha's quitclaim deed would meet the standards of a valid transmutation, Martha's breach of fiduciary claim will undo that transmutation. Because Ron is advantaged by the transaction, the presumption of undue influence arises, and Ron would have the burden of rebutting that presumption. Even though he could show that Martha freely and voluntarily signed the quitclaim deed with knowledge of the consequences, Ron still cannot rebut the presumption. That is because there is another aspect of undue influence that consists of abusing one's position as a "fiduciary and confidant" and that violates the duty to deal with a spouse in "the highest good faith." *Marriage of Fossum*, 192 Cal. App. 4th 336, 121 Cal. Rptr. 3d 195 (2011). Therefore, in this case, Ron has violated that duty by failing to add Martha's name to the title after agreeing to do so. This scenario was based on *Marriage of Starr*, 189 Cal. App. 4th 277, 116 Cal. Rptr. 3d 813 (2010), which was decided a few months before the *Fossum* case. The *Starr* Court also stated that "there is another type of conduct that amounts to undue influence: the use of confidence or authority to obtain an unfair advantage." *Id.* at 284, 116 Cal. Rptr. 3d at 819.

Explanation 7 — The Art Collection Disappears

This scenario is reminiscent of *Fields v. Michael*, where the husband had given gifts that had been dissipated, and the wife had no recourse against the donees. Even though Henri did not "give" the pieces in the art collection away, since he received something of value in return, the drugs, still Mattie has no recourse against the drug dealers. She should be able to sue Henri's estate, claiming breach of fiduciary duty.

Here Henri violated the duty of care found in Corporations Code §16404 that is incorporated into Family Code §721. The duty of care includes "grossly negligent or reckless conduct, intentional misconduct, or a knowing violation of the law." Here, because Henri was purchasing illegal drugs, his conduct at the very least was grossly negligent or reckless and more likely a knowing violation of the law. Mattie has a claim for breach of fiduciary duty, since her one-half interest in the community estate was impaired or that was a detrimental impact on her one-half interest in the community estate. If the breach rises to the level of "oppression, fraud, or malice," Mattie could argue that the appropriate remedy is under §1101(h), where the remedy for breach of fiduciary duty is 100% of "any asset undisclosed or transferred in breach of fiduciary duty." Here, Henri's transfer of the pieces in the art collection was not disclosed to Mattie and thus transferred without her knowledge. Therefore, Mattie has a good argument that Henri violated his duty to disclose and his duty of care and thus breached his fiduciary duty. Under Family Code §1101(h), she could claim the entire $50,000 that was transferred should be awarded to her.

Explanation 8 — Avis Sells Out

After Boris took the job at the auto dealership, Avis became the "primary" manager of the community property business, ACS. Primary management means that Avis may act alone in all transactions regarding the business. Family Code §1100(d). However, Avis was required to give "prior written notice" to Boris of "sale" of the personal property used in the operation of the business. Avis orally informed Boris of the sale but did not give prior written notice.

Failure to give prior written notice does not affect the validity of the sale. Boris's remedies are found in Family Code §1101. The question would be whether Avis's sale of the business without giving prior written notice gives rise to a claim for breach of fiduciary duty. Family Code §1101(a) states that a spouse has a claim for breach of fiduciary duty that results in an impairment of or a detrimental impact to the spouse's interest in one-half interest in the community estate. Because the sale did not result in any loss of their initial investment, it would be difficult to argue that Boris's interest was impaired by the sale of a business that was not profitable. Therefore, it would be doubtful that the failure to give written notice, even though a violation of Family Code §1101(d), would rise to the level of an actionable claim against Avis.

The bottom line is that the sale is valid and cannot be voided. Boris should calm down and be told that he should be happy that Avis was able to sell the business. Avis should be advised of her duty under the Family Code when managing a community property business.

Explanation 9 — Avis Checks Out

Avis wrote three checks from the bank account that contained the proceeds from the sale of ACS, their community property business. Those funds were community property. The issue is whether Avis "transferred" or "disposed" of the property in violation of the TRO. The first check for rent would be considered a "necessity of life," which is an exception to the restraint on a spouse's management and control of the community property during divorce proceedings. The second check to retain a divorce lawyer is also not precluded by the TRO. The third check for tuition for paralegal school is questionable. The TRO prevents a spouse from transferring or "in any way" disposing of community property without the written consent of the other party or an order of court. It seems that Avis did not receive Boris's consent or receive an order of court. If this was an "extraordinary expenditure," Avis was required to notify Boris of any such proposed expenditure and account to the court for that expenditure. It seems that Avis did neither. Thus, it seems that Avis violated the TRO, and that would be considered a violation of the fiduciary duty owed during the period when the divorce is pending.

What is the remedy for that violation? In the *Rossi* case, the remedy for the violation of the fiduciary duty was found in Family Code §1101(h). There the wife had deliberately concealed her winning the California Lottery. The Court awarded the entire winnings to the husband. Like the *McTiernan* case, the court may be somewhat more lenient in this case, where the expenditure was for education. Thus, the remedy would more likely be under Family Code §1101(g), which provides for an award of 50% of the asset "transferred" in violation of the fiduciary duty. Therefore, Avis would be required to reimburse Boris for one-half of the amount, $1,500, that she paid out for the tuition and any court costs and attorney's fees Boris incurred. There would also be a possibility that the court would award an additional penalty, such as bank fees and interest, based on the language in Family Code §1101(g) that the remedies are "not limited" to those listed. Also it should be noted that Avis would have violated the TRO even if she had used her separate property instead of community property.

Explanation 10—Get Out of Jail Free?

Park Place is community property even though the title is in Ira's name. It was purchased with his earnings, community property. Even though either spouse can manage and control community real property, "both spouses must join in executing any instrument by which that community real property . . . is encumbered." Family Code §1102(a). Ira acted alone when he borrowed the money to post the bail, and he alone executed the deed of trust on Park Place. He fits the description of conniving spouse, but the bail bond company also seems to fit the description of innocent lender. The encumbrance is presumed to be valid, because the bail bond company did not know that Ira was married. Even though the bail bond company was a "good faith encumbrancer," Terry's right to join in the encumbrance was still violated. We have two innocent parties: the bail bond company and Terry. She can void the instrument creating the deed of trust as long as she acts within the one-year statute of limitations found in §1102(d). She will be able to void the encumbrance entirely. However, the community will still be responsible for the debt that Ira incurred during their marriage. If or when Terry divorces Ira, she would have a good claim that Ira breached his fiduciary duty. At present, however, Ira got out of jail free of his responsibilities to the community.

Explanation 11 — Terry Hires an Attorney

Yes. This exception to the "joinder" rule is found in §1102(e). Terry can encumber her interest in community real property to pay reasonable attorney's fees in a dissolution proceeding. The interest encumbered is only one-half of the real property.

Explanation 12 — Terry Rents the Beach Cottage

Either spouse has the right to manage community real property. The joinder requirement is limited to major transactions. A lease "for a longer period than one year" is considered a major transaction that requires both spouses to join. Here the lease is for six months, so Terry can enter into a valid lease without Ira's signature. Practically speaking, if Ira never reappears or objects, Terry has the power to lease the beach cottage.

What if We Have Debts? Creditors' Rights and the Community

LIABILITY FOR MARITAL AND PREMARITAL DEBTS

Many chapters of this book are devoted to the characterization of property acquired by married couples. In addition to acquiring property, it is well known that married couples in today's society very often acquire substantial debts. It would be a logical approach to characterize debts just as we characterize property—as community debt or separate property debt. The outcome of that characterization would then be that community property would be liable for community debt, and a spouse's separate property would be responsible for that spouse's separate property debt. Although logical, that is not how married couple's debts are treated. That approach was explicitly rejected in the California Supreme Court case of *Grolemund v. Cafferata*, 17 Cal. 2d 679, 111 P.2d 641 (1941). One reason for the California system is the very strong state policy that creditors should be paid for debts owed to them. Another reason is the history of how the management and control of community property, limited to the husband prior to January 1, 1975, influenced the development of law regarding marital debt. In short, most of the law in this area ensures that creditors can reach as much property, usually the community property, as is available.

Rather than characterizing debts as community or separate, the California system allocates responsibility or "liability" for debts between the community property and each spouse's separate property. The major goal is to ensure that there is property available to meet the obligations of the spouses. The main statutory provision, Family Code §910(a), protects creditors in that "the community estate is liable for a debt incurred by either spouse before or during marriage." That section also states that it does not matter which spouse controls the community property or whether one or both spouses are party to the debt. Think of that—the community property is liable for debts incurred before marriage as well as during marriage! One spouse can obligate the community property for his or her own premarital debt. Think of it this way: "I marry you and your debts!" At this point, you should see that the main debt statute provides very broad protection for creditors.

We should also note that §910(a) refers only to the "community estate," which is defined as community property and quasi-community property. Family Code §§63, 912. See Chapter 10 for the definition of quasi-community property. What about each spouse's separate property? The provision dealing with the liability of each spouse's separate property both expands and limits the liability of a spouse's separate property. Sections 913(a) and (b) provide that a spouse's separate property is liable for his or her own debts but not for the debts of the other spouse. Thus a creditor can reach the community property for a debt incurred by one spouse, and if there is no community property or limited community and quasi-community property, the creditor can also reach the separate property of the spouse who incurred the debt. Again we see the policy of protecting creditors evident in the debt statutes.

However, it is important to note that §913(a) speaks of "a married person's" liability for a debt incurred either by *that person* or by the *person's spouse.* Here we find that the statutes differentiate between the spouse who incurs a debt and the spouse who does not incur the debt. Separate property liability follows the spouse who incurs the debt. Community property liability does not depend on the spouse who incurs the debt. In conclusion, there are two basic principles regarding a married couple's responsibility for debts. The first principle is that the community *estate* is liable for debts incurred by either spouse before or during marriage. The second general principle is that a *spouse's separate property* is liable for debts he or she incurred before or during marriage but not the other spouse's debts.

EXCEPTIONS TO LIABILITY RULES

As soon as those principles are stated, we learn that there is an exception to the second principle—a spouse's separate property is liable for certain types of debts incurred by the other spouse. Sections 914(a)(1) and (2) provide that a married person is "personally liable" for a debt incurred for the "necessaries of life" while the spouses are living together and for the "common necessaries of life" while the spouses are living apart. That section introduces several new phrases that need to be defined. The phrase "personally liable" means that all the person's property, both community and separate, is liable for the other spouse's debts. "Necessaries of life" are defined as living costs consistent with the spouses' station in life; "common necessaries of life" are defined as expenses that are required to sustain life.

Several other definitions are important to understanding the expanse of a couple's liability for debts. First, what is a "debt"? A "debt" includes contract, tort, and other obligations, such as child or spousal support from a prior marriage. Second, when is debt "incurred"? Debt is considered "incurred" at the time a contract is made or a tort occurs or the obligation arises. Family Code §903. Third, how long does the liability for debts last? The answer is "during marriage," which excludes the "period during which the spouses are living separate and apart before a judgment of dissolution of marriage." Family Code §910(b).

At this point, to flesh out the principles and definitions, let us return to our imaginary couple, Harry and Wilma. Like many married couples, as soon as they marry, they begin a life together by incurring debts. Assume that Harry works outside the home, and Wilma has a trust fund that was set up by her parents before she married Harry. She receives monthly checks from the fund, which she deposits in a bank account in her own name. Harry's earnings will be considered community property. Wilma's trust fund checks are her separate property. In order to furnish their apartment, they buy furniture on credit. The debt for the furniture is $10,000. Under the California scheme, the question is whether the community estate is liable for the debt or whether Wilma's separate property would also be liable for the debt. Clearly, the community estate (in this case, Harry's earnings) would be liable for the furniture debt. The debt is a contract debt, incurred during marriage. It does not matter which spouse incurred the debt, and it does not matter who has management and control of Harry's earnings. Wilma's separate property would also be liable for the furniture debt even if Harry was the one who incurred the debt. Even though a spouse's separate property is shielded from debts incurred by the other spouse, a spouse's separate property is liable for necessaries of life incurred by the other spouse. Because furniture would be considered a necessary of life, considering Harry and Wilma's station in life, Wilma's separate property would be liable for that debt even if Harry was the one who incurred the debt.

The next important issue concerns the *timing* of the debt. Both Family Code §910(a) (community estate's liability) and §913 (separate property liability) refer to debts incurred before or during marriage. However, we can understand that a spouse may not want to be responsible for the other spouse's premarital debt. For instance, let's say Wilma had purchased a cottage near Arrowhead before Harry and Wilma married. She has a mortgage on the cottage of over $100,000. According to Family Code §910(a), the *community* estate is liable for a debt incurred by either spouse *before* or during marriage. That means that Harry's earnings would be liable for the payment of the mortgage even though he is not a party to that debt. Perhaps, in an effort to encourage marriage, the debt provisions allow Harry to shield his earnings from liability for Wilma's premarital debt. Family Code §911(a) provides that "the earnings of a married person during marriage are not liable for a debt incurred by the person's spouse before marriage." There are certain requirements for Harry to take advantage of the protection of his earnings from Wilma's premarital debt. He must keep those earnings in an account in which Wilma has no right of withdrawal, and he must not commingle those earnings with any other community property. Thus, Harry can protect his earnings from liability for Wilma's $100,000 premarital debt. Harry's separate property would also not be liable for Wilma's debt, but Wilma's separate property would be liable for that debt. Family Code §913(a) and (b) states that a married person's separate property (Harry's separate property if he has any) is not liable for a debt incurred by the person's spouse (Wilma) before or during marriage, but a married person's separate property (Wilma's trust fund money) is liable for a debt incurred by the person (Wilma) before or during marriage. The exception in §914 dealing with necessaries and common necessaries does not apply in this case, as it is limited to debts incurred during marriage, and Wilma's debt for the cottage was incurred before they married.

CHILD AND SPOUSAL SUPPORT OBLIGATIONS

Another common type of premarital debt in today's society is a child or spousal support obligation from a prior marriage. For instance, in our hypothetical, assume that Wilma was married before and has a spousal support obligation to her former husband, Fred. Obviously, Harry would not want to be responsible for that debt. However, Family Code §915(a) states that "a child or spousal support obligation of a married person that does not arise out of the marriage shall be treated as a debt incurred before marriage." That means that the community estate would be liable for the debt unless Harry shields his earnings as allowed by Family Code §911(a). If Harry does not shield his earnings, then the community estate is liable for Wilma's spousal support obligation. Yet Family Code §915(b) allows for reimbursement to the community estate from Wilma's separate income. Also, Wilma's separate property would be liable for the spousal support obligation, but Harry's separate property (if he has any) would not be liable. Family Code §913(a) and (b). From analysis of the interplay of debt provisions, we can glean that treating child and spousal support obligations as debts incurred before marriage manifests a policy of ensuring that children and spouses of prior marriages will not be disadvantaged by a parent or ex-spouse remarrying. Children and ex-spouses are protected by liability for support obligations being placed on the community estate and the separate property of the parent and ex-spouse. Also, the debt provisions indicate that a new spouse can protect his or her earnings from the other spouse's child and spousal support obligations from a prior marriage. Again we see that the proper way to analyze the debt statutes is to determine what property, community or separate, will be liable for a particular type of debt.

TORT OBLIGATIONS

The next type of debt concerns obligations arising from tort. Debt includes "an obligation incurred by a married person before or during marriage, whether based on contract, tort, or otherwise." Family Code §902. There is no differentiation between the treatment of a tort obligation from other debts. That means that the community estate is liable for the debt incurred before or during marriage. A spouse can shield his or her earnings from a tort debt incurred before marriage by the other spouse. The separate property of the tortfeasor spouse is liable; the separate property of the other spouse is not liable. There is, however, a special "order of satisfaction" for tort obligations involving death, personal injury, or property damage. Under Family Code §1000(b), liability may in some cases be satisfied first from the community estate or in other cases first from the separate property of the tortfeasor spouse. But, let's be clear, the creditor will be "satisfied."

The order of satisfaction depends on whether "the liability of the married person" is or is not "based on an act or omission which occurred while the married person was performing an activity for the benefit of the community." Family Code §1000(b)(1), (2). The order of satisfaction is that if the liability is based on an act or omission that occurred during an activity for the benefit of the community, then the liability "shall first be satisfied from the community estate property and second from the separate property of the married person." In the opposite situation, the order of satisfaction is reversed—first from the separate property of the tortfeasor spouse and then from the community estate property. Thus we see that creditors again are protected. The only question is which property will be reached first.

The interpretation of "performing an activity for the benefit of the community" is somewhat murky. It is clear that the tort itself is not what the statute is referring to. Committing a tort is never for the benefit of the community. Let's say that Harry was involved in a car accident on the way to work. That is an easy case—the negligence is not for the benefit of the community, but the *act* of negligence occurred while Harry was performing an activity for the benefit of the community—going to work. Let's say Harry was involved in a car accident on the way to church. In that case, the activity for the benefit of the community is less obvious, because it seems to be for Harry's personal benefit. Yet it is likely that the activity of going to church would be for the benefit of the community, since Harry's spiritual uplift from church attendance would arguably benefit the community. Let's say Harry was involved in a car accident while going to purchase stolen goods. In that case, the activity was a crime and therefore not a benefit to the community (even though one could attempt to argue that the crime was of monetary benefit to the community). Considering why we have an "order of satisfaction," we see that although creditors of all types must be paid, where a spouse is not benefiting the community through particular activities, the tortfeasor's separate property should be used first to satisfy that type of debt.

LIVING SEPARATE AND APART

One important timing issue concerns debts incurred while the spouses are living separate and apart before a judgment of dissolution of marriage or legal separation. The liability of the community estate includes debts incurred by either spouse before or *during marriage*. What is the definition of "during marriage"? According to Family Code §910(b), "during marriage" extends only until the spouses separate. In other words, "marriage" for purposes of liability of the community estate for debts ends when the spouses separate. See Chapter 8 for the definition of "living separate and apart." There seems to be an exception to that rule found in Family Code §914(a)(2) covering common necessaries of life: "A married person is personally liable for . . . a debt incurred for common necessaries of life of the person's spouse while the spouses are living separately." Since a spouse's earnings are separate property once the spouses are living separate and apart, under this section, a spouse's earnings would still be liable for common necessaries of life incurred by the other spouse. The reason seems to be twofold: (1) a spouse's duty of support extends until the marriage is dissolved; and (2) no spouse should be deprived of the barest necessities of life—food, clothing, housing, medical care—because a creditor may not be assured of payment for debt.

Let us say that Harry and Wilma separate. Harry has lost his job and has a small savings account. He moves into an apartment and uses the last of his savings for the security deposit and the first three months of rent.

The landlord is willing to allow him to stay for three more months on a promise to pay. Wilma will be responsible for that three months' rent. Rent is a "common necessary of life." The spouses are living separately. Wilma is "personally liable," which means her separate property would be liable for Harry's debt even though it was incurred after they were living separate and apart because it is a common necessary of life. Thus, Harry is not out on the street, and the landlord will be paid even though there is no community property available.

SUMMARY

In conclusion, the debt provisions are best understood as protecting creditors of the spouses. The community estate is liable for debts incurred by either spouse before or during marriage. A spouse's separate property is liable for his or her own debts incurred before or during marriage. Regarding premarital debts, a spouse may shield his or her earnings from the premarital debts of the other spouse by keeping those earnings uncommingled with other community property in an account in which the other spouse has no right of withdrawal. After separation, a spouse is liable only for debts for common necessaries of life incurred by the other spouse. A tort obligation is subject to liability of the community estate and the tortfeasor's separate property. The community estate is reached first for tort liability if the tortfeasor spouse was performing an activity for the benefit of the community. The tortfeasor's separate property is reached first if the tortfeasor spouse was not performing an activity for the benefit of the community.

Examples

Example 1 — For Better or Worse and for Debts?

You are at a party, and one of your friends comes to you for advice. He is planning to marry soon but has some doubts about his fiancee. Although she has a very good job, it seems she has a problem with accumulated credit card debt. He wants to know if he will be responsible for her debt after they are married. Advise.

Example 2 — Who's Responsible for Child Support?

Your friend also explains to you that he was married before and has a child support obligation to his children from a prior marriage. He wants to know if his fiancee can be obligated to help pay for that obligation. Advise.

Example 3 — Who's Responsible for the Wreck?

Your friend also explains that he was involved in a car accident about a year ago, and there is a lawsuit pending against him. He is almost sure that he will be held liable for the accident, but it has not yet been decided. If he has a judgment against him, he wants to know if his fiancee can be obligated to help pay the judgment. Advise.

Example 4 — Mickey Wants Minnie to Pay

Mickey and Minnie recently married. Both come from extremely wealthy families and live off trust funds that were set up for them when they were children. They keep the proceeds from their trust funds in separate bank accounts. Mickey owns a large home in the Hollywood Hills. His accountant suggested it would be a tax advantage for him to take a loan to decorate the home before he married Minnie. He hired an interior designer to decorate the home, and the loan was for $100,000. After they married, Mickey asked Minnie to contribute to the repayment of the loan. She asks you if she is obligated to help pay the loan. Advise.

Example 5 — Does Minnie Have to Pay?

Assume the facts are the same as Example 4, except that Minnie decides that Mickey's house needs to be redecorated after they marry. Because Mickey's accountant explains that it would be better for him to undertake the loan, he incurs the loan for $100,000. Would Minnie be obligated to repay the loan from her separate property?

Example 6 — Who Pays the Doctor's Bill?

Ben and Casey were married for several years. Ben worked outside the home, and Casey was a homemaker who took care of their children. Ben moved out of the family home about six months ago. After Ben left, Casey saw Dr. X for a severe case of depression. Over a period of three months, her bill for medical services was over $5,000. Ben has recently received letters from Dr. X demanding payment for Casey's medical treatment. They have not yet filed for divorce and have recently consulted a family counselor about reconciliation. Ben wants to know if he is responsible for Dr. X's bill. Advise.

Example 7 — Does Ben Have to Pay?

Assume the facts are the same as Example 6, except that Ben and Casey have filed for divorce, and there is no hope for reconciliation. Ben wants to know if he is responsible for Dr. X's bill. Advise.

Explanations

Explanation 1 — For Better or Worse and for Debts?

You would answer your friend's question by explaining that the community estate is liable for premarital debts. It would be important to explain also that earnings are community property and would be liable for his wife's premarital debts. Her earnings are also community property and would be liable for her debts. Also, if she has any separate property, it would be liable for her premarital debt. Your friend's separate property would not be liable for her premarital debt. There is a way, you can tell your friend, to shield his earnings from her premarital credit card debt. Tell him to open an account in his own name. Deposit in that account only his earnings and no other property. Make sure that his wife is not on that account, and that account will be shielded from her creditors.

Although that answer is based on the debt statutes in the Family Code, it is also possible to enter into a premarital agreement specifying that all earnings are the separate property of each spouse. If creditors are made aware of that premarital agreement, then the friend's earnings would not be community property and would not be liable for a premarital debt.

Explanation 2 — Who's Responsible for Child Support?

Child support obligations for a child from a prior marriage are treated as premarital debt. That means that the community estate, your friend's earnings, and his soon-to-be wife's earnings, would be liable for that debt. But his soon-to-be wife can also take advantage of the shield for her earnings by putting those earnings in a bank account in her name and keeping them uncommingled with any other community property. However, if your friend has any separate income, and community property is applied to the child support obligation, the community has a right to reimbursement from the debtor spouse's separate property for the amount of community property applied.

Explanation 3 — Who's Responsible for the Wreck?

Assuming that a judgment is entered against your friend after he is married to his fiancee, the issue is when was the debt incurred. It is possible to argue that the debt was not incurred until the judgment was entered, which in this case would make it a marital debt. However, Family Code §903 states that a debt is incurred "in the case of a tort, at the time the tort arose." In this case, that is before the friend's marriage. Thus, the tort judgment would be treated as a premarital debt. Community property and the friend's separate property are liable for a tort debt. However, there is an order of satisfaction.

If the liability of the friend is *not* based on an act or omission that occurred while the married person was performing an act for the benefit of the community, the friend's separate property is reached first and the community property second. Here it is clear that the omission occurred before marriage, and therefore his act would not have been for the benefit of the community. You should note, however, that if the friend has no separate property, community property would be reached by the tort creditor. If the fiancee shields her earnings as provided by statute, those earnings would not be liable nor would her separate property be liable for the friend's tort judgment.

Explanation 4—Mickey Wants Minnie to Pay

In this example, there is no community property involved. Mickey and Minnie's trust funds were set up before they were married and are therefore separate property. The rents, issues, and profits of separate property are separate property. The debt here was incurred by Mickey prior to marriage. According to Family Code §913(a), Mickey's separate property is liable for a debt he incurred before marriage. According to Family Code §913(b), Minnie's separate property is *not* liable for a spouse's debt incurred before marriage. So far, Minnie would not be obligated to pay the premarital debt that Mickey incurred.

There is an issue of whether Minnie would be obligated, because the debt was incurred for a "necessary of life." A married person is "personally liable" (that includes the person's separate property) for a debt incurred for the necessaries of life of the person's spouse. Arguably, interior decoration of a home would be considered a "necessary of life" because of Mickey and Minnie's station in life. However, that liability only covers debts incurred by the person's spouse *during* marriage, while the spouses are *living together.* Mickey incurred the debt *before* marriage. So even though the debt could be considered a necessary of life, Minnie's separate property could not be reached by the creditor who gave Mickey the loan. Whether Minnie wants to help pay the loan for the sake of marital peace is something Mickey and Minnie would have to decide. There is no legal obligation for Minnie to repay the loan.

Explanation 5—Does Minnie Have to Pay?

Generally, a married person's separate property is not liable for a debt incurred by the person's spouse during marriage. Here Mickey incurred the debt during marriage. The exception to the rule is a debt incurred *during* marriage for necessaries of life of the person's spouse while the spouses are *living together.* In this case, it is arguable that redecorating Mickey's house was a necessary of life. Thus, not only would Mickey's separate property be liable for the loan, but also Minnie's separate property would be liable for the loan.

Explanation 6 — Who Pays the Doctor's Bill?

The answer is that Ben would have to pay Dr. X's bill. The community estate is liable for debts incurred by either spouse during marriage. According to Family Code §910(b), "during marriage" does not include the period during which the spouses are living "separate and apart." Because Ben and Casey have not yet reached the point of final parting of the ways, the medical bill would be considered incurred during marriage. In addition, until they are actually living "separate and apart," Ben's earnings are still considered community property. Therefore, Ben would be liable for Dr. X's bill.

Explanation 7 — Does Ben Have to Pay?

The change in facts indicates that Ben and Casey meet the requirements for living "separate and apart." Therefore, the community estate would not be liable for a debt incurred while they are living separate and apart. Also, once Ben and Casey are living separate and apart, Ben's earnings become his separate property. If the medical bill was incurred before they were living separate and apart, as stated in Explanation 6, the community property (Ben's earnings) would be liable for Casey's bill.

If Casey incurred the medical bill after they were living separate and apart, there is still a very good argument that Ben would be liable. Under Family Code §914(a)(2), a married person (Ben) is personally liable (community and separate property) for a debt incurred by the person's spouse (Casey) during marriage, including a debt incurred for common necessaries of life of the person's spouse (Casey) while the spouses are living separately. Under that section, Ben's earnings, even if separate property, would be liable for Casey's medical treatment, which is a common necessary of life. The problem with the analysis is that §914(a) uses the phrase, "during marriage." It is possible that the phrase "during marriage" has a different meaning from "during marriage" in §910(b). During marriage in the section dealing with common necessaries could be interpreted to mean that marriage continues until the marriage is actually dissolved by the court or by legal separation. Thus Ben would be personally liable for Casey's medical bill. There is clearly an ambiguity in the statute concerning the meaning of "during marriage" in the two sections.

It seems that the policies of making sure that a spouse can incur debt for a common necessary of life and that a creditor will be assured of payment for that debt would mandate that the debt statute would make the nondebtor spouse personally liable. Under that analysis, Ben would be liable for Casey's medical bill.

CHAPTER 8

How Do I Leave Thee? Division at Divorce

SEPARATE AND APART

We have often stated that earnings during *marriage* are considered community property. The general community property presumption states that property acquired or possessed during *marriage* is presumed to be community property. Therefore, it is a "given" that earnings or acquisitions by an ex-spouse after the marriage is over would be considered the separate property of that ex-spouse. Still, questions remain. For instance, how are earnings treated during the period of separation before the actual divorce? If they are treated as separate property of the spouse earning them, when does "separation" actually occur?

One logical answer as to how to treat earnings during separation would be to say that those earnings are community property until the actual divorce decree is issued. This is a logical answer, but wrong. Family Code §771 states that "The earnings and accumulations of a spouse . . . while living separate and apart from the other spouse, are the separate property of the spouse." Thus we learn that the crucial time that changes earnings from community property into the separate property of the earning spouse is when spouses are "living separate and apart." The statute does not define "living separate and apart.

Marriage of Baragry

There are many possible points in time that could be used to determine when the couple is "living separate and apart." The most obvious time is when one spouse moves out of the home. Another time would be when the spouses no longer have sexual relations. Another would be the date a dissolution petition is filed with the court. Yet the definition used in the famous *Marriage of Baragry* case, 75 Cal. App. 3d 444, 140 Cal. Rptr. 779 (1977), is "when spouses have come to a parting of the ways with no present intention of resuming marital relations." The Court directs examination of the parties' *conduct* that "evidences a complete and final break in the marital relationship." Even though the definition seems to refer to the parties' intentions, it is the conduct that determines their intentions regarding the marital relationship.

In the *Baragry* case, the determination of "living separate and apart" was the major issue, because the Baragrys had a very long period of time between the date the husband moved out of the house, August 1971, and the time the husband filed his petition for dissolution, October 1975. The issue was the status of the husband's earnings during the period after he moved out of the house. If at that point, the spouses were "living separate and apart," then all his earnings would have been his separate property. If the spouses still had a marital relationship up until the time he filed his petition for dissolution, then all his earnings during that four-year period would have been community property.

The trial court used the earlier date, but the Court of Appeal opted for the later date. Clearly, the wife presented the more sympathetic case according to the appellate court's view. The husband moved out of the family home, stayed on his boat for a while and ended up renting an apartment and staying there with his girlfriend. Yet he maintained the appearances of his marriage. He ate dinner at home often and kept his home as his mailing address. He filed joint tax returns. He took his wife and two daughters on trips and to basketball games after he moved out. He took his wife to social events and regularly brought his laundry home. His wife continued to do his laundry and hoped that he would return to her. They had no marital relations after the husband moved out, but they maintained the "façade of a marital relationship."

The Court of Appeal was unimpressed with the husband's testimony that he maintained the outward appearances of marriage because he wanted to preserve social appearances and keep in touch with his children. Nor was the Court swayed by his statement that he delayed filing for divorce because his upbringing made him reluctant to file for divorce. The Court instead viewed the husband as "enjoying a captain's paradise, savoring the best of two worlds, and capturing the benefits of both." The Court determined that "[d]uring the period that spouses preserve the appearance of marriage, they both reap its benefits, and their earnings remain community property." Thus the couple was not living separate and apart until the husband filed his petition for dissolution in October 1975.

Look at All the Conduct

It is clear from later cases that neither moving out of the house nor filing the dissolution petition are necessarily determinative of the actual date of living separate and apart. Instead, the courts must look at all of the conduct of the spouses to determine the actual date. In *Marriage of Hardin*, 38 Cal. App. 4th 448, 45 Cal. Rptr. 2d 308 (1995), there were 14 years between the husband moving out of the house in 1969 and the dissolution of their marriage in 1983. The wife, Doris, argued that 1983 was the separation date. The husband, Victor, argued for the move-out date of 1969. The trial court agreed with Victor, relying on the facts that after Victor moved out, both parties dated other people; they did not attend business, social events, or family events together; and Doris had filed dissolution petitions specifying the move-out date as the date of separation. The Court of Appeal thought that the trial court had "failed to consider" other relevant evidence such as the parties' continuing economic relationship in the family business and Victor's lack of intention to end the marriage until early 1983. The case was remanded to determine the date of separation.

The date of separation was again at issue in *Marriage of Manfer*, 144 Cal. App. 4th 925, 50 Cal. Rptr. 3d 785 (2006). The husband, Samuel, argued for the later date of March 15, 2005, and the wife, Maureen, argued for the earlier date of July 1, 2004. During that period of time, Maureen's income would have totaled several hundred thousand dollars and would have been considered community property. Thus, the date of separation was crucial.

Samuel argued that the date of separation should be determined based on an "outsider's viewpoint" standard. He reasoned that because he and Maureen agreed to keep their separation secret from family and friends until after the year-end holidays, the date of separation should be close to the date that family and friends were told that they had separated. That was about one month before he filed the petition of dissolution. Maureen argued that it was the spouses' private conduct that controlled the date of separation. Samuel had moved out in June 2004 after they quarreled. They kept up appearances by having some social contacts and taking a trip together, but had no sexual relations and did not commingle funds or support each other after June 2004. Despite determining that their private conduct showed a final and complete break in June 2004, the trial court chose the later date of March 15, 2005 based on an *objective* test: "Would society at large consider the couple separated?" *Id.* at 928, 50 Cal. Rptr. 3d at 788.

The Court of Appeal rejected that standard. Quoting from *Marriage of Hardin* that "[n]o facts are per se determinative," *Id.* at 930, 50 Cal. Rptr. 3d at 789, the Court of Appeal noted that "[t]he best evidence is *their words and actions*." *Id.* (italics in the original). Samuel and the trial court's reliance on the *Baragry* Court's language about "appearance of marriage" misconstrued the test. "The question is not what society at large would have perceived, but what the parties' 'subjective intent' was, as 'objectively determined from *all of the evidence reflecting the parties' words and actions* during the disputed time.'" *Id.* at 934, 50 Cal. Rptr. 3d at 792 (italics in the original).

In conclusion, there is no one fact that will easily determine the date a couple is living separate and apart. As long as a couple is willing to litigate over when the separation occurred, the courts must consider all the facts of *their* relationship to determine when separation actually occurred.

Separate and Apart Under One Roof?

In most cases, one spouse has moved out, and the issue is whether, during the period when the spouses may be attempting to reconcile, one spouse's earnings are community or separate property. One question is whether a couple can live separate and apart while still living under the same roof. This unusual scenario occurred in the case of *Marriage of Norviel*, 102 Cal. App. 4th 1152, 126 Cal. Rptr. 2d 148 (2002). In that case, the husband stated his intention that their marriage was at an end on June 28, 1998. He did not move out of their home until August 15, 1998, and only in September 1998 did he file for dissolution and establish his own bank and credit card accounts. In the time period between June and September, the husband received certain stock options, which would have been his separate property if the spouses were living separate and apart as of June 28, 1998.

The first question facing the Court of Appeal was whether a couple can be considered living separate and apart if they are still physically living in the same residence. The Court concluded that "living apart physically is an indispensable threshold requirement to separation." *Id.* at 1162, 128 Cal. Rptr. 2d at 156. Yet the Court also stated that it is possible that spouses could be physically separated and still be living in the same residence, but it would take "unambiguous, objectively ascertainable conduct amounting to a physical separation under the same roof." *Id.* Sleeping in separate bedrooms was not sufficient. In the Norviel marriage, they had been sleeping in separate bedrooms for nearly four years before the husband stated his intent to end the marriage. The Court cited only one California case, where the couple was found to live separate and apart while living in the same house: The wife had sought an order evicting the husband from the home, occupied separate locked rooms, refused to speak to the husband, and called the police on two occasions when the husband entered her rooms. *Popescu v. Popescu*, 46 Cal. App. 2d 44, 115 P.2d 208 (1941).

There was a vigorous dissent in *Norviel*. The dissent disagreed that physical separation was an absolute requirement of living separate and apart:

> People who have reached a decision as difficult and emotional as ending a lengthy marriage may often be unable to simultaneously engage in such clear-headed conduct as changing legal title on properties, closing bank accounts, dividing funds and establishing new bank accounts, discontinuing and applying for new credit cards, and arranging for new housing. . . . Surely the parties should be allowed a transition period to take the necessary steps to untangle the financial, legal and social ties incident to their decision to change their marital status.

Norviel, 102 Cal. App. 4th at 1166, 126 Cal. Rptr. 2d at 159.

The Supreme Court addressed the issue of the meaning of "living separate and apart" and held that "'living separate and apart' refers to the situation in which spouses are living in separate residences and at least one of them has the subjective intent to end the marital relationship, which intent is objectively evidenced by words or conduct reflecting that there is a complete and final break in the marriage relationship." *Marriage of Davis*, 61 Cal. 4th 846, 864, 352 P.3d 401, 412, 189 Cal. Rptr. 3d 835, 849 (2015). Yet the majority opinion and a concurring opinion left open the possibility that there could be "circumstances that would support a finding that the spouses were 'living separate and apart,' i.e., that they had established separate residences with the requisite objectively evidenced intent, even though they continued to literally share one roof." *Id.* at 412, fn.7, 352 P.3d at 412, fn.7, 189 Cal. Rptr. 3d at 849, fn.7. In most cases, the spouses will have separate residences, and the Supreme Court has purported to give a bright-line rule, yet there will still be some room to argue that separation occurred prior to a spouse actually establishing a separate residence.

The Legislature Abrogates *Davis* and Sets a New Standard

Rather than trying to explore any "room to argue" in *Davis*, California family law attorneys and judges read the decision narrowly. The Supreme Court's bright line rule made separate residences an essential component of the date of separation. This interpretation prevented finding an earlier date of separation for spouses who continued to live together but clearly subjectively and objectively intended to end their marriage. The date of separation typically was fixed on the day when the spouse no longer shared the residence.

The California Legislature resolved the problem by enacting Family Code §70 on January 1, 2017. Family Code §70 explicitly abrogated the decisions of *Marriage of Davis*, 61 Cal. 4th 846 (2015) and *In re Marriage of*

Norviel, 102 Cal. App. 4th 1152 (2002). It also provided a standard, including objective and subjective factors, to determine the date of separation.

Family Code §70 states:

> "(a) Date of separation" means the date that a complete and final break in the marital relationship has occurred, as evidenced by both of the following:
>
> (1) The spouse has expressed to the other spouse his or her intent to end the marriage.
>
> (2) The conduct of the spouse is consistent with his or her intent to end the marriage.
>
> (b) In determining the date of separation, the court shall take into consideration all relevant evidence.

Family Code §70 tells us there must be a complete and final break in that marital relationship. To show that break requires a dual showing:

- First, a spouse must have expressed to the other spouse his or her intent to end the marriage (objective fact).
- Second, that spouse's conduct must be consistent with that intent to end the marriage (subjective conclusion).

The court must consider all relevant evidence. This evidence can include but not be limited to physical separation, social interaction together, maintaining or changing joint or separate bank accounts, attending family events together, vacations, and, to some extent, new intimate relationships, one or both spouses may undertake. Joint or separate tax filing is relevant but not essential as evidence.

Date of Separation and Reconciliation

According to Family Code §70, a married couple doesn't have to physically separate for there to be a date of separation. They can live under the same roof. However, even after filing for divorce, if they are intimate sexually, this may be interpreted as a reconciliation. A court may decide that the break in the marital relationship was not "complete and final." The court likely would no longer recognize the first date of separation, but find a later date based on the dual criteria of Family Code §70 being met. As a consequence, property that would have been one spouse's separate property with an earlier date of separation could be community property because it was acquired before that later date of separation.

Examples

Example 1 — When Did Alan and Barbara Separate?

Alan and Barbara were married in 1999. In 2013, Barbara moved out of their home and filed a petition for dissolution of marriage. She rented an apartment near their home. They continued to have sexual relations even after Barbara moved out. They also saw a marriage counselor in hopes of saving their marriage. Alan and Barbara took several trips together. In 2014, Barbara moved back into their home for a brief period of time. Finally, in 2015, Barbara moved out again and filed another petition for dissolution. They have had no sexual relations since that time. When did Alan and Barbara separate? What are Alan's arguments? Barbara's?

Example 2 — Karl Never Returned

Karl and Judy were married in 1999. In 2012, Karl moved out of their home at Judy's request. Karl several times asked to return home but never did. Karl continued to pay for Judy's support. Judy saw a marriage counselor, but Karl refused to participate in the counseling. However, they maintained a joint checking account and credit cards, filed joint tax returns, and even took title to a car jointly. Karl visited Judy often, sent her gifts on special occasions and holidays, took her out socially, and took her on vacations. They continued to have sexual relations until Karl informed Judy that he intended to stop supporting her when he retired at the end of 2015. Soon after, Judy filed a petition for dissolution. When did Karl and Judy separate? What are Karl's arguments? Judy's?

Example 3 — Patrick and Susan Break Up

Patrick and Susan were married in 1990. Patrick traveled quite a bit for business and had a condo in New York where he stayed while there. They had always kept their financial affairs separate, maintaining separate bank accounts and holding their property in their individual names. In 2013, Susan wrote Patrick a letter while he was in New York on business and told him that she decided to end their relationship. At that time, Patrick moved most of his belongings to his condo in New York but kept a few things at their home. At the end of 2014, Susan moved out of the family home to an apartment and asked Patrick to remove his remaining belongings. Patrick did so. Susan then filed a petition of dissolution in 2015. When did Patrick and Susan separate? What are Patrick's arguments? Susan's?

Example 4—John and Kelly—Bosco's Broken Home

John and Kelly married in 2016. They bought a 2-bedroom townhouse in West Los Angeles, taking title in both their names as Community Property. They shared joint checking bank accounts into which their paychecks were directly deposited. Each had named the other as beneficiary of employment-related benefits, and life insurance. They had a beloved dog, Bosco, a chocolate Labrador retriever. On Valentines Day (February 14, 2020) John told Kelly that he had fallen in love with someone else, named Leslie. John said that, although he would always care deeply for Kelly, he wanted to be with Leslie. Kelly sobbed, "This marriage is over!" and on the same day moved into the second bedroom. John and Kelly had no sexual relationship after February 14, 2020. John and Kelly agreed that Kelly would stay in the townhouse for three months while he found a new place to live because this would be less stressful for Bosco. During those three months, Kelly wrote a children's book titled, Bosco's Broken Home, and sold the rights (book and movie) for $2.5 million. Kelly opened a new bank account in his name only and deposited the first payment of the $2.5 million. He planned to quit his job, but in the meantime arranged for direct deposit of his paycheck and had John's name removed as beneficiary from all his employment-related documents.

On May 4 John and Kelly filed for divorce. John bought out Kelly's interest in the townhouse and removed his name from the title. Leslie is allergic to dogs, so John tearfully agreed that Kelly could have Bosco. John hugged Kelly and whispered that if things didn't work out with Leslie, he would want Kelly back. He told Kelly that he was still the beneficiary on John's employment-related documents and life insurance. With Bosco on a leash, Kelly moved all his belongings to his newly rented apartment.

Are the book and movie rights Kelly's SP or John and Kelly's CP? What is the date of separation? What are Kelly's arguments for February 14? What are John's arguments for May 4?

Explanations

Explanation 1—When Did Alan and Barbara Separate?

The court will probably find that they were not living separate and apart until Barbara refiled her petition for dissolution in 2015. Alan will argue that Barbara's moving out of their home and filing a petition for dissolution the first time demonstrates that they were living separate and apart. He will argue that his earnings after that date were his separate property. Barbara will argue that they were not living separate and apart until she moved out again and filed another petition for dissolution. Although moving out and filing the original petition of dissolution could indicate conduct that "evidences a complete and final break in the marital relationship," there was other conduct that showed their relationship continued beyond that date. The facts indicate that they continued their sexual relationship and traveled together. Barbara moved back into the house, negating separation. Seeing a marriage counselor is objective evidence that they did not consider the marriage to be finished. These facts are loosely based on *Marriage of Marsden*, 130 Cal. App. 3d 426, 181 Cal. Rptr. 910 (1982).

Explanation 2 — Karl Never Returned

The court will probably determine that the complete and final break occurred when Judy filed the petition for dissolution or perhaps when they discontinued sexual relations after Karl informed her that he would no longer support her after the end of 2015. Karl will argue that they were living separate and apart when he moved out of their home in 2012. Judy will argue that their marital relationship continued until she filed her petition for dissolution. Up until that time, they maintained joint economic ties, and there were indications that they attempted to reconcile: Karl wanted to move back into the home, and Judy sought counseling. Also, socially and emotionally, they continued their relationship. These facts are loosely based on *Marriage of von der Nuell*, 23 Cal. App. 4th 730, 28 Cal. Rptr. 2d 447. The Court of Appeal found that the final break did not occur when the husband moved out of the family home because of their "ongoing economic, emotional, sexual and social ties and their attempts at reconciliation." *Id.* at 736, 28 Cal. Rptr. 2d at 450.

Explanation 3 — Patrick and Susan Break Up

It is uncertain what the Court will determine. The facts here show that they maintained separate residences for a good amount of time while Patrick was away on business, so the issues will be when they actually established separate residences and when there is objective evidence of "words or conduct reflecting there is a complete and final break in the marriage relationship" as required by *Marriage of Davis*. Therefore, the Court may find that Patrick and Susan were living separate and apart from the time Susan wrote her letter, which were words that indicated her intention to end the marriage relationship. The Court could also find that they did not actually separate until Susan moved out of the family home and asked Patrick to remove his remaining belongings. At that point, Susan established a separate residence, and Patrick's conduct indicated a final break in the relationship. Since they had always kept their financial affairs separate, that evidence does not indicate a separation in 2013. There is no mention of when their sexual relationship ended or if they maintained any social or emotional ties or if there was any attempt at reconciliation. Those facts may indicate that they separated later than 2013.

If Patrick is the major source of earnings during their marriage, he will argue the earlier date of 2013 so his earnings would be separate property. Despite Susan's letter in 2013, she will argue for the later date of 2015, when she established a separate residence and actually filed the petition of dissolution. Here, the objective evidence regarding moving out and filing the dissolution petition are most likely insufficient to determine the exact date of separation without more evidence of their conduct.

Explanation 4 — Bosco's Broken Home

Are the book and movie rights Kelly's SP or John and Kelly's CP? The answer depends on the date of separation, as defined by Family Code §70. In determining the date of separation, the court must take into consideration all relevant evidence.

Kelly will argue that February 14, 2020, is the date of separation. Kelly "expressed to the other spouse the intent to end the marriage" when, after John confessed his love for Leslie, Kelly sobbed, "This marriage is over!" Kelly's conduct was consistent with that intent, because he moved into a separate bedroom and did not have sexual relations with John after February 14. John and Kelly agreed that Kelly would stay in the townhouse for three months while he found a new place to live. Family Code §70 abrogated the *Davis* decision, so that February 14 could be the date of separation even if Kelly and John both lived in the townhouse. Kelly's conduct was consistent with his intent to end the marriage. He opened a new bank account in his name only and arranged for direct-deposit of his paycheck. He also had John's name removed as beneficiary from all his employment-related documents.

John will argue that the date of separation was May 4, when he and Kelly filed for divorce. Before that date, John's conduct was not consistent with an intent to end the marriage. On February 14, despite announcing his love for Leslie, John said that "he would always care deeply for Kelly." When Kelly moved out of the townhouse, John hugged him and whispered that if things didn't work out with Leslie, he would want Kelly back. He told Kelly that he was still the beneficiary on John's employment-related documents and life insurance. Only after filing for divorce on May 4, did John buy out Kelly's interest in the townhouse, and remove Kelly's name from the title.

Kelly's argument for February 14 satisfies both (1) statement that the marriage is over and (2) conduct consistent with that intent. John can argue that until he and Kelly filed for divorce on May 4, no "complete and final break in the marital relationship" had occurred. John/s conduct before that date was at best inconsistent, in contrast to Kelly's expressed intent on February 14 and consistent conduct. It is most likely that the court will find February 14 to be the date of separation. Kelly will keep the $2.5 million as his separate property.

DIVISION OF ASSETS AND LIABILITIES AT DIVORCE

Once the spouses separate and petition for dissolution of their marriage, the next step is to catalogue and characterize the property they acquired during marriage. That is a major step and is the step that leads to the most litigation in California. Division of community property is straightforward; California law requires "equal division." Under Family Code §2550, "the court shall . . . divide the community estate of the parties equally." There are very few exceptions to the rule of mandatory equal division. Debts are not considered property, yet many couples have accumulated community debts and community property during their marriage. At divorce, those debts that are unpaid at the time of trial must be divided equally or "confirmed" to one of the spouses. Family Code §2551.

Characterizing Debts

The courts are instructed to characterize the liabilities of the parties as either separate or community and then divide them as specified in Family Code §§2620-2627. Some debts are excluded completely from division at divorce. For instance, educational loans are assigned to the spouse receiving the education. Family Code §§2627 and 2641(b)(2). Also, if a spouse is found liable for a tort and "the liability is not based upon an act or omission which occurred while the married person was performing an activity for the benefit of the community," the liability is assigned to the tortfeasor spouse without offset. Family Code §2627. Thus, educational loans and tort liability are not treated like other debts incurred during marriage.

Generally, debts are allocated based on *when* they are acquired. Just as a spouse's separate property includes property owned before marriage, so too debts incurred before marriage belong to the spouse who incurred the debt. Family Code §2621 states that a debt incurred before marriage "shall be confirmed without offset to the spouse who incurred the debt." For instance, assume Jill incurs $60,000 in debt to climb Mt. Everest after graduating from college. On the trip, she meets Jack, and they marry soon after. During the next seven years, they climb all the mountains of the world together and then realize they have nothing left in common and decide to divorce. During their marriage, they worked eight months of the year to earn money to spend the other four months climbing. The value of their community property is about $20,000. If they divorce, the court will confirm the $60,000 debt to Jill as her debt, and the court will divide the community property equally. The debt will be Jill's "without offset." Family Code §2625. That means that that debt will be excluded from the community estate. Jill's debt, because it was incurred before marriage, will be considered her separate debt and is all hers. Thus at divorce, Jill's $60,000 debt will be confirmed to Jill, and the $20,000 community estate will be split equally between Jill and Jack.

A debt incurred during marriage and before separation must be characterized as either a community or a separate debt and then divided accordingly. Community debts are divided equally; separate debts are confirmed without offset to the spouse who incurred the debt. A separate debt can be incurred during marriage and before separation if the debt was "not incurred for the benefit of the community." The statute does not define which debts would be considered for the benefit of the community and which would not. If Harry takes out a loan during their marriage for $10,000 to take Wilma on a vacation around the world, presumably that loan would be for the benefit of the community. The community, Harry and Wilma, benefited from the vacation—travel would probably be considered a benefit to the community, because it expanded the couple's understanding of other cultures and because a vacation usually provides relaxation for the couple.

If during their marriage Wilma buys a new wardrobe costing $10,000 and charges it on her credit card, the question would be whether that debt is for the benefit of the community and thus a community debt that would be subject to division at divorce. Arguably, the wardrobe only benefits Wilma, because she is the only one who will wear that wardrobe. Since the wardrobe is for her personal benefit, then it can be argued that the debt is her separate debt and should be assigned to her. The counterargument is that clothing is usually considered a family expense or a "necessary" that the community should be responsible for, and therefore the debt would be a community debt that would be divided equally at divorce. The term "necessary" is a term of art that refers to a living expense that is appropriate to one's station in life. If a $10,000 wardrobe is appropriate to Harry and Wilma's station in life, then it is possible that a court would consider it a necessary and thus conclude that the debt incurred is a community debt. Neither Family Code §2622, which is entitled "Debts Incurred After Marriage But Before Separation," nor Family Code §2625, which is entitled "Separate Debts" define "benefit of the community," but it is likely that the concept of "necessary" may play a role in fleshing out the definition.

Assume that both the loan and the credit card debt are considered community debts that are to be divided equally. Also assume that Harry and Wilma have other community assets, such as a house valued at $300,000 and a sailboat valued at $20,000. They have sold the house and agreed to divide the proceeds between them. At this point, they have a sailboat worth $20,000 and debts totaling $20,000. To accomplish equal division, one way would be to divide each asset and each debt between Harry and Wilma. If Harry wants to keep the sailboat, the court has the discretion to assign the debt to Harry to "offset" the award of the sailboat to Harry. Family Code §2622 regarding debts incurred during marriage incorporates the Family

Code sections dealing with equal division, which allows awarding an asset to one party "to effect a substantially equal division." Family Code §2601.

One issue regarding debt at divorce involves a judgment for tort liability and the attorney's fees that are incurred to defend against an alleged tort committed by one spouse. Family Code §2627 is clear that liability for a tort "*not* based upon an act or omission which occurred while the married person was performing an activity for the benefit of the community" is assigned to the tortfeasor spouse. What if the liability *is* based on an act or omission that occurred while the married person was performing an activity for the benefit of the community? For instance, a husband is sued for negligence while serving on the Board of Directors of a Bank. He settles the lawsuit and incurs attorney's fees. He also is faced with a divorce petition from his wife. She claims that the settlement and the attorney's fees are separate debts that should be assigned to the husband. According to the Court of Appeal in *Marriage of Hirsch*, 211 Cal. App. 3d 104, 110 259 Cal. Rptr. 30, 44 (1989), the "negligent conduct of a spouse engaged in an activity benefitting the community" would result in a community debt. Thus, both the settlement and the attorney's fees in that case were community debts, rather than the debt of the alleged tortfeasor spouse. The *Hirsch* Court also distinguished an earlier case, *Marriage of Stitt*, 147 Cal. App. 3d 579, 195 Cal. Rptr. 172 (1983), where the wife was assigned the debt for her attorney's fees. She had incurred those fees defending civil and criminal charges of embezzlement from her employer. The *Hirsch* Court stated that *Stitt* was correct if confined to its facts but "An innocent spouse is not required to share in losses incurred by the intentionally tortious or criminal conduct of a spouse where there is no benefit to the community." *Hirsch*, 211 Cal. App. 3d at 110, 259 Cal. Rptr. at 43-44. Therefore, under *Hirsch*, a debt incurred by one spouse that involved intentional tortious or criminal activity would be considered a separate debt, but a debt incurred by one spouse that involved negligence would be considered a community debt.

What if Debts Exceed Assets?

It is not uncommon in California for the community debts incurred during marriage to exceed the community assets. In that situation, Family Code §2623(b) provides:

> To the extent that community debts exceed total community and quasi-community assets, the excess of debt shall be assigned as the court deems just and equitable, taking into account factors such as the parties' relative ability to pay.

This is clearly a deviation from mandatory equal division. It allows the court to take into account equitable factors, such as the parties' differing earning capacities. This Code section is a codification of the holding in *Marriage of Eastis*, 47 Cal. App. 3d 459, 120 Cal. Rptr. 861 (1975). The Court of Appeal stated:

> We construe the proper rule to be that if there are no assets to divide, only obligations, or after the equal division of the assets there remain obligations to be disposed of, the court has the discretion to order the payment of such obligations in a manner that is just and equitable, depending on the respective earning capacities of the spouses and other relevant factors.

Id. at 464, 120 Cal. Rptr. at 864. The Court pointed out that it would be unfair to divide the community debts equally where one spouse has an earning capacity of $1,000 a month and the other has an earning capacity of $500. Therefore, in this one situation, the courts can use their discretion to divide the community debts of the spouses.

Debts After Separation

The next relevant time period concerns debts incurred after the spouses separate but before entry of the judgment dissolving their marriage or legal separation. There are three categories of debts that can be incurred after separation but before dissolution: *common necessaries* of life, *necessaries* of life, and *non-necessaries*. These categories are not defined in the statute. The definitions are derived from common law: A spouse is responsible for the debts incurred by the other spouse if they are for common necessaries or necessaries of life. Common necessaries are considered those items that are necessary to sustain life and include food, clothing, housing, and medical care. Necessaries, as mentioned above, include those items that are necessary to the spouses' station in life. For instance, membership in a country club could be considered a necessary of life if that befitted the spouses' station in life. Non-necessaries would then refer to those items that could not be categorized as either a common necessary or a necessary.

Family Code §2623(a) states that if the debt was for "the common necessaries of life of either spouse or the necessaries of life of the children of the marriage," that debt "shall be confirmed to either spouse according to the parties' respective needs and abilities to pay at the time the debt was incurred." Debts incurred for non-necessaries are treated differently: They are confirmed without offset to the spouse who incurred the debt. Family Code §2623(b). Let us consider a couple, Vidal and Star, who married soon after Vidal styled Star's hair for her upcoming movie. Vidal and Star lived an extravagant life, living mainly off Star's earnings as an actress. Every year they flew to Cannes for the film festival. After Vidal and Star separated, Vidal charged his trip to the film festival on his credit card. He claims that this debt should be confirmed to Star, because she has the ability to pay. A court would reject this argument, because during the period of separation, only debts incurred for common necessaries are confirmed to a spouse based on ability to pay. A trip to Cannes for the film festival is not a common necessary. Common necessaries include only the basics necessary to sustain life. Although Vidal may feel that he needs professionally to travel to the Cannes Film Festival, that would not fit the legal definition of a common necessary. Since the statute refers only to common necessaries and non-necessaries regarding spouses, that debt would be a non-necessary and will be confirmed without offset to Vidal.

After the trip to Cannes, Vidal lost his job as a hairdresser. He moved to an apartment and spent his savings on rent. Over the period of six months, he incurred credit card debt totaling $5,000 for food and clothing. He also claims that those debts should be confirmed to Star. Those debts would be considered common necessaries of life. Since Vidal is unemployed and Star has the ability to pay, those debts would be confirmed to Star based on the "parties' respective needs and abilities to pay." At the time the debt was incurred, because of Vidal's needs and Star's ability to pay, the debt incurred for a common necessary during separation would be confirmed to Star.

If Vidal and Star had a child whom they had enrolled in an exclusive Montessori school in Beverly Hills, the debt incurred for the school tuition would be considered a necessary of life. Considering Vidal and Star's station in life and their child's station in life, exclusive private school would most likely be considered a necessary of life. The debt incurred would be confirmed to Star based on her ability to pay at the time the debt was incurred. Thus, if the debt for school tuition was incurred during the period of separation, and Star had the ability to pay at that time, that debt would be confirmed to Star.

The final time period is after entry of a judgment of dissolution but before the divorce is final. That is a crucial time, because at that time a spouse is responsible for his/her own debts. Any debts incurred during that time period "shall be confirmed without offset to the spouse who incurred the debt." Family Code §2624. After Vidal and Star's judgment of dissolution is entered, Vidal incurs additional credit card debt for food and clothing. Even though that debt is for a common necessary, the debt will be confirmed without offset to Vidal. Once judgment is entered, a spouse's responsibility for a debt incurred by the other spouse ends.

Examples

Example 5 — Barking Up Allison's Tree

Barkley and Allison married in 1990. Barkley, who always loved animals, started a mobile pet grooming business in 2005, using savings from their earnings. Recently, Barkley and Allison have been fighting like cats and dogs. Barkley is considering a divorce from Allison. He comes to you for advice concerning an accident that he had with his pet grooming van. In a civil lawsuit against him, the jury awarded the other driver $200,000 based on Barkley's liability. The judgment has not yet been paid, and he wants to know who will be responsible for that debt if they divorce. How would a court treat the $200,000 judgment?

Example 6 — Who Pays for Herb's Degree?

Herb and Willow were married in 2005. Herb worked as a gardener, and Willow was a waitress and aspiring actress. Willow received a movie contract in 2007 and received more than $100,000 for the movie. Herb had always wanted to go to culinary school, and Willow encouraged him to attend a culinary institute to become a chef. The tuition was very high: $30,000. Willow paid $10,000 from her earnings from the movie, and Herb paid the remaining $20,000 from a student loan. In 2011, Herb completed the two-year program and received a degree in culinary arts. He landed a job as a junior chef at a fancy restaurant. The hours were long and the pay pretty low. Willow was often away on location filming a new movie. Unfortunately, their marriage soured, and they are considering a divorce. Will the student loan be considered a community debt? Who will be assigned the loan? What other issues are relevant?

Example 7 — Herb Graduated Before Marriage

Assume that the facts are the same as Example 6, except that Herb received his degree prior to his marriage to Willow and that the entire loan of $30,000 is still outstanding. Who will be assigned the loan if they divorce?

Example 8 — Will Willow Be Reimbursed?

Assume the facts are the same as Example 6, except that Willow used $10,000 of her earnings during marriage to pay off part of Herb's loan. The loan is now $20,000. Who will be assigned the loan if they divorce? Does Willow have a right to be reimbursed for the $10,000 that was used to pay off Herb's loan?

Example 9 — Who Picks Up the Debt?

While Henry and Wanda were married, Henry bought a pickup truck that he used in his plumbing business. He borrowed $15,000 to pay for the truck. When they separated, $10,000 was still outstanding on the loan. Who will be assigned the loan if they divorce?

Example 10 — Wanda Is Nabbed

Wanda, unfortunately, had a habit of shoplifting. A security officer nabbed her as she was leaving Saks Fifth Avenue in Beverly Hills. Because this was the third time she had been caught shoplifting, she had to stand trial and was in danger of incurring a substantial penalty. She hired an attorney and ran up attorney's fees totaling $15,000. When Henry and Wanda separated, $10,000 in legal fees was still outstanding. Who will be assigned the debt if they divorce?

Example 11 — Wanda Diets and Exercises

In an effort to lose weight, Wanda started on a vigorous exercise and weight loss program. She enrolled at a gym and bought a yearly membership for $1,500. The Dieters' Club she joined provided all the food for six months and cost $3,500. Wanda charged both on her credit card. When Henry and Wanda separated, the total debt of $5,000 was still outstanding. Who will be assigned the debt if they divorce?

Example 12 — Wanda Suffers from High Blood Pressure

After Henry and Wanda separated but before a judgment of dissolution of their marriage was entered, Wanda was hospitalized for high blood pressure. The hospital bills totaled $15,000 and were not covered by health insurance. Who will be assigned the debt for the hospitalization when they divorce?

Example 13 — Henry Seeks Peace on the Pacific

After Henry and Wanda separated but before a judgment of dissolution of their marriage was entered, Henry decided to buy a sailboat. He felt it gave him peace of mind to spend his weekends on the calm of the Pacific Ocean. He took a loan to pay for the sailboat in the amount of $25,000. Who will be assigned that loan when they divorce?

Example 14 — Henry Goes to Palm Springs

The court recently entered the judgment of dissolution of Henry and Wanda's marriage. Before the dissolution became final, Henry bought a condo in Palm Springs and fixed it up. He incurred debts of $10,000 for painting and furniture. Who will be assigned that debt?

Example 15 — Too Many Debts

Assume that all of Henry and Wanda's community property was split equally. Henry received the community business, and Wanda received the community home. At the trial, the court determined that after valuing the community property and the community debts, there was an excess of $50,000 in community debts. How will a court divide those debts?

Explanations

Explanation 5 — Barking Up Allison's Tree

The debt in question here is a judgment for a tort. Family Code §2627 states that only tort liability that is *not* based on an act or omission that occurred while the married person was performing an activity for the benefit of the community (Family Code §1000 (b)(2)) "shall be assigned to the spouse whose act or omission provided the basis for the liability, without offset." Here the judgment against Barkley *was* based on an act or omission that occurred while he was performing an activity for the benefit of the community. That activity was driving the pet grooming van, which was a community business. So it would seem that the judgment would be a community debt. The language of Family Code §2625 and the holding in *Marriage of Hirsch*, 211 Cal. App. 3d 104, 259 Cal. Rptr. 39 (1989), support this position. Under Family Code §2625, a separate debt includes debts incurred during marriage and before the date of separation that were not incurred for the benefit of the community. Since Barkley's judgment was for negligence while performing an activity for the benefit of the community, the *Hirsch* Court would consider it a community debt. Therefore, the court would conclude that the $200,000 judgment was a community debt and would not be assigned to Barkley.

Explanation 6 — Who Pays for Herb's Degree?

The student loan was incurred while Herb and Willow were married. It is for the benefit of the community, even though Herb is the one who benefited from the education. However, educational loans are treated differently from other debts. Family Code §2627 states that educational loans are controlled by Family Code §2641. Under §2641(b)(2), an educational loan "shall be assigned for payment by the party" receiving the education. The remaining portion of the loan will be assigned to Herb. The other issues include (1) whether the community will receive reimbursement for the tuition paid for Herb's education and (2) whether the education that Herb received was one that "substantially enhanced the earning capacity of the party." Family Code §2641(b)(1). These issues are discussed fully in Chapter 5. The second issue is relevant here, because Herb has received an education, but at present is receiving low pay. The statute, however, refers to an education that substantially enhances the earning *capacity* of the party. Before Herb received his degree, he worked as a gardener. Willow would argue that pursuing a degree in culinary arts substantially enhances his earning capacity, even though he does not yet have the experience to capitalize on that education. Thus, a court may consider Herb's education as one that substantially enhanced his earning capacity.

Explanation 7 — Herb Graduated Before Marriage

Herb incurred the loan for his education before they married. This falls under Family Code §2621, Debts Incurred Before Marriage. Those debts, separate debts, "shall be confirmed without offset to the spouse who incurred the debt." That means that Herb's loan will be confirmed to him as his separate debt. You come into a marriage with a debt; you leave the marriage with that debt. Family Code §2641, concerning educational degrees, does not apply because it refers only to "a loan incurred during marriage."

Explanation 8 — Will Willow Be Reimbursed?

The remainder of the loan, $20,000, will be confirmed to Herb as stated in Explanation 7. The question here is whether under Family Code §2641, Community Contributions to Education or Training, the community will receive reimbursement of repayments made from community funds during marriage. That section, discussed in Chapter 5, would allow for the community to be reimbursed for community property used to repay a loan incurred for education or training. The loan does not have to be incurred during marriage, according to *Marriage of Weiner*, 205 Cal. App. 4th 235, 239 Cal. Rptr. 288 (2003).

Explanation 9 — Who Picks Up the Debt?

The court is instructed to characterize loans as separate or community. Family Code §2551. Debts that are incurred by a spouse during marriage and before the date of separation are not automatically community debts. A separate debt is "not incurred for the benefit of the community" and must be "confirmed without offset to the spouse who incurred the debt." Family Code §2625. If the debt is a community debt, it is divided equally. The debt to buy the pickup truck was incurred while Henry and Wanda were married. It clearly was incurred for the benefit of the community, because Henry used it for his business, which benefits the community. The $10,000 debt will be split between Henry and Wanda, even though it was Henry alone who incurred the debt.

Explanation 10 — Wanda Is Nabbed

The court must characterize the debt as separate or community. Family Code §2551. Even though the debt for attorney's fees was incurred during marriage and before Henry and Wanda separated, it would be characterized as a separate debt. The debt was incurred because Wanda was arrested for shoplifting. Even though the attorney may have saved her from a substantial penalty, it is doubtful that the court would consider that the debt was for the benefit of the community. It was for Wanda's benefit and would be confirmed without offset to Wanda. Family Code §2625.

Explanation 11 — Wanda Diets and Exercises

The court must characterize the debt as separate or community. Family Code §2551. The debts for the Gym and the Dieters' Club were incurred during marriage and would probably be considered a community debt. The reason would be that the activities, both to improve Wanda's health and appearance, would be for the benefit of both. On the other hand, Henry would try to argue that the debts were for Wanda's personal benefit and therefore are her separate debts. If the debts are community debts, they are split equally upon divorce. If the debts are considered Wanda's separate debts, they are confirmed to her without offset. Family Code §§2622, 2625.

Explanation 12 — Wanda Suffers from High Blood Pressure

During the period of time between the date of separation and entry of judgment, the court shall confirm the debts for common necessaries of life of either spouse to either spouse "according to the parties' respective needs and abilities to pay at the time the debt was incurred." Family Code §2623(a). Medical care is usually considered a "common necessary of life." Here Wanda incurred the debt, but we can probably assume that she may not be working or have the income to pay the debt. If we also assume that Henry has an ongoing business, he would probably have the ability to pay the debt. If those are the facts, a court has the discretion to assign a portion or the entire debt to Henry. Even though Wanda incurred the debt and the couple had separated, common necessaries of life are still the responsibility of both spouses.

Explanation 13 — Henry Seeks Peace on the Pacific

During the period of time between separation and entry of the judgment of dissolution, a court has some discretion in assigning debts to either spouse. But that discretion covers only "common necessaries of life" for the spouses and "necessaries of life" of the children of the marriage. For "non-necessaries," the debt is "confirmed without offset" to the spouse who incurred the debt. Family Code §2623(b). Although there is therapeutic value in Henry finding peace of mind, it is doubtful that a debt to purchase a sailboat would be considered a "common necessary of life." Even if the sailboat was a "necessary of life," which could include a sailboat if appropriate to Henry and Wanda's station in life, the debt would still be confirmed to Henry. The reason would be that it would be characterized as a separate debt because the debt was not incurred for the benefit of the community. Since Henry and Wanda were separated at the time Henry purchased the sailboat, it would be for his benefit alone and therefore would be confirmed to him without offset. Family Code §2625.

Explanation 14 — Henry Goes to Palm Springs

Even though Henry and Wanda are technically still married until the dissolution is effective, common sense and the Family Code tell us that the debt for painting and furniture will be "confirmed without offset" to Henry. Family Code §2624.

Explanation 15 — Too Many Debts

When community debts exceed total community assets, the court shall assign the excess of debt, "as the court deems just and equitable, taking into account factors such as the parties' relative ability to pay." Family Code §2622(b). If Henry has the ability to pay and Wanda does not, the court could assign more than half or even all of the excess of debt to Henry. Family Code §2622(b) injects "just and equitable" factors into debt division, that are absent in the division of community assets.

Until Death Do Us Part? Division at Death

JOINT TENANCY COMPARED TO COMMUNITY PROPERTY

At divorce, if a married couple owns property held in joint tenancy or community property title, the characterization of that property is controlled by the presumption found in Family Code §2581 (formerly Civil Code §4800.1). That Family Code section applies *only* at divorce. Thus, at death, the presumption follows the title: Joint tenancy property is presumed to be joint tenancy; community property is presumed to be community property. The rationale is that when the couple chose to hold the property and place the deed or title as joint tenancy or community property, that choice reflected their agreement that the property was joint tenancy or community property. If married couples know anything about title, it is that joint tenancy carries with it the right of survivorship. They know that in the event of either spouse's death, joint tenancy property automatically becomes the property of the surviving spouse.

The first question then is whether, at death, community property is treated differently from joint tenancy. If a spouse dies without a will, the results are identical. Under Probate Code §§100 and 6401(a), if a decedent dies without a will (intestate), a surviving spouse is entitled to one-half of the community property and is also entitled to the other one-half that belonged to the decedent. In other words, the surviving spouse has a right to *all* of the community property of the couple. Therefore, in that scenario, community property is like joint tenancy. However, if a decedent dies testate, under Probate Code §6101(b), the decedent has the right to dispose of the decedent's one-half of the community property by will. Thus, in this scenario, there is a difference between joint tenancy property and community property. The joint tenancy property automatically becomes the property of the surviving spouse; one-half of the community property may be devised to someone other than the surviving spouse. The surviving spouse is entitled to only one-half of the community property when the decedent devises the one-half belonging to the decedent to someone other than the surviving spouse.

Presumptions re Joint Tenancy

How does joint tenancy at death FIT into our analysis? Because the *title* controls initially, the funds used to acquire the property do not control. For instance, let's take a couple named Philip and Estelle. They are an older couple, each of whom had children from a prior marriage when they married. Soon after their marriage, they purchased a home and took title in joint tenancy. Philip sold a house he owned prior to their marriage and used those funds to purchase the joint tenancy home. If Philip dies, the presumption regarding the joint tenancy home is that it is joint tenancy. The funds used to buy the home were Philip's separate property, but the joint tenancy presumption cannot be rebutted by *tracing* to Philip's separate property. The presumption can be rebutted by showing the *intentions* of the parties—by their agreement that the property is not joint tenancy but instead is either community property or separate property of either spouse.

In the actual case of Philip and Estelle, *Estate of Levine*, 125 Cal. App. 3d 701, 178 Cal. Rptr. 273 (1981), Philip had his own intentions about the home. He wanted the home to be both joint tenancy and community property. If Estelle died first, he wanted the home to be joint tenancy, which meant that it would automatically become his property. If he died first, he wanted the home to be community property, and then he could devise his one-half to his children. When he discussed this with his lawyer, his lawyer advised him correctly that the title controlled unless there was an agreement between the spouses that the home is other than joint tenancy. Philip told the lawyer that he had such an agreement with Estelle.

Philip's will reflected his understanding of the character of the house, that it was community property, even though the title was in joint tenancy. In the proceeding to determine the character of the home, Estelle testified that they never talked about the character of the property, but that she knew that joint tenancy meant that she would own the house upon Philip's death. Philip's son testified that his father had told him on several occasions that he and his sister would inherit one-half of the funds used to purchase the joint tenancy home. The trial court found that there was no agreement between the crucial parties, Philip and Estelle. Therefore, the joint tenancy presumption was not rebutted by an agreement, and the joint tenancy presumption became the conclusion. The house was joint tenancy and by the right of survivorship became Estelle's property. In conclusion, we learn that, at death, the presumption that joint tenancy property is joint tenancy can be rebutted only by an agreement that the property is other than joint tenancy. Without that agreement, the property is joint tenancy and goes to the surviving spouse.

Oral or Written Agreement?

Let's change the Philip and Estelle scenario. Let's say that Philip and Estelle did have an oral agreement that the joint tenancy home would be community property. Philip dies, and his will leaves his share of the community property to his children. Estelle argues that the house belongs to her because the title is in joint tenancy. The children argue that they have evidence that Philip and Estelle had an oral agreement that the house was community property. The presumption is that the joint tenancy home is joint tenancy, and it can be rebutted by an agreement that the home is community property. The burden of proof is on the party trying to rebut the presumption. In this case, if the children can rebut the joint tenancy presumption, the house will be characterized as community property. The children would then be entitled to one-half of the house, because Philip had a right to devise his one-half of the community property. Estelle would receive the other one-half as the surviving spouse.

The preceding scenario assumes that the agreement was made prior to January 1, 1985. Remember that January 1, 1985 is a significant date, because as of that date all transmutations are valid only if "made in writing by an express declaration" by "the spouse whose interest in the property is adversely affected." Family Code §852(a), (e). The transmutation statute is a general statute that controls how property is changed from separate property to community property and vice versa. In the Philip and Estelle scenario, in order to rebut the joint tenancy presumption, the children would have to show that the oral agreement was made prior to 1985. An oral agreement in 1985 or thereafter would not be sufficient to rebut the joint tenancy presumption. In 1985 or thereafter, the joint tenancy presumption could be rebutted only if there was an express declaration in writing by Estelle that she knew that the character of the property was being changed from joint tenancy to community property. The transmutation statute provides that it is the spouse whose rights are adversely affected who must know that the property's character is being changed. If the oral agreement was in 1985, the children could not succeed in rebutting the joint tenancy presumption.

DIVORCE/DEATH SCENARIO

Estate of Blair

One scenario that has occurred and has been litigated more often than one would expect is when a spouse dies at some stage during the divorce proceedings. The issue was cloudy, because there are differing presumptions regarding joint tenancy at divorce and at death. Upon divorce, Family Code §2581 applies, and joint tenancy property is presumed to be community property. Upon death, joint tenancy property is presumed to be joint tenancy. In *Estate of Blair*, 199 Cal. App. 3d 161, 244 Cal. Rptr. 627 (1988), Ray and Nancy Blair married in 1963 and bought a house in 1972, taking the title in joint tenancy. They separated in 1985, and Nancy executed a new will leaving her entire estate to her sister. Nancy died before their marriage was dissolved. Ray sold the house to a bona fide purchaser. Nancy's sister claimed that Nancy's estate was entitled to one-half of the proceeds of the sale of the house, because the house was community property. Ray claimed that the house passed to him by right of survivorship, because the house was held in joint tenancy. The issue was whether the house was joint tenancy or community property. If it was joint tenancy, it passed to Ray at Nancy's death. If it was community property, Nancy had a right to devise one-half to her sister.

The Court in *Blair* resolved the issue in Ray's favor. Because Nancy died before the couple was divorced, the joint tenancy presumption operative at death controlled. Up until Nancy's death, Ray and Nancy were still married. Even though they had separated and Nancy had changed her will, the court had not dissolved their marriage. When Nancy died, her death was what actually dissolved their marriage. Thus, the Court of Appeal concluded that the case was a death case, and the presumption that should control was that the house was presumed to be joint tenancy. Unless Nancy's sister could produce evidence that rebutted that presumption, the house would be characterized as joint tenancy. If the house was joint tenancy, Ray as the joint tenant received the entire property by right of survivorship, and Nancy's estate was not entitled to any proceeds of the sale of the house.

However, the Court of Appeal recognized that "it is illogical that parties such as Nancy and Ray, awaiting the court's division of property acquired during marriage would envision or desire the operation of survivorship. An untimely death results in a windfall to the surviving spouse, a result neither party presumably intends or anticipates." *Id.* at 169, 244 Cal. Rptr. at 632. In other words, it is clear that Nancy would not have wanted Ray to receive the entire house if she died—they were in the process of getting a divorce and anticipated splitting the house. When she died, instead of splitting the house, Ray received the whole property. The real lesson for lawyers is that when a couple separates, joint tenancy property should be severed so that the property would become tenancy in common. Tenancy in common does not have a survivorship feature. Thus, if the house were tenancy in common, Nancy's share would have gone to her sister through her will.

Marriage of Hilke

Let's change the Ray and Nancy scenario so that Nancy died *after* the Court dissolved their marriage but before the Court had considered division of the joint tenancy house. That was the scenario in the case of *Marriage of Hilke*, 4 Cal. 4th 215, 841 P.2d 891, 14 Cal. Rptr. 2d 371 (1992). Again, the question was whether the joint tenancy presumption that applies at death controls or whether the Family Code §2581 community property presumption that applies at divorce controls. The Supreme Court held that the case was still a divorce case because the trial court had already dissolved the marriage at the time of Mrs. Hilke's death. At divorce, joint tenancy is presumed to be community property and thus is divided equally between the spouses. That decision avoided the illogical result that an ex-spouse would receive the windfall of all the property via survivorship. In the Ray and Nancy scenario, the case would be a divorce case, and thus the joint tenancy house would be presumed to be community property. The presumption could only be rebutted by a writing, either in the deed or a written agreement that the house was other than community property. If not rebutted, the house would be characterized as community property, and one-half would go to Ray and one-half would go to Nancy. Because Nancy died, her one-half would go according to her will.

The Legislature took steps in 2001 to remedy the problem presented in the *Hilke* case. It enacted Probate Code §5601, which states that "a joint tenancy between a decedent and the decedent's former spouse, created before or during marriage, is severed as to the decedent's interest if, at the time of the decedent's death, the former spouse is not the decedent's surviving spouse. . . ." To translate that into understandable English, we will apply that to the Ray and Nancy scenario. A joint tenancy between Nancy (who died) and Ray (who is already divorced from Nancy) is severed when the court dissolves their marriage. That means that divorce automatically severs the joint tenancy and converts it into a tenancy in common. If Nancy had a will leaving her estate to her sister, Nancy's share in the tenancy in common would go to Nancy's sister. If Nancy died without a will, her share in the tenancy in common would go to her heirs. If Nancy's sister were Nancy's only heir, Nancy's entire share in the tenancy in common would go to her sister.

COMMUNITY PROPERTY WITH RIGHT OF SURVIVORSHIP

As discussed in Chapter 4, as of July 1, 2001, a husband and wife may hold property as community property with right of survivorship. This property will be treated as community property during marriage and at divorce, but if one spouse dies, the property will be treated like joint tenancy. In that case, the surviving spouse will own the property through the right of survivorship.

Let us consider our hypothetical couple, Harry and Wilma. Assume that in 2002 Harry and Wilma purchase a home for $100,000 with their earnings during their marriage, and the deed states to "Harry and Wilma as community property with right of survivorship." Assume also that Harry recently died. Since the marriage ended in death, the home will automatically become Wilma's because of the right of survivorship. By creating community property with right of survivorship, both Harry and Wilma confirmed that in the event of either's death, the surviving spouse will receive the home.

Many couples prefer the right of survivorship to traditional community property. The right of survivorship ensures the spouses of automatic transfer of the property to the surviving spouse without probate proceedings. Traditional community property title differs. The surviving spouse will receive all the community property if the decedent dies without a will, but not necessarily if the decedent has a will. If Harry and Wilma held the property as community property, and Harry dies with a will, Wilma would receive her one-half interest, but Harry's one-half interest would go according to the will to whomever Harry specified. So if the property is traditional community property, there is no assurance that the surviving spouse will receive the entire property. Therefore, couples often prefer community property with right of survivorship to traditional community property, because survivorship community property assures the surviving spouse of ownership of the entire property if the other spouse dies.

In addition to this advantage, community property with right of survivorship is also preferred to joint tenancy, because the community property with right of survivorship receives the same beneficial tax treatment as does traditional community property. The important tax concept here is called "basis." Basis is defined as the baseline against which gain is measured. For example, if a piano is purchased for $25 and its value appreciates to $100, when the piano is sold for $100, a taxable gain will be recognized in the amount of $75, the amount by which the sale price exceeds the initial purchase price of the piano. So the basis in this scenario is $25, the baseline against which gain is measured. Therefore, the higher the basis, the smaller the gain will be, and less tax will be owed upon sale of an item.

To illustrate how the characterization of property impacts basis, let us again consider our hypothetical couple, Harry and Wilma. Assume Harry and Wilma purchase a home for $100,000 as joint tenants. At this point, they each have a one-half interest with right of survivorship, and their basis in the property is $100,000. Now assume Harry dies when the property value has increased by $1 million. Wilma gets full ownership of the home, and she decides to sell it. In a joint tenancy, only one-half of the property interest will receive a stepped-up basis, meaning only the decedent's one-half of the property's basis will change to reflect the fair market value of the property at death. Therefore, when Wilma decides to sell the property, her new basis will be $550,000 ($50,000 for the one-half interest she already possessed, and $500,000 for the one-half interest she acquired through the right of survivorship). So if she sells the property immediately after the death of her husband, the gain on sale will be $450,000, the difference between the sale price of $1 million and the $550,000 basis. She will have to pay capital gains taxes on the $450,000 gain.

Now assume that Harry and Wilma purchase the home as traditional community property, rather than joint tenancy. If Harry dies, the IRS will recognize a stepped-up basis for the entire property. So the entire basis of the property will change to reflect the fair market value at death. Therefore, in this scenario, the basis in the property at Harry's death will be $1 million. If Harry died without a will, Wilma, as surviving spouse will also be entitled to the home, just as she would if the house had been in joint tenancy. But there is a definite tax advantage when Wilma decides to sell the property. Assuming that she sells it soon after Harry's death for $1 million, the difference between the basis of $1 million and the $1 million sale price of the property will be zero. Thus there will be no gain, and there would be no taxes due.

The above example clearly illustrates that when a marriage ends in death, property receives preferential tax treatment if the property is characterized as community property, rather than as joint tenancy. Community property with right of survivorship provides the same preferential tax treatment as community property, while at the same time preserving the right of survivorship available at the death of a spouse. Thus community property with right of survivorship preserves the best of both worlds—it allows for preferential tax treatment while simultaneously making the automatic transfer of a property interest available by the operation of law through the right of survivorship. It also is beneficial, since it confirms a spouse's interest in the event of death and automatically terminates the right of survivorship in the event of divorce. See Chapter 4.

Examples

Example 1 — What Are Xavier's Rights?

Hank and Willa married in California in 1970. They saved money from their earnings to purchase a home in Simi Valley. In 1980, they were able to purchase that home. At the suggestion of their real estate agent, they put the title in joint tenancy. The agent explained that in the case either died, the other spouse would receive the home by way of the survivorship feature of joint tenancy. They never discussed the character of the house after they purchased the home and never had any written agreement concerning the character of the home. Recently, Willa died. In her will, she specified that her entire estate should go to her brother, Xavier. Xavier comes to you for advice and wants to know if he has any rights to the Simi Valley home.

Example 2 — They Bought the Home in 1990

Assume that the facts are the same as Example 1, except that Hank and Willa marry in 1985 and purchase the home in 1990. Xavier wants to know if he has any rights to the Simi Valley home.

Example 3 — Who's the Captain of the Yacht?

Eli and Felicia marry in California in 1985. Felicia comes from a wealthy family and she has a trust fund that was set up when she was a child. She receives a monthly check from the trust fund and deposits it in an account in her own name. In 1990, Eli and Felicia purchase a yacht using the money from Felicia's trust fund. They put the title in joint tenancy. Felicia has a will that states all her property goes to her sister Gloria. Felicia recently died, and there is a dispute between Eli and Gloria regarding the yacht. How would a court characterize the yacht? Who will receive the yacht?

Example 4 — Eli and Felicia Agree Orally

Assume that the facts are the same as Example 3, except that Eli and Felicia orally agree that the yacht will be Felicia's separate property. Eli and Felicia make the agreement while all of their families are present at a party on the yacht. How would a court characterize the yacht? Will Gloria receive the yacht?

Example 5 — What Should Felicia Do?

How can Felicia assure that Gloria will receive the yacht if Felicia dies?

Example 6 — Who Owns the XYZ Stock?

Carl and Doreen married in 1985. In 1990, they purchased stock in XYZ Corporation. They put the stock certificates in joint tenancy. They used funds from Carl's earnings to purchase the stock. Recently, Carl and Doreen separated. Before the Family Court dissolved their marriage, Carl died. Carl's brother Barry is claiming that the stock was community property and that Carl devised his share to Barry. How will the stock be characterized? Will Barry receive any of the stock?

Example 7 — Carl Died After the Dissolution

Assume that the facts are the same as in Example 6, except that Carl died after the Family Court dissolved their marriage, but before the property was divided. How will the stock be characterized? Will Barry receive any of the stock?

Example 8 — Edith Is the Survivor

Jon and Edith were married in 2000. In 2003, they purchased their first home in California for $1 million. Their friend Yvette, who is a family law attorney, recommended that they hold the title as community property with right of survivorship. Since they trusted Yvette so much, they took her advice and expressly stated in the deed that the house was community property with right of survivorship. Assume that Jon recently died; also assume that after Jon's death, Edith immediately sold the property at its fair market value of $3 million. How would the property be divided? What are tax implications?

Explanations

Explanation 1 — What Are Xavier's Rights?

Xavier has no rights to the Simi Valley home. At death, the home would be presumed to be joint tenancy property. That presumption is a rebuttable presumption. The burden of proof would be on Xavier to rebut the presumption that the joint tenancy is community property or Willa's separate property. Even though community funds were used to purchase the home, the joint tenancy presumption cannot be rebutted by *tracing*. The joint tenancy presumption can only be rebutted by an oral or implied agreement if the agreement was before January 1, 1985. Since there was no agreement at all, the joint tenancy presumption would be conclusive, and the home would be characterized as joint tenancy. When Willa died, the right of survivorship means that Hank became the owner of the home. The home is not part of Willa's estate, and thus Xavier has no rights to the home.

Explanation 2—They Bought the Home in 1990

The presumption is the same: At death, joint tenancy is presumed to be joint tenancy. Again, Xavier has the burden of rebutting the presumption. Since the home was purchased in 1990, Xavier would need to show that there was a transmutation of the property from joint tenancy to community property. Since Hank and Willa have nothing in writing regarding the character of the home, Xavier could not show a valid transmutation and therefore could not succeed in rebutting the joint tenancy presumption. The conclusion would be that the home is joint tenancy and by way of survivorship became Hank's property. Xavier has no rights to the home.

Explanation 3—Who's the Captain of the Yacht?

The title to the yacht was put in joint tenancy; therefore, at death, the yacht is presumed to be joint tenancy. The funds used to purchase the yacht were Felicia's separate property. Those funds were separate property, because she owned the trust fund before she was married, and the rents, issues, and profits of separate property were her separate property. However, the funds used to purchase the yacht are irrelevant. *Tracing* cannot be used to rebut the joint tenancy presumption. Gloria would have the burden of rebutting the joint tenancy presumption by showing that there was a transmutation of the joint tenancy into community property or Felicia's separate property. Under the transmutation statute, explained in Chapter 2, Family Code §853, a will can be evidence of a transmutation in a probate proceeding. However, in this case, the statement in Felicia's will would not be evidence of a transmutation. The reason is that the "express declaration in writing" required by the transmutation statute Family Code §852(a) must be "by the spouse whose interest in the property is adversely affected." That spouse is not Felicia, but Eli. Therefore, Felicia's will is not evidence of Eli's giving up his interest in the joint tenancy. In conclusion, the joint tenancy presumption becomes conclusive, and the yacht would go to Eli by way of the survivorship feature of joint tenancy. Gloria has no rights to the yacht.

Explanation 4—Eli and Felicia Agree Orally

This example shows the strength of the *title*. The presumption at death is that joint tenancy property is joint tenancy. It cannot be rebutted by *tracing* to Felicia's separate property funds. It cannot be rebutted by an oral agreement as of January 1, 1985. The *intentions* of the parties do not control unless there is an express declaration in writing by the party adversely affected. Here there is only an oral agreement between Eli and Felicia that the yacht will be Felicia's separate property. A court would characterize the yacht as joint tenancy, and Gloria would not receive the yacht.

Explanation 5 — What Should Felicia Do?

If Felicia wants Gloria to inherit the yacht, she should not have put the yacht in joint tenancy. If she had put the title to the yacht in her name, the general community property presumption would have applied. It applies at death and at divorce. The separate property proponent would be Gloria, and she could rebut the presumption by *tracing* to Felicia's separate property funds. That would rebut the community property presumption, and the yacht would be characterized as Felicia's separate property. Then, according to Felicia's will, all "her" property would go to Gloria, and Gloria would receive the yacht.

If the title is put in joint tenancy, as of January 1, 1985, Gloria would have to produce an "express declaration in writing" showing that Eli knew that he was giving up his interest in the yacht. That express declaration in writing would be sufficient to show a transmutation of the yacht from joint tenancy to Felicia's separate property. Otherwise the joint tenancy presumption could not be rebutted. *Tracing* to Felicia's separate property funds would not work. Neither would an oral agreement suffice to rebut the joint tenancy presumption.

Explanation 6 — Who Owns the XYZ Stock?

It is clear that this case will be treated as a death case. Carl and Doreen's marriage was not yet dissolved when Carl died. Any divorce proceedings are considered "abated" by Carl's death. The presumption that applies at death is that joint tenancy is presumed to be joint tenancy. That presumption cannot be rebutted by *tracing*. Therefore, the purchase of the stock with Carl's earnings that are community property is irrelevant to characterizing the stock. The only way for Barry to rebut the joint tenancy presumption is by showing a transmutation. There is no mention of any "express declaration in writing." Since Barry cannot rebut the presumption, the conclusion will be that the stock is joint tenancy property. Joint tenancy property goes by survivorship to the surviving spouse. In this case, the stock belongs to Doreen. Barry has no rights to the stock. This seems unfair. Carl most likely would not have wanted Doreen to receive the stock once they separated and initiated divorce proceedings. However, the legal procedure for preventing this type of unfairness is for joint tenancies to be severed once the spouses separate.

Explanation 7 — Carl Died After the Dissolution

This case seems to be controlled by the Supreme Court case of *Marriage of Hilke*, where the Court treated the same scenario as a divorce case. That meant that the presumption at divorce, Family Code §2581 (formerly Civil Code

§4800.1), controlled the characterization of the joint tenancy property. At divorce, joint tenancy property is presumed to be community property. That presumption can only be rebutted by a writing, either in the title or in a written agreement. Since there is no writing in Carl and Doreen's case, the stock would be considered community property. One-half would belong to Doreen, and one-half would belong to Carl. Since Carl died, his share would go to Barry according to Carl's will.

However, the Legislature passed Probate Code §5601, which covers this exact situation. Here we have a joint tenancy between a decedent, Carl, and the decedent's former spouse, Doreen. At the time of the decedent's death, the former spouse, Doreen, is not the decedent's surviving spouse—their marriage was dissolved by the Court, and therefore Doreen is not Carl's surviving spouse. Section 5601 states that the joint tenancy is severed, which means that it is converted to a tenancy in common. Carl could devise his share of the tenancy in common to Barry, or without a will Carl's share would go to Carl's heirs. Under either the *Hilke* analysis or Probate Code §5601, Barry will receive one-half of the stock.

Explanation 8—Edith Is the Survivor

At Jon's death, Edith receives full ownership of the property through the right of survivorship. As for the tax implications, Edith will get a stepped-up basis of the property's full fair market value, $3 million. Therefore, Edith will not recognize any taxable gain since the difference between the sale price and the stepped-up basis is zero.

Quasi-Community Property

Often, married couples acquire property out-of-state in common law jurisdictions *before* they become domiciled in California. There is a question about how California is going to treat this property, because the acquiring spouse, at the time of acquisition, was subject to the laws of another state and may have had no intention of eventually becoming domiciled in California. The laws of the prior domicile might have afforded the spouses property rights that are radically different from those of California law. If the property was acquired in a common law state, for example, then under the laws of that state, it is exclusively owned by the acquiring spouse, absent an agreement to hold the property otherwise. There is no such thing as an automatic "present, existing, and equal interest" of the other spouse in the property. Upon death or divorce, the nonacquiring spouse may have rights in the property through operation of equitable distribution and elective share laws. But until those occurrences, the property is under the sole ownership, management, and control of the acquiring spouse. This is essentially what separates the common law system from the community property system.

WHAT DOES "QUASI" MEAN?

To avoid having to treat the property as the separate property of the acquiring spouse and having to apply the law of the prior domicile to determine how it is distributed, the California Legislature in 1917 broadened the definition of community property to include property acquired during the marriage while the spouses were domiciled elsewhere. The effect of this legislation was to alter the property rights of any married person who purchased property in a common law state before moving to California. Basically, what was once the property of an individual spouse in a common law state became "community property" in California the moment that a couple became domiciled here. This amendment to the community property statute did not last long. In *Estate of Thornton*, 1 Cal. 2d 1, 5, 33 P.2d 1, 3 (1934), the California Supreme Court held that it would be unconstitutional to consider such property "community property." Specifically, the Court held that if property is acquired as his or her individual property in a common law state, the acquiring spouse had obtained "vested" rights in sole ownership and control of that property. Such "vested" rights could not constitutionally be forfeited simply by bringing the property to California and/or by the couple's changing their domicile to California. *Id.*

The *Thornton* decision created a predicament. If California courts had to give deference to property rights "vested" by the law of the state where the property was acquired, it might mean that the nonacquiring spouse may have *no* interest in the property whatsoever upon termination of the marriage. This was often the case before common law states adopted equitable distribution laws, under which the nonacquiring spouse would be granted a portion of the acquiring spouse's property upon divorce. Before equitable distribution laws, when the marriage ended in divorce, the acquiring spouse's property was just that—his or her own property. The nonacquiring spouse was left out in the cold.

To better illustrate this problem, assume that our hypothetical couple, Harry and Wilma, had a marriage where Harry worked outside the home and Wilma was a homemaker. They lived in a common law state that did not have an equitable distribution statute. Harry purchased all of their property from his earnings and held it in his name alone. The couple then moved to California and soon after sought a divorce. Applying the law of the state where the property was acquired, since the couple's prior state did not have an equitable distribution law, the California court would be bound to treat the property as Harry's property and to give *all* of the marital assets to him. This would impoverish Wilma, which could in turn burden the state, as Wilma might become a public charge.

In response to *Thornton*, the California Legislature created a new classification for out-of-state property acquired when the spouses were domiciled elsewhere. The classification is called "quasi-community property." In the divorce context, that classification reaches "all real or personal property, wherever situated" if:

1. the property was acquired by either spouse while domiciled elsewhere, and

2. the property would have been community property if the acquiring spouse had been domiciled in California at the time of acquisition, or
3. in exchange for real or personal property, wherever situated, which would have been community property if the spouse who acquired the property had been domiciled in this state at the time of acquisition.

Family Code §125(a).

In the context of death, the classification reaches "all personal property wherever situated, and all real property situated in this state," if:

1. the property was acquired by a decedent while domiciled elsewhere, and
2. the property would have been community property of the decedent and the surviving spouse if the decedent had been domiciled in California at the time of acquisition, or
3. in exchange for real or personal property, wherever situated, that would have been community property of the decedent and the surviving spouse if the decedent had been domiciled in California at the time the property so exchanged was acquired.

Probate Code §66(a).

The quasi-community property classification has the unique effect of treating property like community property *only upon death or divorce*. When a couple changes their domicile to California, the property rights they have from the prior domicile remain intact throughout the life of their marriage. No vested rights are forfeited solely upon the spouses' change of domicile to California. Upon death or divorce, however, California law applies. If the property is classified as quasi-community property, it is treated as if it were community property. At divorce, it is divided equally between the spouses, because quasi-community property is included in the community estate. Family Code §§63, 2550. At death, if the decedent dies intestate, the surviving spouse will take all of the decedent's quasi-community property. Probate Code §§101, 6401(b). The decedent also has the right to devise one-half of the decedent's quasi-community property.

Probate Code §§101, 6101(c).

Let us apply the quasi-community statutes to Harry and Wilma's situation. First, assume that after Harry and Wilma become domiciled in California, Wilma seeks a divorce. She would want a share of the property acquired during the marriage. However, that property was all acquired from Harry's earnings in a common law state and was held in his name. According to the law of that state, all the property would belong to Harry absent an equitable distribution statute. If California followed that law, Wilma would have no rights to the marital property. Enter the quasi-community statute. If the property fits the statutory definition of quasi-community property, it will be divided as if it is community property, and Wilma will have a right to one-half of the quasi-community property. It FITs the definition! The marital property is real or personal property. It is acquired by a spouse, Harry, while domiciled elsewhere. The property would have been community property if the acquiring spouse had been domiciled in California at the time of acquisition. If Harry had been domiciled in California at the time of acquisition, his earnings would have been considered community property. Any property acquired with those earnings, even if the title was in his name, would have been community property. Since the marital property fits the definition of quasi-community property, Wilma will have a right to one-half of that property.

At death, if Harry dies domiciled in California, the quasi-community property will be treated like community property. Again the property must FIT the definition. It does. All personal property wherever situated and real property that is situated in California is covered by the definition. Therefore, it is certain that at least Harry's personal property fits the definition. Under our facts, the property was acquired by Harry, the decedent, while domiciled elsewhere. The property would have been Harry and Wilma's community property if Harry had been domiciled in California at the time of acquisition. The property was acquired from Harry's earnings. Those earnings would have been community property if Harry had been domiciled in California when he earned them. Therefore, Harry's property would fit the definition of quasi-community property. If Harry died intestate, Wilma would be the surviving spouse and would be entitled to all the quasi-community property. If Harry died with a will, leaving his property to his sister Gertrude, only one-half of the quasi-community property would go to her. Wilma is entitled as surviving spouse to one-half of the quasi-community property. Harry has the right to devise one-half of the quasi-community property. Please note that here quasi-community property differs from community property. Wilma has no right to devise the quasi-community property that Harry acquired. Only the "decedent" has the right to devise one-half of the "decedent's" quasi-community property.

The third part of the quasi-community property definition is called the "exchange" provision. To understand what "exchange" means, let's return to Harry and Wilma, who have moved to California. While here, Harry took some of his savings that he earned in a common law state and purchased a fishing boat. He put the title in his name. If Harry and Wilma divorce, let us try to characterize the fishing boat. It was acquired while Harry and Wilma were domiciled in California, and California law seems to control. Harry would argue that even though California law would presume that the fishing boat is community property, he can rebut the presumption by tracing to the funds used to buy the boat. According to the law in a common law state, the funds that came from his earnings would be Harry's property. Thus comes the "exchange" provision of Family Code §125(b), which would consider the fishing boat quasi-community property. The fishing boat is personal property acquired "in exchange" for personal property (Harry's earnings) that would have been "community property" if Harry had been domiciled in California at the time of its acquisition. Harry's earnings and thus the fishing boat are quasi-community property. The "exchange" provision in Probate Code §66 operates in a similar manner.

In conclusion, we see that the quasi-community property definitions are only quasi-difficult. Understanding quasi-community property entails a step-by-step analysis of each part of the statutory provisions. Once the determination is made that the property is quasi-community property, it is in almost all circumstances treated like community property.

IS QUASI-COMMUNITY PROPERTY CONSTITUTIONAL?

The constitutionality of the new "quasi-community property" classification was upheld by the California Supreme Court in *Addison v. Addison*, 62 Cal. 2d 558, 399 P.2d 897, 43 Cal. Rptr. 97 (1965). In *Addison*, the Court noted that "the concept of quasi-community property is applicable only if a divorce or separate maintenance action is filed here after the parties have become domiciled in California. Thus, the concept is applicable only if, after acquisition of domicile in this state, certain acts or events occur which give rise to an action for divorce or separate maintenance." Id. at 566, 399 P.2d at 902, 43 Cal. Rptr. at 102. Upon that point, "the interest of the state of the current domicile in the matrimonial property of the parties *is substantial*," such that "[v]ested rights . . . *may be impaired* . . . ." *Id.* at 566, 567, 399 P.2d at 902, 43 Cal. Rptr. at 102 (emphasis added).

In *Addison*, both the husband and the wife were domiciled in California at the time of divorce, causing California to have a "substantial interest" in the spouses' respective property rights. Twenty-three years after *Addison*, a different case arose in which only one of the spouses was domiciled in California, while the other remained in the common law state where the property was acquired. In that case, *Marriage of Roesch*, 83 Cal. App. 3d 96, 147 Cal. Rptr. 586 (1978), the Court of Appeal held that, if only one spouse was domiciled in California, the application of the quasi-community property classification to their property would be unconstitutional. There, the Court squarely stated that for the quasi-community property classification to apply, two prerequisites had to be met. First, *both parties* would have to change their domicile to California. Second, subsequent to that change, the parties would have to seek the legal alteration of their marital status in a California court. *Id.* at 106-107, 147 Cal. Rptr. at 592.

The two-prong test of *Roesch*, defining when the quasi-community property classification is constitutionally applicable, has remained substantially in place. There are some exceptions that allow the classification of property as quasi-community property. In *Marriage of Fransen*, 142 Cal. App. 3d 419, 190 Cal. Rptr. 885 (1983), it was noted that only one spouse had to seek legal alteration of marital status in the California court. This is necessarily so because, in the words of the *Fransen* Court, "[t]o require otherwise would enable one spouse to defeat a quasi-community property claim of the other spouse by merely refusing to seek a dissolution, annulment or legal separation." *Id.* at 431, 190 Cal. Rptr. at 892. More significantly, in *Marriage of Jacobson*, 161 Cal. App. 3d 465, 207 Cal. Rptr. 512 (1984), the Court of Appeal held that where only one spouse was domiciled in California and the other remained in the prior domicile, as long as that other spouse *consented to the jurisdiction of the California court* and *to the application of California law*, the quasi-community classification could be applied. *Id.* at 472, 207 Cal. Rptr. at 516. To date, *Fransen* and *Jacobson* are the only exceptions to the *Roesch* rule that both parties have to be domiciled in California and have to seek out alteration of their marital status in California for the quasi-community property classification to apply.

Where it is unconstitutional to apply the quasi-community property classification, by implication, the property is still governed according to the laws of the domicile of the acquiring spouse at the time of acquisition. The nonacquiring spouse may still have rights in that property, afforded by the equitable distribution statutes of that jurisdiction.

In conclusion, there are two steps in characterizing property that spouses acquire while domiciled out of state. First, we apply the classification statutes to see whether the property can be classified as quasi-community property. Second, we see whether the constitutional prerequisites established in *Roesch*, or the *Jacobson* or *Fransen* exceptions, are met. If the statute is applicable and the constitutional prerequisites are met, then the property is quasi-community property, subject to California law, and it will be distributed as if it were community property upon divorce or death. If the constitutional prerequisites are not met, then the property remains subject to the law of the acquiring spouse's domicile at acquisition, and it will be distributed according to those laws upon divorce or death.

Examples

Example 1 — Wendy Flees to San Diego

Harry and Wendy were married in Maryland in 1990. They both worked at the Department of Labor. Neither had any assets when they were married; however, over the years they have managed to purchase a house in joint tenancy and some furniture and have managed to save a few thousand dollars in a joint savings account. Also, each has accumulations in a retirement account. Last year, Wendy decided that she had enough of the cold winters and petitioned for a transfer to San Diego. Harry, however, did not want to leave since his family lived close by. Six months after Wendy became domiciled in San Diego, she filed for dissolution of marriage in California family court. Can a California court characterize the Maryland property as quasi-community property? If it cannot, how will it be distributed?

Example 2 — Harry Appears and Stipulates

Assume that the facts are the same as in Example 1, except that when Harry received notice that Wendy filed for dissolution, he was in agreement that they should divorce and wanted the process to be as painless as possible. Therefore, Harry made a general appearance in the court in San Diego through counsel and stipulated that California law governed the distribution of all their assets. How should the court classify their assets in Maryland?

Example 3 — Harry and Wendy Move West

Assume that the facts are the same as in Example 1, except that both Harry and Wendy move to San Diego. Also assume that while they are in San Diego, they buy a condo overlooking the Pacific Ocean. The condo is in Harry's name, and they used savings from his earnings in Maryland to buy it. Wendy files for dissolution. How will the condo be characterized?

Example 4 — Hank and Willa Leave the Big Apple

Hank and Willa were married in New York in 1990. While domiciled there, they purchased an apartment in Manhattan using Hank's earnings. The title was in Hank's name. In 2014, they retired in California but kept the Manhattan apartment. Hank recently died intestate. Would the Manhattan apartment be classified as quasi-community property?

Example 5 — Howard Is Always on the Golf Course

Howard and Wanda were married in 1990 in Olympia, Washington, a community property state. In Washington, they purchased a house in Howard's name and accumulated substantial savings from Howard's earnings. Two years ago, they decided to retire in Palm Springs. They sold the house and purchased a condo in Howard's name on the ninth hole of a golf course in Palm Springs. They left the savings account in Washington. Distressed at how much time Howard was playing golf, Wanda filed for dissolution in California. How will the court classify the condo and their savings?

Example 6 — Howard Meets His Maker on the Golf Course

Assume the facts are the same as in Example 5, except assume that Howard had an unfortunate accident with a golf cart and died before Wanda filed for divorce. If Howard died without a will, what are Wanda's rights in the accumulated savings if the savings were attributed to his efforts only? Try to analyze this by reference to Probate Code §28(b), which states:

> "Community Property" means:
>
> (b) All personal property wherever situated, and all real property situated in this state, heretofore or hereafter acquired during the marriage by a married person while domiciled elsewhere, that is community property, or a substantially equivalent type of marital property, under the law of the place where the acquiring spouse was domiciled at the time of acquisition.

Explanations

Explanation 1 — Wendy Flees to San Diego

Statutory Analysis

The property satisfies the definition of quasi-community property, found in Family Code §125. The property is "real and personal property, wherever situated" and meets two elements of subdivision (a):

1. The property was acquired while Harry and Wendy were domiciled in Maryland.
2. If Harry and Wendy were domiciled in California when they acquired the property, it would have been community property.

Consider first their furniture, savings, and retirement accounts. According to the facts, neither had "assets" when they were married. Thus, the furniture, accumulated savings, and retirement accounts were acquired during the marriage. In California, property acquired by a married person during marriage is presumed to be community property unless it can be traced to separate property sources. Here, there are no facts indicating that the property comes from a separate property source.

Next, consider the house, which Harry and Wendy held as joint tenants. If that home had been purchased in California as joint tenants, then that home would be presumed to be community property, absent a writing that states that the property interests are separate. Family Code §2581. The facts do not say that such a writing exists; thus, the home would be community property if they had been domiciled in California.

In conclusion, the property would be considered "community property" if Harry and Wendy were domiciled in California when they acquired it. Under the statute, thus, the property can be classified as "quasi-community property" that would be divided equally at divorce.

Constitutional Analysis

Even though the statute is satisfied, on these facts, the statute cannot be constitutionally applied. The facts here are the same as *Marriage of Roesch*, and the result must be the same. In *Roesch*, the Court held that a quasi-community property classification is permissible only if (1) both parties changed their domicile to California, and (2) the parties seek in a California court an alteration of their marital status. Here, only Wendy has changed her domicile to California.

On these facts, the California court will have to look to Maryland law to determine Harry and Wendy's respective ownership interests, even though their property fits the definition of quasi-community property.

Explanation 2 — Harry Appears and Stipulates

The court will determine whether the quasi-community property statute can apply. Indeed it can.

Statutory Analysis

The statutory analysis is the same as in Explanation 1.

Constitutional Analysis

On these facts, the court can apply the statute without offending the Constitution. Even though Harry is not domiciled in California, he is consenting to California jurisdiction by making a general appearance, and he has stipulated to the application of California law. *Marriage of Jacobson* established that where the spouse is domiciled elsewhere and acquires property elsewhere, but nonetheless *consents to California jurisdiction and to have the substantive law of California applied*, the court can characterize the property as quasi-community property. *Jacobson* created the "consent exception" to the normal *Roesch* requirement that both spouses have to be domiciled in California for the quasi-community property statute to apply. Thus application of Family Code §125 is constitutionally permissible on these facts, and the Maryland property will be classified as quasi-community property and divided equally because quasi-community property is part of the "community estate."

Explanation 3 — Harry and Wendy Move West

Statutory Analysis

The condo in San Diego satisfies the definition of quasi-community property found in Family Code §125. The property is "real property, wherever situated." Even though it was acquired in California and while they were married, Harry would try to trace it to his earnings from Maryland. He would argue that the condo is therefore his property under Maryland law. This is where the "exchange" provision, Family Code §125(b) applies. The condo is real property acquired in exchange for personal property, wherever situated (Harry's earnings from Maryland), that would have been community property (earnings are considered community property under California law) if the spouse who acquired the property (Harry) had been domiciled in California at the time of acquisition. Therefore, tracing to Harry's funds would be tracing to quasi-community property, which makes the condo quasi-community property that would be divided equally at divorce.

Constitutional Analysis

On these facts, the court can apply the statute without offending the Constitution. *Marriage of Roesch* established two requirements for constitutional application that (1) both parties have changed their domicile to California, and (2) subsequent to the change of domicile, the spouses sought legal alteration of their marital status in a California court.

Here both Harry and Wendy moved to California and seem to have established their domicile here. Thus the first *Roesch* requirement is satisfied. As stated in *Marriage of Fransen*, the second *Roesch* requirement is satisfied when either spouse initiates a legal proceeding to alter their marital status in California. Here Wendy is petitioning for dissolution. Both *Roesch* requirements are therefore satisfied. The court will be able to classify and divide the quasi-community property without offending constitutional principles.

Explanation 4 — Hank and Willa Leave the Big Apple

This hypothetical highlights the difference between the quasi-community property definitions at divorce and at death. Under Family Code §125, the definition of quasi-community property includes real property "*wherever situated*." Under Probate Code §66, the definition of quasi-community property includes "all real property *situated in this state*." Therefore, since the Probate Code would control this case, the Manhattan apartment would *not* be defined as quasi-community property because it is situated in New York, not in "this state," meaning California. The laws of New York would control the character and distribution of the Manhattan apartment in a probate proceeding.

Explanation 5 — Howard Is Always on the Golf Course

Statutory Analysis

Here we have property that was acquired by Howard and Wanda before they became domiciled in California. But the relevant fact is that they acquired the home and the savings in a community property state. Depending on how Washington community property law treats the home and the savings, there may be no need to resort to the quasi-community statute. For instance, if Washington classifies the house in Howard's name as community property and Howard's earnings as community property, then anything purchased with those earnings will also be considered community property using tracing rules. Therefore, the condo in Palm Springs would be characterized as community property. The savings account in Washington would also be characterized as community property. Under Family Code §770, community property includes personal property, "wherever situated." Thus we can see that the quasi-community property statute is only necessary if the state of the spouses' prior domicile would treat the property acquired there differently from California law.

Constitutional Analysis

There is no constitutional problem here, since both Howard and Wanda are domiciled in California when Wanda filed for dissolution.

Explanation 6 — Howard Meets His Maker on the Golf Course

Classification

In Example 5, the accumulated savings were classified as "community property." However, at death, the Probate Code, rather than the Family Code, applies. Given that Washington is a community property jurisdiction, the financial assets will be classified as "community property" under Probate Code §28(b) rather than "quasi-community property" under Probate Code §66.

Probate Code §28(b) provides that if property is considered "community property" in the domicile of the spouse at the time of acquisition, then it is likewise "community property" here in California. According to the facts, the financial assets were accumulated in Washington, a community property state. Since those savings were accumulated during the marriage, and there are no facts indicating that they are traceable to separate property sources, Washington would likely consider them to be "community property." They are likewise "community property" here in California.

Wanda's Interest

By the operation of two Probate Code sections, Wanda will receive all of the financial assets upon Howard's death.

Probate Code §100 provides that "[u]pon the death of a married person domiciled in this state, one-half of the decedent's community property belongs to the surviving spouse and the other half belongs to the decedent." When Howard died, he was domiciled in California. Thus, by operation of that statute, Wanda owns one-half of the accumulated savings, and Howard owns the other half.

Probate Code §6401(a) provides that in intestate succession, "the intestate share of the surviving spouse is one-half of the community property that belongs to the decedent." Thus, by operation of §6401, Wanda gets the other one-half of the accumulated savings that Howard owned.

In conclusion, because Wanda owned one-half by operation of §100, and because she takes Howard's one-half by operation of §6401, Wanda gets the entire accumulation upon Howard's death.

CHAPTER 11

Putative or Partners: Problems That Arise When Couples Are Not Married

UNMARRIED COHABITANTS

Many Californians have the mistaken belief that there is "common law" marriage in this state. They believe that if a couple lives together for a number of years, they will be legally married. That is untrue. California abolished common law marriage in 1895. The unavailability of common law marriage has influenced the development of the law regarding those couples who choose to live together but do not meet the formal requirements for marriage. As more and more couples lived together without marrying, the courts had to address the ownership of the property acquired during the relationship.

The most typical scenario was where a couple lived together in a situation that resembled what is sometimes called a *traditional marriage*. One would work outside the home, and the other would be a homemaker. If they were married, the working spouse's earnings would be community property, and any property acquired with those earnings would be community property. However, if they were not married, the working cohabitant's earnings would belong to that person. Also, any property acquired in the working cohabitant's name would belong to that person. If the relationship ended, the stay-at-home cohabitant would have no rights to the property earned or titled in the working cohabitant's name. In a long relationship that resembled marriage in every way except the marriage license and ceremony, the property rules that applied to unmarried cohabitants created an inequity. One cohabitant could leave the relationship with all the accumulated wealth, and the other cohabitant would have no rights to that wealth.

Two approaches to the marriage-like relationship were possible. The first was to recognize that some cohabitants had an "actual family relationship" and treat the couple as if they were married. That would mean that property acquired during their relationship would be treated according to the laws governing community property. The second approach was to examine the cohabitants' intentions toward the accumulated property and to find either an express or an implied-in-fact contract to share that property. The second approach was adopted by the California Supreme Court in the landmark decision of *Marvin v. Marvin*, 18 Cal. 3d 660, 557 P.2d 106, 134 Cal. Rptr. 815 (1976).

Marvin v. Marvin

The *Marvin* Court rejected the first approach that was taken in the earlier Court of Appeal case, *Cary v. Cary*, 34 Cal. App. 3d 345, 109 Cal. Rptr. 862 (1973). The *Cary* Court had opted to treat a marital-like relationship as an "actual family relationship" with rights similar to those of married couples. The *Marvin* Court instead adopted the second approach and held:

1. Distribution of property acquired during a nonmarital relationship is governed by judicial decision, not community property statutes.
2. Express contracts between nonmarital partners will be enforced unless based on meretricious sexual services.
3. If there is no express contract, the courts will examine the conduct of the parties to determine whether they had an implied contract, agreement of partnership or joint venture, or some other tacit understanding.
4. Quantum meruit and other equitable remedies may be available for nonmarital partners.

The landmark *Marvin* case involved allegations by Michelle Triola Marvin that she and screen actor Lee Marvin had an oral agreement to share property. She alleged that she agreed to give up her career and serve as Lee's companion, homemaker, housekeeper, and cook, and he agreed to provide for her financial support for the rest of her life.

Lee argued that their relationship was an illicit one and therefore was based on "meretricious sexual services." Meretricious sexual services is a euphemism for prostitution. In other words, property given in exchange for sexual relations would be barred. It was illicit in this case, argued Lee, because they were having sexual relations outside of marriage. According to the Court, that was insufficient to invalidate an agreement relating to their property. Those agreements fail only to the extent that they rest upon a consideration of meretricious sexual services. If the sexual relationship could be severed from other consideration, the agreement would stand.

The *Marvin* Court held that both express and implied-in-fact agreements as well as equitable remedies were available to cohabitants. On remand, Michelle could not prove her allegations. The trial court found that they never agreed to share property nor did Lee agree to provide Michelle with financial support for the rest of her life. The difficulty of proving an "oral" agreement is obvious when there is a "he said, she said" battle. An implied agreement is also difficult to prove when there is no sharing of assets or other activity that indicates sharing. The equitable remedy of quantum meruit is the most difficult to prove. Quantum meruit permits recovery of the reasonable value of the services rendered less the reasonable value of support received. In a case like Michelle Marvin, a court is likely to find that although Michelle did render services through her household activities, she received the equivalent of that value merely through living at the standard of living of the wealthier cohabitant.

Implied Contracts to Share Property

The best case for recovering on an implied-in-fact contract is the long-term, marital-like relationship. For instance, in the *Cary* case, Janet and Paul lived together for more than eight years. They held themselves out as a married couple. They purchased a home and other property and conducted all business as husband and wife. They had four children together. Paul worked outside the home, and Janet stayed at home caring for the house and children. All their property was acquired through Paul's earnings. Even if Paul testified that he did not agree to share the property accumulated from his earnings, his conduct contradicted his words. A court would likely find an implied-in-fact contract to share the home and all other property acquired during their relationship. It would be based on conduct separate from their sexual relationship. The court could look at their conduct of holding themselves out as husband and wife and having children together as tacitly agreeing that one would work outside the home and the other inside the home. That conduct would indicate an implied agreement to share the property accumulated during their relationship.

Some later courts have required additional conduct besides a long-term marital-like relationship to show an implied-in-fact contract. In the case of *Maglica v. Maglica*, 66 Cal. App. 4th 442, 78 Cal. Rptr. 2d 101 (1998), the Court of Appeal stated that a marital-like relationship was insufficient without other conduct that indicated sharing. In *Maglica*, Claire Maglica had a long-term relationship with Anthony Maglica, where she took his name, and they held themselves out as a married couple. However, Claire also worked in his business and made significant contributions to its success. Additional sharing conduct helps establish an implied agreement to share that business. A similar approach was taken in the case of a same-sex couple. In *Whorton v. Dillingham*, 202 Cal. App. 3d 447, 248 Cal. Rptr. 405 (1988), the

Court of Appeal found that Whorton's allegation of business-related conduct was sufficient consideration for a contract that included a promise to act as "companion, confidant, travel and social companion, and lover." The Court considered the sexual part of the allegation as severable from the rest of the contract. The Court's focus on Whorton's allegation that he acted as "chauffeur, bodyguard, social and business secretary, partner and counselor in real estate" reinforces the inference that additional business conduct will support an implied-in-fact contract between unmarried cohabitants.

Even though marriage and domestic partnership are now legal options for same-sex couples, couples who chose not to take advantage of those options may be able to establish shared property rights through *Marvin* principles. What relief is available if no contract is proved? The *Marvin* Court states that party can recover in quantum meruit for the value of services performed. But *Maglica* says that the measure of recovery is the reasonable value of services rendered, provided they were of direct benefit to the defendant, not the total amount of benefit to the defendant. For example, Anne provides a variety of career support services for Brenda, including scheduling appointments, organizing business-related and social events, managing media coverage, and more. When Brenda ends the relationship with Anne, Brenda's earnings average $5 million per year. Anne cannot prove an agreement to share both parties' earnings 50-50. Anne will argue for an implied-in-fact contract to compensate her for her services. Under *Maglica*, Anne's recovery in quantum meruit is the only the fair market value (what a paid employee would have earned) for this work. Had Anne and Brenda been married, or registered domestic partners, she could recover one-half the income Brenda earned during the period.

Examples

Example 1 — Henri Meets Jeanne

Henri and Jeanne met while Henri was on a business trip to Los Angeles. They soon began a sexual relationship, and Henri rented an apartment for Jeanne. Whenever Henri came to Los Angeles, he stayed in the apartment with Jeanne. She often accompanied him on business trips and to many social events. While he was away, she took care of the apartment, and when he visited, she cooked and performed other homemaking tasks. After their relationship terminated, Jeanne wishes to sue Henri, claiming that he promised to support her as long as she was in need.

Example 2 — Almost Like Husband and Wife

Steve and Joan lived together for 12 years. They had three children during their relationship. They held themselves out as husband and wife, and Joan took Steve's last name. Steve worked outside the home and put his earnings in a joint bank account. They purchased a home and other properties and put the titles in both their names as "husband and wife." Joan managed the properties by collecting rents, paying bills, and arranging repairs. When their relationship terminated, Steve claimed that all the property was purchased with his earnings and therefore belonged to him. Joan claimed that they had an implied-in-fact agreement to share the property accumulated during their relationship.

Example 3 — Terri Needs Back Support

Terri and Elliot lived together for more than 15 years. They had two children during their relationship. Terri worked at the beginning of their relationship but stayed at home after they had the children. Elliot practiced law, and Terri cared for their home, took care of the children, and planned entertainment for social events. They also took title to their home jointly. At the end of their relationship, Terri filed a lawsuit asking for support from Elliot because she had sustained a back injury. She based her claim on an agreement to support her for the rest of her life. Would she be successful?

Example 4 — Jan and Leslie Live Together

Before same-sex marriage became legal in California, Jan and Leslie were same-sex lovers. They believed that their relationship was a committed one and had a "marriage" ceremony before friends. They knew they could not be legally married in California, but they used the occasion to proclaim their love for each other. They took a vow to "share their love, lives, and property" until "death do us part." Soon after the ceremony, Leslie moved in with Jan. During their relationship, Jan, who was a doctor, opened a professional practice. Leslie served as the receptionist and did all the billing for the practice. Leslie received a salary. That salary and the fees Jan received from the practice were deposited in a joint checking account. They bought a condo using the funds from that account, but the title was taken in Jan's name because Jan had a better credit rating. They lived in the condo for ten years. Fifteen years after their ceremony, Leslie moved out of the condo. Leslie is seeking a share of the condo as well as support from Jan. Would Leslie be successful?

Explanations

Explanation 1 — Henri Meets Jeanne

Unfortunately for Jeanne, it is highly unlikely that she will be able to recover. The court may hold that they were not even "cohabitants" given the sporadic nature of the relationship. They lived together only when Henri was in Los Angeles and thus did not have the type of relationship that would give rise to cohabitant status. Also, the court may view their relationship as "meretricious" in that Henri provided the apartment for Jeanne in return for their sexual relationship. Here the domestic tasks she performed could be considered part of the meretricious relationship and thus not adequate consideration for their agreement. Therefore, their agreement would not be found to be an implied-in-fact agreement. Even if the "cohabitation" and "meretricious" requirements could be met, Henri would undoubtedly deny that he ever agreed to support Jeanne thus foreclosing the possibility of an oral agreement. Finally, Jeanne would not be able to recover in quantum meruit, since a court would consider the support she received during their relationship was adequate compensation for the services she rendered. This scenario is based on the case of *Bergen v. Wood*, 14 Cal. App. 4th 854, 18 Cal. Rptr. 2d 75 (1993).

Explanation 2 — Almost Like Husband and Wife

This scenario presents the most favorable facts for finding an implied-in-fact agreement. Even if Steve denies that they ever had an oral agreement to share the home and other property, their conduct shows an agreement to share. Here their relationship is marital-like in that they shared the same last name, had three children together, and their relationship lasted as long if not longer than most marriages. That is in Joan's favor. In addition, there is conduct apart from their relationship that demonstrates an agreement to share property. They bought the properties together and put them in both their names. Steve provided the funds, while Joan provided business services regarding the property. Because the courts since *Marvin* seem to require additional conduct to show an implied-in-fact agreement, Joan would be able to meet that requirement by showing business as well as domestic services. This scenario closely tracks the case of *Alderson v. Alderson*, 180 Cal. App. 3d 450, 225 Cal. Rptr. 610 (1986).

Explanation 3 — Terri Needs Back Support

Although Terri and Elliot had a long-term marital-like relationship, Terri would not succeed. First, there are no rights to support after a cohabitation relationship ends as there may be after divorce. Second, it is highly doubtful that she could prove that they had an oral agreement of support. Not only would Elliot deny that they discussed support after termination of their relationship, but most cohabiting couples do also not expect that they have any obligations to each other after they split up. Third, it is possible that a court could find an implied-in-fact agreement to share the home considering that Terri not only took care of the home but also planned entertainment for social events for the couple. That is the slimmest evidence of additional conduct but may be sufficient considering the length of the relationship and their marital-like conduct. However, it is almost impossible to show an implied-in-fact agreement to support after the relationship has terminated. Even if Elliot did support Terri for a year after they split up, that support does not necessarily indicate an agreement to support for a longer period of time. Therefore, Terri would not succeed in receiving an award of support. This scenario is based on the case of *Friedman v. Friedman*, 20 Cal. App. 4th 876, 24 Cal. Rptr. 2d 892 (1993).

Explanation 4—Jan and Leslie Live Together

Since same-sex couples could not marry in California at the time Jan and Leslie lived together, same-sex couples had to rely on *Marvin* principles to assert any rights. Here, Leslie could attempt to base a lawsuit on an oral agreement to share their property. At their ceremony, they agreed to share their "love, lives, and property." This was said in front of friends, and therefore, it would be difficult to deny that Jan promised to share property. Jan might attempt to attack the agreement, since it was based on "meretricious sexual services," but only a homophobic court would look at their relationship as one where property was given in return for a sexual relationship. In addition, their conduct demonstrates an implied-in-fact contract to share, despite Jan's name on the title. Here, they had a long-term relationship. Leslie worked in Jan's medical practice, and they deposited their earnings in a joint account. They lived for over ten years in the condo they bought. Therefore, a court could find an agreement to share the property even without an oral agreement to share. Finally, Leslie would have the most difficulty proving an agreement for support after the relationship ended. Even though they agreed to share their "lives" at their ceremony, an agreement for support after termination of their relationship would probably have to be more specific for a court to enforce it. Thus, Leslie would have a good chance to have a share of the condo, but may not receive support from Jan. If same-sex couples do not marry nor register as domestic partners, they would still need to rely on *Marvin* principles to claim property rights.

PUTATIVE SPOUSE DOCTRINE

Defects in Marriage

Sometimes a couple marries and later finds out that a defect renders their marriage void or voidable. Usually, they learn of the defect when one "spouse" dies or the couple decides to divorce. The most common defect is that one "spouse" was not divorced or properly divorced from a former spouse. In that situation, the second "marriage" is void, even though the couple complied with all the formal requirements of marriage. The second marriage is considered bigamous, and no property rights arise from that marriage. The other, less-common, scenario of a void marriage is an incestuous marriage that violates the limits on marrying certain relatives. Again, that marriage is void, and no property rights arise from that marriage.

Some marriages may also be defective but can become valid by one spouse ratifying the marriage. Those marriages are voidable. For instance, one spouse could convince the other spouse to marry based on a misrepresentation. When the "defrauded" spouse finds out about the misrepresentation, she would have the option of having the marriage annulled. If the "defrauded" spouse instead continues to live with the other spouse despite the fraud, that would constitute ratification of the marriage and the marriage would be valid. Thus the "wronged" spouse would have the option of voiding the marrying or ratifying it. In most older cases, the fraud had to be related to the sexual or procreative aspects of marriage, such as a wife concealing from her husband that she was pregnant by another man. *Hardesty v. Hardesty*, 193 Cal. 330, 223 P. 952 (1924). In a more recent case, *Marriage of Ramirez*, 165 Cal. App. 4th 751, 81 Cal. Rptr. 3d 180 (2008), the Court of Appeal faced the issue of whether the Ramirez's marriage was voidable because husband Jorge had a "simultaneous" sexual relationship with wife Lilia's sister. The court found that Jorge had committed fraud and therefore Lilia was entitled to a judgment of annulment. *Id.* at 751, 81 Cal. Rptr. 2d at 185-186. Because the marriage was void, no community property rights would arise and Jorge would have no property rights arising from the marriage.

In conclusion, in a voidable marriage, the "wronged" spouse has the option of voiding the marriage or ratifying it. If the marriage is annulled, no property rights arise from that marriage. If the marriage is ratified by the "wronged" spouse, the marriage is valid, and property rights will attach. Some other defects that render a marriage voidable include being under the age of consent, of unsound mind, or physical incapacity. The requirements concerning validity of marriages are found in Family Code §§2200, 2201, and 2210.

Property Rights When Marriage Is Void or Voidable

The question presented in this section concerns the property rights of parties to a void or voidable marriage. If the marriage is invalid, then there were traditionally no property rights because there was no marriage. Yet this lack of property rights, especially after a long relationship, will often result in an inequity. For instance, consider our couple Harry and Wilma. Assume that they married 20 years ago by obtaining a marriage license, having a ceremony, and complying with all the technical requirements of California law. However, at the time of their marriage, Wilma's divorce from her former spouse, Fred, was not yet final. Both Harry and Wilma assumed that Wilma's divorce was final and acted on that assumption. During their relationship, Harry worked outside the home, and Wilma cared for their home and their three children. Their home and all their property were accumulated from Harry's earnings and kept in Harry's name. When they filed for dissolution, it was discovered that their marriage was actually a bigamous marriage, because Wilma was still married to Fred at the time she married Harry. Harry would want to argue that because their marriage was void, Wilma has no rights to his earnings and to the property acquired with those earnings. Community property rights only arise if there is a valid marriage. To allow Harry's argument to prevail would result in an inequity to Wilma. Thus came the "putative spouse doctrine." Although it originated in equity, it was codified in Family Code §2251:

> (a) If a determination is made that a marriage is void or voidable and the court finds that either party or both parties believed in good faith that the marriage was valid, the court shall:
>
> (1) Declare the party or parties to have the status of putative spouse.
>
> (2) If the division of property is in issue, divide, in accordance [with equal division], that property acquired during the union which would have been community property or quasi-community property if the union had not been void or voidable. This property is known as "quasi-marital property."

Therefore, if Harry and Wilma's marriage is void and either or both had a "good faith belief" in the validity of the marriage, they could be considered putative spouses. If they are declared to have the status of putative spouses, any property that would have been community property if they had been validly married will be treated as if it was community property. Because a putative spouse is not actually married, the property cannot be called community property. Instead, it is denominated as quasi-marital property.

In Harry and Wilma's case, it is clear that their marriage is void. Wilma was still married to Fred until their divorce decree became final. Thus, when she married Harry, she was entering into a bigamous marriage. "Good faith belief" is more difficult to define, but it is probably met in Harry and Wilma's case. A court will find that both Harry and Wilma did have a good faith belief that their marriage was valid. They went through all the formal requirements thinking that their marriage was valid. They both assumed that they were free to marry. For 20 years, they acted as if they were married. Therefore, they had a good faith belief that they were married and will have the status of putative spouses. The next step would be to analyze whether the property accumulated during their marriage would have been considered community property if they had been validly married. Here Harry's earnings and all the property acquired with those earnings would have been considered community property even though the property was in Harry's name. The property would be called quasi-marital property and would be divided at divorce as if it was community property. Therefore, Wilma and Harry would have a 50/50 share of the quasi-marital property.

A final issue concerns how long putative spouse status lasts. The right to recover as putative spouse depends on "good faith" state of mind. What happens when a "good faith" wife discovers her marriage is invalid?

For instance, if Wilma finds out that Harry was not divorced from Fran, she no longer has a "good faith" belief in her marriage to Harry. She then loses her status as a putative spouse. Therefore, any property acquired by Harry after she loses putative spouse protection belongs to Harry. If she continues to live with Harry, she would be treated as an unmarried cohabitant and would only have the rights provided to unmarried couples.

To preserve possible putative status after the date she discovered that the marriage was invalid, Wilma should promptly retain a lawyer, and file for a decree of nullity. The attorney will advise her to collect evidence that she had a good faith belief before the date of discovery. This evidence could include documents which identify her as married to Harry, and testimony from friends, co-workers, neighbors, etc., that her speech and conduct were consistent with a good faith belief that she was married to Harry.

Good Faith Belief Requirement in a Valid Marriage

The putative spouse doctrine requires that one or both of the parties have a good faith belief that the marriage is valid. The good faith belief is judged by a "a subjective standard that focuses on the alleged putative spouse's state of mind to determine whether he or she maintained a genuine and honest belief in the validity of the marriage." *Ceja v. Rudolph & Sletten, Inc.*, 56 Cal. 4th 1113, 1116, 302 P.3d 211, 213, 158 Cal. Rptr. 21, 23 (2013). The *Ceja* case rejected the objective test used by earlier Court of Appeal cases. The Supreme Court held that trial courts must look at the "totality of the circumstances" with attention to the following: (1) the efforts to create a valid marriage, (2) the alleged putative spouse's personal background and experience, and (3) all the circumstances surrounding the marriage. *Id.* The court noted that the reasonableness or unreasonableness of the belief is a factor in whether the belief was genuinely and honestly held. *Id.*

In *Ceja*, Robert and Nancy married in 2003. They obtained a marriage license and had a church wedding attended by 250 people. However, at the time of the wedding, Robert was still married to his former wife, Christina. Three years later, Robert died in a work accident. Nancy filed a wrongful death action against Robert's employer, Rudolph & Sletten, claiming she was Robert's putative spouse. The major issue was whether Nancy had a good faith belief. The trial court found she did not, based on the objective test and granted summary judgment for the employer. The Court of Appeal reversed and rejected the objective test found in *Marriage ofVryonis*, 202 Cal. App. 3d 712,

248 Cal. Rptr. 807 (1988). The Supreme Court agreed and disapproved the objective test of *Vryonis* and its use in later Court of Appeal cases.

Under the *Ceja* standards, several facts favor Nancy. First, Robert and Nancy took steps to create a valid marriage, obtaining a marriage license and holding a church wedding. Second, they acted as a married couple by wearing wedding rings, sharing a joint checking account, living together, and filing taxes as married. She testified that she would not have had the wedding had she not believed that her marriage was legal and valid. This was despite the fact that she faxed a copy of the divorce judgment to Robert's employer showing that Robert's divorce was not final at the time of the wedding. If Nancy was credible, it was likely that she would attain putative spouse status.

In the earlier *Vryonis* case, it is possible that even under a subjective standard, the putative wife, Fereshteh, would not have had putative spouse status. Fereshteh and Speros had a private *muta* religious ceremony. Although Fereshteh was educated, she did not have knowledge of California marriage law and relied on Speros's assurances that they were husband and wife. They did not live together. Fereshteh knew that Speros dated other women. She did not use his name. They filed separate tax returns, claiming single status. Two and a half years later, Fereshteh went public about their marriage when Speros told her he was to be married to someone else. Under the *Ceja* standards, the first problem for Fereshteh is that there were no efforts to create a valid marriage. The second problem is that the circumstances of the marriage indicate that she had almost no married life together with Speros. Her personal background is cloudy in that she was educated but not familiar with California law. Even if she testified that she believed that they were married, it seems the reasonableness of her belief could be called into question. Therefore, even under the *Ceja* "totality of circumstances" test, Fereshteh would not have putative spouse status.

According to the California Domestic Partner Act, the putative spouse doctrine applies to domestic partnerships. *In re Domestic Partnership of Ellis & Arriaga*, 162 Cal. App. 4th 1000 (2008). Darren Ellis and David Arriaga complied with the first step in the procedure for creating a Registered Domestic Partnership (RDP) — the completion of the registration papers. Arriaga was supposed to mail the registration to the Secretary of State, but he never did. When Ellis filed a petition to dissolve the domestic partnership, Arriaga asked the trial court to dismiss Ellis' action on the ground that no RDP in fact existed. The trial court agreed with Arriaga, but the appellate court reversed the trial court's ruling. The appellate court held that a person's reasonable, good faith belief that his or her RDP was validly registered with the Secretary of State entitled that person to the rights and duties of an actual registered domestic partner under the putative spouse doctrine. Parties who qualify for putative spouse and putative domestic partnership status may be entitled to all of the benefits and burdens of marital partners or RDP's. This includes rights to property acquired during marriage, responsibilities for debt incurred during marriage, and support benefits. However, the court in *Arriaga* applied the objective standard to test the rule of putative spouses, not just by what one party believed, however genuinely. The court reasoned that, for instance, if both parties know that the registration was never mailed, neither can qualify as putative domestic partners. Unless one party believed in the mailing it would not be objectively reasonable to conclude an RDP existed. The *Ceja* subjective standard is, "When the question is whether a party acted in good faith, the inquiry concerns the party's **subjective** state of mind and: whether it is genuine and sincere or tainted by fraud, dishonesty, collusion, deceit, and unfaithfulness." Applying this standard, the court could very likely find Ellis to be a putative spouse, based upon his sincere belief that the registration had been mailed. Ellis knew that it had not been mailed, and so could not be a putative spouse.

In 2024 the Court of Appeal issued a new family law opinion regarding the rights of a putative spouse. *Marriage of Gilbert-Valencia and McEachen* (2024) 2024 DJDAR 132. In this case, the parties obtained a marriage certificate in 2008 despite the fact that husband ("Daniel") had not finalized his divorce from his previous spouse until 2011. The "new" wife ("Kate") was unaware that Daniel was still married to his previous spouse. However, after Daniel finalized his divorce from the previous spouse, Kate and Daniel had another ceremony in July 2011. David's stated reason for the second wedding was so that he could change his name. The trial court found that, from the initial invalid marriage in 2008 until the second ceremony in July 2011, Kate had a "good faith" belief that she was legally married to Daniel. Therefore, Kate was a "putative spouse" for purposes of dividing the parties' quasi-marital property. In 2009 Daniel had purchased a house with a Veterans Affairs home loan. He took title in his own name as an unmarried man. Kate agreed to this title because she believed that adding her name could lead to Daniel being discharged from the Air Force. If the Air Force learned that Daniel, as a transgender man, had married a woman, he would promptly be discharged, likely with loss of benefits. Kate and Daniel relied upon Daniel's continued Air Force career, including future earnings, as a primary source of income. In 2016, following the parties' separation, Daniel filed a petition for divorce. Despite the family court's automatic temporary restraining orders (ATROS), Daniel sold the house in May 2017 and used the sale proceeds for his personal use. In early 2018, Daniel pleaded no contest to four counts of contempt regarding his initial declaration of disclosure required in family law cases and failure to obey a deposition subpoena. Kate agreed to waive all other possible counts of contempt including Daniel's failure to comply with the trial court's order regarding the proceeds from the sale of the house.

In October 2019, the trial court concluded that the house was purchased during the time period when Kate was a putative spouse and so, the house was quasi-marital property subject to division by the court. The trial court further ruled that Daniel sold the home in violation of his fiduciary duty to his putative spouse, Kate. The court awarded 100% of the proceeds from the sale to Kate, pursuant to Family Code §1101(h). Daniel appealed, arguing that the trial court should not have awarded 100% of the house proceeds to Kate. Because he had pleaded no contest to the four counts of contempt (and all other charges or possible charges were waived by Kate), he could not be punished again for his breach of fiduciary duty regarding the house. However, the Court of Appeal disagreed, reasoning that the stipulation the parties entered into made no mention of division of property and only intended to give Daniel a "fresh start" as to matters of contempt, which is a type of criminal proceeding. The appellate court did, however, agree with Daniel that the trial court incorrectly awarded Kate 100% of the house proceeds. The appellate court acknowledged that as a putative spouse Kay was entitled to the division of the home as if she were a legal spouse. Community property must be divided unless the trial court finds good cause that the interest of justice requires unequal division. If a breach of fiduciary duty by one spouse is "oppressive, fraudulent, and/or malicious," Family Code §1101 requires that property be divided unequally against the offending spouse. However, a spouse's breach of his or her fiduciary duty to the other spouse does not prevent the family court from dividing the property 50-50. Only if the offending spouse not only breaches his or her fiduciary duty but does so oppressively, fraudulently, and/or maliciously, is the court empowered to award 100% of the asset to the nonoffending spouse. The appellate court found that although Daniel breached his fiduciary duty to Kate and violated the ATROS, there was no finding by the trial court that Daniel's breach or violation constituted oppression, fraud, or malice. Without such a finding, the trial court could not award Kate more than her 50% share of the proceeds from the sale of the home.

Only One in Good Faith?

There was an important disagreement between two District Courts of Appeal on the issue of whether a bad faith spouse can claim putative spouse status. In *Marriage of Tejeda*, 179 Cal. App. 4th 973 (2009), the Court of Appeal held that only one party to the union must maintain a good faith belief in the validity of the "marriage." The putative spouse doctrine protects the "innocent" spouse (the wife). Until her husband revealed that they were not married, she had complied with the formal requirements of a California marriage, and she had a "good faith" belief that they were married. As a putative spouse she would be entitled to the same property rights that she would have from a valid marriage. The property accumulated by either spouse during the putative marriage would be considered quasi-marital property and divided

50/50 according to the laws of community property. The result was that the "bad faith" spouse also would receive 50% of the quasi-marital property. *In re Marriage of Guo & Sun*, 186 Cal. App. 4th 1491 (2010), the "good faith" wife (Go) petitioned for divorce and later amended it to seek a judgment of nullity. At the time of their marriage, in 2001, "husband" (Sun) told her that he had divorced his first wife, although in fact he only divorced first wife after the "second marriage." The marriage was void. The "good faith wife" (Go) did not petition for putative spouse. The "bad faith" husband (Sun) did. The trial court denied his petition, and he appealed. The Court of Appeals interpreted the language of the Family Code §2251 that gives the trial court "the party or parties" who believed in good faith that the marriage was valid. That language meant that "only an innocent party can seek to be a putative spouse." *Id.* at 1499, 112 Cal. Rptr. 3rd at 913.

The conflict between the holdings in *Marriage of Tejeda* (only one party to the union must maintain a good faith belief in the validity of the "marriage") *Marriage of Guo* (only the innocent party, could be considered a putative spouse) was resolved by the California Legislature. Family Code §2251(a)(2) was amended to read: "If the division of property is in issue, [the court shall] divide, in accordance with Division 7 (commencing with Section 2500), that property acquired during the union that would have been community property or quasi-community property if the union had not been void or voidable, only upon request of a party who [was] declared a putative spouse. This property is known as 'quasi-marital property.'" Pursuant to Family Code §2251(a)(2), only a putative spouse may request a division of quasi-marital property. Alternatively, the putative spouse may simply accept the decree of nullity, which restores both parties to unmarried status as of the date of the invalid "marriage." Thus, each party is entitled to as separate property all that party's earnings and acquisitions bought with earnings during the void "marriage."

Why might someone eligible for putative spouse status decide not to claim it or to request a division of quasi-marital property?

For example, spouse Herbert is a high wage earner and has a valuable pension plan. He discovers that his spouse Will knowingly went through a ceremony of marriage with him even though he had not divorced his first spouse. Moreover, Will's earnings have been less than one-fourth of Herbert's. Will loves to shop and has has incurred a large amount of credit card debt. Herbert bought a house before he and Will went through the ceremony of marriage and has made mortgage payments every month from his earnings. If Herbert files for a declaration of nullity, and chooses not to seek putative spouse status, he can keep all his wages and employment benefits earned during the invalid "marriage"—because they are his SP. The mortgage payments on his house were made from his SP earnings, and only increased his interest in the house. If Herbert gets putative spouse status and asks for property division, he is only entitled to what he would have received had the marriage been valid: one-half of quasi-marital property. Will, although not a good faith spouse, will get the other half of the quasi-marital property. If the court finds that Herbert's mortgage payments were quasi-marital property, Will could claim one-half of the total amount payments made during the "marriage." The quasi-marital property would be liable for both spouses' debts. In this case, Herbert would be well advised to file for a decree of nullity, but as a putative spouse, not to seek division of any quasi-marital property.

Putative Spouse Doctrine at Death

The California Probate Code does not have a specific provision regarding putative spouses, as it speaks only of the "surviving spouse." The question that the California courts struggled with was how to interpret "surviving spouse" to include a "putative spouse." The problem was that a surviving partner of an invalid marriage was in actuality not a *spouse*. The courts turned to equity to help provide for a spouse who would receive nothing under the Probate Code, particularly if their "spouse" died without a will (intestate). Let us review briefly the rights of a surviving spouse under the Probate Code. Under Probate Code §§100 and 6401(a), the surviving spouse is entitled to one-half of the community property as the surviving spouse and is entitled to the other one-half that belonged to the decedent. In short, if the decedent died intestate, the surviving spouse has a right to *all* of the community property of the couple. As to the separate property of the decedent, if the decedent died intestate, the surviving spouse has a right to all, one-half, or one-third, depending on the other heirs of the decedent. Probate Code §6401(c).

If a "spouse" has a good faith belief in the validity of the marriage, that spouse attains putative spouse status and has a right to both quasi-marital property and the separate property of the decedent. Usually the dispute in these cases involves the surviving putative spouse and the children of the decedent. For instance, in the California Supreme Court case of *Estate of Leslie*, 37 Cal. 3d 186, 689 P.2d 133, 207 Cal. Rptr. 561 (1984), William Garvin and Fay Reah Leslie married in Tijuana, Mexico. The marriage was invalid. The Court accepted William's argument that he had a good faith belief in the validity of the marriage. However, Fay Reah Leslie's children from a prior marriage contested the concept that as a putative spouse, he had a right to a portion of her separate property. It was clear that precedent allowed him as a putative spouse to share in the quasi-marital property, which would have been community property but for the invalidity of the marriage. The Supreme Court held that the putative spouse should have the same rights as a legal spouse, meaning both quasi-marital and separate property. The logic of that is sound—if there is a good faith belief in the marriage, that in essence makes the marriage valid. Therefore, the putative spouse should have the same rights as a legal spouse.

What happens when it turns out that a decedent has both a legal spouse and a putative spouse? That scenario occurred in the case of *Estate of Vargas*, 36 Cal. App. 3d 714, 111 Cal. Rptr. 779 (1974). Juan Vargas married Mildred in 1929 and raised three children with her. In 1945, Juan "married" Josephine and raised four children with her. The property at issue in the case was all acquired through Juan's earnings after he "married" Josephine. He died in 1969, seemingly living a double life for 24 years. One wonders how he kept up the deception! In any case, the Court of Appeal had to deal with disposition of Juan's estate. It was clear that Mildred was the legal spouse, and under the Probate Code, she was entitled to all of Juan's estate. Juan's marriage to Josephine was void because it was a bigamous marriage. It was also clear that the trial court had found Josephine credible and that she had a good faith belief in the validity of her marriage to Juan.

Under prior precedent, California courts had developed the theory of quasi-marital property, which equated property rights acquired during a putative marriage with community property acquired during a legal marriage. Thus, the Court faced the dilemma of two parties, Mildred the legal spouse and Josephine the putative spouse, who both had a legitimate claim to all of the property. Another possible theory yielded another result. That theory treated Juan and Josephine's marriage as a partnership, with each partner having a one-half share of the property accumulated during the partnership. That meant that Josephine would have a one-half share of the partnership property, and Juan would have the other half. Juan's one-half would be considered community property, and Mildred as the legal spouse would be entitled to that half. Finally, equity could be called on to divide the property as the court saw fit.

The court even theorized that both Mildred and Josephine could be entitled to three-quarters of the property. For instance, on the one hand, as the legal surviving spouse, Mildred would receive one-half as the community property, and, under equity, Mildred would receive one-half of the other half because she was the long-suffering legal wife. On the other hand, under the partnership theory, Josephine would receive one-half as the partner in the enterprise, and, under equity, Josephine would receive one-half of the other half because the property was accumulated while Juan had a relationship with her.

The Court of Appeal upheld the decision of the Probate Court to divide the estate equally, "presumably on the theory that innocent wives of practicing bigamists are entitled to equal shares of property accumulated during the active phase of the bigamy." *Id.* at 719, 111 Cal. Rptr. at 781.

Examples

Example 5 — Mark Was Never Divorced from Laura

Mark and Pauline met in 2000. At that time, Mark told Pauline that he was separated from his wife, Laura. They began living together, and in 2001, Mark told Pauline that his divorce from Laura was final. Soon after, they decided to marry. After obtaining the marriage license, they had a small ceremony at the courthouse. The marriage was recorded. They acted as if they were married. Pauline changed her name, and they filed joint tax returns. Pauline's earnings were spent on household expenses. Mark's earnings were used to buy several parcels of property, and they were all put in Mark's name. Recently, Pauline was cleaning Mark's office and found cards and letters from Laura. When Pauline confronted Mark, Mark admitted that when they married in 2000, his divorce from Laura was not final. Pauline immediately demanded a "divorce." She comes to you for advice. What are Pauline's rights to the property accumulated during their "marriage"?

Example 6 — Pauline Bought Parcels of Property

Assume the facts are the same as Example 5, except that Mark's earnings were spent on household expenses. Pauline's earnings were used to buy several parcels of property, and they were all put in Pauline's name. After Mark and Pauline separate, Mark comes to you for advice. What are Mark's rights to the property accumulated during their "marriage"?

Example 7 — Roger and Sarah Live in Fantasyland

Roger and Sarah both work behind the scenes at Disneyland. They both love the rides and have vivid imaginations. They start living together in 2014. The following year, they decide to have a costume party where everyone comes dressed as their favorite person at a wedding. One of Roger's friends dresses as a justice of the peace. Roger dresses as a groom and Sarah as a bride. At the party, Roger's friend performs a ceremony for all the "brides" and "grooms." Roger and Sarah even wrote out wedding vows for all those who want to "marry." After the party, Roger and Sarah went away together for a "honeymoon" to Hawaii. When they discuss the wedding and honeymoon, Roger tells Sarah, "You are living in Fantasyland." Sarah tells him, "Our marriage is for real." Recently, Roger died in an accident on one of the rides he was working on. According to his employment contract, "Death benefits are payable to the surviving spouse of the decedent or to the putative spouse of the decedent." Putative spouse is defined as "the surviving spouse of a void or voidable marriage who is found by the court to have believed in good faith that the marriage to the decedent was valid." Sarah is heartbroken about Roger's death. She comes to you for advice about whether she could claim to be Roger's surviving spouse or putative spouse. Would Sarah have any rights to Roger's death benefits?

Example 8 — Will Betsy Collect the Flags?

Sam and Betsy met at a Fourth of July celebration in 2010. Sam told Betsy that he was celebrating his independence from his ex-wife, Britannia. They found that they shared an interest in collecting historical artifacts. Betsy was particularly impressed with his extensive collection of antique American flags. They soon married according to California procedures, but Sam did not tell Betsy that his divorce from Britannia was not yet final at the time Sam and Betsy "married." Sam recently died without a will, and his children from his marriage to Britannia are contesting Betsy's rights to Sam's collection of antique flags. Britannia has conceded that she has no rights to Sam's estate. What rights does Betsy have to Sam's flag collection?

Example 9 — Who Collects the Art?

Michael was an art history teacher in San Francisco when he married Angela in 2000. In 2005, he began giving lectures twice a month in Los Angeles. There he met Pam and also "married" her. He told Pam that he was divorced from Angela but still saw her often because they had joint custody of their two children. In 2010, Michael acquired an art collection using a savings account containing funds that were earned from his lectures in Los Angeles. Michael recently died without a will, and Pam then discovered that Michael was never divorced from Angela. In a probate proceeding, both Angela and Pam are claiming the art collection. What theories support Angela's claim to the art collection? Pam's? How would a court decide?

Example 10 — Pam Discovers the Truth

Assume the facts are the same as Example 9, except that Pam discovered in 2014 that Michael is still married to Angela. Does Pam have any rights to the art collection acquired in 2010?

Explanations

Explanation 5 — Mark Was Never Divorced from Laura

Pauline will not obtain a divorce. Because Mark was still married to Laura when he "married" Pauline, their marriage is a bigamous one and is considered void. (The court can issue a finding of nullity that restores her to her status as of the date of the invalid marriage.) The issue is whether Pauline qualifies as a putative spouse. To be considered a putative spouse, it must be determined if Pauline had a "good faith" belief in the validity of a lawful marriage. Under the *Ceja* "totality of the circumstances" test, the court will examine their efforts to create a valid marriage. Here that was met because they had a marriage license and a ceremony. The marriage was also recorded. Next, the court will look at the circumstances surrounding the marriage. Here they acted as a married couple: They lived together, filed joint tax returns, and shared the responsibilities of marriage. Regarding Pauline's background and experience, she could testify that she relied on Mark's representation that his divorce from Laura was final, and she never had any reason to doubt him until she found the letters from Laura.

Mark would claim that his earnings and the property in his name belong to him. Because they were not "legally" married, he will claim his earnings are his property. However, Pauline has the better argument that the property acquired during their "marriage" is "quasi-marital" property. Quasi-marital property is property that would be considered community property if they had been legally married. Had the marriage been valid, Mark's earnings would have been considered community property, and property bought with community property is still community property even though it is held in Mark's name. Therefore, Pauline as a putative spouse has a right to one-half of the property. Ironically, Mark will keep the other half even though he was not in "good faith."

Explanation 6 — Pauline Bought Parcels of Property

Again, Mark and Pauline's marriage is a bigamous one and is void. The issue here is whether Mark can be considered a putative spouse. Although they attempted to comply with the procedural requirements and lived as if they were married, Mark knew he was not divorced from Laura at the time he "married" Pauline. Therefore, he would not be considered to be acting in "good faith." The conflict between the holdings in *Marriage of Tejeda* (only one party to the union must maintain a good faith belief in the validity of the "marriage") *Marriage of Guo* (only the innocent party, could be considered a putative spouse) was resolved by the California Legislature. As amended, Family Code §2251(a)(2) provides: "If the division of property is in issue, [the court shall divide . . .] property acquired during the union that would have been community property or quasi-community property if the union had not been void or voidable, only upon request of a party who [was] declared a putative spouse."

Pauline can qualify as a putative spouse, so she may request a division of quasi-marital property. Alternatively, she may accept the decree of nullity, and claim as her separate party all her earnings and acquisitions bought with her earnings during the void "marriage."

Explanation 7 — Roger and Sarah Live in Fantasyland

Sarah most probably will not be considered Roger's surviving spouse. They did not make efforts to create a valid marriage, such as obtaining a marriage license, having a ceremony, and recordation. Even though they had a ceremony of sorts, they never applied for nor received a license. This case has some similarities to the *Vryonis* case, where the couple did not comply with the procedural requirements of California law. There the couple exchanged private vows to be married. Here, the couple exchanged vows before friends and lived together before Roger died. Sarah may be willing to testify that she thought they were married because they had a ceremony and lived together after their honeymoon. However, under the *Ceja* standards, a court would have to test *her subjective* state of mind and: "whether it is genuine and sincere or tainted by fraud, dishonesty, collusion, deceit, and unfaithfulness."

Most courts would doubt that Sarah had a genuine and honest belief in the validity of a marriage that took place at a costume party. The likelihood of her recovering death benefits is very doubtful.

Explanation 8 — Will Betsy Collect the Flags?

For Betsy to inherit from Sam, she must be deemed to be Sam's surviving spouse. Under the Probate Code, a surviving spouse has at least a one-third share of a decedent's separate property if that spouse dies without a will. Here, Sam's flag collection would have been considered separate property, because Sam acquired it before they married. However, their "marriage" was void because Sam was still married to Britannia at the time they went through the California marital procedures. Unless she can be considered a putative spouse, Betsy has no rights to Sam's flag collection as a surviving spouse.

In the *Leslie* case, the California Supreme Court held that a putative spouse has the same rights as a surviving spouse to the decedent's separate property. The issue is whether Betsy would be considered a putative spouse. Sam and Betsy followed the California procedures and lived as husband and wife. Betsy could testify that she believed in good faith that they were lawfully married. She believed Sam when he described Britannia as his ex-wife. Therefore, a court could consider Betsy to be a putative spouse. She would be entitled to Sam's separate property as if she were a surviving spouse. Sam's flag collection would be split between Betsy (one-third) and his children (two-thirds).

Explanation 9 — Who Collects the Art?

Angela was legally married to Michael. Under the Probate Code, she would be considered the surviving spouse. The surviving spouse is entitled to all the community property when the decedent dies without a will. The art collection was acquired during their marriage from Michael's earnings. It is community property. Angela claims that she deserves the art collection based on being Michael's legal spouse.

Pam claims that she has the status of putative spouse. They went through a marriage ceremony, and she believed in good faith that Michael was divorced from Angela. The art collection was acquired with funds from Michael's earnings during their putative marriage. Those earnings would have been community property if they had been validly married. As a putative spouse, she would be entitled to the quasi-marital property if there were no legal spouse.

Those are the two major theories that would allow Angela and Pam to claim the entire art collection. However, since the Probate Code does not have a provision regarding quasi-marital property, the court must resort to its equitable power to do what is fair in a situation where both the legal and putative spouses are innocent parties. If that were the case, the most equitable course is to split the art collection between Angela and Pam or to sell the collection and split the proceeds between them.

If the court favors Angela, the court could find that Pam was not a putative spouse. The court could use the "reasonable person" standard and determine that a reasonable person would not have believed that Michael was spending so much time in San Francisco with his ex-wife without still being married to her. If Pam did not attain putative spouse status, she would not be entitled to any property.

Explanation 10 — Pam Discovers the Truth

When Pam finds out that Michael is still married to Angela, she no longer has a good faith belief in her marriage to Michael. Her status as putative spouse lasts only as long as her good faith belief lasts. Since she had a good faith belief at the time the art collection was acquired, she will have rights if the court considers her a putative spouse at that time.

If Pam continued to live with Michael after she found out about his marriage to Angela, she would have no rights to property then acquired with his earnings. Once she lost putative spouse status, Michael and Pam would be treated as unmarried cohabitants and would only have rights as provided in the doctrine developed from *Marvin v. Marvin*.

CHAPTER 12

Domestic Partnerships

HISTORY OF DOMESTIC PARTNERSHIPS IN CALIFORNIA

The history of domestic partnerships cannot be separated from the legal and political movements for or against same-sex marriage. In 1999, California became the first state to recognize domestic partnerships for same-sex couples. The California Senate Judiciary Committee passed Assembly Bill 26, which defined domestic partnerships and provided limited rights to health benefits and hospital visitation. (These were two critically important rights that *Marvin* independent living agreements could not ensure.) The California Domestic Partner Rights and Responsibilities Act (effective January 1, 2005) expanded the 1999 law, establishing property rights, parental rights, and a more formalized process for dissolving a domestic partnership.

In California and in some other states, over the next decade, domestic partnerships gradually evolved to provide almost the same rights and benefits (at least under state law) as marriage. During the same period, many states and the federal government debated whether to prohibit or legalize same-sex marriage. Given the uncertain status of same-sex marriage, domestic partnerships remained a popular option for many couples throughout the state

From 1996 to 2013, the federal Defense of Marriage Act (DOMA) prevented the United States government from recognizing any same-sex marriage, even if the couple's marriage was legally recognized by their home state. In *United States v. Windsor*, 570 U.S. 744 (2013), widow Edith Windsor sued for a refund of the $363,058 federal estate taxes she was required to pay because her deceased spouse was a woman; she would not have had to pay any tax as the widow of a man. In *Windsor* the Supreme Court struck down §3 of the federal DOMA, finding that it deprived same-sex couples who are legally married under state laws, of their Fifth Amendment rights to due process and equal protection. (DOMA was formally repealed by the federal Respect for Marriage Act of 2022, which defined marriage for the purposes of federal law as a legal union between individuals and required states to recognize same-sex marriages and interracial marriages validly performed in other jurisdictions.)The right to same-sex marriage under the United States Constitution was determined by the Supreme Court in *Obergefell v. Hodges*, 576 U.S. 644 (2015).The Court held that the fundamental right to marry is guaranteed to same-sex couples, and that the Fourteenth Amendment requires states to (1) license same-sax marriages, and (2) recognize same-sex marriages validly made in other jurisdictions.

Once same-sex marriage became legal, many registered domestic partners in California chose to marry. Some have terminated their domestic partnership before they married, while others have not.

DOMESTIC PARTNERS ACT AS OF JANUARY 1, 2005: RIGHTS AS IF MARRIED

On January 1, 2005, the California Domestic Partner Rights and Responsibilities Act of 2003 (2005 Act) became effective, thereby granting domestic partners most but not all the same rights and obligations as spouses. *Knight v. Superior Court*, 128 Cal. App. 4th 14, 26 Cal. Rptr. 3d 687 (2005), *rev. denied*, June 29, 2005. That meant that any property domestic partners acquire would be characterized and divided as if they were married. As of January 1, 2005, domestic partners were subject to community property law at both death and dissolution of the domestic partnership.

Upon the death of a registered domestic partner, the surviving partner has the same rights, protections, and benefits as a widow or widower. Family Code §297.5(c).The surviving domestic partner is entitled to his or her one-half of the community property under Probate Code §100. If the domestic partner died without a will, the decedent's one-half share of the community property will also pass to the surviving domestic partner via Probate Code §6401(a). If the decedent died intestate, the surviving domestic partner will receive all of the community property just as a surviving spouse would. Depending on whether there are other heirs, the surviving domestic partner will inherit either one-third, one-half, or all of the decedent's separate property. If the decedent has no surviving relatives, the surviving domestic partner will inherit all of the decedent's separate property. Probate Code §6401(c).

As of 2005, community property law fully applied to domestic partners both during the partnership and upon separation or dissolution of the partnership. Family Code §297.5(a)(b). Domestic partnership terminations are subject to the same court proceedings applicable to spouses who file for dissolution of their marriage. Unlike marriage dissolutions, however, the Family Law court has jurisdiction over the dissolution of a domestic partnership even if neither partner is a resident of or domiciled in California. Family Code §299(d).

The 2005 Act required the Secretary of State to send letters to all those domestic partners who had registered prior to 2005, explaining their new rights and obligations. The letter also explained that registered domestic partners who did not want to be subject to the new rights and obligations *must* terminate their domestic partnership prior to January 1, 2005. Family Code §299.3(a).

The main section of the 2005 Act defining the rights and obligations of domestic partners does not directly address the issue of retroactivity. However, retroactivity of Family Code amendments is now "the general rule." That was the holding of *Marriage of Fellows*, 39 Cal. 4th 179, 138 P.3d 200, 46 Cal. Rptr. 3d 49 (2006), based on the California Supreme Court's interpretation of Family Code §4(c). The general rule, however, is subject to other sections of §4 that codify the constitutional protection of due process. See Chapter 2 on retroactivity of family code amendments.

According to the California Domestic Partner Act, the putative spouse doctrine applies to domestic partnerships. *In re Domestic Partnership of Ellis & Arriaga*, 162 Cal. App. 4th 1000 (2008). Parties who qualify for putative spouse and putative domestic partnership status may be entitled to all of the benefits and burdens of marital partners or registered domestic partners. This includes rights to property acquired during marriage, responsibilities for debt incurred during marriage, and support benefits. Although the court in *Arriaga* applied the objective standard to test the rule of putative spouses, it should have used the *Ceja* subjective standard. "When the question is whether a party acted in good faith, the inquiry concerns the party's *subjective* state of mind and: whether it is genuine and sincere or tainted by fraud, dishonesty, collusion, deceit, and unfaithfulness."

DOMESTIC PARTNERS ACT EFFECTIVE JANUARY 1, 2020

During the fifteen years since the passage of the 2005 Act, the Legislature made amendments and changes to the Domestic Partners Act, which *were effective January* 1, 2020.

(Amended by Stats. 2019, Ch. 135, Sec. 1. (SB 30) Effective January 1, 2020.)

Family Code §297

(a) Domestic partners are two adults who have chosen to share one another's lives in an intimate and committed relationship of mutual caring.

(b) A domestic partnership shall be established in California when both persons file a Declaration of Domestic Partnership with the Secretary of State pursuant to this division, if, at the time of filing, all of the following requirements are met:

(1) Neither person is married to someone else or is a member of another domestic partnership with someone else that has not been terminated, dissolved, or adjudged a nullity.

(2) The two persons are not related by blood in a way that would prevent them from being married to each other in this state.

(3) Both persons are at least 18 years of age, except as provided in Section 297.1.

(4) Both persons are capable of consenting to the domestic partnership.

The 2020 Act incorporated several important changes. It (1) eliminates the 62 years of age or older requirement for opposite-sex couples to register as domestic partners; (2) opens the registration of a domestic partnership to all partners over the age of 18; and (3) confirms that the 2011 elimination of the common residence requirement applies to persons under the age of 18. A person under the age of 18 who otherwise meets the requirements for a domestic partnership can establish a domestic partnership with a court order granting permission. Unlike when a minor petitions a court to marry, parental consent is not required. The distinction addresses the possibility that a minor seeking a domestic partnership may not be living with the intended domestic partner, but in the parents' home, in foster care, in a youth shelter or group home, or other residence.

NON-CALIFORNIA RESIDENTS

There is no California residency requirement in the domestic partnership law, and no distinction made concerning the requirements to register a domestic partnership. A California resident and out-of-state partner, or two out-of-state residents, are eligible to file a declaration of domestic partnership valid in California. They must complete the application form online, print it, and have their signatures notarized.[1] They should be aware, however, that their

1. A notary public in any state can notarize the signatures. However, if the out-of-state notary public cannot use the preprinted acknowledgment form, the notary public can complete a

California domestic partnership may not be recognized or enforced by the federal government or by other states. See Federal Application and Full Faith and Credit, below.

DOMESTIC PARTNERSHIP PLUS MARRIAGE

The 2020 Act specifically addressed the common situation where a couple who were domestic partners, entered into a lawful marriage, without terminating the domestic partnership.

> §297.5 (k))(1) For purposes of the statutes, administrative regulations, court rules, government policies, common law, and any other provision or source of law governing the rights, protections, and benefits, and the responsibilities, obligations, and duties of registered domestic partners in this state, as effectuated by this section, with respect to community property, mutual responsibility for debts to third parties, the right in particular circumstances of either partner to seek financial support from the other following the dissolution of the partnership, and other rights and duties as between the partners concerning ownership of property, *any reference to the date of a marriage shall be deemed to refer to the date of registration of a domestic partnership with the state.*

This language provides that for all the listed purposes, a domestic partnership plus marriage will be treated as one relationship, starting at the date when the domestic relationship was registered. This approach would avoid difficulties at divorce when community property, enabling the court to treat as a whole community assets or debts acquired partly during the domestic partnership and partly during the marriage. Another important effect of this language is to qualify a combined domestic partnership plus marriage as a "marriage of long duration" for purposes of spousal support.

Some couples who registered as domestic partners before 2005 also entered into an agreement similar to a premarital agreement, prior to 2005. The 2020 Act provides that such an agreement is enforceable, so long as it was completed and in effect as of June 30, 2005.

> §297.5(k)(2) Notwithstanding paragraph (1), for domestic partnerships registered with the state before January 1, 2005, an agreement between the domestic partners that the partners intend to be governed by the requirements set forth in Sections 1600 to 1620 [Premarital Agreement Act], inclusive, and which complies with those sections, except for the agreement's effective date,

separate certificate and attach the separate certificate to the registration form. The registration form and required filing fee must then be returned by mail or in person to the California Secretary of State office in Sacramento or Los Angeles.

> shall be enforceable as provided by Sections 1600 to 1620, inclusive, if that agreement was fully executed and in force as of June 30, 2005.

Partners in a registered domestic partnership who also are married to one another may file a petition in California Superior Court to dissolve both the domestic partnership and the marriage in a single proceeding. California also authorizes a judgment for dissolution, nullity, or legal separation of a marriage between persons of the same sex to be entered if the marriage was entered in California and neither party to the marriage currently resides in a jurisdiction that will dissolve the marriage.

FEDERAL LAW APPLICATION

The purpose of both the Domestic Partner Act of 2005 and of 2020 was to extend to registered domestic partners all the rights, benefits, and obligations of married persons, with the exception of the rights, benefits, and obligations accorded only to married persons by federal law. . . . While California generally treats registered domestic partners and married couples equally in terms of rights and responsibilities, the federal government does not always treat registered domestic partners the same as spouses for legal or tax purposes. As an example, *registered domestic partners are not considered married for federal tax purposes.* https://www.sos.ca.gov/registries/domestic-partners-registry. California does regard domestic partners as eligible to file as a married couple for state taxes.

FULL FAITH AND CREDIT

A marriage contracted outside this state that would be valid by laws of the jurisdiction in which the marriage was contracted is valid in California. Family Code §308. California also recognizes domestic partnership equivalents from other jurisdictions. "A legal union of two persons, other than a marriage, that was validly formed in another jurisdiction, and that is substantially equivalent to a domestic partnership as defined in this part, shall be recognized as a valid domestic partnership in this state regardless of whether it bears the name domestic partnership" Family Code §299.2. However, if another state offers domestic partnerships that are totally different from California domestic partnerships, California will not recognize the out-of-state partnership.

Why would someone choose a domestic partnership rather than marriage? Although the purpose of California's domestic partnership legislation was to create substantial legal equality between domestic partners and spouses, domestic partnership is not marriage under California law. *In re Villaverde*, 540 B.R. 431 (Bankr. C.D. Cal. 2015). Plus, as discussed above, other jurisdictions may not recognize and give full faith and credit to a California domestic partnership. A couple who has been comfortable with their domestic partnership since 2005 or more recently, and who intends to remain California residents, may regard marriage as unnecessary. A widow or widower who vowed never to remarry, or whose adult children would oppose a new marriage, may find domestic partnership an acceptable alternative.

Examples

Example 1 — Jungle Love

Julie and Carla met while on an African safari tour. Amid all the excitement of seeing elephants, zebras, giraffes, and lions, they learned a lot about each other. As luck would have it, both lived in San Francisco. In 2003, they registered their domestic partnership with the State of California. During their partnership, they decided to buy a house. Both Julie and Carla wanted their names on the title, so they decided to take title in joint tenancy. Also in 2003, Carla bought a boat so they could go whale watching and enjoy nature. The boat was in Carla's name. In 2004, they received a letter in the mail explaining how, in 2005, registered domestic partners would be subject to community property law. After discussing it, Julie and Carla terminated their domestic partnership before the 2005 law took effect. They decided they did not want to be subject to community property law since they were happy with their lives as they were. As time went on, however, their love faded. Carla recently moved out of the house. Who gets the house and the boat?

Example 2 — Domestic Partners Till Death Do Us Part

Keith and David met, fell in love, and decided to register their domestic partnership with the State of California on February 14, 2014. They had been living together in an apartment, but after they registered, they decided to buy a West Hollywood condominium together, taking title as joint tenants. The condominium cost $500,000, and David made the down payment of $100,000 using his earnings from before they registered as domestic partners. Keith worked as an interior designer and furnished their new condominium using his earnings from after they registered as domestic partners. Keith paid for all of the new oak furniture, which cost $50,000. Keith also had a bank account in his own name, which contained $10,000 of his earnings from before they registered as domestic partners. Suppose that on January 1, 2020, Keith died unexpectedly without a will. Who owns the condominium, the furniture, and the bank account?

Example 3 — I'm Leaving You — Let's Go to Court

Assume the same facts as Example 2, except suppose that Keith and David broke up on their eighth anniversary (February 14, 2022) and are seeking dissolution of their domestic partnership. Who owns the condominium, the furniture, and the bank account?

Example 4 — Oscar and Penny Play Bridge Together

Oscar and Penny both live at a 55+ retirement village near San Diego. Oscar has never married, served in the Navy for many years, and lives comfortably on his military service-related benefits. Penny is a widow who recently sold her San Diego condominium and moved into a one-bedroom apartment in the retirement village. She receives Social Security benefits. Oscar and Penny have mutual friends who love to play bridge. Those friends introduced them, and they immediately hit it off. They want to give up their small one-person apartments and move into one of the village's larger apartments for couples. They are considering marriage, but Penny is concerned that she will lose her Social Security benefits if they marry. Recently, they were talking to their friends who had read an article about the domestic partnership law in California. They were told, "It's just like marriage, but it's not. Maybe you should investigate." Oscar and Penny come to you for advice. Could they register as domestic partners? Should they? Oscar mentions that they are thinking about moving to Florida in a year or two. What questions would you ask them and what advice would you give?

Example 5 — Marriage Too

Chris and Neil met while in college. They played on the Frisbee team together. After college they moved in together, and since things were going so well, they decided to register for a domestic partnership in 2005. Chris started working as an investment banker straight out of college and earned a good salary. Rather than waste money paying rent, in 2006 they bought a small house in Venice Beach right next to the water. The purchase price was $800,000. They took title to the house in joint tenancy, and Chris contributed $200,000 as a down payment from an inheritance he received from his parents. They got married in 2016 after the Supreme Court decision in *Obergefell v. Hodges*, 576 U.S. 644 (2015).

Neil was unhappy in his job and decided to go to law school. Chris supported Neil both financially and emotionally throughout law school. Financially Chris paid $30,000 a year for three years of tuition ($90,000 total) until Neil graduated in 2020. Unfortunately, the pressure Chris was under at work and Neil's stress of failing the bar exam three times and not finding employment in any law-related position — wrought havoc on their relationship. In 2023, Chris and Neil decided to dissolve their domestic partnership and marriage and go their separate ways. The fair market value of the house is currently $1.5 million. How will a court characterize and divide the house? Will Chris get his $90,000 tuition back? Will Neil be eligible for spousal support from Chris?

Example 6 — Political Bedfellows

Marcy and Nancy met at a political demonstration in San Francisco. They shared the same political beliefs and soon decided they wanted to share their life together. They moved in together and, in 2012, registered as domestic partners with the State of California. At the time they registered their partnership, Marcy's divorce from Larry Luckless was not final. She had told Nancy that she was divorced when they first moved in together. Marcy and Nancy invited all their politically active friends to a ceremony that declared their commitment to each other for life. They treated each other in all ways as if they were married. Marcy had a good job at an advertising agency, and Nancy worked at the San Francisco office of a member of Congress. During their relationship, Marcy invested her salary in a mutual fund that steadily grew in value. During the campaign for president in 2015, Marcy and Nancy had many arguments about the merits of the candidates. In January 2016, they separated. Nancy filed a petition for dissolution of their domestic partnership. Nancy claims that she has a right to one-half of Marcy's mutual fund. Marcy responded to Nancy's petition, claiming that Nancy has no rights to her mutual fund because their domestic partnership registration was defective. Marcy was still married to Larry when they registered as domestic partners. Can Nancy get one-half of Marcy's mutual fund despite the defective domestic partnership?

Explanations

Explanation 1 — Jungle Love

Since Julie and Carla took title to the house in joint tenancy, upon termination of their domestic partnership in 2004, each would own a proportional ownership in the house. Joint tenancy is a form of equal ownership; therefore, each would be entitled to one-half of the house. The boat was acquired in Carla's name while they were domestic partners. During that time period, domestic partnership provisions did not create any "community" property rights for the domestic partners. The applicable doctrines were those for unmarried cohabitants. Julie has no rights to the boat. It is Carla's property.

Explanation 2 — Domestic Partners Till Death Do Us Part

Keith and David's relationship under the 2005 Act and the 2020 Act will be governed as if they were spouses. Family Code §297.5(k)(1) provides that "any reference to the date of marriage shall be deemed to refer to the date of registration of a domestic partnership with the state." Keith and David registered their domestic partnership in February 2014, after the effective date of the 2005 Act. From the date of registration, they would be treated as if married in almost all respects.

Keith died intestate on January 1, 2020. David will be treated as a surviving spouse. Under Family Code §297.5(c), a surviving domestic partner has the "same rights, protections and benefits . . . as are granted to . . . a widow or widower." Under the Probate Code, if a decedent dies intestate, the surviving spouse receives all of the community property and one-third, one-half, or all of the separate property, depending on whether there are other heirs. All joint tenancy property goes to the surviving joint tenant. The condominium was in joint tenancy and David will receive the condo because he is the surviving joint tenant. Because this is a death situation, not divorce, the $100,000 down payment is considered transmuted to joint tenancy.

The furniture was purchased during their domestic partnership with Keith's earnings during that time. Earnings would be treated as community property under the law applicable to married couples. Keith's earnings and the furniture purchased with those earnings would be considered community property. David would be entitled to the furniture. Keith's bank account is in his own name and the earnings that he deposited in that account were from before they registered as domestic partners. Since the registration date is deemed to be the date of marriage, earnings from before the date of registration would be considered separate property. It would be the funds, not the title, that would control characterization of the property. David would be entitled to as least one-third of those funds, depending on whether Keith had other heirs.

The condominium would still go to David as the surviving joint tenant. Keith's earnings and the furniture purchased with those earnings would be considered "community" property under the law applicable to spouses. If so, then under prior law, David would have no rights to the earnings and the furniture purchased with Keith's earnings. Keith's heirs would take that position. Even if those earnings would be considered "separate" property because they were not actually married and unmarried cohabitants' earnings are their own property, David would still be entitled under the 2005 and 2020 Acts to at least a one-third share of the earnings.

Explanation 3 — I'm Leaving You — Let's Go to Court

Keith and David's relationship will be governed by the 2005 and 2020 Acts, both of which give rights and obligations to registered domestic partners as if they were spouses. Family Code §297.5(k)(1) provides that "any reference to the date of marriage shall be deemed to refer to the date of registration of a domestic partnership with the state." Keith and David registered their domestic partnership in February 2014, after the effective date of the 2005 Act. From the date of registration, they would be treated as if married in almost all respects. Therefore, upon termination of Keith and David's domestic partnership, each partner owns his or her own separate property. Each partner has a present, established one-half interest in community property. Property acquired during the partnership is generally presumed to be community, unless it was traced to separate property funds or was the subject of a valid agreement to the contrary. The property held in joint tenancy would be presumptively community for purposes of divorce, unless a party could rebut that presumption by showing a written agreement, valid at the time made, to hold the property as other than community. Family Code §2581. Keith and David never made such an agreement, so the community property presumption will stand. Keith contributed $100,000 separate property to the down payment, and under Family Code §2640 he is entitled to reimbursement without interest.

The furniture was purchased during the partnership, so it is presumptively community property. Keith cannot rebut the presumption because he purchased it with funds that he earned during the domestic partnership. Concerning the bank account in Keith's name, it would also initially be presumed to be community property, because it was acquired during the domestic partnership. However, Keith would be able to rebut the presumption by tracing to separate property funds, those earned before the domestic partnership. The bank account would belong to Keith. The condominium would be split 50/50, subject to David's right to reimbursement. The furniture would also be split 50/50, but the bank account would be Keith's separate property.

Explanation 4—Oscar and Penny Play Bridge Together

Under the 2005 Act domestic partnership was available not only for same-sex couples, but for opposite-sex couples one of whom was over age 62 and eligible for Social Security benefits. The 2020 Act has no age or gender restrictions. You can reassure Penny that she and Oscar are eligible for a domestic partnership. She and Oscar have met the requirement of "an intimate and committed relationship of mutual caring" since they are considering marriage. Oscar assures you that he has never been married. Penny produces her marriage certificate and her husband's death certificate. You confirm that they are not related in a way that would prevent them from getting married.

If Oscar and Penny do become registered domestic partners, you explain to them that California will treat them as a married couple for most purposes. For example, they will be able to file jointly when paying California state tax, but not for federal tax. Because the Navy is a branch of the military, you will research how Oscar's service-related benefits will be affected by his domestic partnership. You briefly explain separate property and community property and the difference the characterization makes at death or divorce. You advise them to keep each of their separate funds separate, and avoid any commingling of funds. If they buy property which they want to own jointly, they should take title in both their names. (They should consult you or another lawyer first to make sure the title correctly reflects their intention.)

You ask them if they have any businesses, stocks, pensions, and other property to evaluate the effect of the domestic partnership. For estate planning purposes, you ask if they have any children or other relatives. If they have made wills or named beneficiaries on insurance policies or other assets, you want to review them. If they become domestic partners, they will have to make new wills and consider whether to change beneficiaries. Finally, you tell them that other states may not recognize their California domestic partnership. You will research Florida's law and tell them about it at your next meeting. You recommend that, in the meantime, they consider whether domestic partnership is right for them.

Explanation 5 — Marriage Too

Chris and Neil acquired the Venice house during their domestic partnership, taking title in joint tenancy. At dissolution, the court, applying Family Code §2581, will presume the house taken in joint tenancy to be community property. Since there is no written agreement to rebut the community property presumption, the court will confirm the house as community property. Any appreciation in value of the house would be split between Chris and Neil. Second, the court will consider whether Chris has a right to reimbursement without interest of the $200,000 downpayment under Family Code §2640. Chris can trace the funds to his inheritance which is his separate property; the court will confirm his right to reimbursement.

Chris supported Neil during three years of law school. He paid $90,000 total in tuition plus ordinary living expenses. Neil graduated with his Juris Doctor degree in 2020. He failed the bar exam three times and has never been employed in a law-related job. Fewer than 10 years have passed between Neil's 2020 graduation and the 2023 action for dissolution. Under Family Code §2641, there is a presumption that the community has not benefited from its investment in Neil's education. Neil's failure to pass the bar exam or be employed in a law-related position does not rebut this presumption. The community is entitled to the $90,000 invested in Neil's education; Chris is entitled to one-half of that amount, $45,000. The community is not entitled to compensation for the ordinary living expenses.

Neil's petition for spousal support asserts that the court must reserve jurisdiction over it because Chris and Neil's relationship is a "marriage of long duration." According to Family Code §297.5 (k)(1), "any reference to the date of a marriage shall be deemed to refer to the date of registration of a domestic partnership with the state." This language provides that for all the listed purposes, a domestic partnership plus marriage will be treated as one relationship, starting at the date when the domestic relationship was registered. Whether or not the court orders Chris to pay spousal support to Neil at the time of divorce, it will retain jurisdiction over the issue for the future.

Explanation 6 — Political Bedfellows

If Marcy and Nancy were married, their situation would resemble a putative "spouse" scenario. The "marriage" would be defective because Marcy was still married to Larry at the time Marcy and Nancy attempted to marry. Similarly, the "domestic partnership" was defective because Marcy was still married to Larry at the time Marcy and Nancy attempted to register as domestic partners. One of the requirements of establishing a domestic partnership is that "neither person is married." Family Code §297(b)(3). If a marriage is void, a party who has a sincere subjective good faith belief in the validity of the marriage will be considered a putative spouse who has rights to quasi-marital property. Quasi-marital property is property that would be community property if there was a valid marriage. Nancy could claim to have a sincere, subjective good faith belief in the validity of their domestic partnership. If she did not know that Marcy was still married to Larry when they registered their partnership, Nancy qualifies as a "putative" domestic partner/spouse and would have a one-half right to the mutual fund as quasi-marital property.

The End!

Table of Cases

Table of Statutes

Index

www.ingramcontent.com/pod-product-compliance
Lightning Source LLC
Chambersburg PA
CBHW081124180926
51611CB00004B/50
* 9 7 8 1 5 4 3 8 0 5 7 0 3 *